Second-Trimester Abortion

Perspectives After a Decade of Experience

Edited by

Gary S. Berger, MD, MSPH, FACOG
William E. Brenner, MD, FACOG
Louis G. Keith, MD, FACOG

Forewords by

Irvin M. Cushner, MD, MPH
and
Jeffrey E. Grossman

John Wright • PSG Inc
Boston • Bristol • London

Library of Congress Cataloging in Publication Data

Main entry under title:

Second-trimester abortion.

   Bibliography: p.
   Includes index.
   1. Abortion. 2. Pregnancy--Trimester, Second. I. Berger, Gary S. II. Brenner, William E. III. Keith, Louis G. [DNLM: 1. Abortion, Induced. 2. Pregnancy trimester, Second. WQ 440 S445]
RG734.S42   618.8'8   80-25584
ISBN 0-88416-256-7

Medicine is an ever-changing science. As new research and clinical experience broaden our knowledge, changes in treatment and drug therapy are required. The authors and the publisher of this work have made every effort to ensure that the treatment and drug dosage schedules herein are accurate and in accord with the standards accepted at the time of publication. Readers are advised, however, to check the product information sheet included in the package of each drug they plan to administer to be certain that changes have not been made in the recommended dose or in the indications and contraindications for administration. This recommendation is of particular importance in regard to new or infrequently used drugs.

Copyright © 1981 by Gary S. Berger, William E. Brenner and Louis G. Keith

All rights reserved. No part of this publication may be reproduced or transmitted in any form or by any means, electronic or mechanical, including photocopying, recording, or any information storage or retrieval system, without permission in writing from John Wright • PSG Inc.

Printed in the United States of America.

International Standard Book Number: 0-88416-256-7

Library of Congress Catalog Card Number: 80-25584

Dedication

This book is dedicated to Christopher Tietze, MD, who, over the course of several decades, has pursued with scientific objectivity the investigation of health problems facing women, their physicians and society at large.

Photo © 1981 Warren Martin Hern

Christopher Tietze moves among us as a colleague, friend, teacher, constant student, world citizen, and inspiration to clear thought. He fixes a steady and unyielding gaze on a landscape littered with random events and helps us understand it with the power of his mind. He gives us courage by staring down ignorance, showing us the way to marshal the facts that are there, and demonstrating that a work of precision can be a witness to compassion and the love of justice. He is the modern and timeless scholar whose devotion to his craft will speak to us and demand the best from us as long as we are searching for answers in this confused world.

Warren Martin Hern

THE EDITORS

Dr. Gary S. Berger is Clinical Assistant Professor of Obstetrics and Gynecology and Adjunct Associate Professor of Maternal and Child Health at the University of North Carolina. Dr. Berger serves as the Director of the Menstruation and Reproduction History Research Program at the Center for the Advancement of Reproductive Health, Chapel Hill, North Carolina. He is a Diplomate of the American Board of Preventive Medicine as well as the American Board of Obstetrics and Gynecology.

Dr. William E. Brenner is Upjohn Distinguished Professor of Obstetrics and Gynecology at the University of North Carolina. He is a Diplomate of the American Board of Obstetrics and Gynecology.

Dr. Louis G. Keith is Professor of Obstetrics and Gynecology at Northwestern University Medical School and The Prentice Women's Hospital and Medical Center, Chicago, Illinois. He is also Executive Director, The Charles A. Fields Medical Foundation, Chicago, Illinois. Dr. Keith is a Diplomate of the American Board of Obstetrics and Gynecology.

CONTRIBUTORS

Milagros F. Atienza, MD is a member of the Department of Gynecology and Obstetrics, Johns Hopkins Medical Institutions, Baltimore, Maryland.

Willem Beekhuizen, MD is a staff physician at the Center for Human Reproduction, Leiden, The Netherlands.

Kurt Benirschke, MD is Professor of Pathology and Reproductive Medicine at the University of California at San Diego, La Jolla, California.

Gary S. Berger, MD, MSPH, FACPM is Assistant Professor of Obstetrics and Gynecology and Adjunct Associate Professor of Maternal and Child Health at the University of North Carolina, Chapel Hill, North Carolina. He also is the Director of the Menstruation and Reproduction History Research Program of the Center for the Advancement of Reproductive Health, Chapel Hill, North Carolina.

Ronald T. Burkman, MD is Associate Professor of Gynecology and Obstetrics, at the Johns Hopkins Medical Institutions and Director of the Johns Hopkins Program for International Education in Gynecology and Obstetrics, Baltimore, Maryland.

Marc A. Bygdeman, MD, PhD is Professor of Obstetrics and Gynecology at the Karolinska Hospital, Stockholm, Sweden.

Willard Cates, Jr, MD, MPH is the Chief of the Abortion Surveillance Branch, Family Planning Evaluation Division, Bureau of Epidemiology, Department of Health and Human Services, Public Health Service, Centers for Disease Control, Atlanta, Georgia.

Elizabeth B. Connell, MD is a Lecturer in Obstetrics and Gynecology at the Northwestern University Medical School, Chicago, Illinois.

Henry P. David, PhD is Associate Clinical Professor of Psychiatry at the University of Maryland Medical School; and Director, Transnational Family Research Institute, Baltimore, Maryland.

Marijke du Plessis-Alblas, MD is a staff physician at the Center for Human Reproduction, Leiden, The Netherlands.

David A. Edelman, PhD is Adjunct Associate Professor of Obstetrics and Gynecology at the University of North Carolina, Chapel Hill, North Carolina and Associate Director for Research, International Fertility Research Program, Research Triangle Park, North Carolina.

Julian Gold, MB, BS is Epidemic Intelligence Service Officer with the Abortion Surveillance Branch, Family Planning Evaluation Division, Bureau of Epidemiology, Department of Health and Human Services, Public Health Service, Centers for Disease Control, Atlanta, Georgia.

David A. Grimes, MD is Clinical Assistant Professor of Gynecology and Obstetrics at Emory University School of Medicine and Assistant Chief, Abortion Surveillance Branch, Family Planning Evaluation Division, Bureau of Epidemiology, Department of Health and Human Services, Public Health Service, Centers for Disease Control, Atlanta, Georgia.

Charles H. Hendricks, MD is Professor and Chairman Emeritus of the Department of Obstetrics and Gynecology at the University of North Carolina, Chapel Hill, North Carolina.

Nancy B. Kaltreider, MD is Associate Clinical Professor of Psychiatry at the University of California at San Francisco, San Francisco, California.

Louis G. Keith, MD is Professor of Obstetrics and Gynecology at Northwestern University Medical School and The Prentice Women's Hospital and Maternity Center; he also is Executive Director of The Charles A. Fields Medical Foundation, Ltd., Chicago, Illinois.

Thomas D. Kerenyi, MD is Professor of Clinical Obstetrics and Gynecology, Chief of Obstetrics and Director of the Division of Perinatology at the Mount Sinai School of Medicine, City University of New York, New York.

Evert Ketting, PhD is Research Director of STIMEZO (Netherlands National Abortion Federation) and Research Fellow, NISSO (Netherlands Institute for Socio-Sexological Research), Zeist, The Netherlands.

Theodore M. King, MD is Professor and Chairman of the Department of Obstetrics and Gynecology at the Johns Hopkins Medical Institutions, Baltimore, Maryland.

Jean Pakter, MD, MPH is Director of the Bureau of Maternity Services and Family Planning of the New York City Department of Health, New York.

Malcolm Potts, MB, B Chir, PhD, D Obst is Executive Director of the International Fertility Research Program, Research Triangle Park, North Carolina.

Jack W. Provonsha, MD is Professor of Philosophy of Religion and Christian Ethics and Co-Director of the Student Health Services at the Loma Linda University, Loma Linda, California.

Judith P. Rooks, CNM, MS, MPH is with the Office of the Assistant Secretary for Health in the Department of Health and Human Services, Washington, DC.

Carol J. Rowland Hogue, PhD is Associate Professor of Biometry at the University of Arkansas for Medical Sciences, Little Rock, Arkansas.

Jeannie I. Rosoff is President of the Alan Guttmacher Institute, Washington, DC.

Rudy E. Sabbagha, MD is Associate Professor of Obstetrics and Gynecology and Director of the Diagnostic Ultrasound Center at Northwestern University Medical School and The Prentice Women's Hospital and Maternity Center, Chicago, Illinois.

Kenneth F. Schulz, MBA is Assistant Chief of the Statistical Services Branch, Family Planning Evaluation Division, Bureau of Epidemiology, Department of Health and Human Services, Public Health Service, Centers for Disease Control, Atlanta, Georgia.

Richard M. Selik, MD is an Abortion Surveillance Officer with the Abortion Surveillance Branch, Family Planning Evaluation Division, Bureau of Epidemiology, Department of Health and Human Services, Public Health Service, Centers for Disease Control, Atlanta, Georgia.

Jack C. Smith, MS is Chief of the Statistical Services Branch of the Family Planning Evaluation Division, Bureau of Epidemiology, Department of Health and Human Services, Public Health Service, Centers for Disease Control, Atlanta, Georgia.

Phillip G. Stubblefield, MD is Assistant Professor of Obstetrics and Gynecology at the Harvard Medical School and Chief of the Division of Ambulatory and Community Medicine of the Department of Obstetrics and Gynecology, Brigham and Women's Hospital, Boston, Massachusetts.

Christopher Tietze, MD is a Senior Consultant of The Population Council, New York, New York.

Carl W. Tyler, Jr, MD is Director of the Family Planning Evaluation Division, Bureau of Epidemiology, Department of Health and Human Services, Public Health Service, Centers for Disease Control, Atlanta, Georgia.

Louise B. Tyrer, MD is Vice President for Medical Affairs of Planned Parenthood Federation of America, New York, New York.

Dirk A.F. van Lith, MD, DPH is a staff physician at the Center for Human Reproduction, Leiden, The Netherlands.

Kees J. van Schie, MD is a staff physician at the Center for Human Reproduction, Leiden, The Netherlands.

Judith A. Widdicombe, RN, BA is Executive Director of Reproductive Health Service in St. Louis, Missouri.

Gerald I. Zatuchni, MD is Associate Clinical Professor of Obstetrics and Gynecology and Director of Technical Assistance with the Program for Applied Research on Fertility Regulation at Northwestern Unviersity Medical School and The Prentice Women's Hospital and Maternity Center, Chicago, Illinois.

CONTENTS

Contributors vii

Foreword Irvin M. Cushner xv

Foreword Jeffrey E. Grossman xix

Preface xxi

PART I Overview

1 Second-Trimester Abortion: A Global View 1
Christopher Tietze

2 Second-Trimester Induced Abortion in the United States 13
Carl W. Tyler, Jr., Willard Cates, Jr., Kenneth F. Schulz, Richard M. Selik, and Jack C. Smith

3 The Availability of Second-Trimester Abortion Services in the United States 27
Jeannie I. Rosoff

PART II The Second Trimester of Pregnancy

4 Anatomy 39
Kurt Benirschke

5 Ultrasonic Evaluation 57
Rudy E. Sabbagha

6 Physiology 69
Charles H. Hendricks

PART III Methods of Second-Trimester Abortion

7 Hypertonic Saline Instillation 79
Thomas D. Kerenyi

8 Prostaglandin Procedures 89
Marc A. Bygdeman

9 Hyperosmolar Urea 107
Ronald T. Burkman, Theodore M. King, and Milagros F. Atienza

10 Dilatation and Evacuation 119
David A. Grimes and Willard Cates, Jr.

11 **Laminaria and Other Adjunctive Methods** 135
Phillip G. Stubblefield

PART IV Evaluation

12 **Morbidity and Mortality** 163
Willard Cates, Jr. and David A. Grimes

13 **Future Reproduction** 179
Carol J. Rowland Hogue

14 **The Role of Health Agencies** 189
Jean Pakter and Julian Gold

15 **Recommended Procedures for Evaluation of Abortion Techniques** 205
David A. Edelman

PART V Related Issues

16 **How Much is a Fetus Worth?** 213
Jack W. Provonsha

17 **Social Issues** 221
Henry P. David

18 **Psychological Impact on Patients and Staff** 239
Nancy B. Kaltreider

19 **Emotional Issues for Professionals** 251
Judith P. Rooks

20 **Counseling Issues** 259
Judith A. Widdicombe

21 **Postabortal Contraception** 265
Louis G. Keith and Gary S. Berger

PART VI International Considerations: The Dutch Abortion Experience

22 **Second-Trimester Abortion Services in the Netherlands** 285
Evert Ketting

23 **Aspirotomy** 295
Dirk A.F. van Lith, Willem Beekhuizen, Kees J. van Schie, and Marijke du Plessis-Alblas

24 **Complications of Aspirotomy** 301
Willem Beekhuizen, Dirk A.F. van Lith, Kees J. van Schie, and Marijke du Plessis-Alblas

PART VII Future Directions

25 The Future of Second-Trimester Abortion
    in the United States   309
    Louise B. Tyrer

26 The Future of Second-Trimester Abortion
    Throughout the World   315
    Malcolm Potts

27 Preventing the Need for Second-Trimester
    Abortion   325
    Elizabeth B. Connell

28 Contragestational Agents   331
    Gerald I. Zatuchni

    Index   337

FOREWORD
Irvin M. Cushner, MD, MPH

It is both remarkable and, at the same time, a sign of this era of rapid change that one can refer back to the "infancy" of a field which has existed for barely more than a decade. Yet, one now reads of the "maturing" of the family planning and abortion fields, both of which were incorporated into our society and integrated into our health care system within the past ten years. Indeed, in the very year that this book is being prepared, we note the tenth anniversaries of several significant events of 1970: 1) the enactment of Title X of the Public Health Service Act, establishing a Federal program in family planning; 2) the first issuance by a major health-related organization (the APHA) of a policy statement advocating repeal of all abortion laws; and 3) the enactment, by New York State, of an abortion law whose only restriction was that it be performed by a licensed physician and the subsequent action, the first by any local health department (New York City), to assure both its implementation and its quality.

They were, indeed, eventful days. These three events seemed to presage a then-unprecedented acceptance of fertility regulation as a right and as a needed service. Since milestones frequently occasion reflection and evaluation, it is not untimely to note that, while most of our best guesses turned out to be correct, some of our most ardent hopes have yet to be realized. This is no more true for any component of fertility regulation than for second-trimester abortion.

As the availability of contraceptive and first-trimester abortion services increased, the proportion of abortions performed in the second trimester decreased. We expected that. Yet, there are still more than 100,000 such procedures performed annually in the United States.

We expected that, with continued research, surveillance, and service delivery improvement, the risks of morbidity and mortality would decrease. They have. Yet, the level of risk with first-trimester procedures remains significantly less than with second-trimester abortion.

We hoped that, with time, we would learn more about the reasons for delay in obtaining desired abortion services and that intervention strategies could be developed to further reduce the need for this less-than-ideal approach. While we have identified certain groups at highest risk of delay, we still know little about their reasons and we still have no intervention technique with a particularly outstanding record of success.

Finally, we expected that, even with an increased acceptance of abortion as a health-related service, second-trimester abortion would remain particularly less acceptable. While essentially correct in this projection, we still find ourselves in the midst of a continuous struggle to maintain that level of public support for all legal abortion which was achieved in the past decade.

Within the pages of this book, the reader will find three recurring themes: 1) contraception is preferred over abortion; 2) first-trimester is preferred over second-trimester abortion; 3) the need for second-trimester abortion will not "go away," much as we might wish it would. This latter reality (rather than the mere passage of a decade) is the primary justification for and purpose of the book. The higher levels of risk, both physical and psychosocial, will make this contemporary review of particular value to all who are concerned with women's health and with reproductive health.

In this volume, the continuing need for second-trimester abortion services is dealt with in realistic terms. The declining but continuing utilization is clearly outlined by Tietze and by Tyler and his group. The quandry in which many clinicians currently find themselves is best seen through the descriptions of the various methods at the disposal of women and their physicians, their comparative levels of mortality and morbidity risks as reviewed by Cates and Grimes, and the psychologic dilemmas experienced by women and by health professionals as described by Rooks and by Kaltreider. The paradox of minimal acceptance of second-trimester abortion, on the one hand, and the socio-political factors which will surely force a greater need for it, on the other, are explained by David and by Potts. The effects of all of these issues are felt, ultimately, on the availability and quality of these desperately needed services, and some varying approaches toward their improvement are taken by Rosoff and by Pakter and Gold. The extremely difficult ethical issues are sensitively reviewed by Provonsha who gives us a brief glimpse at what, in the opinion of this writer, may very well be the next phase in the public debate over abortion; namely, abortion policy based *again* on the reason for the request. Shades of the 1960s, perhaps; but the current trend, nonetheless, and especially so in relation to second-trimester abortion.

This book, the most extensive volume currently available on this subject, addresses all of these issues and more. In it, the reader will find complete and detailed coverage of every facet of second-trimester abortion: availability, utilization, clinical management, social and psychosocial issues, and evaluation.

As significant as the content itself is the list of contributing authors, about each of whom one can truly say, "They wrote the book." Each of them has previously distinguished herself/himself in the area about which they write.

In this list there is one whose distinction stands out and stands alone. It is particularly fitting that this important work is dedicated to him—Christopher Tietze.

There is hardly a significant event in the recent history of abortion in the United States in which Chris Tietze did not play some important and effective role: researcher, expert witness, advocate, speaker, activist, consultant, committee member, and on and on and on. Some of these roles he played through his inherent skills as a brilliant statistician, articulate orator, perceptive policy-maker, and intelligent debater. But, perhaps, his most important contributions have been the result not so much of his inherent skills as of his inherent values. His tenacity in his unyielding demand for truth, for justice based on truth, and for human dignity has been an inspiration to all of us who labor in this field. Dedicating this book to this remarkable person is but one measure of the respect and love felt for him by those who have been among the beneficiaries of his efforts.

To Berger, Brenner, and Keith, our colleagues who were responsible for the conference whose proceedings formed the basis for this book and who assumed the task of producing it, should go the commendation and gratitude of both health professionals and the women they serve. They surely have mine.

Irvin M. Cushner, MD, MPH
Professor, Obstetrics/Gynecology and Public Health,
University of California, Los Angeles
Former Deputy Assistant Secretary for Population Affairs,
US Department of HEW

FOREWORD

Jeffrey E. Grossman

Problems related to the control of reproduction and particularly to the termination of unwanted pregnancies have always been serious health concerns facing women during the larger part of their adult lives. It is only in recent years that effective medical methods of contraception have been available to liberate women from the specter of compulsory childbearing. Even today, excessive fertility remains the burden of millions of women. In many areas of the world, this problem relates to the unavailability of contraceptive technology. In the United States, where access to contraceptive services is widespread, significant numbers of women at risk of pregnancy still use no contraception or select a method which may not afford them the protection they need. Among those women who become pregnant and seek abortion, approximately 10% undergo induced abortion in the second trimester of pregnancy.

The task of all who are concerned with providing women high quality health care would be much easier if indeed there were no differences between the first and second trimester of pregnancy with regard to the ease and safety of induced abortion. Substantial differences do exist, however, making abortion in the second trimester more difficult, more costly and potentially more hazardous to the pregnant woman. In addition, the social, political and ethical issues surrounding "later" pregnancy interruption have polarized American society in recent years and imposed an additional hardship on some individuals.

With these considerations in mind, the officers and directors of The Charles A. Fields Medical Foundation, Ltd., decided to provide the financial support for a national conference on second-trimester abortion, which would permit the most qualified medical experts to gather and provide a comprehensive review of this subject. That conference was held September 27–28, 1979 at Chapel Hill, North Carolina.

We are grateful to each of the participants of the conference for their efforts in rigorously adhering to the principles of medical scholarship. It is hoped that the information in this monograph will help to clarify the myriad of issues which exist. If this indeed is the case, we will have succeeded in what we set forth to do.

Jeffrey E. Grossman
Chairman, Board of Directors
The Charles A. Fields Medical Foundation, Ltd.

PREFACE

Medical literature has considered the subject of second-trimester abortion in some detail since the worldwide liberalization of abortion laws during the last two decades. Nonetheless, there is no consensus regarding the relative risks and benefits of the available medical or surgical procedures for termination of pregnancy in the second trimester.

Some years ago, Dr. Emanuel Friedman of Harvard University was instrumental in pointing out to us the need for a comprehensive monograph on the subject of second-trimester abortion. He proposed that the editors prepare the entire manuscript based on their own experiences and a review of the literature. Because of other commitments, we were unfortunately unable to do this. Our interest in the subject remained, however, and when Mr. Jeffrey E. Grossman, Chairman of the Board of Directors of The Charles A. Fields Medical Foundation, Ltd., approached us with the idea of holding a national conference on the subject of abortion, we agreed to do this if arrangements could be made to publish a thoroughly referenced text of the discussions presented at the conference. He agreed, and what followed lies within the pages of this volume.

The central theme of this book relates to the question, "What have we learned after a decade of experience?" Although the accumulated data are considerable, the state of the art is changing rapidly in this specialized area of medicine. Certain trends are clear, however; i.e., while the proportion of women requesting second-trimester procedures is diminishing in the United States, highly specialized care must be available during the abortion procedures. Similarly, even though there have been improvements in the technical approach to abortion in the second trimester, concerns for patient safety still exist. Furthermore, our knowledge of the physiology of the second trimester of pregnancy remains imperfect and there is therefore no universally agreed upon method to assure totally safe abortion in the second trimester.

The editors wish to thank each contributor for complying with numerous revisions and editorial changes. The final manuscript could not have been prepared without the considerable talents of Paula Hamilton and Associates.

As usual, our wives Barbara, Beverly, and Gail generously afforded us their typical encouragement by giving of their time so that this book could be produced.

Thanks to all.

Gary S. Berger
William E. Brenner
Louis G. Keith
Chapel Hill, North Carolina
and
Chicago, Illinois

PART I
Overview

1 Second-Trimester Abortion: A Global View

Christopher Tietze

Second-trimester abortion is responsible for a disproportionate share of adverse experiences associated with pregnancy termination. In the United States during 1972–1977, abortions performed at 13 weeks' gestation or later accounted for 11% of all legal abortions, while causing an estimated two-thirds of all major complications and over one-half of all known abortion-related fatalities. Because of these circumstances, it is important to review the numbers and trends of second-trimester abortions as they are performed throughout the world, the demographic and socioeconomic characteristics of the women obtaining them, and the methods used to perform them by medical practitioners in different locales.

Such a review is, of necessity, limited to data on legal abortions, because no information is available from any country on the timing of illegal and self-induced abortions. Survey data are not reliable sources of information on the timing of illegal abortions, nor are hospital records, because the risk of complications requiring medical attention is higher after a later abortion than after an early one.

COMPARATIVE DATA

Numbers and Trends

Unfortunately, pregnancy duration is not uniformly reported in official statistics on abortion. In some countries, e.g., England and Wales, the notification form used includes an entry for the date of onset of the last menstrual period, and gestational age is tabulated in terms of complete weeks. As shown in Table 1-1, a declining pattern of abortions by single weeks of gestation is observed. In Czechoslovakia and Scotland, pregnancy duration is reported by physicians in terms of weeks; since physicians may interpret "weeks" as ordinal week, nearest week, or completed week, which for "12 weeks" corresponds from 77 to 83 days, 81 to 87 days, or 84 to 90 days, respectively, the reported figures tend to bunch at even numbers of weeks and especially at multiples of four which correspond to lunar months. Because of this reporting preference, many abortions performed at 13 weeks of gestation are reported as being only 12 weeks, and the number of second-trimester procedures is thus reduced. On the other hand, Sweden requires reporting in terms of completed weeks but provides careful instructions which define pregnancy duration. This maneuver largely avoids the "heaping phenomenon" at even numbers of weeks. An additional consideration of this problem is that

Table 1-1
Legal Abortions at 10 to 16 Weeks Gestation, by Single Weeks: Selected Countries and Years

Weeks of Gestation	Czecho-slovakia 1975	England and Wales 1973	Scotland 1976	Sweden 1977
10	15,223	18,419	1699	5205
11	4987	15,899	510	3100
12	8049	11,682	871	1431
13	133	7331	215	399
14	208	4339	361	393
15	65	2632	130	303
16	105	1828	260	266

while many physicians follow the tradition of counting the duration of pregnancy from the first day of the last menstrual period, others count from the estimated day of conception. For all these reasons, information on time trends and group differences within countries is more reliable than comparisons between countries.

The overall frequency of legal second-trimester abortion depends on the applicable law. All countries authorizing abortions on the basis of medical or fetal indications permit these abortions in the second trimester, but few countries permit second-trimester abortions simply at the request of the pregnant woman or on social or social-medical indications. As of mid-1979 the latter indications were valid in some of the states of Australia, Great Britain, Hong Kong, India, Israel, Japan, Singapore, Sweden (up to 18 weeks), the United States, and Zambia.[1]

Table 1-2 shows the percentages of second-trimester procedures among all legal abortions in nine countries and New York City for each year of the 1968 to 1977 decade or for those years for which data were available. A shift toward earlier abortion has occurred in almost all areas. This has been most dramatic in Sweden, where the proportion of second-trimester abortions dropped from 57% in 1968 to 6% in 1977. This trend probably reflects the increasing availability of abortion services, and a growing awareness among women as well as physicians that abortion is safer early in pregnancy. Exceptions to the general trend toward earlier abortions were recorded in Czechoslovakia and Hungary, where the proportions of second-trimester abortions rose when access to abortion on request—but not to abortion on medical grounds—was restricted.

In recent years the proportion of second-trimester abortions by country was highest in India (averaging 24% from 1972 to 1975). This was followed by Scotland, Canada, and England and Wales where the proportion varied between 16% to 18%. The comparable figures for the United States, Sweden, and Japan ranged from 4% to 9%. In Hungary and Czechoslovakia, where second-trimester abortions are generally limited to those performed for medical reasons, the proportion of all second-trimester abortions was less than one per 100 legal abortions.

In New York City, for the years 1973 to 1975, the increased proportions of second-trimester procedures among nonresident women stand in contrast to the downward trend for residents. This suggests a selective migration of patients from other geographic locations in order to obtain second-trimester abortions. By 1976 the great majority of nonresident women came from nearby suburban areas, thus reducing the selection by pregnancy duration. In 1977 the trend was reversed, indicating a tightening of hospital policies in other areas,

Table 1-2
Second-Trimester Abortions per 100 Legal Abortions: Selected Areas, 1968 to 1977

Area and Characteristics	1968	1969	1970	1971	1972	1973	1974	1975	1976	1977
Canada[5]	na†	na	na	na	na	na	21.2	18.7	16.9	15.8
Czechoslovakia[6]	0.5	0.5	0.5	0.5	0.6	0.6	0.5	0.4	0.5	0.8
England and Wales[7,8]										
Residents	38.0	34.3	28.7	23.3	20.4	18.1	17.2	17.4	16.5	16.4
Nonresidents	36.3	38.1	26.9	21.6	18.9	22.7	25.6	28.5	32.0	32.0
Hungary[9,10]	na	na	na	0.5	0.5	0.5	1.0	0.8	0.7	0.8
India[11]	na	na	na	na		"nearly 24"			na	na
Japan[12]*	5.0	4.8	4.5	4.1	3.8	3.4	3.2	3.2	4.1	4.2
New York City[13]										
Residents	na	na	na	20.7	16.1	15.1	14.5	11.7	9.7	9.1
Nonresidents	na	na	na	18.8	18.2	25.8	25.6	24.1	19.6	22.4
Scotland[14]	na	35.0	28.0	25.6	20.9	19.2	16.9	18.0	17.8	na
Sweden[15]	57.1	49.3	40.5	32.6	26.6	19.7	13.3	7.0	6.4	6.0
United States[16,17]	na	na	na	na	15.3	14.5	12.0	10.8	9.7	9.0

*Gestation reported in months. Second-trimester abortions (four months or more) were 19.2% in 1951 and 13.6% in 1952; they dropped gradually to 5.0% in the late 1960s.
†na = not available.

and in 1978 the proportion of second-trimester abortions for nonresidents again reached 25.4% (not shown in Table 1-2). In that year about 600 *more* women came to New York City to obtain second-trimester abortions than in 1976, compared to about 100,000 who were able to obtain these services elsewhere. First-trimester abortions to nonresidents *declined* by 2400 from 1976 to 1978, thus driving up the percentage of second-trimester procedures. A marked increase in the proportion of second-trimester abortions among nonresidents also occurred in England beginning in 1974 as first-trimester abortion became increasingly available to many European women, first in the Netherlands and later in other countries as well.

Table 1-3 presents a different approach to the statistics of second-trimester abortions. They are shown as a rate per 1000 women, 15 to 44 years of age, for selected areas and for the 1968 to 1977 decade rather than as a percentage of all legal abortions. Computed in this manner, the incidence of second-trimester abortion is higher in England and Wales than in Scotland, higher in the United States than in Canada or in England, still higher in Japan, and highest in New York City. The highest second-trimester abortion rate, 16 per 1000 women, 15 to 44 years of age (not shown in Table 1-3), has been reported from Seoul, Korea, based on a survey of providers of abortion services conducted in 1977 to 1978.[2] The rapidly declining proportions of second-trimester abortions among all legal abortions in Sweden in 1968 to 1972 and in the United States from 1972 to 1977, as shown in Table 1-2, are not reflected in Table 1-3 because these declines coincided with increases in the overall abortion rate.

Table 1-3
Second-Trimester Abortions per 1000 Women, 15 to 44:
Selected Areas, 1968 to 1977

Area	1968	1969	1970	1971	1972	1973	1974	1975	1976	1977
Canada	na	na	na	na	na	na	2.0	1.8	1.7	1.7
Czechoslovakia	0.2	0.2	0.2	0.2	0.2	0.1	0.1	0.1	0.1	0.2
England and Wales*	1.3	1.8	2.3	2.4	2.3	2.1	2.0	1.9	1.8	1.7
Hungary	na	na	na	0.4	0.4	0.4	0.4	0.3	0.3	0.3
Japan†	5.4	5.1	4.7	4.3	3.9	3.3	3.1	3.0	3.8	3.8
New York City*	na	na	na	8.2	6.7	7.3	7.4	5.7	4.8	4.7
Scotland	na	1.3	1.5	1.6	1.6	1.4	1.3	1.3	1.2	na
Sweden	4.0	4.3	4.1	4.0	4.0	3.2	2.6	1.4	1.3	1.2
United States	na	na	na	na	2.0	2.4	2.4	2.4	2.4	2.3

*Residents only.
†Based on Muramatsu's estimate of actual number of legal abortions in 1970 (2,780,000) and trend of reported abortions 1968–1977.[18]

Sociodemographic Characteristics

Women of low socioeconomic status (Table 1-4)—and especially younger women (Table 1-5)—had the highest proportions of late abortions. The strong inverse association of gestation period and the woman's age probably reflects the inexperience of the very young in recognizing the symptoms of pregnancy, their unwillingness to accept the reality of their situation, and their ignorance about where to seek advice and help, as well as their hesitation to confide in adults.

Table 1-4
Second-Trimester Abortions per 100 Legal Abortions by Occupation Group, within Marital Status: England and Wales, 1968 and 1973*

Occupation Group	Single Women by Own Occuptation		Married Women by Husband's Occupation	
	1968	*1973*	*1968*	*1973*
Professional	23.3	14.4	23.0	8.9
Intermediate	31.7	15.0	29.1	10.3
Skilled	37.5	19.1	41.2	14.5
Semi-skilled	41.0	23.5	42.6	16.2
Unskilled	48.0	26.6	48.5	20.4

*Residents.

Table 1-5
Second-Trimester Abortions per 100 Legal Abortions by Woman's Age: Selected Areas and Periods

	Period	Woman's Age (years)							
		14 or less	*15–17*	*18–19*	*20–24*	*25–29*	*30–34*	*35–39*	*40 or more*
Canada	1976	33.5	27.2	21.7	16.3	11.5	10.4	10.7	14.1
England and Wales*	1976	30.6	23.2		18.2	13.8	10.6	10.0	12.3
Hungary	1977		3.3		0.5	0.5	0.5	0.3	07
India†	1972–75		41.9		15.6	10.8	14.0	17.0	
Japan	1977		19.1		8.0	4.1	2.6	2.4	2.8
New York City*	1977	27.6	18.4	12.3	9.0	6.9	5.9	6.1	6.5
Sweden	1975–76		10.6	9.1	6.9	5.0	4.1	4.3	6.7
United States‡	1972–75		18.6		12.2	9.9	9.7	10.0	

*Residents only.
†Karnataka State.[19]
‡Distribution by age and gestation estimated by iterative adjustment of a known distribution (JPSA/CDC) to marginal totals for the United States.[20]

Economic considerations and, in many places, regulations prohibiting surgery on minors without parental consent also undoubtedly contributed to delays.

The very high proportions of second-trimester abortions shown in Table 1-5 for the youngest women actually understate the situation. For example, a woman who conceives at 14 years and nine months and has a first-trimester abortion will appear in the "14 or less" age group; if she has a second-trimester abortion, she will be in the next higher age group. Since over half of all pregnancies conceived before age 15 which were aborted in the United States and in England and Wales in 1976 occurred after 14 years and six months, this distortion is a significant one.

The slight increases in proportions of second-trimester procedures observed in all areas among the oldest women shown in Table 1-5 reflect the association of high order pregnancies with low socioeconomic status. Abortions for medical reasons are also more common among older women. Moreover, some women in their forties may have misinterpreted the amenorrhea of pregnancy as the onset of menopause.

Methods

The various methods used to terminate pregnancy in the second trimester can be grouped under three general headings: dilatation and evacuation (D&E), major surgery (hysterotomy and hysterectomy), and medical induction.

As shown in Table 1-6, dilatation and evacuation by the vaginal route is employed primarily in the early part of the second trimester (13 16 weeks). Over the past several years its use has increased in the United States as well as in England, where it is utilized to a greater degree than in any other country, especially in the private sector, as compared with the hospitals of the National Health Service (NHS). D&E is used substantially less frequently in Sweden and is limited almost exclusively to pregnancies of less than 14 weeks' gestation.

Hysterotomy and hysterectomy, in contrast to D&E, are performed more often in the later than in the earlier part of the second trimester in England and Wales and also in Sweden. Utilization of these major surgical procedures has declined dramatically in the United States as well as in England, where it had been very prevalent during the period immediately following the implementation of the 1967 Abortion Act. This situation clearly was associated with a strong tendency to perform abortion and sterilization concurrently. In 1977, abortions by hysterotomy or hysterectomy and surgical sterilizations were performed much more often in NHS hospitals than in the private sector.

Table 1-6
Percent Distribution of Second-Trimester Abortions by Type of Procedure, Within Weeks of Gestation: Selected Areas and Periods

Area, Period, and Weeks of Gestation	Dilatation and Evacuation*	Hysterotomy or Hysterectomy	Medical Induction	Other Procedures
Canada, 1977				
13–16	68.9	3.8	27.3	na
17 or more	9.5	3.9	86.6	na
England and Wales, 1968†				
13–16	50.0	42.5	7.5	
17 or more	16.7	68.5	14.8	
England and Wales, 1977†				
13–16	77.4	2.7	19.6	0.3
17 or more	40.6	3.2	55.9	0.3
NHS-hospitals, 1976‡				
13–16	57.6	6.2	35.6	0.6
17 or more	24.7	9.1	65.8	0.4

Area, Period, and Weeks of Gestation	Dilatation and Evacuation*	Hysterotomy or Hysterectomy	Medical Induction	Other Procedures
Private sector, 1976				
13–16	90.3	0.3	9.2	0.2
17 or more	46.2	1.2	52.4	0.2
Sweden, 1975–1977#				
13–16	18.2	9.2	72.6	na
17 or more	2.1	27.2	70.7	na
United States, 1970–1971§				
13–16	39.4	7.9	51.4	1.3
17 or more	0.0	4.4	94.5	1.1
United States, 1977¶				
13–16	66.7	0.9	32.1	0.3
17 or more	10.0	0.8	88.5	0.7

*Reported as suction or surgical curettage. Includes dilatation and evacuation (D&E) at 13 or more weeks of gestation.
†Residents and nonresidents.
‡National Health Service hospitals.
#Hysterotomy or hysterectomy refers to cases reported as "other one-step methods," and medical induction to those reported as "two-step methods."
§Data from the Joint Program for the Study of Abortion.[21] Medical induction refers only to intraamniotic instillation of hypertonic saline solution. The "0.0" entry at 17 weeks or more under dilatation and evacuation is an artifact since a few cases so reported were coded as of unknown gestation.
¶Based on reports from 28 states. Medical inductions include saline and prostaglandin in 90% of "other procedures." Abortions at 16 weeks subtracted from 16 weeks and over and added to 13–15 weeks by formula.

Of all second-trimester abortions performed by major surgery (hysterotomy or hysterectomy), 4% were done by hysterectomy in 1968 and 10% in 1977 in England and Wales, and 14% in 1977 in Canada, compared with 37% in 1970–1971 and 55% in 1977 in the United States. Thus, the proportion of hysterotomies for second-trimester abortion appears on the decline.

Medical induction includes mainly the use of prostaglandin, hypertonic saline, and urea. In general, these procedures are selected more often in the later than in the earlier part of the second trimester. The exception to this is observed in Sweden, where extraovular instillations are more widely practiced than in the other three countries. The use of medical induction has increased in England and Wales at the expense of hysterotomy. In the United States, however, D&E is replacing many medical induction procedures.

Table 1-7 shows that the relative ranking of prostaglandin, saline, and urea within the category of medical induction is quite different in different settings. Prostaglandin is the clear favorite in England's NHS hospitals, while hypertonic saline predominates in the United States and Canada. In the private sector in England and Wales, all three methods are used with about equal frequency.

No national statistics on methods of abortion are collected in Japan. According to Professor Manabe[3] of the Kyoto University School

Table 1-7
Percent Distribution of Second-Trimester Medical Inductions by Method, Within Weeks of Gestation: Selected Areas, 1971

Weeks of Gestation	Prostaglandin	Saline	Urea
Canada			
13–16	39.6	48.8	11.6
17 or more	33.4	57.5	9.1
England and Wales*			
13–16	75.1	11.0	13.9
17 or more	48.6	21.0	30.4
NHS-hospitals			
13–16	92.1	0.7	7.2
17 or more	88.1	1.8	10.1
Private sector			
13–16	32.1	36.9	31.0
17 or more	31.2	29.5	39.3
United States†			
13–16	25.1	66.3	8.6
17 or more	29.1	64.2	6.7

*All "other medical inductions" assumed to refer to urea.
†Ninety percent of "other methods" assumed to refer to urea.

of Medicine, a combination of laminaria and metreurynter (balloon) currently is the most frequently used method for second-trimester abortion (probably over 80%). This procedure gradually is replacing extraamniotic instillation of ethacridine lactate (Rivanol).[3] The use of prostaglandin is increasing in Japan, but according to Muramatsu, it is still mainly limited to academic institutions.[4] Hypertonic saline and urea are not used for medical induction procedures in Japan.

The different patterns exhibited in Tables 1-6 and 1-7 reflect, among other things, differences and changes in medical opinion and attitudes, generated in turn by the collective experience (or lack of it) of the medical profession, passed along in medical schools and teaching hospitals. Attitudes are modified occasionally by communication of research findings through the network of professional channels of communication and by the personal experience (or lack of it) of providers of abortion services. Other and more subtle factors include the organization of abortion services in the public and private sectors, the economic benefits or costs of specific procedures to providers and consumers, and the real or perceived risks of legal complications or administrative censure.

COMMENT

It is unfortunate that so many women must resort to second-trimester abortion. Their need to do so reflects a personal and/or social failure: a failure on the part of the pregnant woman, her family, or her doctor, the educational system, the medical system, the legal system; in fact, a failure of society at large. Any action, inaction, or deliberate policy which tends to delay the decision to seek an abortion or to implement that decision increases the risks to maternal life and health associated with it.

REFERENCES

1. Tietze C: *Induced Abortion 1979.* New York, The Population Council, 1979.
2. Hong SB, Tietze C: Survey of abortion providers in Seoul, Korea. *Stud Fam Plann.* 10:161, 1979.
3. Manabe Y: Personal communication, 1979.
4. Muramatsu M: Personal communication, 1979.
5. Canada: *Statistics Canada* and *Therapeutic Abortions,* 1977.
6. Czechoslovakia: Institute for Health Statistics. *Zdravotnicta Statistika CSSR,* Potraty, 1977.
7. United Kingdom: Office of Population Censuses and Surveys. *The Registrar General's Statistical Review of England and Wales.* Supplement on Abortion, 1973.

8. United Kingdom: Office of Population Censuses and Surveys. *Abortion Statistics: Legal Abortions Carried Out Under the 1967 Abortion Act in England and Wales,* 1976.

9. Hungary: Central Statistical Office. *A Vetelesek Adatai,* 1974-1975.

10. Hungary: Central Statistical Office. *Terhesseg-megszakitasok es Spontan Vetelesek Adatai,* 1976-1977.

11. India: National Institute of Family Planning. *Director's Report,* 1975-1976.

12. Japan: Ministry of Health and Welfare. *Statistics of Eugenic Protection:* Showa 52.

13. Pakter J, Nelson F, Svigir M: Legal abortion: a half decade of experience. *Fam Plann Perspect.* 7:248, 1975.

14. United Kingdom: Scottish Home and Health Department. Abortion statistics. *Health Bul.* 35:282, 1977.

15. Sweden: National Board of Health and Welfare. *Aborter,* 1977. Statistiska meddelanden, HS 1979:5.

16. Forrest JD, Tietze C, et al: Abortion in the United States, 1976-1977. *Fam Plann Perspect.* 10:271, 1978.

17. Center for Disease Control: *Abortion Surveillance, 1977.* Altanta, issued September, 1979.

18. Muramatsu M: An analysis of factors in fertility control in Japan—an updated and revised version. *Bull Inst Pub Health* 22:228, 1973.

19. Rao NB, Kanbargi R: Legal abortion in an India state. *Stud Fam Plann.* 8:311, 1977.

20. Cates W Jr, Tietze C: Standardized mortality rates associated with legal abortion: United States, 1972-1975. *Fam Plann Perspect.* 10:109, 1978.

21. Tietze C, Lewit S: Joint Program for the Study of Abortion (JPSA): Early medical complications of legal abortion. *Stud Fam Plann.* 3:97, 1972.

2 Second-Trimester Induced Abortion in the United States

Carl W. Tyler, Jr.
Willard Cates, Jr.
Kenneth F. Schulz
Richard M. Selik
Jack C. Smith

INTRODUCTION

Second-trimester legal abortion is an important public health problem in the United States because:

- These surgical procedures are performed almost 100,000 times each year
- They have been responsible for more than half of the abortion-related deaths among women in this country since 1972
- Most of the disability and the deaths associated with these procedures can be prevented

The data in Figure 2-1 demonstrate that, as pregnancy duration increases, the risk of death from induced abortion also increases.[1] It is clear that abortion deaths in the United States could be reduced by more than 50%, if all abortions were performed in the first trimester of pregnancy instead of the first two trimesters.

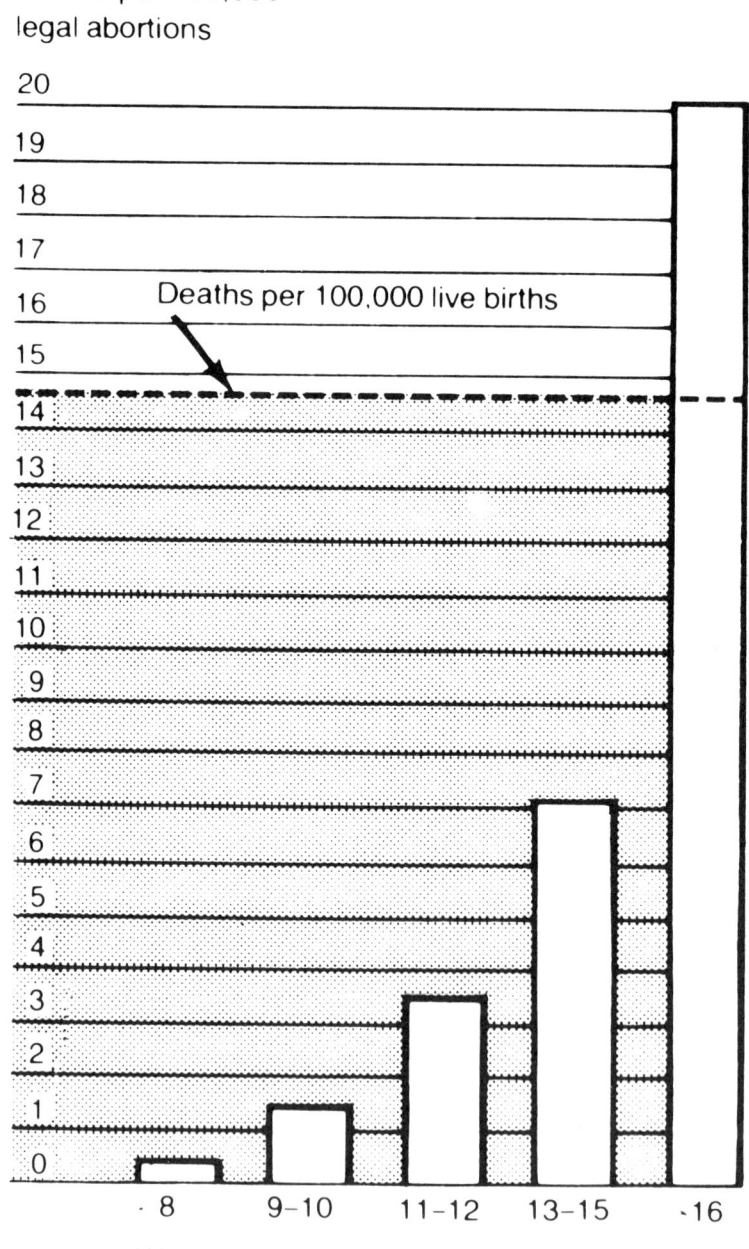

Figure 2-1 Standardized death-to-case rates per 100,000 legal abortions, by weeks of gestation, compared with standardized birth-related mortality rate, United States, 1972–1975.

Because second-trimester abortion has been a problem in the past decade and is likely to continue to be a problem in the future, this chapter will examine several of the current trends in the practice of late pregnancy termination. It also will consider possible changes for the future and the factors which will affect them.

CURRENT TRENDS

The practice of legal abortion in the United States has increased at an astonishing rate. In 1969, hospitals and health departments reported fewer than 23,000 abortions to the Center for Disease Control (CDC) (Table 2-1).[2] In 1970, more than 190,000 legal abortions were reported. One year later in 1971 the number had increased to more than 485,000. Each year since then, the total number of reported legal abortions has been greater than it was in the preceding year. By 1977 CDC for the first time received reports of more than one million legal abortions. Early reports to CDC for 1978 show no decline or leveling off in the number of legal abortions performed in the United States.

Table 2-1
Reported Legal Abortions—United States, 1967–1977

Year	Abortions	Increase from Previous Year	
		No.	%
1969	22,670	...	...
1970	193,491	170,821	753.5
1971	485,816	292,325	151.1
1972	586,760	100,944	20.8
1973	615,831	29,071	5.0
1974	763,476	147,645	24.0
1975	854,853	91,377	12.0
1976	988,267	133,414	15.6
1977	1,079,430	91,163	9.2

Source: Center for Disease Control: *Abortion Surveillance Annual Summary, 1977.*[2]

The total number of abortions actually performed in this country almost certainly is greater than that stated in CDC's reports, even though an almost 50-fold increase in the number of such operations has been documented in less than a decade. The Alan Guttmacher Institute (AGI), for example, reported 18% more abortions being performed in 1977 than did CDC.[3]

The national trend for second-trimester abortions contrasts

strikingly with that for the total number of legal abortions (Table 2-2). From 1972 to 1977, the percentage of all abortions reported as having been performed in the second trimester declined from 17.9% to 8.6%. Thus, while the total number of reported legal abortions increased by 80% and the number of first-trimester abortions more than doubled, the number of second-trimester abortions actually declined by 12%. In terms of the health and safety of American women choosing to terminate unplanned pregnancies, this change is favorable.

Table 2-2
Estimated Number of Second-Trimester Legal Abortions in the United States, 1972–1977

Year	Reported Abortions	Second-Trimester Abortions	
		Percent	*Number*
1972	586,760	17.9	104,971
1973	615,831	16.6	102,170
1974	763,476	13.2	100,722
1975	854,853	12.1	103,378
1976	988,267	10.5	103,709
1977	1,079,430	8.6	92,778
Total	4,888,617	12.4	607,728

Source: Center for Disease Control: *Abortion Surveillance Annual Summary 1977.*[2]

Despite this decline during the recent years, any operation performed nearly 100,000 times a year on American women of reproductive age has important implications. According to the National Hospital Discharge Survey for 1975, fewer women of 15–44 years of age underwent appendectomies or surgery of the muscles, tendons, fascia, and bursae, and fewer had lesions of the skin and subcutaneous tissue removed in hospitals than underwent second-trimester abortions.[4] This same survey recorded that women having second-trimester abortions were hospitalized an average of 1.4 days per patient. If an average hospital day cost $175 at that time, then the hospitals caring for women undergoing these operations incurred costs of more than $25 million in a single year. Adding professional fees substantially increases this cost estimate to at least $50 million.

Second-trimester abortions are particularly important from a public health point of view because they are responsible for more than half of the preventable abortion deaths. In the years from 1972 to 1977, 74 (57%) of the 129 legal abortion deaths reported to CDC occurred in women whose pregnancies were advanced beyond the first 12 weeks. The overall trend in mortality during these same years has nonetheless been favorable (Table 2-3). Between 1972 and 1975 deaths averaged nearly 15 a year, but there were only 15 deaths in 1976 and 1977 combined. The death-to-case rates have declined as well, averaging 14.4 per 100,000 second-trimester abortions each year between 1972 and 1975, and only 7.6 per 100,000 in 1976 and 1977 combined.

Table 2-3
Estimated Death-to-case Rates* for Second-Trimester Legal Abortions in the United States, 1972–1977

Year	Deaths	Rate
1972	12	11.4
1973	18	17.6
1974	13	12.9
1975	16	15.5
1976	9	8.7
1977	6	6.5
Total	74	12.2

*Rates are number of deaths per 100,000 second-trimester legal abortions.

Any discussion of the recent decline in the death-to-case rate of second-trimester abortions raises two questions. First, how do the characteristics of the people undergoing second-trimester abortions influence this trend? Second, what role do changes in medical practice play in this recent decline? National reporting of abortion data to the Center for Disease Control does not characterize women undergoing second-trimester abortions. Such an analysis, however, can be performed, based on use data from the Joint Program for the Study of Abortion/CDC.

Death-to-case rates for women undergoing second-trimester abortions increase with age, are higher for black women than for white, and are higher for married than for unmarried women (Table 2-4). Adjusting for the effect of age eliminates significant differences associated with marital status. The differences between race, however, are unchanged. Black women still have an age-adjusted death-to-case rate more than three and one-half times that recorded for whites. Since black women constitute a growing rather than a declining proportion of women undergoing abortion (23% in 1972 vs 34% in 1977), the age-adjusted rates do not explain a declining death-to-case rate. The racial differences in these rates must, therefore, be investigated further.

The procedures used for second-trimester abortions changed substantially between 1974 and 1977. The use of hypertonic saline instillation has declined, while the use of other techniques has increased. The data in Table 2-5 and Figure 2-2 are from the 16 states that reported abortion techniques and weeks of gestation for the entire

Table 2-4
Estimated Death-to-case Rates* of Second-Trimester Legal Abortions by Age, Race, and Marital Status, United States, 1972–1977

Demographic Characteristics	Rate
All women	12.2
Age	
Younger than 20	6.5
20–24	14.8
25 and older	18.9
Race	
White	6.8
Black	24.1
Marital status	
Married	17.7
Unmarried†	10.1

*Rates are number of deaths per 100,000 second-trimester legal abortions.
†Includes never married, separated, widowed, and divorced.

Table 2-5
Percentage of Reported Second-Trimester Abortion by Weeks of Pregnancy and Procedure, Selected States,* United States, 1974–1977

Weeks of Pregnancy and Procedure	1974	1975	1976	1977
13–15 weeks	100.0	100.0	100.0	100.0
D&E	65.3	69.9	76.5	80.8
Saline	28.9	22.9	18.9	11.8
Pg and other	5.8	7.3	4.6	7.4
Number of abortions	5,969	7,543	8,893	10,143
≥ 16 weeks	100.0	100.0	100.0	100.0
D&E	11.8	15.8	19.4	20.4
Saline	73.3	62.4	55.3	45.9
Pg and other	14.9	21.8	25.3	33.7
Number of abortions	10,220	12,313	13,071	13,038

*The 16 states selected for this tabulation are all of those which have reported weeks of pregnancy and procedure data for the four years, 1974–1977.
Source: Center for Disease Control: *Abortion Surveillance Annual Summaries for 1974, 1975, 1976, and 1977.*[5]

period of 1974 through 1977.⁵ Of the methods of legal abortion performed on women with 13- to 15-week pregnancies, dilatation and evacuation has become increasingly more popular. This technique was used for almost two-thirds of early second-trimester abortions in 1974 and four-fifths in 1977. Saline, on the other hand, was used for almost 30% of the cases in 1974, and only 12% in 1977. Prostaglandin and other agents showed no clear change in their use in 13- to 15-week abortions during the years 1974 to 1977; these agents were used in only about 6% of early second-trimester abortions.

For abortions performed on women with pregnancies of 16 or more weeks' gestation, 73% involved saline in 1974; by 1977 that proportion had decreased to 46%. The percentage of abortions performed with prostaglandin and other agents more than doubled during these same years. In 1974, prostaglandin and other agents were used in 15%

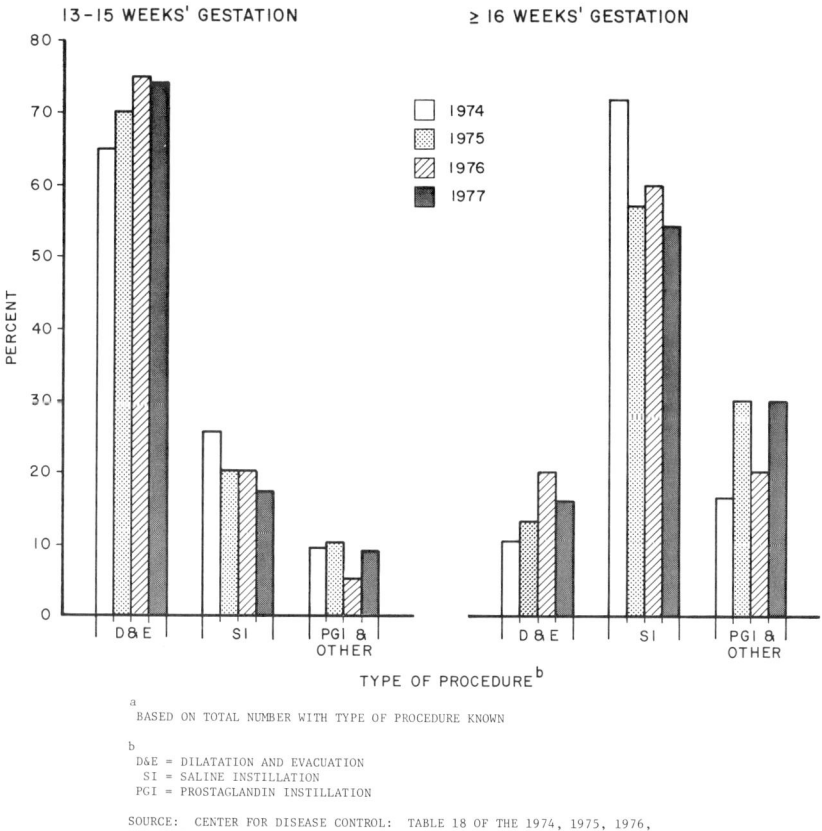

Figure 2-2 Percent distribution of legal abortions performed at ≥ 13 weeks' gestation, by type of procedure, United States, 1974–1977.

of late second-trimester cases; by 1977 that proportion had increased to 34%. The use of dilatation and evacuation increased steadily over the same time period from 12% of late second-trimester abortions in 1974 to 20% in 1977. It seems most likely that these changes in the procedures used to terminate second-trimester pregnancies are a major factor in the declining death-to-case rate noted above.

FUTURE TRENDS

Future trends in second-trimester abortions will be affected by demographic, social, behavioral, and biologic factors. The number of teenage American women reached a peak in the middle of the 1970s.[6] As these women reach their most fertile years in the coming decade, birth planning will become important to them. The expected increase in the number of women aged 20 to 29 in the 1980s probably will mean that the number of legal abortions will increase accordingly. It also is reasonable to speculate that the number of second-trimester abortions will increase.

Changes in frequency of sexual activity will continue to influence the risk of unplanned pregnancies. National surveys have indicated that the proportion of sexually active teenage American women is increasing.[7] This could mean that, even though there will be fewer women aged 15 to 19 in the coming decade, there may be more unplanned pregnancies.

Recently reported changes in contraceptive usage also favor an increase in unplanned pregnancies. The 1976 National Survey of Family Growth indicates that large numbers of women are turning away from highly effective modern contraceptives with their inherent risks and are using the safer but less effective "traditional" contraceptives.[8]

Approval of diagnostic tests for congenital disorders also will lead to more legal abortions in the second trimester. If such screening procedures are used routinely for women who are not at high risk for the disorders which can be detected by these tests, then some women with normal fetuses will have false positive test results and undergo unnecessary abortions.

Legal and judicial actions at the national, state, and local level also are likely to increase abortion delay and, therefore, the need for second-trimester abortions. Recent decisions to restrict the use of public funds to pay for abortions have been associated with delay in obtaining abortion.[9,10] New state laws and local ordinances have introduced mandatory waiting periods and complex consent procedures[11] that also could cause abortions to be delayed until the second trimester of pregnancy.

On the other hand, some influences potentially should decrease the number of second-trimester abortions. For example, involuntary infertility may decrease the number of unwanted pregnancies and the need for abortion. Sexually transmitted infections such as gonorrhea probably will cause substantial numbers of cases of infertility.[12] Pelvic inflammatory disease associated with use of the intrauterine device also may lead to infertility.[13]

The use of over-the-counter pregnancy test kits may allow some unplanned pregnancies to be diagnosed and terminated early. Although most consumers using these tests probably will make early and correct diagnoses of pregnancy more often than not, a false-positive test could lead to unnecessary surgery and a false-negative test could lead to a delay in seeking an abortion for an unintended pregnancy.

The role of behavioral and biological determinants of trends in second-trimester abortion was highlighted by a study in which more than 1000 women undergoing abortion in 1976 in Washington, DC, were interviewed.[14] Psychological processes, such as decisional conflict, and repression, or denial of pregnancy all caused women to delay seeking abortion. Social factors, such as the duration of a woman's relationship with her sexual partner and use or lack of use of contraception also played an important role. Inadequate knowledge about the availability and legality of abortion also correlated significantly with delay. This was a surprising finding since the interview respondents lived in our nation's capital and were questioned only three years after the Supreme Court decision. The low level of education which was associated with delay in seeking abortion "probably reflects competency rather than simply knowledge or socioeconomic status."[14] Of the biologic factors the most strongly associated with delay in seeking abortion was a history of irregular menstruation. Lack of perception of pregnancy symptoms was another important factor.

This study indicates that both improved contraceptive use as well as the provision of more accurate information on the legal status of abortion might further reduce the number of legal second-trimester abortions. Moreover, it demonstrates that biologic factors are important determinants of abortion delay. Until these factors can be effectively managed, second-trimester abortions will continue to be a major health care problem.

It is clear that extensive research on abortion delay will be needed in the future in order to understand more fully the reasons behind this phenomenon. Despite the careful planning of this study and the sophisticated analysis of its data, the factors described by the authors explained only a small proportion (17%) of the variance between women who did and those who did not delay seeking abortion.

This lack of understanding of the reasons for delaying abortion strengthens the contention that second-trimester abortions will continue to be an important health problem.

SOLVING THE PROBLEM: THE NEED TO CHANGE CURRENT TRENDS

There are two major means of resolving the health problems associated with second-trimester abortions. The first is to prevent the need for such operations altogether. A program of contraceptive development leading to safer, more effective, and more acceptable means of preventing unplanned pregnancy could substantially reduce the need for second-trimester abortion. Promoting early decision-making on the continuation or termination of pregnancies also could be effective if free pregnancy tests were available through public health facilities. Furthermore, effective and frequent dissemination of current and accurate information on the legal status of abortion also could help avoid delay in seeking abortion. In addition, extensive health education regarding the signs and symptoms of early pregnancy might help some women to seek medical advice early in pregnancy.

Making second-trimester abortion a safer procedure is the second means of resolving the health problems related to delayed abortions. In this regard, there are two possible approaches. The first is to use the safest available technique for performing second-trimester abortion. The second requires a critical analysis of deaths from second-trimester abortions. Since 1975, CDC has begun to analyze all reported legal abortion deaths.[15] The analysis carried out at CDC examines the roles played by physicians, patients, health care facilities, and the community in which the death of the woman occurred. A review of fatal cases indicates that 86% of the deaths might have been prevented if there had not been some problem in carrying out the tasks needed to avoid the death. In most cases several factors simultaneously contributed to death (Figure 2-3). In 68% of these cases there was a problem with the physician's performance. In 62% of cases a critical performance problem was ascribed to the patient. In 44% of cases both the physician and the patient had a critical performance problem. In most cases multiple performance problems were identified (Figure 2-4). Of the performance problems identified, the four most common were: 1) patient's failing to use contraception, 2) patient's delaying obtaining a first-trimester abortion, 3) physician's failing to empty the uterus completely, and 4) physician's perforating the uterus. The most common patient problem was delay in obtaining an abortion in the first trimester (Figure 2-5). Only 14% of abortion-related deaths analyzed to date were judged not to have been preventable.

If analysis of cases is to be effective in making second-trimester abortions safer, other actions also are necessary. Medical histories, for example, will need to focus not only on the immediate diagnosis and treatment of a particular problem, but also consider community,

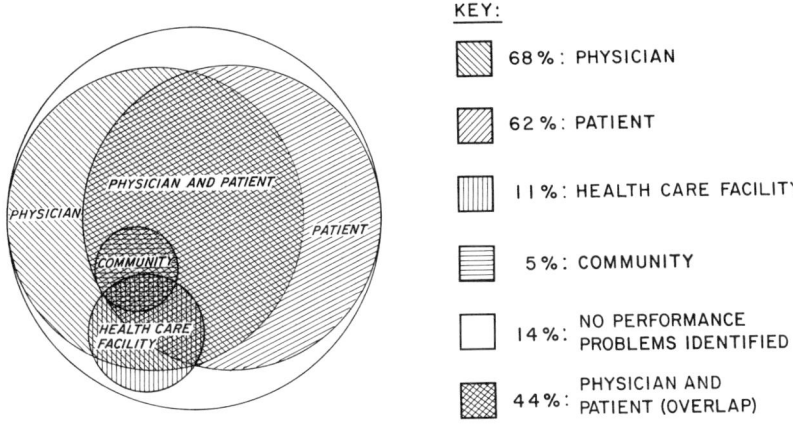

Figure 2-3 Percent distribution of abortion-related deaths in 1975–1977, by person(s) responsible for performance problems.

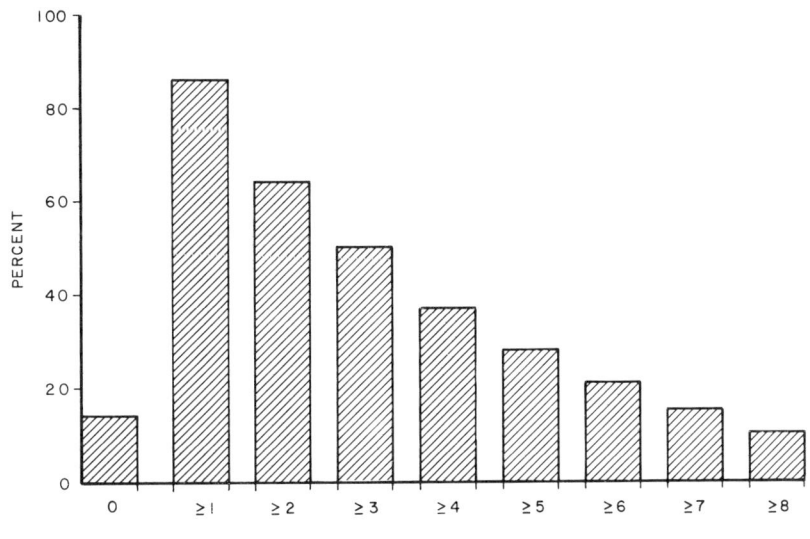

Figure 2-4 Percentage of abortion-related deaths to which multiple performance problems contributed in 1975–1977.

health care facility, and patient and physician factors which might lead to the prevention of that problem in the future. Epidemiologic analysis of groups of cases must be performed to improve the power of individual case analysis. Wide dissemination of these findings will be essential in order to effect changes in health care practices throughout the country. Finally, new trends in health problems related to second-trimester abortion must be assessed frequently in order to assure that critical case analysis is having the desired effect.

SUMMARY

Second-trimester abortion is an important health problem because of the large number of procedures performed and because the associated morbidity and mortality are largely preventable. Fortunately, the current trends in performance of second-trimester abortion are favorable to the health of American women. Recent changes in medical practice, such as wider utilization of D&E for early second-trimester abortions, have been an important part of these salutary changes.

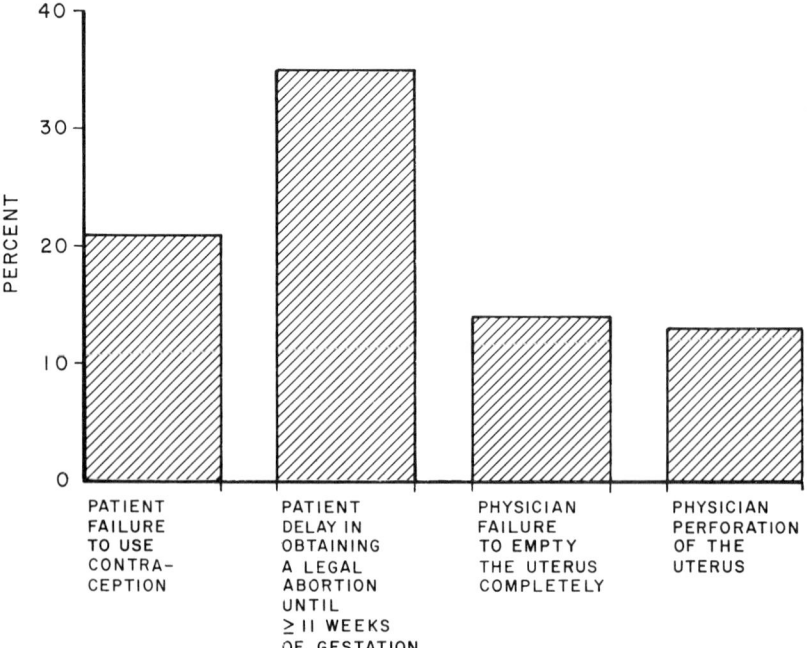

Figure 2-5 Percentage of abortion-related deaths to which selected performance problems contributed in 1975–1977.

These favorable trends could be further strengthened by more effectively preventing unplanned pregnancies, as well as by providing the safest possible abortion services. Critical evaluation of both commonly practiced and newly developed abortion techniques and detailed epidemiologic analysis of abortion deaths hold prospects for safer second-trimester abortions in the future.

REFERENCES

1. Cates W Jr, Tietze C: Standardized mortality rates associated with legal abortion: United States, 1972-1975. *Fam Plann Perspect.* 10:109, 1978.
2. Center for Disease Control: *Abortion Surveillance, 1977.* Atlanta, issued September, 1979.
3. Forrest JD, Tietze C, Sullivan E: Abortion in the United States, 1976-1977. *Fam Plann Perspect.* 10:271, 1978.
4. Ranofsky AL: *Surgical Operations in Short-stay Hospitals, United States, 1975.* Vital and Health Statistics: Series 13, Data from the National Health Survey, No. 34, DHEW Pub No. (PHS) 78-1785.
5. Center for Disease Control: *Abortion Surveillance, 1974, 1975, 1976 and 1977.* Atlanta, issued April, 1976; April, 1977; August, 1978; and September, 1979.
6. U.S. Bureau of the Census, Current Population Reports Series P-25, No. 601, *Projections of the Population of the United States: 1975 to 2050.* US Government Printing Office, Washington, DC, 1975.
7. Zelnik M, Kantner JF: Sexual and contraceptive experience of young unmarried women in the United States, 1976 and 1971. *Fam Plann Perspect.* 9:55, 1977.
8. Ford K: *Contraceptive utilization in the United States: 1973 and 1976.* Advance Data, National Center for Health Statistics, No 36, August 18, 1978.
9. Cates W Jr, Kimball AM, Gold J, et al: The health impact of restricting public funds for abortion, October 19, 1977-June 10, 1978. *Am J Pub Health* 69:945, 1979.
10. Rubin GL, Gold J, Cates W Jr: Response of low income women and abortion facilities to restriction of public funds for abortion: a study of a large metropolitan area. *Am J Pub Health* 69:948, 1979.
11. Cates W Jr, Gold J, Selik RM: Regulation of abortion services—for better or worse? *N Engl J Med.* 301:720, 1979.
12. Center for Disease Control: Results of culture testing for gonorrhea—United States, 1978. *Morbidity Mortality Weekly Rep.* 28:290, 1979.
13. Faulkner WL, Ory HW: Intrauterine devices and acute pelvic inflammatory disease. *JAMA* 235:1851, 1976.
14. Burr WA, Schulz KF: Delayed abortion in an area of easy access. *JAMA* 244:44, 1980.
15. Selik RM: *Performance problems associated with abortion deaths: an epidemiologic analysis.* Presented at the Epidemic Intelligence Service Conference, Atlanta, April 2-6, 1979.

3 The Availability of Second-Trimester Abortion Services in the United States

Jeannie I. Rosoff

The total number of women obtaining legal abortions has grown steadily during the past ten years. The proportion of abortions performed in the second trimester of pregnancy, however, has declined sharply from 17.9% in 1972 to 10.4% in 1976 and even further in 1977.[1] While a causal relationship cannot be established, it is likely that one of the factors leading to this decline has been the relatively rapid increase in the availability of first-trimester abortion services.

In 1972 slightly more than half of all abortions were performed in the woman's state of residence; by 1976 90% of women obtaining abortions were able to do so in their own state.[2] It remains true, however, that many women still have to travel considerable distances to obtain their abortions, and that a considerable number of women are unable to obtain an abortion within their own states. To some unknown degree, delay may be caused by difficulties in securing a convenient, low-cost abortion early in pregnancy. One might anticipate, however, that with increased education, widespread availability of low-cost or free pregnancy tests, more complete geographic availability of abortion services, *and* subsidized abortions for the poor, the proportion of abortions performed in the second trimester might decline even further in the future. In addition, the availability of early second-trimester abortions in specialized clinics at a cost lower than that charged in hospitals also might result in more, if not *most*, second-trimester abortions being performed in the very early part of that gestation period. On the other hand, should the future see an increased use of prenatal screening with amniocentesis or other procedures to detect birth defects as recently recommended in the Surgeon General's Report on Health Promotion and Disease Prevention,[3] a small rise in the number of late second-trimester abortions might be expected.

Only three of the many issues related to availability of second-trimester abortions will be considered in this chapter:

- The extent to which second-trimester abortions are legally regulated
- The geographic distribution of abortion services and, in particular, of abortion services in the second trimester
- Relative costs in hospitals vs clinics

REGULATION

The Supreme Court, in *Roe v. Wade*,[4] prohibited state restrictions on abortions in the first trimester, permitted states to regulate abortion in the second trimester for purposes "reasonably related" to the protection of the woman's health, and prohibited abortion after viability of the fetus except "when it is necessary to preserve" the woman's life or health. The Supreme Court said that viability generally occurs between the 24th and 28th week of gestation but refused to define it further, leaving the decision to be made by the physician on a case-by-case basis. In spite of this, laws still remain on the books (although some are under court challenges) which prohibit abortion, except to preserve the woman's life or health, after the 20th week in North Carolina, and after 24 weeks in Massachusetts, Nevada, New York, South Carolina, and South Dakota. In Oklahoma, special conditions are imposed after the 24th week. Seventeen other states, more attuned to the Supreme Court decisions, prohibit abortion "after the second trimester" or "in the third trimester" or after "viability," except to preserve the woman's life or health. Kentucky does so when the fetus "is expected to be viable;" in Utah the concern centers on a reasonable chance of survival. The remaining majority of states have no laws on how late in pregnancy abortions may be performed (Table 3-1).

Table 3-1
State Laws Relating to Third-Trimester Abortions

	No. of States	Abortion Only to Preserve Woman's Life or Health	Abortion Only to Preserve Woman's Life	Additional MD Certification Required	Additional MD Presence Required	All Attempts Must be Made to Preserve Life of Fetus
Third-Trimester Abortions	3					
Connecticut		X				
Florida		X		X		
Washington			X			
After Second Trimester	2					
Georgia		X		X		
Iowa		X				
After Viability	13					
Idaho			X			
Illinois						X
Indiana		X*				X
Louisiana		X		X*	X*	X
Missouri		X		X		
Montana		X				X
Nebraska		X		X		X
North Dakota		X				
Pennsylvania		X				
Rhode Island			X			
Tennessee		X		X		
Virginia		X				X
Wyoming		X				

Table 3-1
State Laws Relating to Third-Trimester Abortions *(continued)*

	No. of States	Abortion Only to Preserve Woman's Life or Health	Abortion Only to Preserve Woman's Life	Additional MD Certification Required	Additional MD Presence Required	All Attempts Must be Made to Preserve Life of Fetus
"Is Expected to be Viable"	1					
Kentucky		X				X
Reasonable Chance of Survival	1					
Utah		X				X
After 24 Weeks	6					
Massachusetts		X				X
Nevada		X				
New York			X			
Oklahoma		X[‡]			X	X
South Carolina		X		X[§]		
South Dakota		X				
After 20 Weeks	4					
Iowa						X
Minnesota					X[†]	
New York					X	
North Carolina		X				

*Law temporarily enjoined.
†Under court challenge.
‡If an abortion is performed to preserve the woman's mental health, the certification of a financially independent psychiatrist is required.
§After the 24th week a physician must certify, in writing and before the abortion is performed, the precise criteria upon which the judgment that the fetus was not viable is based.

Besides attempting to regulate, in some cases impermissibly so, *when* second-trimester abortions may be performed, some 22 states limit, by law, *where* they may be performed (Table 3-2). Fourteen states require that they take place in hospitals, but in Idaho this requirement applies only from 14 weeks on. Some states also specify that certain additional conditions must be met, some of which may be more or less restrictive. In Connecticut the hospital must have both a Department of Obetetrics and Gynecology and a Department of Anesthesiology. Massachusetts requires that abortions after the first 13 weeks be performed in a hospital equipped for general surgery. The Illinois law specifies only that life support equipment must be available. In eight other states, the law specifies that second-trimester abortions may also be performed in nonhospital facilities, in some cases with additional requirements which may be onerous to a greater or lesser degree or, in some cases, ambiguous. For example, in South Dakota, if a hospital is unavailable, second-trimester abortions may be performed in clinics or even doctors' offices if there are an adequate supply of blood for transfusions and facilities for Rh testing and for administration of Rh immune globulin. In Kentucky, however, the clinic must offer a full range of obstetrical and surgical facilities in which the operating physician has privileges in obstetrics and gynecology. In Utah second-trimester procedures may be performed in clinics and facilities capable of providing "the same degree of care as a hospital."

Table 3-2
State Laws Regulating Second-Trimester Abortion Facilities

Hospitals Only	Hospitals or Other Facilities
Connecticut*	Georgia†
Hawaii†	Kentucky*
Idaho‡	Minnesota†
Illinois*	Nevada*†
Indiana	North Carolina†
Louisiana†	South Carolina†
Massachusetts*	Utah
Missouri	South Dakota*
Montana	
New York§	
North Dakota	
Oklahoma	
Tennessee†	
Virginia†	

*Additional requirements other than licensed by state or publicly operated.
†Law specifies hospital or facility must be licensed or publicly operated.
‡Between 14 and 25 weeks.
§Between 12 and 20 weeks.

It is not known with precision at this time exactly how many states—both among those several which have specific laws regarding the regulation of second-trimester abortions and the majority which do not—have administrative regulations dealing specifically with the performance of abortion in the first and second trimesters, with the regulation of outpatient surgery, or with the licensing of nonhospital health facilities. For example, in Pennsylvania and several other states, the departments of health by *regulation,* not law, require that second-trimester abortions be performed in hospitals. Many of these regulations have been challenged in the courts with varying degrees of success and outcome. In a recent case involving the regulation of first-trimester abortions, the U.S. Court of Appeals for the First Circuit ruled on June 19, 1979, that states may require facilities offering only first-trimester abortions to be licensed. This reversed a district court ruling that permanently enjoined enforcement of Massachusetts' clinic licensure law and the licensing regulations issued by the Department of Public Health, insofar as they applied to abortion clinics. The district court held in October, 1978, that the regulations constituted an imposition of special requirements on first-trimester abortion clinics and, pursuant to *Roe v. Wade,* exceeded state authority to regulate early abortions.[5] "There is room," the court said, "for states to apply the same licensing standards to abortion facilities as they apply to like facilities performing medically analagous procedures, as long as they do not do so in a way that evades *Roe* by impinging on a woman's right to elect and obtain an abortion during the first trimester. The fact that [Massachusetts'] provisions apply generally to health care facilities of all kinds, and do not single out abortions," the court continued, "suggests that they reflect a neutral evaluation and selection of standards deemed necessary to safeguard the public."

Previously, on May 21, 1978, a New Jersey Supreme Court had ruled that regulations limiting the performance of second-trimester abortions on an outpatient basis are within a state's purview.[6] The decision upheld the "termination of pregnancy rule" issued in 1978 by the New Jersey State Board of Medical Examiners. This rule provided that, beyond the first trimester and within a period not exceeding 16 menstrual weeks and/or 14 gestational weeks, abortions by the dilatation and evacuation (D&E) procedure were allowed to be performed in a hospital or licensed clinic on an outpatient basis. Second-trimester abortions by any other method or beyond the specified period were required to be performed in a hospital on an inpatient basis.

The court said that testimony and documentary evidence indicated that saline abortions "presented significantly greater risk frequency for complications" such as hemorrhage, infection and fever, and other "extrinsic" risks when performed on an outpatient basis. There was "more than sufficient credible evidence," it added, "upon which the Board could act, and in light of the conflicting nature of the proofs, we are constrained to defer to their expertise." Finally, the plaintiff's argument that the in-hospital restriction would effectively bar many needed second-trimester abortions was found "equally unavailing." While recognizing the need for such abortions (estimated by the Board to range from 5000 to 7000 annually) and "the problem of admittedly higher hospital costs for inpatient procedures, which will restrict young and poor women from obtaining treatment," the court concluded that "it does not follow . . . that the Board must advocate a rule which in its opinion would be deleterious to maternal health."[6]

The main contested areas of the law regarding the performance of abortions in the second trimester are thus: *when* they may be performed, *where* they may be performed, and *under what conditions* the states may require they be performed. Further litigation may be expected for some extended period while clarification is sought for all these questions.

GEOGRAPHICAL DISTRIBUTION OF SERVICES

Legal limitations on the availability of abortion, however serious by themselves, apply only to a limited number of states and are only *one* of the elements shaping trends in the availability of abortion services in the second trimester. It can be expected, therefore, that some of the patterns of distribution which became apparent in the availability of first-trimester abortions will be reflected in the ease or difficulty with which abortion can be obtained later in pregnancy. In general, abortion services have become more widely diffused among the diverse regions of the country. In the first quarter of 1973, 84% of all abortions were performed in the three census divisions (Middle Atlantic, South Atlantic, and South Pacific) where New York, the District of Columbia, and California already had liberalized their abortion laws. In the first quarter of 1977, however, only 58% were performed in these same census divisions.[7] While significant disparities still exist between census divisions, disparities which are even more apparent at the community level, the percentage of abortion needs which were met in each census division in 1977 was much closer to the percentage of all women in need of abortion services than was the case in 1973.

Although abortion services presently are more widely available than they were in the year after the Supreme Court decisions, service providers have remained heavily concentrated in metropolitan areas, particularly in the very largest metropolitan areas. This statement is especially true for second-trimester procedures. Even among those few hospitals reporting performance of abortion procedures, there were significant disparities between metropolitan and nonmetropolitan areas. Sixty-three percent of hospital providers in metropolitan areas reported performance of second-trimester abortions, but only 38% in nonmetropolitan areas did so.

The widespread availability of first-trimester abortion services after 1973 was due largely to the expansion of a network of outpatient or "free-standing" clinics. By 1976, these facilities accounted for 62% of all reported abortions in the United States.[7] During that same year, only eight out of ten public hospitals and six out of ten non-Catholic hospitals performed *any* abortions. With the exception of a few large medical centers, those hospitals which did provide abortions reported performing very few procedures. The providers of abortion services which had relatively large (400 or more reported abortions in 1976) caseloads, however, were more likely to perform late abortions. Throughout the United States, only 50% of those hospitals reporting fewer than 400 abortions in 1976 performed any second-trimester abortions, while 91% of those reporting more than 400 abortions performed second-trimester abortions.

The trends observed in the provision of first-trimester abortion services—i.e., the slow, but real diffusion of availability of services geographically, the emergence of a nonhospital delivery system, and the concentration of specialized reproductive health services in a rather limited number of facilities located mainly in metropolitan areas—all are being reflected in the current patterns of the provision of second-trimester abortions. A special survey of the characteristics and service features of abortion providers conducted by the Alan Guttmacher Institute (AGI) in 1977 indicated that only about one-quarter of ambulatory care clinics reported performing abortions in the second trimester.[8] As with hospitals, the larger the abortion caseload of the clinic, the more likely it was to perform second-trimester procedures. Taking into account the estimates from the Center for Disease Control of about 118,500 second-trimester procedures performed in the United States in 1977[9] and the data obtained through the AGI 1977 survey of the characteristics and services provided by abortion providers (chiefly clinics), it appears that about 80,000 second-trimester abortions were provided in hospitals versus 38,500 in clinics. In 1977, clinics accounted for about one-third of all second-trimester abortions in the United States and undoubtedly a higher proportion in the 13th and 15th weeks.

COMPARATIVE COSTS

In 1976, the median cost of a first-trimester abortion performed in a clinic was $165.[8] As shown in Table 3-3, the cost of a second-trimester abortion not only was substantially higher but also increased with the length of gestation. A clinic abortion at 12 to 14 weeks cost an average of $254; at 15 weeks, the average cost was $340. The average fee for a second-trimester abortion performed in a hospital was even higher, since the average hospital charge alone was $435 without the physician's fee, which frequently was as high as $300. It is clear that the quoted average greatly understated the total cost to a woman of an in-hospital second-trimester abortion, and that a second-trimester abortion was substantially less expensive if performed in a clinic. The increasing numbers of second-trimester abortions being performed in clinics rather than hospitals may be expected, in time, to reduce the average expense facing a woman who seeks a second-trimester abortion.

Table 3-3
Average Charges for Second-Trimester Abortions in Hospitals and Clinics, 1978

Clinics†	
Average total charge for all D&E abortions (40 providers)	$284
Average total charge for D&E abortion at 12-14 weeks (14 providers)	$254
Average total charge for D&E abortion at 15 weeks and over (7 providers)	$340
Hospitals‡	
Average hospital charge for second-trimester abortion	$435*

*Amount significantly understates the *total* average charge since 84% of respondant hospitals reported that the physician's fee (typically between $200 and $300) is not included.
Sources:
†*Membership Directory, 1978,* National Abortion Federation, New York, New York. (Forty of its 118 abortion provider members report performing second-trimester abortions.)
‡From unpublished AGI sample survey of US abortion provider hospitals and clinics conducted in late 1976, inflated by the 8.7% increase in the medical care component of the Consumer Price Index between 1976 and 1977.

Any discussion of average costs may fail totally to describe the true and often desperate situation faced by an individual woman seeking a second-trimester abortion in a given city in the United States. Even if outpatient clinics exist in her local area, they may not perform second-trimester abortions because of clinic policy or state laws restricting the provision of second-trimester abortions to hospitals. There is no assurance of access either to a local clinic or to a local hospital which can provide second-trimester abortion services. In some cases, the cost of travel to an abortion facility must be added on to the already high cost of a second-trimester abortion.

The restrictive combination of laws and policies, and the geographic distribution of providers willing and legally capable of providing second-trimester abortion services, most severely affects those women with low incomes. Although currently under review in various courts, at the time of this writing the federal Medicaid program provides funds for abortions only in cases in which the woman's life would be endangered, or severe and long-lasting physical health damage would result if the pregnancy were carried to term, or in reported cases of rape or incest. Only a few states have bridged this gap by using local funds to provide abortions for low-income women.[7] In the remaining states, low-income women seeking second-trimester abortions are faced with carrying their pregnancies to term, obtaining illegal abortions, seeking providers who will perform abortions at reduced fees or finding sufficient personal funds. The average Aid to Families with Dependent Children (AFDC) monthly payment for a family of four is $241, a figure which is substantially below the average clinic fee for an abortion performed at 15 weeks' gestation.[7] If second-trimester abortions are unavailable from clinics, low-income women have to face the even higher costs of hospital abortions. In the many communities without hospitals where second-trimester abortion procedures are unavailable. Low-income women also have to incur substantial travel costs. Thus the combination of Medicaid policies and the present geographic distribution of service providers easily might serve to make second-trimester abortions prohibitively expensive and thus realistically unavailable for large numbers of low-income women.

The recent impetus to require a one- to two-day delay in obtaining an abortion has been upheld by some courts[10]; this procedure leads to even further delays and increases the total costs of the procedure. Besides the medical costs, the patient additionally must incur doubled transportation expenses to which must be added the cost of days lost from work. Provisions for parental notification cause many teenagers to delay in seeking abortions for fear of parental reaction. Such activities encourage the teenager's postponement of her decision or perhaps even denial of her pregnancy until late in gestation.

COMMENT

Although the percentage of abortions performed in the second trimester has diminished rapidly in the five years following the landmark 1973 Supreme Court decisions, many women still are denied the abortions they desire because they are unable to overcome the major obstacles of travel to the provider and high cost.

It is unlikely that hospitals will make second-trimester abortion services more available or accessible in the immediate future. However, further expansion of the network of abortion clinics which has developed rapidly in the past years is possible. It now appears that some procedures can be provided safely in ambulatory clinic settings between 13 and 16 weeks.[10] Expansion of the clinic network, while possible, is not without certain limitations. These limits may be defined by law and/or regulations, both of which may need to be challenged repeatedly and at considerable cost. Similar limits also will be set by the economics of the situation, since the existence of a free-standing clinic requires a potential caseload large enough to be able to sustain it financially.

Nevertheless, certain steps must be taken if the following two goals are to be met: 1) to reduce further the percentage of those abortions which are performed during the second trimester, and 2) to enable all women who need abortions in the second trimester to obtain them. The steps are:

- Massive educational programs by public health authorities and the media regarding the early signs of pregnancy, and the importance of very early pregnancy detection. This is important not only in view of what we know of the significance of environmental factors on the health and well-being of the child if a birth is desired, but also because of the steadily increasing risks, week by week, of delayed abortions. A special effort in this educational campaign should be made to reach teenagers
- Development of a broad network of facilities for pregnancy detection, with free or very low-cost services, subsidized by local, state, and federal governments
- Assuming that safety can be maintained, lifting legislative or regulatory restrictions on the performance of early second-trimester abortions in clinics

- Elimination of confounding legal factors, such as required waiting periods and parental notification, which tend to delay obtaining an early abortion
- Removal of restrictions on the funding of abortions in private health insurance plans
- Finally, and perhaps most importantly, removal of federal and state restrictions on the funding of abortions for the poor through Medicaid and other publicly funded programs. In addition to the public funding of abortions for those women who are medically indigent, funding of transportation to medical care facilities requires particular attention in light of the inequities in the geographic availability of abortion services and, in particular, second-trimester abortion services

REFERENCES

1. Forrest JD, Sullivan E, Tietze C: Abortion in the United States, 1977-1978. *Fam Plann Perspect.* 11:329, 1979.
2. Forrest JD, Tietze C, Sullivan E: Abortion in the United States, 1976-1977. *Fam Plann Perspect.* 10:271, 1978.
3. *Healthy People, The Surgeon General's Report on Health Promotion and Disease Prevention 1979.* DHEW Pub No (PHS) 79-550091, p 7.
4. *Roe v. Wade,* Supreme Court, 410 U.S. 113 (1973).
5. *Baird v. Department of Public Health of Massachusetts,* 48 U.S.L.W. 2007 (lst Cir).
6. *Livingston v. New Jersey State Board of Medical Examiners,* A-596-77 (N.J. Super. Ct., App. Div.).
7. Alan Guttmacher Institute: *Abortions and the Poor: Private Morality, Public Responsibility,* 1979, p 6.
8. Lindheim BL: Services, policies and costs in U.S. abortion facilities. *Fam Plann Perspect.* 11:283, 1979.
9. Center for Disease Control: *Abortion Surveillance, 1976.* Atlanta, issued August, 1978.
10. Cates W Jr, Gold J, Selik R: Regulation of abortion services—for better or worse? *N Engl J Med.* 301:722, 1979.

PART II
The Second Trimester of Pregnancy

4 Anatomy

Kurt Benirschke

The purpose of this chapter is to synthesize existing information about the size and development of the human fetus and its placenta, membranes, cord, and amniotic fluid during the second trimester of pregnancy, or the gestation period from approximately 13–25 weeks.

It should be appreciated at the outset, however, that for numerous reasons, this is a difficult task. To begin with, when spontaneous abortion occurs in the second trimester, it usually is due to some pathologic event which may have had serious impact on normal development. Second, malformations of the uterus with consequent placental abruption and disturbances of nidation represent additional factors that may seriously affect developmental parameters without necessarily being recognized at the time of spontaneous abortion. Third, the recent vast experience with second-trimester induced abortions frequently employs hypertonic solutions which not only have a profound impact on fluid volume but also lead to fetal distortions and alterations of placental structure. On the other hand, if dilatation and evacuation is used, the fetus and placenta are destroyed.

Thus, it is difficult to obtain truly normal conceptuses from the second trimester. Embryological studies are scarce because the major developmental phases have ended, and the fetal growth phase constitutes less of a challenge to embryologists. Perhaps the best analysis of existing material has been performed by Boyd and Hamilton, whose primary concern was the development of the placenta, but who presented sufficient detail of fetal development as well as much pictorial support to their extensive studies.[1,2] These problems notwithstanding, this chapter will attempt to place the existing information in perspective from a clinical point of view.

THE FETUS

Because the fetus grows rapidly during the second trimester, careful attention must be paid to the data upon which determination of the fetal age is based. The obstetrician conventionally refers to the menstrual age of a pregnancy, connoting the length of time elapsed from the date of onset of the last menstrual period. Frequently, however, this determination may be inaccurate. Menstrual age exceeds the ovulation or fertilization age, i.e., the true fetal age, by two weeks unless implantation bleeding at the time of the trophoblastic invasion of the maternal vascular bed is mistaken as a new menstruation. In this case, the perceived gestational age would be in error by one month. How often this phenomenon occurs is not known with certainty. It is clear, however, from clinical practice that it may be more common than was previously thought.

Gruenwald and Minh have discussed the difficulty in obtaining normative data early in pregnancy for body and organ weights.[3] Moore has described the confusion that continues to exist when lunar and calendar months are used, suggesting that, because of the rapidity of fetal growth, one ideally should state whether one means the beginning or the end of "the tenth week."[4] Boyd and Hamilton also have discussed the pitfalls of accurate ascertainment of size and weights early in pregnancy. The nature of the delivery, the length of time elapsed before weighing, and the extent of blood loss when the cord is cut, all have a profound influence on weights of the fetus and placenta at this stage of pregnancy.

Frequently, not only are menstrual dates uncertain, but pathologic circumstances are not fully taken into consideration as well. For example, 23% of Wingate's 47 fetuses of *spontaneous* second-trimester abortions had congenital anomalies.[5] In addition, some studies indicate the occasional presence of decidual vascular lesions diagnostic of preeclampsia. Presumably these have a restrictive action on any placental perfusion that may already exist at this time.[6] Furthermore, the fetal weight changes profoundly upon immersion in formalin solution. In our own experience with weights, determined on identical scales before and after formalin fixation, there was a 5% to 8% increase following fixation, which possibly was dependent upon the strength and buffer of the formalin. Boving also found a 5% difference.[7] Unfortunately, such information frequently either is not available in the published compilation of fetal weights or is not adjusted in the tables from which normal weights are deduced. It is therefore impossible to define accurately the expected normal weight of a fetus which may have been subjected to any one or more of these variables. Extraneous factors such as race[3] and maternal smoking[8] also often enter into these considerations.

In clinical practice it has been more convenient to express correlations with sitting height or crown-rump (CR) length. Overall length (crown-heel or CH) is more difficult to assess, as the fetal legs often are difficult to straighten. Even though Streeter measured CR length by straightening the fetus at later stages,[9] other authors have measured the fetus with the natural curvature intact. Trolle reviewed this topic in detail and compared his large quantity of material from legal second-trimester abortions with data from the literature. He found considerable variation in the curves constructed from these data. He concluded that the best assessment of fetal age could be derived from Streeter's foot and CR length curves and Scammon's CH length measurements.[10] Trolle strongly recommended using foot length as the measurement standard, as little variation was found, and dismembered fetuses also could be assessed for their age. According to Streeter, from 12 to 21 weeks' menstrual age, the foot length increases from 1 to 3.8 cm.[9] Anyone who has attempted to measure the *accurate* length of a midterm fetus will know that extension of the neck region causes the measurement to vary considerably. This problem is greatly enhanced even with early maceration. The weight of the fetus is perhaps the most variable parameter, and thus the least accurate measure by which to gauge gestational age.

In the final analysis, one has to make a choice of whose data best fit one's bias. Figure 4-1 graphically reproduces the crown-rump length and fetal weight with standard deviation (SD) as plotted from Potter and Craig's table.[11] These data are nearly identical to the findings of Boyd and Hamilton, and are shown related to menstrual age. When a comparison is made with Streeter's curves, both length and weight are found to be larger than those quoted from Boyd and

Hamilton. It is not possible to ascertain the reasons for this discrepancy from the published records. It can be seen from Figure 4-1 that the fetus grows remarkably in length (60–180 mm) as well as weight (25–394 g) during menstrual weeks 12–26. The CR length increases almost linearly by approximately 1 cm per week, while weight increases more rapidly in the middle portion of this trimester.

Virtually all of the major differentiative embryological events have been completed prior to the onset of the second trimester. The physiologic umbilical hernia retracts abruptly in the 10th week when the embryo is approximately 42 mm in length; the external genitalia can be distinguished readily as male or female; fine lanugo hair is present on the forehead; and the extremities have a typically human quality. If anything is typical of the fetal development in the second trimester, it is the lengthening of the body in relation to the cranium. In contrast, at the outset of the third trimester, the fetal head is disproportionally large and, according to Boyd and Hamilton, represents one-third of the CR length.[2] At the end of the fourth month the

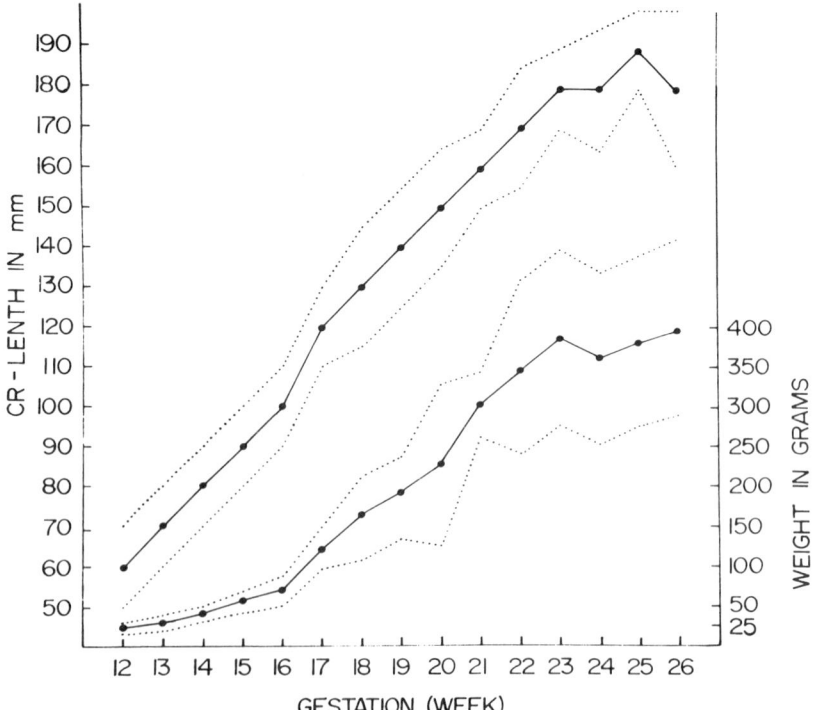

Figure 4-1 This graph plots the data of Potter and Craig[11] for crown-rump (CR) length in millimeters and fetal weight in grams for gestation weeks 12 to 26. The stippled lines give the standard deviations.

umbilical cord takes its origin at just above the symphysis in order to move upward into its "normal" position as a result of the growth of the lower abdomen during the ensuing two months. At the end of the fifth month the fetus weighs just under 500 g and has reached one-half the size of its term length. Fetal movement is perceived by the pregnant mother, lanugo hair covers the entire body, and sebum is from adnexal skin glands. Ossification of bones increases rapidly, brown fat forms in periadrenal, substernal, and cervical regions, and the skin is shiny and translucent (Figure 4-2). Hereafter, length increases by nearly 50 mm monthly, and the weight even more rapidly. For a month or so the skin is characteristically wrinkled, only to be filled out by the deposition of subcutaneous fat in the seventh month.

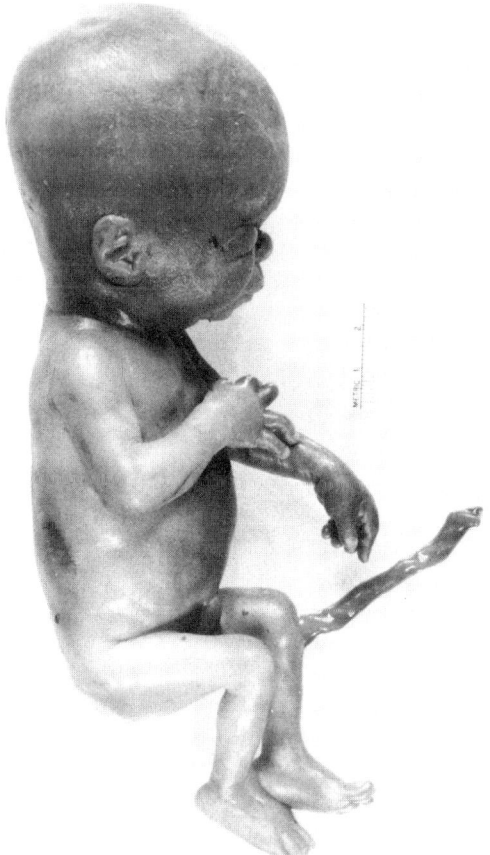

Figure 4-2 Second-trimester fetus from spontaneous abortion. Note glistening, translucent skin, fine facial and scalp lanugo, congested head from delivery, and truncal petechiae. Crown-rump (CR) length 17 cm, foot length 3.2 cm, estimated menstrual age 22 weeks.

Any pathologic interpretation of specific organ abnormalities must rest upon an understanding of standard normal weights.[11,12] For example, the particularly large "size" of the fetal adrenal gland is due to the presence of a fetal cortical zone that is destined to undergo atrophy following birth.[13] Similarly, the pathologist faced with tissue sections alone may turn to the developing renal cortex as an additional rough guide to placing a fetus of unknown size into an approximate developmental age group, even though fairly wide ranges in glomerular counts have been found.[14] Illustrations of the normal morphology of second-trimester fetal kidneys are provided in Potter's comprehensive study.[15]

Finally, the maturation processes of testes and ovaries involve specific changes that help to date fetuses. The early abundance of testicular interstitial cells reaches its peak at 13 cm CR length; atrophy rapidly ensues thereafter.[16] Likewise, the breaking up of sex cords and continuous centrifugal transformation of "Eiballen" into individual granulosa cell-invested primordial ova takes an orderly and superficially datable course. Testicular descensus into the scrotal sac normally occurs between the sixth and eighth months, and the process occurs slightly earlier on the right than on the left side.[17]

The size of the fetal head is another important parameter by which to estimate fetal growth in relation to length of gestation. Few accurate data from anatomical studies exist, however, and they are likely to be distorted by artifacts. Thus, vaginally delivered second-trimester fetuses frequently have extensive galeal and facial congestion, edema, and petechiae, as is evident from Figure 4-2. Fetuses obtained after introduction of hypertonic solutions into the amniotic cavity likewise often have petechiae and distortion of the fetal skin, as evidenced by the inability of skin cells to proliferate in tissue culture.[18] In recent years, skull size and CR length have been measured accurately in utero by ultrasonography.[19] Since this procedure will be discussed extensively elsewhere in this volume, suffice it to say that the exponential growth of the fetus in the first trimester becomes linear in the second trimester. Biparietal skull measurements show very little variation, conform closely to caliper measurements after delivery, and give a very accurate placement as to gestational age. From 12–26 weeks from ovulation, the biparietal diameter increases from 23–75 mm.

THE UMBILICAL CORD

There is considerable variability in the length of the umbilical cord; to define its "normal" length is difficult. Probably the most extensive data for the second trimester are the measurements by Boyd and

Hamilton.[2] As will be seen from Table 4-1, the length of the cord doubles during the second trimester. Thereafter, relatively little growth is recorded.

Table 4-1
Cord Length During Fetal Development

Lunar Month	Fetal Length in mm	Average Cord Length in cm	Range in cm
Fourth	61–100	15	5–25
Fifth	101–150	25	14.5–45
Sixth	151–200	28	21–48

Source: Boyd and Hamilton (1970).[2]

In contrast to the short, straight umbilical cord of species with bicornuate uteri, the human umbilical cord has a characteristic spiraling structure. This helical arrangement is present early in gestation; it becomes more pronounced with increasing gestational age. In the majority of cases a left spiral is taken; rarely is spiraling absent altogether. The cause of this helical arrangement has been debated widely. Malpas and Symonds concluded that it is most likely the result of differential fiber growth with a helical twist, and is genetically determined.[20] On the other hand, monozygotic twins do not necessarily have identical helices; the twist may reverse or it may be lost, and arteries may turn around veins and vice versa. Genetic explanations, differential blood flow arrangements, living in northern or southern hemispheres, and the many other theories invoked to explain the spirals fail to do so adequately. The helices probably are primarily the result of fetal movements. Quantitation of some of this fetal movement comes from the recent report by Sørensen, Hasch and Lange.[21] Using ultrasonography, they demonstrated a steady decline of breech presentation from 40% at 23 weeks to 15% at 32 weeks.

Spirals are found almost exclusively in primates; in the only other studied animal with a uterus simplex, the nine-banded armadillo twists are probably prevented by the tight packing of the longitudinally oriented quadruplets.

Human umbilical cords frequently are looped about the neck or extremities at this gestational age, and fetal deaths from such looping, knotting, or excessive spiraling have been described.[22] False knots ("varicosities") containing looped vessels are frequent.

In addition to variations in length and helical arrangement, the cord shows variations in structure and content. The amount of Wharton's jelly is extremely variable, and a false impression can be obtained from inspection of cords after removal of fetal blood. Reynolds has shown clearly that very little jelly is present when the fetal cord vessels are normally distended.[23] Numerous studies have searched for nerves in the cord. It is presently believed that no nerves traverse the length of the cord, and only some nerves pass from the fetal abdominal wall into the most proximal portions of vessels. The presence of remnants of omphalomesenteric and allantoic ducts must be considered a frequent normal variant of cord development, and even tiny remnants of muscleless vitelline vessels may exist in the second-trimester cord.

The umbilical vessels differ in many respects from large caliber arteries and veins at other bodily sites. Thus, no internal elastic lamella is present in the arteries, as is the case with the very permeable and loosely structured veins. The umbilical vessels freely permit the passage of leukocytes, are highly contractile, and have a different muscle bundle arrangement from other vessels.[2] Normally, two arteries and one larger vein are present, but a single umbilical artery occurs in 0.7% to 1% of fetuses. Two veins rarely are found. The two umbilical arteries have characteristic anastomoses of various types within 3 cm of the placental surface in about 96% of cases.[24] This finding is also made with different frequencies in most, but not all, primates studied by Young.[25]

The point of attachment of the cord to the chorionic plate is of interest. In over 90% of term placentas, the cord is situated on the main body; it lies at the margin in some 7% and on the membranes in about 1%. Velamentous insertion at term is correlated with lighter placentas, an increased frequency of fetal anomalies, postpartum hemorrhage, and twinning.[2,22] At earlier stages of pregnancy, on the other hand, the frequency of velamentous insertion apparently is much greater. Monie studied 183 questionably spontaneous abortion specimens. Of 18 specimens from the ninth to twelfth weeks of gestation, six (33.3%) had velamentous cords; of 34 specimens from the 13th to 16th weeks, nine (26.5%) were so constituted, and of 63 specimens from the 17th to 38th weeks only seven (11.1%) demonstrated this anomaly.[26] In addition to this finding, the incidence of fetal abnormalities was higher in the earlier gestational material. Monie's preference in explaining the high incidence of velamentous insertion goes to the theory of oblique implantation; irregular expansion (placental wandering, trophotropism) is an equally likely possibility, however. This can be inferred from marginal regressive changes in term placentas and from findings in multiple placentation. Numerous ultrasonographic studies since King's original description[27] have confirmed the high frequency of apparent placenta previa in the second trimester (Figure 4-3). This situation changes toward term, and the "migration" of the placenta presumably comes about by marginal atrophy and expansion at the contralateral side. Rizos, et al. have reviewed their own sonographic studies and most of the literature. At 16 weeks' gestation 58 (5.3%) of 1098 sonograms demonstrated placenta previa. Fifty-two patients were followed, but only five eventually had placenta previa at term. Ninety percent converted to normal placentation.[28] Similar marginal atrophic changes developing in migrating placentas have been observed by Winter.[29] When cervical markers are used for the exact localization of placental positional changes, on rare occasions the placenta also may demonstrate downward movement in the uterus.[30] Norlander, et al. as well as Rizos, et al. have shown not only that anterior location is considerably more common among low-lying placentas, but also that anterior location is more common overall.[28,30]

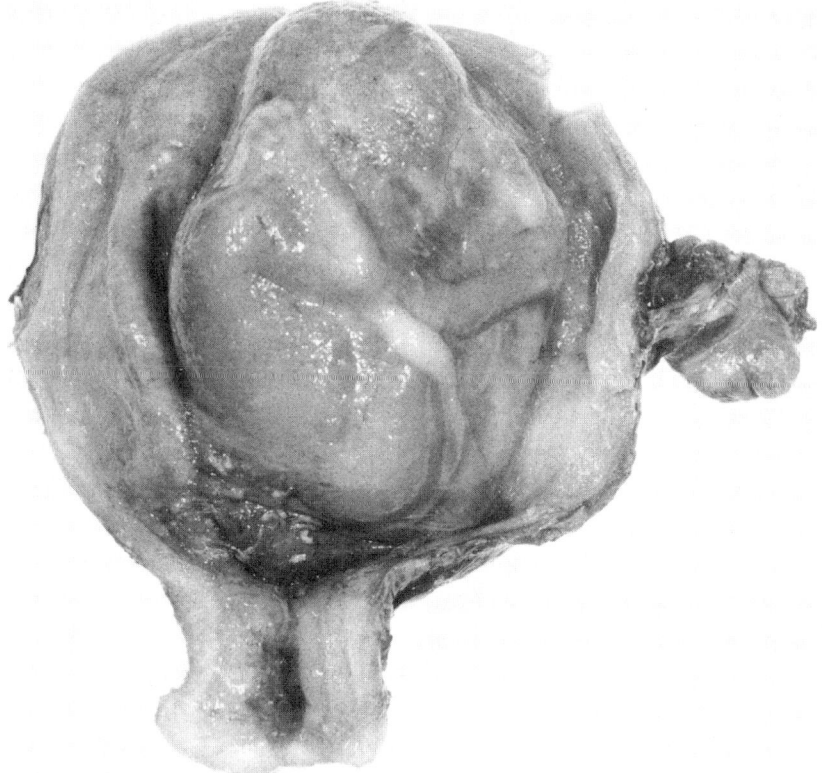

Figure 4-3 Hysterectomy specimen at 15 weeks' menstrual age with crown-rump (CR) length of 10 cm. The internal cervical os is overlain by a dark sickle-shaped segment of placenta. This represents a placenta previa.

THE PLACENTA

The placenta grows considerably during the second trimester. Prior to this time, its differentiation has largely been completed. In a study of the mitotic acivity of the cytotrophoblast or the Langhans layer, Tedde and Piras unequivocally demonstrated that the number of mitoses falls dramatically following the 12th week and reaches a low by the 17th week[31] (Figure 4-4). The size and volume of the developing placenta have been assessed by several investigators. Among the earliest were Boyd and Hamilton.[1] Abramovich[32] later criticized the lack of statistical evaluation of their data; this discrepancy subsequently was corrected by Grimes and Hamilton.[33] The graphs in this second publication give percentile curves over the entire range of development, which do not differ appreciably from the findings of the 47 hysterotomy specimens examined by Abramovich.[32] His table of accurately staged pregnancies indicates considerable variation in fetal and placental sizes. Nevertheless, when fetal weight and fetal/placental sizes are plotted with the logarithm of placental weight, a straight line relationship emerges. This series, albeit small, is valuable in that

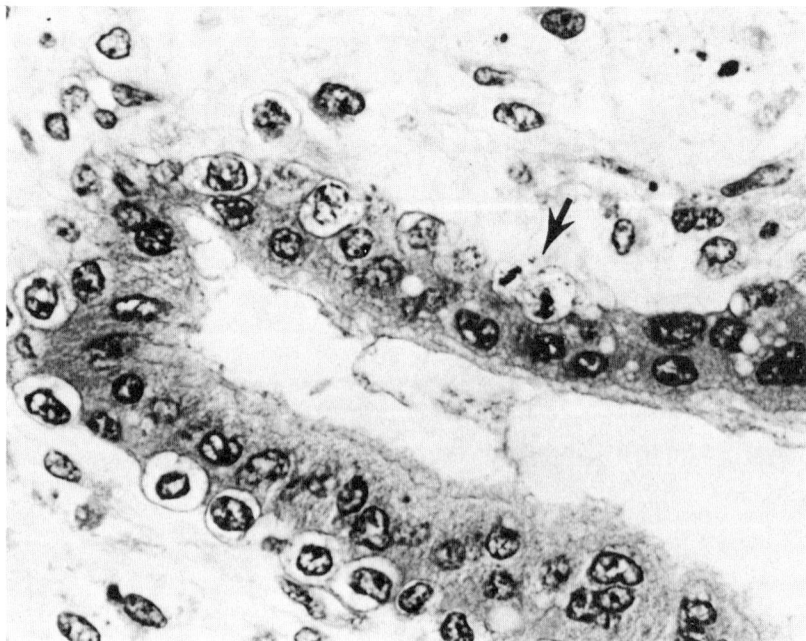

Figure 4-4 The villous surface at 12 weeks' gestation with syncytium (microvillous surface) lining the cleft-like maternal intervillous space. Cytotrophoblast with mitoses (arrow) forms a nearly continuous layer beneath. (H and E × 650.)

the organs were collected prospectively and treated uniformly by draining the small quantity of blood. Under these conditions, the placental weight increased from 68 to 305 g from weeks 12–23½ of menstrual age. It must be recognized that after delivery the placenta is "deflated" because of the absence of fetal vascular tone and the lack of intervillous blood content. This phenomenon readily becomes apparent when one injects the placenta with fluid and observes its thickness increase. Thus, the placenta is more likely to have a greater volume in utero than can be estimated after its removal. This situation has been examined by sonography before birth and by volumetry after birth. In all but two of 12 cases, the ultrasonographic volume was considerably greater than that of the delivered placenta.[34]

Considerable effort has been spent on estimating the extent of the placental villous surface area and on the quantitative aspects of the development of new villi during the placental growth phase. Aherne and Dunnill performed the most meticulous studies; they found that the placental exchange surface grows until term but that the average villous diameter remains constant from 18 to 40 weeks at 40μ to 49μ. They concluded that this augmentation was the result of continuous new villus formation, a suggestion which has not been accepted by all students of this question.[35]

The macroscopic morphology of the placenta also undergoes characteristic changes during the second trimester. At the outset, the type of chorionic vascular pattern has been established; the "disperse" type is much more common and is associated with more vascular divisions, more cotyledons, and heavier placentas than is the "magistral" pattern which is found more often with marginal cords.[36] Almost invariably the arteries pass over the chorionic veins and have dichotomous divisions. The number of "perforating" arteries determines the number of fetal cotyledons, generally around 20.

Aside from growth, the following changes occur during the second trimester. The decidua basalis becomes very much attentuated; septation is initiated from the floor by the growth of "X-cells," which produce the ultimate cotyledons visible from the maternal side (Figure 4-5); the spaces around amnion and decidua capsularis are obliterated. These latter processes are important. Up to the 12th week of development, the amnion does not completely fill the chorionic sac. This phenomenon is best appreciated in younger specimens (Figure 4-6).

The totally avascular amnion, therefore, is nourished by the nutrients and oxygen contained within the amniotic fluid and the magma reticulare or viscous chorionic liquid. Through continuous amnion expansion, this membrane becomes passively applied to the chorion in the 12th week. The membranes never completely fuse, however, and

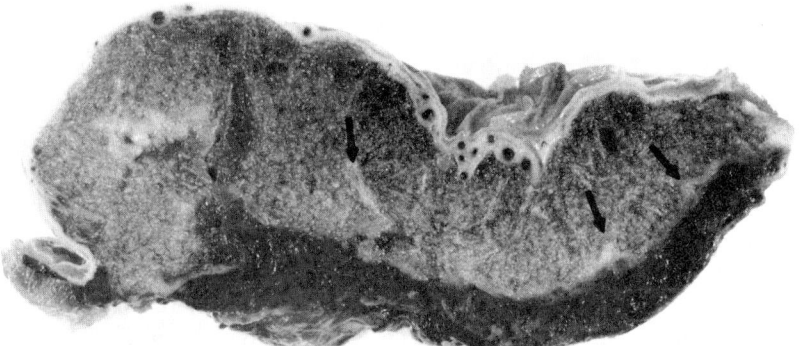

Figure 4-5 Spontaneously delivered placenta at 23 weeks' gestation with 500 g fetus. Characteristically, this placenta had intense chorioamnionitis. The large fresh clot (bottom) does not constitute an abruption. Note pale nature of villous tissue in immature placenta and incipient septum formation at arrows.

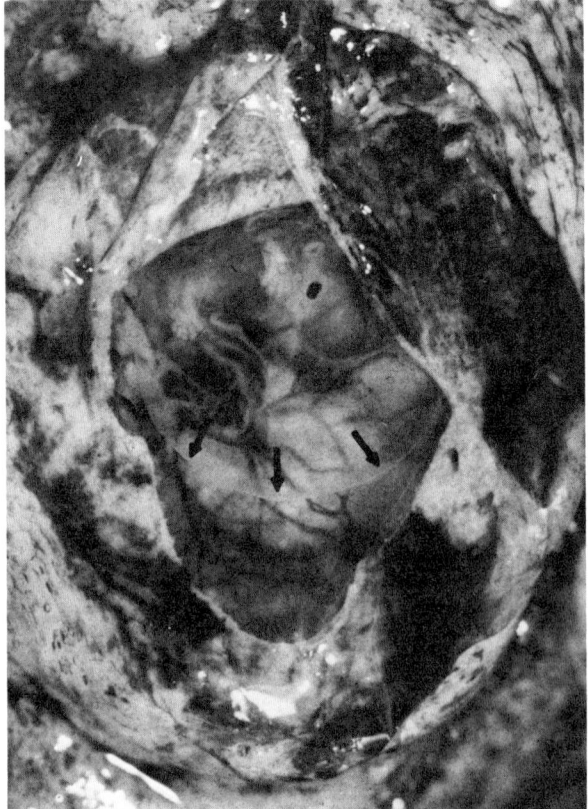

Figure 4-6 Eight-week conceptus in situ with 2 cm fetus. The chorion laeve has been laid open to disclose amnionic sac which will displace chorionic fluid in direction of arrows.

remain easily separable at term. This process of demi-fusion is important, since early disruption of the amnionic membrane may lead to the formation of amnionic bands.

The abolition of the extramembranous uterine space is more complex and less well understood. Boyd and Hamilton state that all of the decidua capsularis regresses, that the surface epithelium of the decidua vera atrophies, and that the uterine space is obliterated in the fifth month by "fusion" of the chorion laeve with the decidua vera.[2] In the author's opinion, actual cellular fusion does not occur between these two membranes; they are only passively joined and capable of atraumatic extrauterine separation.

Of special interest is a brief consideration of those changes occurring in the placenta as a result of chemical methods of pregnancy termination. The most frequently employed technique, intraamnionic injection of hypertonic solutions, leads to a very characteristic coagulation necrosis of the placental surface (Figure 4-7). Edema and cellular disruption of the amnion and chorion occur with formation of a thin layer of subchorionic intervillous thrombus. Superficial vessels frequently are thrombosed, and occasional infiltration by leukocytes is seen. Similar changes occur when the hypertonic solutions are injected extraamniotically.[37]

From the preceding considerations, one can infer that 15- to 20-week abortions of this type are induced by extramembranous rather than truly extraamniotic injection. The extent of the placental injury testifies to the enormity of water and solute fluxes taking place. Villi that are trapped within this superficial coagulation necrosis lose their immunologic markers, whereas the remaining 80% of peripheral villi remain normal.[38] Exactly what triggers the abortion in such cases has been in dispute; some authors favor placental damage, others a disturbance in the "progesterone block." Still other explanations have been advanced as well.

The situation differs with mechanically induced abortions. Manabe, Okamura and Yoshida convincingly show in bougie-induced

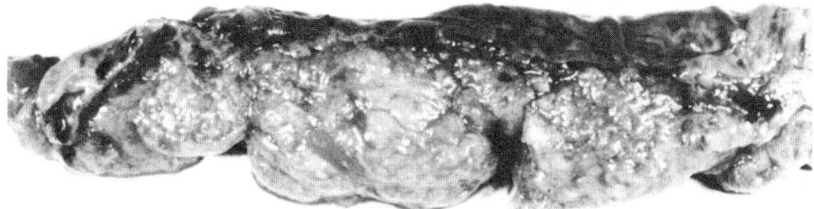

Figure 4-7 Placenta at 18 weeks delivered after intraamnionic saline instillation. Note narrow band of darker subchorionic thrombosis and coagulation necrosis. The amnion and chorion have a hemolyzed appearance.

abortions that the placental surface is not disturbed.[39] Moreover, after bougie-induced abortion, the steroid 3β-ol-dehydrogenase activity of the placenta appears to remain intact. With instillation methods, needle puncture marks in the placenta occasionally may be observed upon careful study; these occur in anterior as well as posterior placentas (Figure 4-8). Similar injury to the fetus has been documented by Broome, et al.[40] In spontaneous second-trimester abortions, on the other hand, chorioamnionitis is the most common finding, followed by circumvallation and other rare abnormalities.

THE MEMBRANES

Reference has been made to the fusion of amnion and chorion by the fourth month. At the same time, the fine vasculature of the chorion laeve, which formerly supplied the villi of the membranous portion of the placenta, undergoes atophy.[41] The amniotic epithelium presently is clearly recognized as being single-layered, having a microvillous surface from early pregnancy, and showing degenerative changes

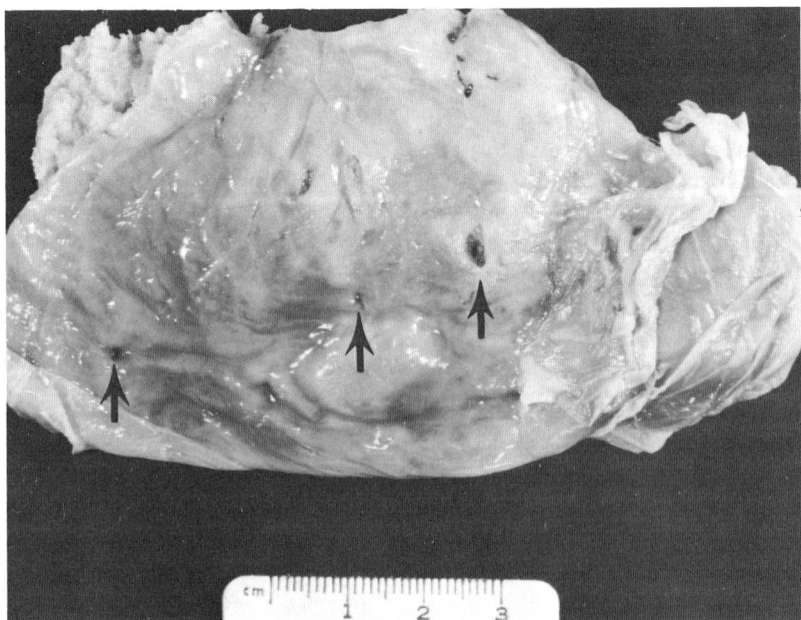

Figure 4-8 Immature (30 weeks) placenta four days following amniocentesis for Rh disease. Fetus died following last intrauterine transfusion presumably from exsanguination through one of three needle marks (arrows). This placenta had a posterior uterine location.

toward the end of pregnancy.[42] Scanning electronmicroscopic studies indicate that neither the size of the amniotic epithelial cells nor that of their microvilli changes appreciably during the course of pregnancy, and that minute intercellular channels develop near the end of the first trimester. They are largest in midpregnancy, and are interpreted as having importance in the mechanism of fluid exchange. Hoyes has observed similar channels electronmicroscopically and has hypothesized that they may enable active fluid absorption from the amnionic cavity.[41] Other details of anatomy and pathology lie outside this review and may be found in Bourne's monograph.[43]

THE AMNIOTIC FLUID

The volume of amniotic fluid varies considerably at all gestational ages. When the work of Tervilä is considered, accurate determination by the familiar dye-dilution studies must be seriously questioned. Tervilä found that injected dye mixes very irregularly within the fluid compartment.[44] Moreover, the volume is quickly affected by changes in fetal and maternal well-being. Abramovich has provided the best review; he found that a linear exponential relationship exists which best fits the CR-length and weight of fetus. When menstrual age is correlated, the relationship is less linear but still significant.[45] When actual values obtained by hysterotomy are plotted, a curve develops. At 12 weeks the average value is 58 ml (range 35 to 103 ml), at 16 weeks, 171 ml (range 159 to 342 ml), and at 20 weeks, 500 ml (range 226 to 515 ml).[2] Reliable figures from 20 to 28 weeks are scarce, but Wagner and Fuchs suggest that fluid accumulates at a rate of 50 ml per week.[46]

CONCLUSIONS

During the second trimester of pregnancy the feto-placental unit grows rapidly, all differentiative embryologic events having been completed. Reasonably good information presently exists that allows estimation of the length of gestation from fetal measurements. Crown-rump length remains the most reliable measurement; foot length is equally valid but more difficult to use in assignment of gestational age. Fetal weight is a more variable function of age and is subject to multiple distorting influences. Placental weight and size correlate well with fetal size and age. Remarkable variability exists in the growth of the umbilical cord and accumulation of amniotic fluid volume. Aside from demonstrating growth of the placenta, recent sonographic studies have confirmed that placental migration is a frequent phenomenon of late pregnancy. Most recent measurements on therapeutic terminations suggest that the time-honored tables of Streeter show fetuses to be somewhat larger than current data demonstrate.

REFERENCES

1. Boyd JD, Hamilton WJ: Development and structure of the human placenta from the end of the 3rd month of gestation. *Br J Obstet Gynaecol* 74:161, 1967.
2. Boyd JD, Hamilton WJ: *The Human Placenta.* Cambridge, W. Heffer and Sons, 1970.
3. Gruenwald P, Minh HN: Evaluation of body and organ weights in perinatal pathology. I. Normal standards derived from autopsies. *Am J Clin Pathol.* 34:247, 1960.
4. Moore KL: *The Developing Human.* Philadephia, WB Saunders, 1973.
5. Wingate MB: Anatomic studies on midtrimester abortion. *Am J Obstet Gynecol.* 102:901, 1968.
6. Nadji P, Sommers SC: Lesions of toxemia in first trimester pregnancies. *Am J Clin Pathol.* 59:344, 1973.
7. Boving BG: Anatomy of reproduction, in Greenhill JP (ed): *Obstetrics.* Philadelphia, WB Saunders, 1965.
8. Dawes GS, (ed): *Size at Birth,* Ciba Symposium 27. Amsterdam, Elsevier, Excerpta Medica, 1974.
9. Streeter GL: Weight, sitting height, head size, foot length and menstrual age of the human embryo. *Carnegie Contrib Embryol.* 11:143, 1921.
10. Trolle D: Age of foetus determined from its measures. *Acta Obstet Gynecol Scand.* 27:327, 1948.
11. Potter EL, Craig JM: *Pathology of the Fetus and the Infant.* Third Ed, Chicago, Year Book Medical Publ, 1975.
12. Stowens D: *Pediatric Pathology.* Baltimore, Williams and Wilkins, 1959.
13. Swinyard CA: Growth of the human suprarenal glands. *Anat Rec.* 87:141, 1943.
14. MacDonald MS, Emery JL: The late intrauterine and postnatal development of human renal glomeruli. *J Anat.* 93:331, 1959.
15. Potter EL: *Normal and Abnormal Development of the Kidney.* Chicago, Year Book Medical Publ, 1972.
16. Gillman J: The development of the gonads in man, with a consideration of the role of the fetal endocrines and the histogenesis of ovarian tumors. *Carnegie Contrib Embryol.* 32:81, 1948.
17. Scorer CG: The incidence of incomplete descent of the testicle at birth. *Arch Dis Child.* 31:198, 1956.
18. Park IJ, Wentz AC, Jones HW: The viability of fetal skin of abortuses induced by saline or prostaglandin. *Am J Obstet Gynecol.* 115:274, 1973.
19. Campbell S: Physical methods of assessing size at birth, in Dawes GS (ed): *Size at Birth.* Ciba Symposium 27. Amsterdam, Elsevier, Excerpta Medica, 1974.
20. Malpas P, Symonds EM: The direction of the helix of the human umbilical cord. *Ann Hum Genet.* 29:409, 1966.

21. Sørensen T, Hasch E, Lange AP: Fetal presentation during pregnancy. *Lancet* 2:477, 1979.
22. Benirschke K, Driscoll SG: *The Pathology of the Human Placenta.* New York, Springer-Verlag, 1967.
23. Reynolds SRM: The proportion of Wharton's jelly in the umbilical cord in relation to distention of the umbilical arteries and vein, with observation on the folds of Hoboken. *Anat Rec.* 113:365, 1952.
24. Andrade A: Anatomical and radiographic study on the anastomosis and branching of the umbilical arteries in white and non-white Brazilians. *Acta Anat.* 70:66, 1968.
25. Young A: The primate umbilical cord with special reference to the transverse communicating artery. *J Hum Evol.* 1:345, 1972.
26. Monie IW: Velamentous insertion of the umbilical cord in early pregnancy. *Am J Obstet Gynecol.* 93:276, 1965.
27. King DL: Placental migration demonstrated by ultrasonography. *Radiology* 109:167, 1973.
28. Rizos N, Doran TA, Miskin M, et al: Natural history of placenta previa ascertained by diagnostic ultrasound. *Am J Obstet Gynecol.* 133:287, 1979.
29. Winter R: Die Rolle regressiver Veranderungen der Plazenta bei der sogenannten Plazentamigration. *Geburtsh Frauenheilkd* 38:4–23, 1978.
30. Nordlander S, Sundberg B, Westin B, et al: Scintigraphic studies of uterine and placental growth and placental migration during pregnancy. *Acta Obstet Gynecol Scand.* 56:483, 1977.
31. Tedde G, Piras AT: Mitotic index of the Langhans' cells in the normal human placenta from the early stages of pregnancy to the term. *Acta Anat.* 100:114, 1978.
32. Abramovich DR: The weight of placenta and membranes in early pregnancy. *Br J Obstet Gynaecol.* 76:523, 1969.
33. Grimes DH, Hamilton WJ: Tolerance limits for fetal and placental growth relationships. *Br J Obstet Gynaecol.* 78:620, 1971.
34. Bleker OP, Kloosterman GJ, Breur W, et al: The volumetric growth of the human placenta: a longitudinal ultrasonic study. *Am J Obstet Gynecol.* 127:657, 1977.
35. Aherne W, Dunnill MS: Morphometry of the human placenta. *Br Med Bull.* 22:5, 1966.
36. Bhargava I, Raja RTK: An anatomical study of foetal blood vessels on the chorial surface of the human placenta. *Acta Anat.* 75:13, 1970.
37. Gustavii B, Brunk V: A histological study of the effect on the placenta of intraamniotically and extraamniotically injected hypertonic saline in therapeutic abortion. *Acta Obstet Gynecol Scand.* 51:121, 1972.
38. Christie JL, Anderson ABM, Turnbull AC, et al: The human placenta and membranes: a histologic and immunofluorescent study of the effects of intra-amniotic injection of hypertonic saline. *Br J Obstet Gynaecol.* 73:399, 1966.
39. Manabe Y, Okamura H, Yoshida Y: Bougie-induced abortion at midpregnancy and placental function: histological and histochemical study of the placenta. *Endokrinologie* 57:389, 1971.
40. Broome DL, Wilson MG, Weiss B, et al: Needle puncture of fetus: a complication of second trimester amniocentesis. *Am J Obstet Gynecol.* 126:274, 1976.
41. Hoyes AD: Ultrastructure of the mesenchymal layers of the human chorion laeve. *J Anat.* 109:17, 1971.

42. Ludwig H, Metzger H, Korte M, et al: Die freie Oberflache des Amnionepithels. *Arch Gynak.* 217:141, 1974.

43. Bourne G: *The Human Amnion and Chorion.* London, Lloyd-Luke, 1962.

44. Tervilä L: Transfer of water from maternal blood to amniotic fluid of live and dead fetuses in health and in some pathological conditions of the mother. *Ann Chir Gynaecol Fenn.* 53:1, 1964.

45. Abramovich DR: Liquor amnii, in Shearman RP (ed): *Human Reproductive Physiology.* Oxford, Blackwell, 1972.

46. Wagner G, Fuchs F: The volume of amniotic fluid in the first half of human pregnancy. *Br J Obstet Gynaecol.* 69:131, 1962.

5 Ultrasonic Evaluation

Rudy E. Sabbagha

The woman who desires a second-trimester pregnancy termination should seek an appropriate health care facility. Subsequently, the usual course of events includes: a history, physical examination, and appropriate counseling.

When pregnancy dates are uncertain or when an abnormality is suspected because of the history or the clinical examination, further evaluation becomes mandatory. Often ultrasound is chosen to help clarify the situation. In the absence of any abnormality, an abortion is performed by one of several methods. The selection of a specific method depends in part on the experience of the physician. If a decision is made to use intraamniotic instillation of an abortifacient, many physicians prefer to examine the pregnancy by ultrasound prior to amniocentesis. The rationale for such an examination is threefold. First, knowledge of placental position enhances the chance of successful amniocentesis by defining the best area of the maternal abdomen for insertion of the needle. Second, the length of pregnancy can be defined objectively and the potential for error reduced to a minimum. Third, those abnormalities of pregnancy which have escaped clinical detection may be recognized ultrasonically, and thus overall patient care can be improved. Lastly, if D&E is selected, ultrasound is valuable to assist in accurately determining the fetal size.

This chapter examines the role of ultrasound as a biophysical test used to define gestational age and assesses the nature of any pregnancy abnormality.

DEFINITION OF ULTRASOUND

Ultrasound is a noninvasive biophysical modality used for the diagnosis of a variety of medical conditions. The sonar apparatus consists of two main parts: a transducer and an oscilloscope or a TV monitor. The transducer is constructed from one or more piezoelectric crystals which range in frequency from 2–5 MHz, and are used to emit sound and receive echoes from a multitude of interfaces within the tissues being examined. These echoes then are transformed into electrical impulses which appear as two-dimensional images on the face of an oscilloscope or a TV monitor.

In pregnancy, ultrasonic examination of the uterus and maternal pelvis yields valuable information, including:

- Fetal biparietal diameter (BPD)
- Fetal abdominal circumference (AC)
- Placental size, location, and macroscopic characteristics
- Amniotic fluid volume
- Number of fetuses
- Presence of adnexal or uterine masses
- Presence of fetal congenital anomalies

BPD AND GESTATIONAL AGE

In the second trimester of pregnancy the ultrasonically derived fetal BPD can be used to determine gestational age. The accuracy of the prediction is such that, in relation to a given BPD (obtained from 16–26 weeks), the length of pregnancy can be calculated within ±11 days in 95% of the population.

The objective determination of gestational age is important because assessment of pregnancy duration based upon the first day of the presumed last menstrual period (LMP), or from the fundal size, or from both, is subject to a wide margin of error.[1-3] Physicians who base their management of second-trimester pregnancy solely on clinical criteria occasionally estimate gestational age incorrectly, fail to select the most appropriate method for terminating the pregnancy, and may find themselves in the position of delivering a viable, premature fetus.

BPD STANDARDIZATION

Early ultrasound charts showed a marked variation in the specific BPD values used to predict mean gestational age.[4] The variations were assumed, at least in part, to represent population differences. Previously, it had been shown that the mean BPDs obtained from a large number of fetuses of black women and white women were almost identical, particularly in the first half of pregnancy.[5] Additional careful analysis of a number of well-designed studies, however, in which BPDs were derived by similar ultrasound methodology, showed no statistically significant differences in the cephalic measurements of a heterogenous population of fetuses.[4] These findings led to the development of a composite mean BPD chart shown in Table 5-1.[4] Although this composite BPD chart can be used universally to predict menstrual fetal age, its applicability to gravidas residing in geographic areas of very high altitude, where mean fetal BPDs may be smaller, remains to be elucidated.

Composite BPD values can be used to determine gestational age if the following guidelines are used:

1. The BPD is measured from the outer to the inner (O–I) aspects of the skull tables (representing the true interfaces producing the biparietal echo-complex) by one of two methods. The first is in relation to 1-cm scale markers which are projected electronically onto the screen adjacent to the plane of the BPD (Figure 5-1). The second is by electronic calipers. When either method is used, the sonar and actual BPD values will correlate with each other because the effect of parallax (apparent reduction of BPD due to the grid over the oscilloscope) is reduced to a minimum.
2. The velocity of ultrasound used to obtain the BPD should be 1540 meters per second (mps). In some European countries the electronic calipers used to measure the BPD are calibrated to 1600 mps and thus inflate the measurement of the BPD. When such machines are used, the BPD measurement should be readjusted to a velocity of 1540 mps. For example, a BPD of 6.0 cm derived by calipers calibrated to a velocity of 1600 mps is readjusted to a value of approximately 5.8 cm (6.0 × 1540/1600).

Table 5-1
Mean Sonar BPDs* Obtained from 14th to 30th Week of Pregnancy, Representing Four Studies with Uniform Methodology

Week	Composite Mean cm
14	2.8
15	3.2
16	3.6
17	3.9
18	4.2
19	4.5
20	4.8
21	5.1
22	5.4
23	5.8
24	6.1
25	6.4
26	6.7
27	7.0
28	7.2
29	7.5
30	7.8

*BPD = biparietal diameter. All BPDs are measured from outer to inner aspects of fetal head (O-I BPD), using an ultrasonic tissue velocity of 1540 meters per second.[4]

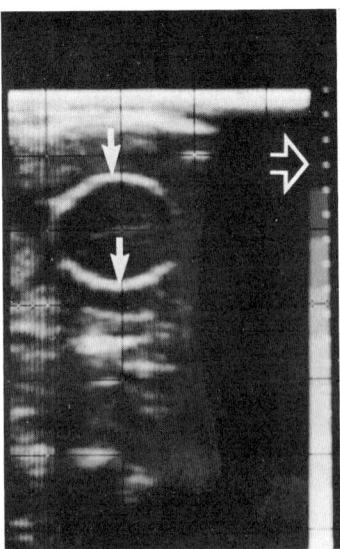

Figure 5-1 Real-time ultrasound image of fetal head in the plane of the biparietal diameter (BPD). Key: solid arrow = the outer and inner aspects of the parietal echo complex used for obtaining the BPD measurement; open arrow = the 1-cm scale markers used for BPD measurement.

BPDs vs 24-WEEK LIMIT

Interruption of a pregnancy after 24 weeks' gestation (26 menstrual weeks) occasionally may result in the delivery of a viable infant. Thus, it is important to define the upper limit of the BPD beyond which pregnancy should not be terminated. A BPD of 6.1 cm is equivalent to a mean menstrual gestational age of 24 weeks (Table 5-1). This prediction varies, however, by ±11 days (2 times standard deviation),[6] or from 22 and 3/7 to 25 and 4/7 weeks. Fetuses with biologically small BPDs thus are more advanced in gestational age than is apparent from the mean BPD chart (Figure 5-2). By the same token, fetuses with biologically large BPDs are less mature than is apparent from the mean BPD chart (Figure 5-2).

Since the gestational age in a particular fetus can only be assessed within a margin of ±11 days with 95% confidence, the validity of terminating pregnancy in gravidas with a fetal BPD of 6.1 cm may be

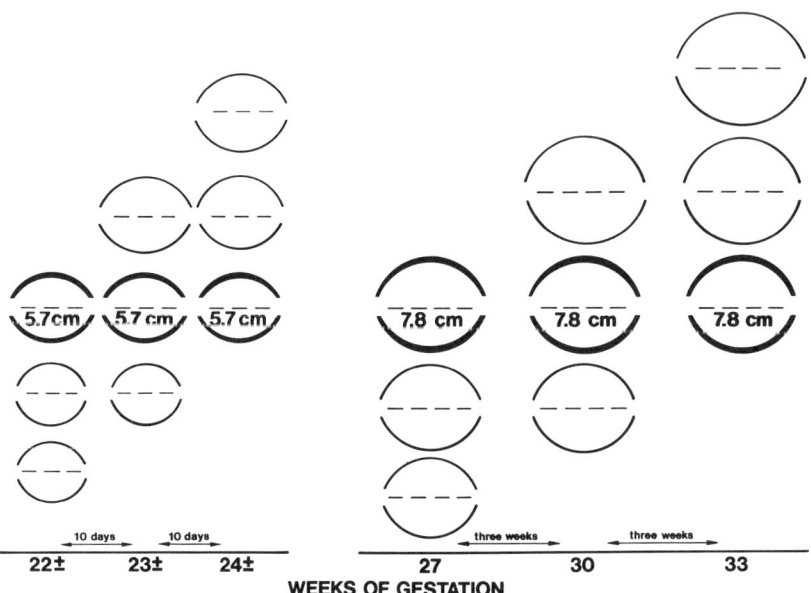

Figure 5-2 Fetuses of the same gestational age normally have different biparietal diameters (BPDs). Thus, assigning all fetuses with a BPD of 5.7 cm, a mean gestational age of 23 weeks causes the duration of pregnancy to be overestimated in the young fetus with a large BPD and underestimated in the older fetus with a small BPD. The range of error is ±11 days (2 × SD) in 95% of fetuses. By assigning all fetuses with a BPD of 7.8 cm, a mean gestational age of 30 weeks, the range in duration of pregnancy is increased to ±3 weeks with 90% confidence. Source: Sabbagha and Hughey.[4]

questioned. Some fetuses (statistically estimated to represent 20% of the group with a BPD of 6.1 cm) may be more advanced in gestational age by 7 to 11 days. Similarly, the duration of pregnancy in 20% of gravidas with a fetal BPD of 6.4 cm (or 25 weeks' mean gestation) may, in fact, fall within the 24-week range.

It is clearly apparent that the absolute BPD value predicting the 24th week of gestation or the limit beyond which pregnancy ordinarily is not aborted is difficult to ascertain. Nonetheless, where strict adherence to an upper limit of 24 menstrual weeks is mandatory, the selected BPD should not exceed 5.6 to 5.7 cm.

ABDOMINAL CIRCUMFERENCE

The fetal abdominal circumference (AC) value is useful in the second trimester of pregnancy for the diagnosis of fetal congenital anomalies. For example, a discrepancy between fetal BPD and AC is one of the criteria used to diagnose hydrocephalus. Furthermore, the diagnosis of abnormalities of the fetal abdomen including gastrointestinal, renal, and abdominal wall defects is enhanced by careful attention to the AC.[7] The importance of the detection of fetal anomalies in gravidas seeking termination of pregnancy is discussed elsewhere in this chapter.

PLACENTA

Ultrasonic placental localization prior to intraamniotic instillation of any abortifacient agent has the following advantages:

- an increase of the likelihood of obtaining amniotic fluid from the first tap (Figures 5-3, 5-4)
- a decrease of the chance for sensitization of the Rh-negative gravida with Rh-positive fetal red blood cells
- the discovery of a molar placenta (Figure 5-5)

Currently, vacuum aspiration is the procedure of choice for emptying the uterus in gravidas with hydatidiform mole. On rare occasions, however, molar pregnancy is associated with a live fetus beyond 12 weeks' gestation.[3] This complicated diagnosis can be facilitated by ultrasound. In such a situation, vacuum aspiration may increase the risk for uterine hemorrhage or perforation, and the use of vaginal prostaglandin E_2 (PGE_2) suppositories or, in some cases, hysterotomy may be warranted.[8]

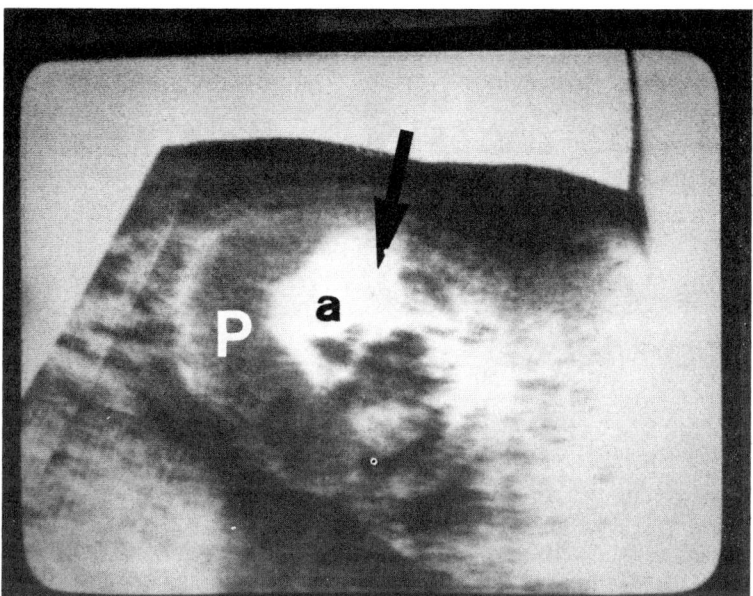

Figure 5-3 Longitudinal scan of a second-trimester pregnancy shows fundal placenta (p). Arrow points to the best area for obtaining amniotic fluid (a).

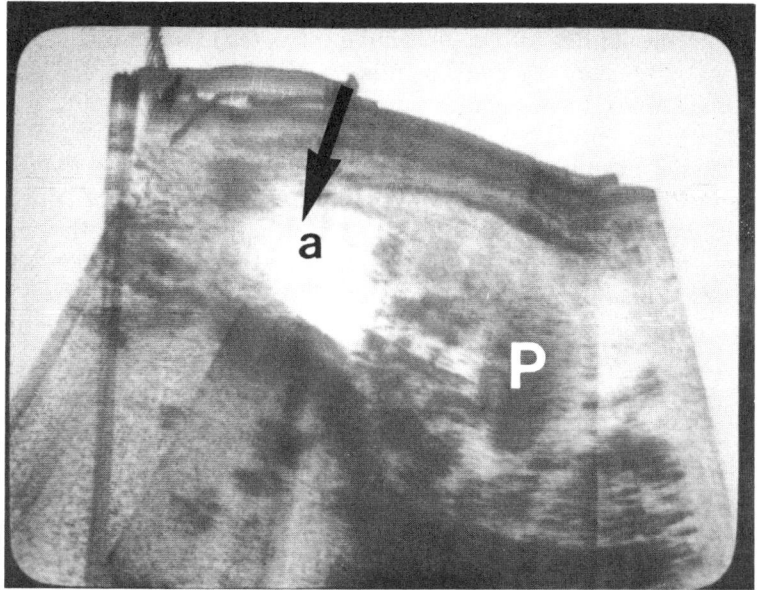

Figure 5-4 Longitudinal scan of a second-trimester pregnancy shows placenta (p) in lower uterine area. Arrow points to the best area for obtaining amniotic fluid.

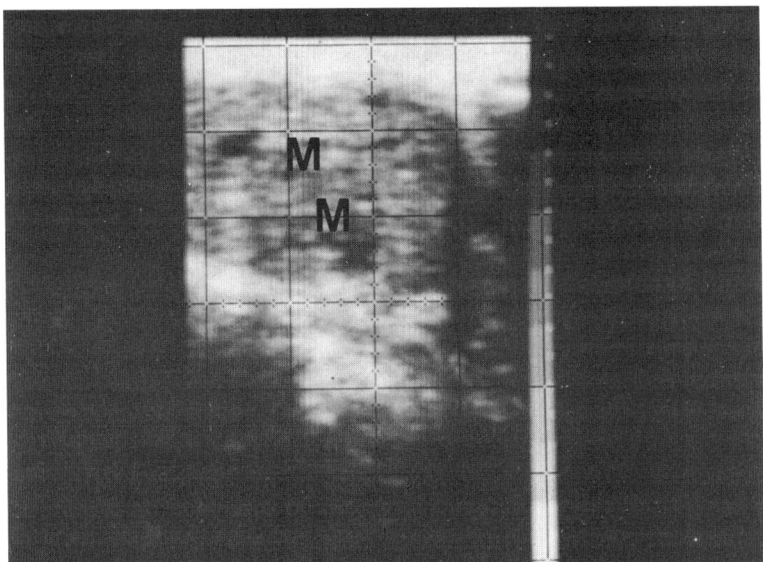

Figure 5-5 Longitudinal real-time image of molar pregnancy (M). Note uniform "snow storm" appearance.

UTERUS LARGE FOR DATES

The uterine fundus will appear large for dates in several conditions: molar pregnancy, polyhydramnios, multiple gestation, uterine myoma, adnexal mass and inaccurate dates. Whereas the differentiation of these entities may not always be clinically feasible, accurate ultrasonic examination almost invariably facilitates the correct diagnosis and will help the physician manage the patient appropriately. For example, in the presence of multiple gestation, the fundal height may extend to the midumbilical area in pregnancies where the gestational age is only 12 weeks. Similarly, in the presence of a uterine or adnexal mass, fundal height will extend beyond the limits ordinarily associated with given dates (Figures 5-6, 5-7).

When pregnancy is associated with an adnexal cyst, the physician performing amniocentesis prior to instillation of an abortifacient agent should ultrasonically localize an area over the maternal abdomen for entry into the amniotic sac without penetrating the cyst. Failure to differentiate the cyst may lead to instillation of the abortifacient into the cyst cavity. Additionally, careful attention should be given to the nature of the cyst, because on some occasions the adnexal mass may be a tubal or abdominal pregnancy or a teratoma. In such patients, ultrasonic findings should alert the physician to the need for further evaluation by laparoscopy or laparotomy.

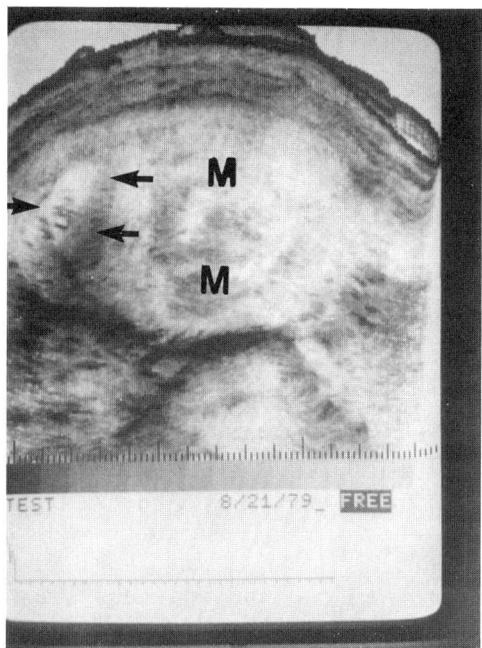

Figure 5-6 Transverse scan shows a markedly enlarged uterus because of myomas (M). Arrows point to a small 8-week gestational sac in the left aspect of the uterus.

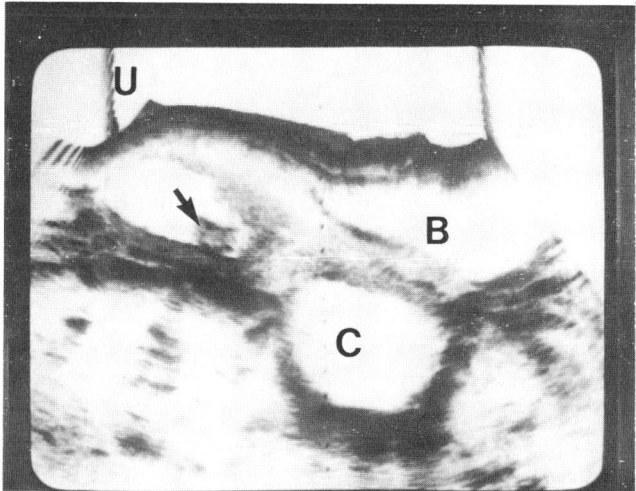

Figure 5-7 A longitudinal scan shows bladder (B), ovarian cyst (C), and a 10-week gestational sac. Arrow points to fetal part inside gestational sac. The uterine fundus is seen extending to the umbilicus (U). The fundal height receded to the mid-umbilical area when the bladder was emptied, but was still very large for dates.

UTERUS SMALL FOR DATES

The uterine fundus will appear small for dates in several conditions: inaccurate dates, oligohydramnios, and intrauterine fetal death (IUFD). In the latter two instances, intraamniotic instillation of an abortifacient agent may be difficult and the use of PGE_2 vaginal suppositiories may be preferred.[8]

CONGENITAL ANOMALIES

Several fetal anomalies now can be ultrasonically diagnosed in utero, including defects of the renal, gastrointestinal, skeletal, and neural systems. The sonographer should search for the presence of congenital anomalies, particularly those of multifactorial etiology, in gravidas who are at high risk for producing offspring with birth defects. The criteria used for placing gravidas in such a high-risk category include historical data, elevated levels of α-fetoprotein in maternal serum or in amniotic fluid, and the presence of hydramnios or oligohydramnios documented by ultrasound.

The ultrasonic discovery of any fetal anomaly in women requesting an abortion because of adverse socioeconomic factors is significant because the justification for the procedure becomes more apparent. In this way the emotional impact and guilt sometimes associated with abortion may be dramatically alleviated, particularly in those women whose feelings are ambivalent to start with.

SUMMARY

Because of the variety of conditions encountered in the second trimester which could complicate the intended interruption of pregnancy, ultrasonic evaluation should be used liberally by the clinician.

REFERENCES

1. Dewhurst CJ, Beazley JM, Campbell S: Assessment of the fetal maturity and dysmaturity. *Am J Obstet Gynecol.* 113:141, 1972.
2. Campbell S: The assessment of fetal development by diagnostic ultrasound. *Clin Perinatol.* 1:507, 1974.
3. Sabbagha RE: Ultrasound in managing the high-risk pregnancy, in Spellacy WN (ed): *Mangement of the High-Risk Pregnancy.* Baltimore, University Park Press, 1976.
4. Sabbagha RE, Hughey M: Standardization of sonar cephalometry and gestational age. *Obstet Gynecol.* 52:405, 1978.

5. Sabbagha RE, Barton FB, Barton BA: Sonar biparietal diameter: I. Analysis of percentile growth differences in two normal populations using same methodology. *Am J Obstet Gynecol.* 126:479, 1976.

6. Sabbagha RE, Turner JH, Rockette H, et al: Sonar BPD and fetal age: Definition of the relationship. *Obstet Gynecol.* 43:7, 1973.

7. Tamura R, Sabbagha RE: Percentile ranks of sonar fetal abdominal circumference measurements. Unpublished data.

8. Southern EM, Gutknecht GD: Management of intra-uterine fetal demise and missed abortion using prostaglandin E_2 vaginal suppositories. *Obstet Gynecol.* 47:602, 1975.

6 Physiology

Charles H. Hendricks

The second trimester of pregnancy has been studied far less intensively than have the trimesters preceding and following it. That the first and third trimesters have received academic emphasis is not surprising. Physiologically speaking, the concerns of early pregnancy center on fertilization, ovum transport, the mechanics of implantation, and the need to provide a nutrient supply for the embryo as well as a place for further growth and development. From the pathophysiologic point of view, there is a fear of early pregnancy loss which focuses heavily upon the relatively large risk of spontaneous abortion and the risks of teratogenic influences. By the third trimester, concern centers on the final spurt of fetal growth, the weeks of prelabor, and the process of labor itself. All of these considerations have been studied extensively in the past two decades. Particular attention has been focused on problems of premature labor, intrapartum death, unanticipated hemorrhagic processes, and dysfunctional labor.

By contrast, the second trimester of pregnancy is expected to be quite uneventful. Obstetricians long have assumed that a pregnancy which has successfully survived the first trimester was destined to go forward into the third before the appearance of additional threats to pregnancy stability or viability.

During the second trimester, hyperplasia of the myometrium—to the extent that it exists at all—is completed. The process of myometrial hypertrophy advances steadily, but at a decreasing pace. Placentation also is completed, and the basis is laid for the conditions which permit successful housing of the fetus within the uterine cavity as the pregnancy advances. During the middle trimester, the uterus becomes an abdominal organ, begins to assume a more cylindrical rather than spherical shape, and accommodates to radical changes in volume without threatening its blood supply and without going into premature labor.

Fortunately, only relatively infrequently do things go seriously amiss during the second trimester. Spontaneous abortions, when they do occur, are due primarily to cervical incompetency, occasional premature rupture of the membranes and, even less frequently, major obstetric accidents. It is only toward the very end of the second trimester that the threat of premature labor begins to cloud the horizon. Despite its seeming predictability and relative quiescence, however, the second trimester is of critical importance. It is somewhat unfortunate that it has been relatively neglected from an academic point of view because it usually goes so well, because disasters are rare, and because the obstetrician's sense of a need to intervene arises so seldom. This chapter deals principally with two issues: *uterine contractility* and *cervical resistance,* since they pertain directly to second-trimester abortion.

UTERINE CONTRACTILITY

The process of uterine contractility has been studied more intensively than cervical resistance. Braxton Hicks reported in 1872 that the uterus contracts from the late first trimester all the way through pregnancy.[1] His study methodology was the utmost in simplicity. Where the uterus could be palpated abdominally, he followed contractions by abdominal palpation. Earlier in pregnancy he felt for contractions through what today would seem almost painfully prolonged sessions of bimanual pelvic examination. He observed that if the uterus were palpated "without friction or any pressure beyond that necessary for full contact of the hand continuously over a period of from five to twenty minutes, it will be noticed to become firm if relaxed at first, and more or less flacid if it be firm at first." Contractions usually occurred spontaneously at least once every 20 minutes, and most frequently within the 5- to 10-minute time range. Hicks believed the contractions tended to last from two to five minutes. He also noticed that from the third month on, contractions could be elicited by stimulating the uterus manually or by other means of "excitement."

Finally, Hicks made an important statement, one which modern physicians sometimes fail to appreciate. He said, "When the contractions are more than usually powerful, the woman is conscious of their presence and by watching these, we shall convince ourselves that the contractions, which were before unnoticed by her, are really the same as the 'pains' of premature expulsion of the fetus and also of true labor." Thus, there is every evidence to believe that Hicks understood that the uterine contractility pattern of midpregnancy, while different in certain respects from that found in active labor, is, nevertheless, part of the continuum of uterine contractility which is maintained throughout early and midpregnancy, and which, when enhanced and supplemented physiologically or pharmacologically near term, brings about the objective changes seen in prelabor and labor itself.

It is now possible to record in women spontaneous, physiologic, and pharmacologic responses of uterine contractility during all stages of pregnancy. An intrauterine pressure recording of uterine contractility in very early pregnancy (6 weeks) is illustrated in Figure 6-1. In this typical record, relatively prolonged periods of very small and weak contractions are interspersed at intervals by "bursts" of larger contraction complexes which certainly would be palpable to examining fingers, and which would be quite compatible in duration with the contraction times described by Hicks from his clinical evaluation alone.

Other examples of this phenomenon of relative uterine quiescence are shown in the top part of Figure 6-2 at 11 weeks' gestation and in the top portion of Figure 6-3 at 14 weeks' gestation. Only after

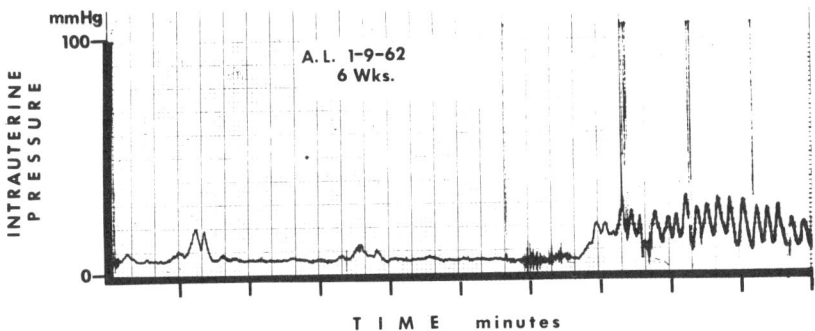

Figure 6-1 Uterine contractility at six weeks' postconception. Source: *Sandorama* Congress Edition, Basle, Switzerland, Sandoz, Ltd. September, 1967.

about 22 weeks of pregnancy or when abortion threatens, do consistently higher intermittent contraction patterns begin to emerge. When substantial contractility appears in normal pregnancy, the uterine volume already has expanded significantly, and further rapid volume distention with its accompanying myometrial stretch is associated with a continuously increasing uterine contractility pattern.

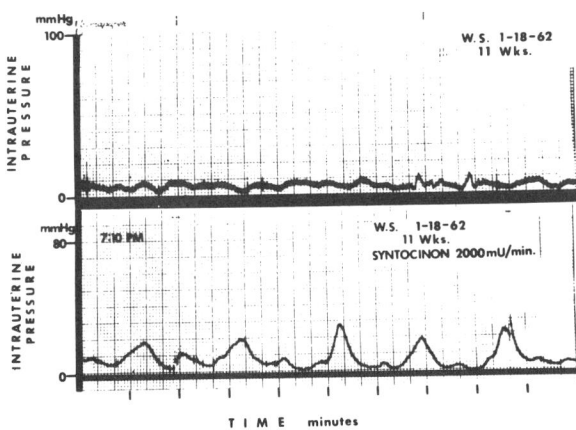

Figure 6-2 Uterine contractility at 11 weeks' gestation. Top line: Spontaneous activity. Bottom line: Tracing during administration of synthetic oxytocin at 2000 mU/min. Source: *Sandorama* Congress Edition, Basle, Switzerland, Sandoz, Ltd. September, 1967.

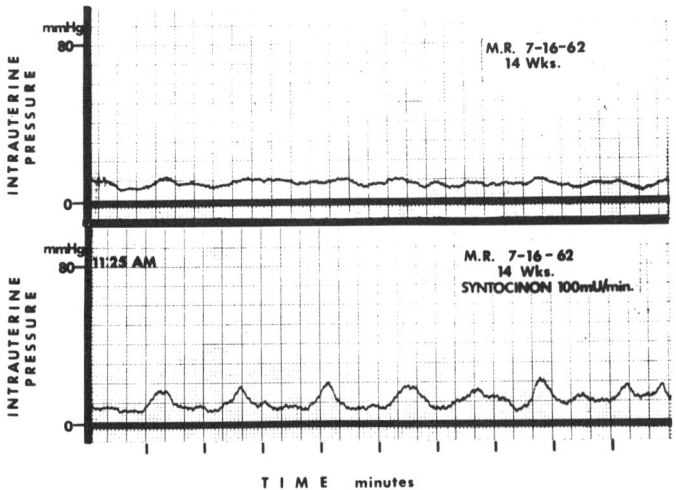

Figure 6-3 Uterine contractility at 14 weeks' pregnancy. Top line: Spontaneous activity. Bottom line: Activity during infusion of synthetic oxytocin at 100 mU/min. Source: *Sandorama* Congress Edition, Basle, Switzerland, Sandoz, Ltd. September, 1967.

Along with observations on uterine contractility, other studies have determined that various substances stimulate the myometrium to greater contractile efforts. It has been known for many years that the uterus in early pregnancy responds to oxytocin and vasopressin more like the nonpregnant uterus, and the uterus throughout pregnancy responds quite consistently to small doses of vasopressin. The response to oxytocin in the nonpregnant state and the first half of pregnancy, however, is surprisingly modest, when it can be demonstrated at all.

In 1915 W. Blair Bell extended his earlier observations on the effect of posterior pituitary extracts upon uterine contractility.[2] He stated that posterior pituitary extracts were capable of "sensitizing the uterus before labor" by repeated administration. Because he knew from prior experience that very early induction of labor might be difficult and time consuming, he advocated administration of pituitary extract intermittently over the span of a few days "in order to sensitize the uterus," before further measures were taken to induce very premature labor. After sensitization, labor would be induced by the insertion of bougies, which are closely related in function to modern laminaria.

After the isolation of the active pituitary principle, oxytocin, and the development of methods to study uterine contractility, it became possible to demonstrate and quantify the limits of oxytocin responsiveness in earlier pregnancy. The bottom line of Figure 6-2 demonstrates the almost overwhelming resistiveness of the uterus to oxytocin stimulation at the 11th week of pregnancy. Synthetic oxytocin, at the rate of 2000 mU/min, was administered by intravenous infusion. Despite this excessive dose, far beyond any pharmacologic range, the uterine contractility response, while present, was somewhat incoordinate in quality and insufficient in quantity to present any resemblance to any normal threatened abortion or preliminary stages of normal labor.

A more typical type of oxytocin response, this time at 14 weeks' gestation, is shown in the lower half of Figure 6-3. Here the administration of 100 mU/min of oxytocin produced fairly regular uterine contractility patterns, but they still fell far short of what one would anticipate in threatened spontaneous abortion. The threshold dose below which no response may be elicited is usually about 60 mU/min in the early part of the second trimester.

In spontaneous abortion, uterine contractility and oxytocin sensitivity develop concomitantly, just as they do in later pregnancy with a viable fetus. At the end of the extrusion of the products of conception, the uterus goes into the equivalent of a "postpartum contractility pattern." Figure 6-4 shows a uterine contractility tracing from a woman who had aborted spontaneously several hours before the record began. This contractility pattern looks like a tracing from a uterus which has successfully completed normal term labor a few hours previously.

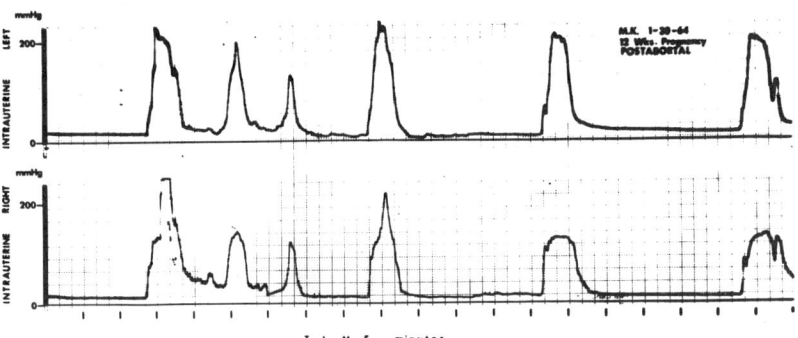

Figure 6-4 Spontaneous uterine contractility after spontaneous abortion. Activity is being recorded from catheters placed in right and left cornual regions. Source: *Sandorama* Congress Edition, Basle, Switzerland, Sandoz, Ltd. September, 1967.

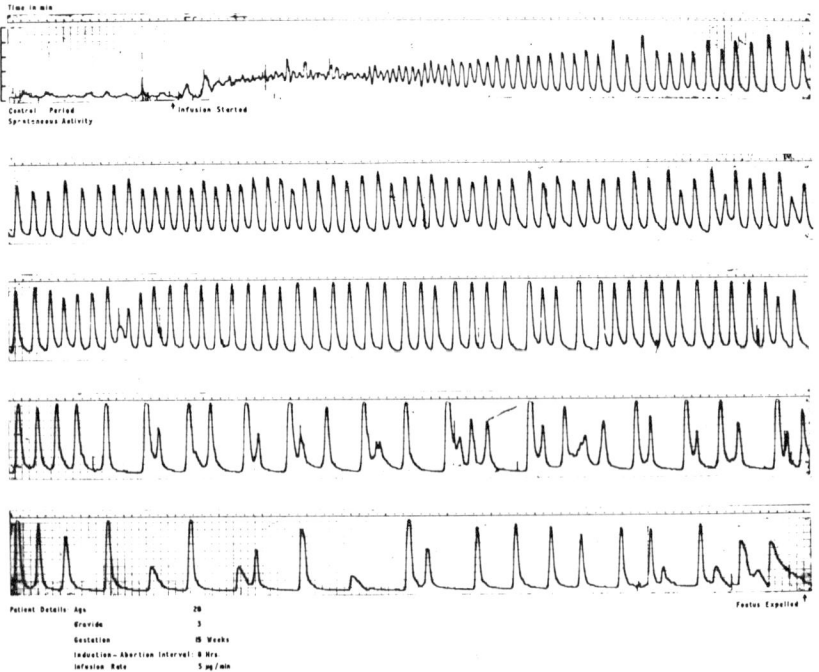

Figure 6-5 Therapeutic abortion with infusion of prostaglandin E_2 at 15 weeks' gestation. Source: Karim.[3]

Despite all the attention that has been given to the development of an understanding of the physiology of oxytocin and its relationship to uterine contractility, it has become increasingly evident that oxytocin *by itself* is not the prime determinant of preterm labor, spontaneous abortion, or successful therapeutic abortion. Something appears to be lacking. It presently is thought that the missing ingredient may be the activation of one or more prostaglandins in the contractile process.

In 1970 Professor S. Karim published a graph (see Figure 6-5) showing the uterine contractility profile of a 15-week therapeutic abortion induced by a continuous infusion of PGE_2 at the rate of 5 µg/min.[3] Initiation of the infusion altered the contractility within a period of two minutes. Within ten minutes a phase of hypercontractility had begun, and within an hour labor-like contractility had appeared. The entire process was completed within eight hours. This performance could never be duplicated by use of oxytocin alone. During the past decade numerous prostaglandin studies have yielded sufficient insight into the process of uterine evacuation to cause suspicion that the prostaglandins may be more deeply involved in the process of labor than is oxytocin. The many stimuli which result in the elaboration of prostaglandins, and thus increased uterine contractility, help to explain the potential role of prostaglandins, not only in the induction of premature labor but also in spontaneous and therapeutic abortion. If this concept is correct, the fetus is removed from obligatory participation in the initiation of midterm pregnancy termination.

CERVICAL RESISTANCE

Specific resistances impede the evacuation of the uterus. The pregnant cervix represents a formidable counterforce to uterine contractility because of its anatomic structure. As pointed out by Danforth,[4] the cervix is composed predominantly of connective tissue, and contains only a thin shell of organized smooth muscle tissue. It is a matter of interest that as early as 1873 Haughton[5] calculated that the unaided uterus at term simply was not strong enough to overcome the enormous resistance of the cervix. He could not have known then that the process of parturition is actively aided by a chemical alteration and physical rearrangement of the cervical structure itself. These processes later were described under the general term of "cervical ripening." The classic works of Danforth et al.[6-8] laid the foundation for our present state of understanding of this phenomenon. Danforth and coworkers showed that the collagen fibers of the cervix become separated, disrupted, and widely scattered by the end of labor. This observation marked the beginning of unraveling of the mystery of cervical preparation. Danforth subsequently demonstrated an increased synthesis of glycosaminoglycans and a decrease in the collagen/total protein ratio based on the hydroxyproline content. The work of Danforth et al recently has been largely confirmed and supplemented by Kleissl and colleagues, who observed that the collagen characteristics in second-trimester pregnancy more closely resembled those of the nonpregnant cervix than of the cervix at term or in labor.[9] While the nature of the initiation, control, and limitation of degradation of collagen in the cervix is only slowly being worked out, it finally is becoming apparent that the process of collagen degradation makes possible the normal cervical dilatation pattern. Furthermore, the appropriate cervical dilatation pattern occurs at any stage of gestation when labor or spontaneous abortion takes place.

Central to this issue is the question of what initiates the collagen degradation process. Putting the matter in more clinical terms, the question is: What is it that initiates cervical ripening? For almost 30 years clinical obstetricians have assumed that oxytocin used sequentially had some effect upon "cervical ripening" before term.[10] But the evidence that oxytocin, so exquisitely effective in controlling uterine contractility in pregnancy at term, can also perform cervical ripening effectively, has never been very convincing. Perhaps this is because the methods of applying oxytocin are not efficient, the time required to bring about a measurable change is long, and the quantitation of cervical ripening is an imprecise clinical exercise.

During the past several decades physicians have searched for some sort of unifying theory to explain exactly what initiates labor and permits it to be carried out spontaneously and successfully. Until relatively recently, the search has been tedious and basically unrewarding. With the recognition that prostaglandins relate to the reproductive process, hopes were renewed that somehow the prostaglandins—such obviously powerful agents for the production of uterine contractility—might be proven equally effective in producing cervical ripening and thus in removing the last obstruction to uterine evacuation. Liggins has shown that small dose infusion of PGF_2 can ripen the sheep cervix within less than 24 hours without increasing uterine contractility.[11] Recent work by Calder, Embrey and Tait[12] at Oxford, and by Ulmsten and Wingerup in Lund[13] has begun to provide some evidence that prostaglandins indeed play a role in cervical ripening both at term and during the second trimester. Calder and Wingerup and their respective colleagues have produced limited, but impressive, evidence that cervical preparation, independent of alterations in uterine contractility, can be brought about by the intracervical application of prostaglandin E_2 gels in the second trimester.

SUMMARY

Both historically and in modern terms it has been demonstrated that pharmacologic methods can be used to "sensitize" and thus enhance the uterine contracility pattern leading to uterine evacuation. The demonstration of cervical ripening, in a very minor sense by oxytocin and in a much more impressive sense by prostaglandin E_2, begins to offer both a physiologic and a pharmacologic explanation of how the formidable cervical barrier can be acted upon successfully prior to the onset of labor. Finally, the fact that prostaglandins in many respects are stronger oxytocic agents than is oxytocin itself, improves the prospect of reaching some sort of unified explanation for the onset of labor where 1) myometrial sensitization, 2) increase of uterine contractility and 3) connective tissue preparation are all induced by the same physiologic agent; that is, a prostaglandin. If this is indeed the case, it must be recognized that the process is by no means limited to term pregnancy, but applies equally to spontaneous or pharmacologic uterine evacuation in the second trimester.

REFERENCES

1. Hicks JB: On the contractions of the uterus throughout pregnancy: their physiological effects and their value in the diagnosis of pregnancy. *Trans Obstet Soc London* 13:216, 1872.
2. Bell WB: Infundibulin in primary uterine inertia and the induction of labour. *Proc Royal Soc Med.* 8:71, 1915.
3. Karim S: Action of prostaglandin in the pregnant woman, in Ramwell P, Shaw JE (eds): *Prostaglandins* vol. 180, NY Academy of Sciences, 1971.
4. Danforth N: The fibrous nature of the human cervix, and its relation to the isthmic segment in gravid and nongravid uteri. *Am J Obstet Gynecol.* 53:1, 1947.
5. Haughton S: *Principles of Animal Mechanics.* London, Longmans, Green & Co., 1873. Cited by Reynolds SRM: *Physiology of the Uterus,* Second ed, New York, Hafner, 1965.
6. Danforth DN, Buckingham JC, Roddick JW: Connective changes incident to cervical effacement. *Am J Obstet Gynecol.* 80:939, 1960.
7. Danforth DN, Veis A, Breen M, et al: The effect of pregnancy and labor on the human cervix: changes in collagen, glycoproteins, and glycosaminoglycans. *Am J Obstet Gynecol.* 120:641, 1974.
8. Danforth DN, Buckingham JC, in Blandau RJ, Moghissi I (eds): *The Biology of the Cervix.* Chicago, University of Chicago Press, 1973, p. 351.
9. Kleissl HP, Van der Rest M, Naftolin F, et al: Collagen changes in the human uterine cervix at parturition. *Am J Obstet Gynecol.* 130:748, 1978.
10. Mauzy CH, Donnelly JF: The induction of premature labor by means of pitocin in patients with toxemia of pregnancy. *Am J Obstet Gynecol.* 64:517, 1952.

11. Liggins GC: Personal communication.

12. Calder AA, Embrey MP, Tait T: Ripening of the cervix with extra-amniotic prostaglandin E_2 in viscous gel before induction of labour. *Obstet Gynaecol.* 84:266, 1977.

13. Ulmsten U, Wingerup L: Cervical ripening induced by prostaglandin E_2 in viscous gel. *Acta Obstet Gynecol Scand.* (suppl 84), 1979.

PART III
Methods of Second-Trimester Abortion

7 Hypertonic Saline Instillation

Thomas D. Kerenyi

Instillation of hypertonic saline (20% NaCl) into the amniotic sac was one of the first methods used in this country to perform legal abortion by amnioinfusion. Even today, it probably is the most widely used method for late second-trimester abortions. When performed by experienced physicians, amnioinfusion with hypertonic saline is an effective method for second-trimester abortion, with live births occurring only rarely.

Introduced in Rumania by Aburel in 1939, the procedure was used widely in Japan from 1946 to 1952. After this time, it fell into disrepute because of high rates of complications and mortality.[1] According to Wagatsuma, however, these high complication rates probably resulted from infusions performed by inexperienced practitioners in ill-equipped facilities on patients who were not screened for preexisting medical disorders.[2]

Saline instillation was reevaluated and popularized in the 1960s by Csapo and others,[3,4] who established the method as an effective alternative to major surgical procedures such as hysterotomy.[5,6] In the United States, the saline method has been performed almost exclusively by transabdominal instillation of the hypertonic solution directly into the amniotic sac. The exact mechanism of action by which hypertonic saline induces abortion is still not clear. The following theories have been proposed:

1. Suppression of placental progesterone synthesis, thus suspending the block to uterine activity [3,4,6-9]
2. Release or production of prostaglandins which cause uterine contractions and explusion of the fetus [10,11]
3. Acute sodium intoxication of the products of conception (hypertonicity and dehydration of the fetal-placental unit) resulting in fetal death [12,13]
4. Release of oxytocin from the pituitary gland which stimulates the uterine musculature to contract [14]

The significance of theory #4 and the primary nature of #3 are doubtful. Theories #1 and #2 most likely play important roles in the activation of myometrial contractility. When combined, these theories probably become the final pathway of all endogenous and exogenous uterine stimulants. This comprehensive theory, as advanced by Csapo, accommodates spontaneous as well as induced parturition at all stages of pregnancy, and is known as the "seesaw theory."[9]

Careful screening of patients for preexisting medical conditions, such as sickle cell anemia, and cardiac or renal disorders, is advisable before carrying out the amnioinfusion procedure. A difference of opinion exists regarding the need for hospitalization following saline instillation. In some clinics, women have been permitted to leave shortly after their instillation and advised to return when uterine contractions begin.[15,16] Most physicians, however, have maintained that patients should be hospitalized in a fully-equipped, well-staffed facility following the instillation procedure.[17-19]

TECHNIQUE

Prior to the instillation of saline the patient should empty her bladder. Her abdomen then is wiped or sprayed with an antiseptic solution and draped with sterile towels. Local anesthetic is used in the region of the instillation site. A spinal needle (usually 18 gauge) then is inserted transabdominally into the amniotic sac. In order to be sure that the needle is in the amniotic sac, a free flow of amniotic fluid must be established before instillation of the saline solution.[18] Most physicians withdraw 50–250 ml of amniotic fluid prior to the amnioinfusion. This technique may prevent a sudden increase in intraamniotic pressure that might rupture the fetal membranes and produce leakage from the vagina. Another advantage of aspirating fluid is that it permits the production of a concentration of saline which is sufficient to cause fetal death and expulsion.[6]

The amount of saline infused varies according to the week of gestation and the amount of amniotic fluid withdrawn. Most physicians instill 150–250 ml of 20% saline.[20] To reduce the chance of the needle's displacement during instillation, some practitioners instill saline via a catheter placed through a large bore needle (for example, 14 gauge).[21] Others use the gravity drip technique of infusion (without pressure from a syringe), introduced by Kerenyi and associates, which requires an elevated solution bottle connected to the spinal needle by a standard plastic IV infusion tubing. The saline is then infused slowly, over approximately a ten-minute period. This infusion method also allows the operator to discontinue administration if there is any adverse reaction before the total dose is administered and the problem becomes severe or irreversible.[22]

Saline also may be infused by inserting a long needle through the vaginal portion of the cervical myometrium into the amniotic sac.[23,24] This technique may be useful when the transabdominal approach is technically difficult; for example, when there has been previous abdominal surgery. Some physicians, however, have found transcervical instillation difficult to perform and associated with high complication rates.[25]

EFFECTIVENESS

Reports of the instillation-abortion time vary considerably, but most mean times fall within a 24- to 36-hour range (see Table 7-1). About 97% of patients expel the fetus within 72 hours.[19,26] The use of oxytocics and/or laminaria tents augments the effect of hypertonic saline and shortens instillation-to-abortion intervals. In less than 1% of the cases, a second amnioinfusion with hypertonic saline may be necessary after 48 hours, because of failure of expulsion. Further progress depends on the degree of cervical effacement and dilatation. In fact, should partial cervical dilatation permit it, amniotomy is preferred to reinfusion. Before repeating the instillation, it is important to establish the presence or absence of the fetal heart sound. If detectable, the amount of saline infused must be greater than in cases where fetal death already has occurred. Total absence of labor should alert the operator to the possibility of ovarian cyst infusion, and this should be ruled out.[22]

Table 7-1
Second-Trimester Pregnancy Termination with Intraamniotic 20% Saline

Author Date (Ref No.)	No. of Pts.	Weeks Gest.	AF Out (ml)	NaCl 20% (ml)	Oxy (a)[†]	Selected Studies IAT*	Retained placenta	Patients with Complications and Side Effects (%)						
								GI	Hemor-rhage	Fever	Lac.	Coagulo-pathy	Failed	Live AB
Kerenyi et al 1973[22]	5000	14–24	50–500	150–250	yes	25	12.9	3.0	2.3	2.3	0.3	0.3	0.4	0.06
Cohen and Ballard 1974[22]	4112 807	16–20 16–20	30–50 30–50	200 200	yes yes	37.9 22.1	NS‡ NS	NS NS	2.2 2.2	NS NS	NS NS	0.12 0.62	NS NS	NS NS
Berger and Kerenyi 1975[27]	4069	17–20	50–500	200	yes	NS	12	NS	2.4	1.1	NS	0.3	0	0
WHO 1976[38]	769	15–20	5–10	200	no	30.4	31.8	1.7	1.5	NS	0.1	NS	19.5	NS
JSPA CDC 1977[39]	10,013	13–24	NS	200	yes	29.2	28	3.3	1.9	5.0	0.6	0.3	2.4	0

*IAT = mean installation time in hours
†(a) = started after instillation
‡NS = Not stated

MORBIDITY

Several major medical complications have been associated with the saline abortion method. These include:

- hypernatremia (increase in serum sodium, above 160 mEq/liter)
- coagulopathy
- hemorrhage (blood loss greater than 500 ml)
- infection and/or fever
- uterine injury, including rupture
- cervical fistula or cervical laceration

Signs and symptoms of mild hypernatremia—which appear in about one of 200 patients—include facial flushing, restlessness, thirst, headache, and cardiorespiratory abnormalities such as hypotension, bradycardia, and apnea.[19,22] Hypernatremia usually results from the inadvertent injection of saline into the patient's vascular system. Severe hypernatremia, on the other hand, is characterized by the development of central nervous system abnormalities such as seizures or coma, and may be life threatening. If proper instillation techniques are used, severe hypernatremia should be completely avoidable.[18] Suspected hypernatremia should be treated by intravenous infusion of normal saline, 5% dextrose solution or, in milder cases, oral administration of fluids. Treatment should be followed by careful monitoring of vital signs, urinary output, and serum electrolytes.[19]

Although many patients experience subclinical changes in blood coagulation factors 6 to 12 hours after intraamniotic instillation of saline, most parameters of clotting return toward normal in 24 hours. Severe clotting disorders are rare.[19,28] In a six-year review of almost 5000 saline-induced abortions, Cohen and Ballard found only ten cases of clinically evident coagulopathy.[29] In another large series of saline inductions, the incidence was 0.3%.[22] Early oxytocin administration increases the risk of coagulopathy. If a clotting disorder occurs, treatment consists of transfusions of fresh frozen plasma or cryoprecipitate, and uterine evacuation to ensure that all products of conception have been removed.[19,29]

Hemorrhage and infection are the most frequent complications following intraamniotic instillation of hypertonic saline. In a study of over 4000 patients, Berger and Kerenyi reported an overall rate of 5.5 complications per 100 cases; 96% of all complications were due to hemorrhage and/or infection.[27]

Hemorrhage requiring transfusion has been reported in 2% to 7% of patients.[28] It is more likely to occur when oxytocin is used to augment saline or when the placenta is retained for several hours following expulsion of the fetus. The risk of hemorrhage can be reduced substantially when the placenta is manually or surgically removed if it has not been expelled within two hours after delivery of the fetus.[27-29]

Fever, presumably due to infection, has been reported in 2.2% to 16.6% of patients.[28] The risk of infection increases when abortion time exceeds 48 hours.[27-29] Some physicians, therefore, advocate the use of augmenting agents, such as oxytocin or laminaria, which may shorten the instillation-to-abortion interval.[30] The risk of bacterial infection can be reduced further by a high standard of sterile technique.[28] Treatment of infection consists of antibiotic therapy. If infection persists, a more precise diagnosis may be made, based on cultures taken from the patient. Persistent fever due to infection may require surgical evacuation of the uterine contents.

Injuries to the uterus, such as cervical lacerations, rarely are associated with intraamniotic instillation of saline alone. They occur more frequently when the cervix dilates rapidly, such as when high concentrations of oxytocin are used to stimulate additional activity.[31,32] Should uterine injuries occur, they may be repaired vaginally or via laparotomy, depending on their location and extent.[19,22]

Water intoxication can be avoided by the use of electrolyte-containing solutions for intravenous infusions and by restricting oxytocin dosage to no more than 40 mU oxytocin/min (2 ampules = 20 IU per 1000 ml over a period of eight hours).[33] If electrolyte-containing solutions are the vehicle for oxytocin, even with high doses added (5-10 ampules per liter), water intoxication does not occur if the volume does not exceed 1000 ml per eight hours.[5]

The delivery of a live fetus after saline induction is rare. Following saline instillation, cessation of the fetal heart beat usually occurs within 30 minutes.[5,18] In a series of 5000 consecutive cases, only three fetuses were born with evidence of cardiac or skeletal muscle activity, none of which lasted more than a few hours. All three had occurred in cases for which the amnioinfusion was not completed, due to loss of the cavity by inadvertent movements (i.e., cough, IV pole knocked away and needle pulled out by connecting tube, etc.). If the fetal heart beat is detectable two hours later, a partial or total reinstillation is advised.

Another factor associated with delivery of a live fetus may be an underestimation of gestational age and the consequent overdilution of the hypertonic solution by the large amount of amniotic fluid present. Such an error can be minimized by routine ultrasonic estimation of the gestational age in all second-trimester abortions. Even the most experienced clinicians frequently are mistaken by several weeks in the second trimester of pregnancy.[34]

Utilizing ultrasound cephalometry and an upper limit of 24 weeks' gestation (menstrual age), it is reasonable to conclude that only those pregnancies which exhibit a fetal biparietal diameter (FBPD) measurement of less than 64 mm (from outer table to outer table) are candidates for abortion.[4]

MORTALITY

According to Schiffer et al., the main factors which result in maternal death are the complications secondary to incomplete abortion with bleeding and sepsis, complications which arise from the use of other agents to shorten the instillation-to-abortion time, and complications secondary to preexisting medical conditions which contraindicate the saline method of abortion.[35]

The risk of death is highest for women with sickle cell disease, moderate to severe anemia, cardiac or cardiovascular disease, and renal disorders.[17-19] According to data reported to the Center for Disease Control during the years 1972-1976, 36 deaths were associated with approximately 200,000 saline-induced abortions. This resulted in a mortality rate of 18.3 per 100,000 procedures.[36] Considering these statistics, it may be worthwhile to reconsider the question posed by Zuspan to a panel of experts: "Are second-trimester abortions safer than letting the patient continue to term for delivery?"[17] The majority of experts answered in the affirmative. One of the quoted statistics puts the amnioinfusion figures (18.3 per 100,000) in the proper perspective. "Maternal mortality associated with pregnancy, childbirth and puerperium, excluding induced abortions: 20 deaths per 100,000 pregnancies."[37]

FINAL COMMENTS

Whether hypertonic saline or other agents are used for amnioinfusion, a similarity exists between the basic processes of second-trimester abortion and term delivery. Both events depend on the active participation of the uterine musculature in the process of self-evacuation. In cases of malfunction, the greater the uterine size, the more severe are the ensuing complications. This is especially evident in the case of hemorrhage and infection, the two leading obstetrical complications at almost any stage of gestation. Therefore, expectant "labor floor" management should be employed, including the continuous presence of obstetrically trained nursing and physician staff under the supervision of experienced attending physicians "on call" on a 24-hour basis.

In the author's opinion, these measures represent, for a woman in labor, the best safeguard at four to six months, as well as seven to nine months of gestation.

REFERENCES

1. Csapo AI: Termination of pregnancy by the intraamniotic injection of hypertonic saline, in Greenhill JP (ed): *The Yearbook of Obstetrics and Gynecology, 1966-1977,* Chicago, Year Book, 1966, p 126.
2. Wagatsuma T: Intra-amniotic injection of saline for therapeutic abortion. *Am J Obstet Gynecol.* 93: 743, 1965.
3. Bengtsson L, Csapo AI: Oxytocin response withdrawal, and reinforcement of defense mechanism of the human uterus at midpregnancy. *Am J Obstet Gynecol.* 83:1083, 1962.
4. Jaffin H, Kerenyi TD, Wood EC: Termination of missed abortion and the induction of labor in midtrimester pregnancy. *Am J Obstet Gynecol.* 84:602, 1962.
5. Kerenyi TD: Midtrimester abortion, in Osofsky HJ, Osofsky JD (eds): *The Abortion Experience.* Hagerstown, Md, Harper & Row, 1973, p 383.
6. Kerenyi TD, Muzsnai D: Volume and sodium concentration studies in 300 saline-induced abortions. *Am J Obstet Gynecol.* 121:590, 1975.
7. Csapo AI, Knobil E, Pulkkinen M, et al: Progesterone withdrawal during hypertonic saline-induced abortions. *Am J Obstet Gynecol.* 105:1132, 1969.
8. Tyack AJ, Parsons RJ, Millar DR, et al: Plasma progesterone changes in abortion induced by hypertonic saline in the second trimester of pregnancy. *Br J Obstet Gynaecol.* 80:548, 1973.
9. Csapo AI: The "see-saw" theory of the coagulatory mechanism of pregnancy. *Am J Obstet Gynecol.* 121:578, 1975.
10. Gustavii B: The distribution within the placenta, myometrium, and decidua of ^{24}Na-labelled hypertonic saline solution following intra-amniotic or extra-amniotic injection. *Br J Obstet Gynaecol.* 82:734, 1975.
11. Honore LH: The mechanism of midtrimester abortion induced by intra-amniotic instillation of hypertonic saline: a modification of Gustavii's lysosomal hypothesis. *Am J Obstet Gynecol.* 126:1011, 1976.
12. Galen RS, Chauhan P, Wietzner H, et al: Fetal pathology and mechanism of fetal death in saline-induced abortion: a study of 143 gestations and critical review of the literature. *Am J Obstet Gynecol.* 120:347, 1974.
13. Myers RE, Symchych P, Strauss L, et al: Morphologic changes of uterine wall following intra-amniotic injection of hypertonic saline in the rhesus monkey. *Am J Obstet Gynecol.* 119:877, 1974.
14. Short RV, Wagner G, Fuchs AR, et al: Progesterone concentrations in uterine venous blood after intra-amniotic injection of hypertonic saline in midpregnancy. *Am J Obstet Gynecol.* 91:132, 1965.
15. Kerenyi TD: Outpatient intra-amniotic injection of hypertonic saline. *Clin Obstet Gynecol.* 15:124, 1971.
16. Tietze C, Lewit S: Highlights of the Joint Program for the Study of Abortion (JPSA): Early medical complications of legal abortion, in Lewit S (ed): *Advances in Planned Parenthood,* vol 8, Amsterdam, Excerpta Medica, 1973, p 173.
17. Zuspan FP, Ballard CA, Bieniarz J, et al: Second trimester abortion—a symposium by correspondence. *J Reprod Med.* 16:47, 1976.

18. Kerenyi TD: Technique of late abortion, in Lewit S (ed): *Abortion Techniques and Services.* Proceedings of the Conference, New York, June 3-5, 1971. Amsterdam, Excerpta Medica, 1972, p 17.

19. Brenner WE: Second trimester interruption of pregnancy, in Taymor ML, Green TH (eds): *Progress in Gynecology,* vol 6. New York, Grune & Stratton, 1975, pp 421-444.

20. Singh KB: Midtrimester abortion by three-percent and five-percent saline amnioinfusion. *Adv Plann Parent.* 10:114, 1975.

21. Perry G, Schulman H, Wong TC: Modified saline abortion for medically high-risk patients. *Obstet Gynecol.* 44:571, 1974.

22. Kerenyi TD, Mandelman N, Sherman DH: Five thousand consecutive saline inductions. *Am J Obstet Gynecol.* 116:593, 1973.

23. Kurzon AM: Transcervical amniocentesis-hypertonic saline instillation for midtrimester abortion. *Adv Plann Parent.* 10:1, 1975.

24. Ruttner BT: Termination of midtrimester pregnancy by transvaginal intra-amniotic injection of hypertonic solution. *Obstet Gynecol.* 28:601, 1966.

25. Mitra M, Chakrabarty B, Poddar D: Intra-amniotic infusion of hypertonic saline through cervical os; preliminary report on fifteen cases. *J Obstet Gynecol. (India)* 25:161, 1975.

26. Schulman H, Kaiser IH, Randolph G: Outpatient saline abortion. *Obstet Gynecol.* 37:521, 1971.

27. Berger GS, Kerenyi TD: Control of morbidity associated with saline abortion. *Adv Plann Parent.* 9:31, 1975.

28. Burnett LS, Wentz AC, King TM: Techniques of pregnancy termination. Part 2. *Obstet Gynecol Surv.* 29:7, 1974.

29. Cohen E, Ballard CA: Consumptive coagulopathy associated with intraamniotic saline instillation and the effect of intravenous oxytocin. *Obstet Gynecol.* 43:300, 1974.

30. Lauersen NH, Schulman JD: Oxytocin administration in midtrimester saline abortions. *Am J Obstet Gynecol.* 115:420, 1973.

31. Horowitz DA: Uterine rupture following attempted saline abortion with oxytocin in a grandmultiparous patient. *Obstet Gynecol.* 43:921, 1974.

32. Hirsch JS: Cervical fistula as a complication of midtrimester abortion. *Obstet Gynecol.* 41:478, 1973.

33. Lauersen NH, Birnbaum SJ: Water intoxication associated with oxytocin administration during saline-induced abortion. *Am J Obstet Gynecol.* 121:2, 1975.

34. Kerenyi T: Unpublished data.

35. Schiffer MA, Pakter J, Clahr J: Mortality associated with hypertonic saline abortion. *Obstet Gynecol.* 42:759, 1973.

36. Center for Disease Control: *Abortion Surveillance 1976.* Atlanta, August 1978.

37. Tietze C: Induced abortion: A fact book. *Rep Popul Fam Plann.* 4:47, 1973.

38. Comparison of intra-amniotic prostaglandin F_2 alpha and hypertonic saline for induction of second trimester abortion. *Br Med J.* 1:1373, 1976.

39. Grimes DA, Schulz KF, Cates W, et al: Midtrimester abortion by intraamniotic prostaglandin $F_2\alpha$: Safer than saline? *Obstet Gynecol.* 49:612, 1977.

8 Prostaglandin Procedures

Marc A. Bygdeman

Although effective contraceptive methods are available, induced abortion remains important as a means of fertility control all over the world. Considerable efforts have been devoted to the study of and improvements in abortion technology. Further refinements are still possible, however, in terms of greater effectiveness, diminished complications, enhanced technical ease, greater convenience, and lower costs. This is particularly true for second-trimester procedures, where the techniques currently in use result in significantly higher maternal morbidity and mortality compared to first-trimester abortions. For many years the most widely used method for terminating pregnancy in the second trimester has been the intraamniotic administration of hypertonic saline. More recently, however, intraamniotic prostaglandins have been used with increasing frequency and considerable success. At present, the use of $PGF_2\alpha$ has been approved by drug safety regulating authorities in approximately 50 countries.

This chapter discusses the risks and benefits of inducing second-trimester abortion by prostaglandins. The experience of intrauterine administration is summarized, but the emphasis will be on the development of abortion methods based on administration of prostaglandin analogues by noninvasive routes, since such techniques can be used during all parts of the second trimester.

INTRAUTERINE ADMINISTRATION

Extraamniotic Administration

Classical prostaglandins Instillation of prostaglandin into the extraamniotic space produces adequate myometrial stimulation while maintaining low plasma levels of the drug. Interruption of pregnancy by extraamniotic administration of PGE_2 or $PGF_2\alpha$ can be accomplished with total doses from one-tenth to one-twentieth less than those which are required by the intravenous route and, as a result, with markedly reduced systemic side effects.

Effective and well-tolerated multiple dose schedules of PGE_2 and $PGF_2\alpha$ have been developed for extraamniotic administration. In initial clinical trials using primary prostaglandins, two-hourly doses of 750 µg $PGF_2\alpha$ or 200 µg PGE_2 were instilled via a transcervically placed extraamniotic Foley catheter. A success rate of between 85% and 95% within 36 hours was reported.[1,2] Equally effective was a continuous infusion of these compounds into the extraamniotic space.[3]

Very few comparative studies of classical prostaglandins with other methods exist. Lange, Secher and Thomsen-Pedersen compared extraamniotic administration of $PGF_2\alpha$ with hypertonic saline. They reported that minor side effects occurred in about 50% of the cases treated with $PGF_2\alpha$; nonetheless, the method was superior to hypertonic saline with regard to the number of complications and length of stay in the hospital.[4]

The advantages of extraamniotic administration of classical prostaglandins are:

- The individual dose is low and well tolerated even if injected intravenously by mistake
- The total cumulative dose is low
- The frequency of prostaglandin-specific side effects such as vomiting and diarrhea are lower than those following intraamniotic administration of the same compound
- The procedure is suitable during the first weeks of the second trimester when intraamniotic administration is technically difficult

Data indicate that the frequency of cervical laceration is lower following extraamniotic than intraamniotic administration of prostaglandins.[5] The major limitations of the method include the need for repeated injections and the inconvenience of an indwelling catheter, which also enhances the risk of uterine infection.

Prostaglandin analogues The need for repeated instillation can be overcome either by administration of a higher single dose of PGE_2 (1.5 mg) incorporated in 9 ml of a 5% viscous solution of hydroxy-methyl cellulose[6] or by using single doses of different prostaglandin analogues which have a longer lasting stimulatory effect on uterine contractility. The results of studies of two analogues, together with those of classical prostaglandins, are summarized in Table 8-1. In a multicenter international study, one single injection of 920 μg 15-methyl $PGF_2\alpha$ diluted in Hyscon induced abortion successfully in 530 or 80.3% of 660 second-trimester patients.[7] Karim, and Karim and Ratnam[8,9] have reported that 1 mg of the analogue $2\alpha,2\beta$-dihomo-15-methyl $PGF_2\alpha$ methyl ester given as one single extraamniotic injection resulted in abortion within 24 hours in 82% of the patients. The mean induction-to-abortion interval was 14.3 hours. In the majority of patients, however, the abortion was regarded as incomplete, and surgical evacuation of placental tissues was required. Most of the patients were in the early part of the second trimester. As a result, the failed cases generally were easy to manage, since treatment resulted in sufficient cervical dilatation to enable the evacuation of the uterus by vacuum aspiration and curettage.

Table 8-1
Results of Extraamniotic Administration of Prostaglandins for Termination of Second-Trimester Pregnancy in Selected Studies

Compound	No. of Patients	Type of Treatment	Dose per Injection (μg)	Mean Induction-Abortion Interval (hours)	Success Rate (%)
$PGF_2\alpha$[2]	50	Repeated	750	24.2	92*
$PGF_2\alpha$[1]	93	Repeated	750	24.9	85*
PGE[1]	70	Repeated	200	19.3	93*
15-methyl $PGF_2\alpha$[7]	660	Single	920	14.1	80.3*
$2\alpha,2\beta$-dihomo-15-methyl $PGF_2\alpha$ methyl ester[8,9]	300	Single	1000	14.3	82†

*Abortion within 36 hours
†Abortion within 24 hours

Extraamniotic administration of prostaglandin has been used only to a limited extent and mainly in countries which had prior experience with this route of administration. In these locations it partly has replaced Rivanol and hypertonic saline. Its clinical usefulness, however, is not so great as abortion methods based on noninvasive administration of prostaglandin analogues.

Intraamniotic Administration

Classical prostaglandins Intraamniotic administration of $PGF_2\alpha$ for termination of second-trimester pregnancy has been used routinely at the Karolinska Institute since 1973. Prostaglandin $F_2\alpha$ (5 mg/ml) often is administered through a small flexible polyethylene catheter without removal of amniotic fluid. An initial 5 mg is given as a test dose. Several satisfactory dose schedules have been utilized. Among these are 25 mg repeated after six hours, or a single dose of 40 mg or 50 mg. Reinstillation of 20–40 mg $PGF_2\alpha$ may be required after 24–48 hours. If the primary method fails, an intravenous infusion of oxytocin also may be added. Repeated intramuscular injections of 15(S), 15-methyl $PGF_2\alpha$ have been found to be effective to complete the abortion process in patients demonstrating poor uterine contractile response to intraamniotic $PGF_2\alpha$ as a consequence of early rupture of the membranes or for other reasons.[10,11]

The intraamniotic instillation of $PGF_2\alpha$ is most effective for terminating pregnancy at 15 to 20 menstrual weeks' gestation.[12,13] The results often are not comparable, however, when different dose schedules are used, since various investigators have selected different methods of patient management and different criteria for evaluation of complications and incomplete abortion rates. Multicenter studies have been organized by the World Health Organization (WHO) to evaluate the efficacy and safety of different dose schedules of intraamniotic administration of $PGF_2\alpha$. Since the criteria for accepting the patients, the general management, and the reporting formulas have been the same in all these studies, the results may be more comparable than the results of single-center studies.[14,15]

The WHO studies have shown that a single intraamniotic dose of 50 mg $PGF_2\alpha$ was as effective in inducing abortion as a 25 mg dose of $PGF_2\alpha$ repeated after six hours, but superior to 40 mg. Side effects and complications generally were of the same magnitude for the three dosage schedules used. The frequency of hemorrhage and blood transfusion was slightly lower for 50 mg $PGF_2\alpha$ than for either 40 mg or 25 mg repeated after six hours. A higher efficacy of a repeated 25 mg dose than of 50 mg $PGF_2\alpha$ in a random comparison has been reported only if the initial two doses were supplemented by 25 mg

PGF$_2\alpha$ at 24 and 30 hours in those patients who had not yet aborted.[16]

Prostaglandin analogues A drawback to intraamniotic administration of PGF$_2\alpha$ is that additional treatment is needed in some patients, even if the initial dose is increased to 50 mg. This disadvantage may be reduced by using different prostaglandin analogues, which are more potent and have a longer duration of action than the classical prostaglandins.

One such analogue is 15(S), 15-methyl PGF$_2\alpha$, which is approximately 20 times more potent in stimulating uterine contractility than is PGF$_2\alpha$.[17] The introduction of a methyl group at C-15 protects the compound from rapid metabolic degradation following systemic or intraamniotic administration. The half-life time of 15-methyl PGF$_2\alpha$ in the amniotic fluid is significantly longer than for the parent compound; this results in prolonged duration of the uterine response (Figure 8-1).[18]

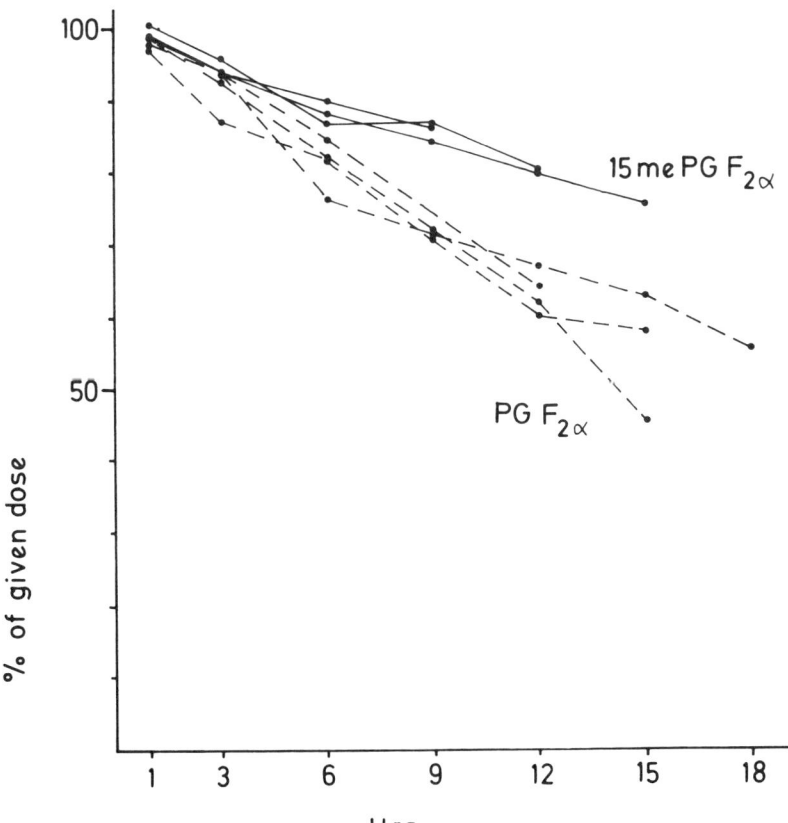

Figure 8-1 Disappearance of PGF$_2\alpha$ and 15(S),15-methyl PGF$_2\alpha$ following intraamniotic administration. Source: Green et al.[22]

In a multicenter study involving 1521 patients, $PGF_2\alpha$ (40 mg or 50 mg) and 15-methyl $PGF_2\alpha$ (2.5 mg) were compared; both were administered intraamniotically.[15] Almost 95% of the patients who received 15-methyl $PGF_2\alpha$ aborted without additional treatment. The corresponding figures for 40 mg and 50 mg $PGF_2\alpha$ were significantly lower (Figure 8-2 and Table 8-2). The frequency of gastrointestinal side effects in this study was slightly higher and the incidence of hemorrhage and blood transfusion lower with 15-methyl $PGF_2\alpha$ than with either of the two doses of $PGF_2\alpha$. Thus, both experimental data and clinical results indicate that 15-methyl $PGF_2\alpha$ is a better agent than $PGF_2\alpha$ for a single treatment method via the intraamniotic route of administration.

Table 8-2
Results of Intraamniotic Administration of Prostaglandin $F_2\alpha$ for Termination of Second-Trimester Pregnancy in Selected Studies

Compound	No. of Patients	Dose (mg)	Mean Induction-Abortion Interval (hours)	Success Rate (%)
$PGF_2\alpha$[14]	719	25 + 25 (6-hr interval)	19.7	85.6
$PGF_2\alpha$[15]	251	40	21.6	81.7
$PGF_2\alpha$[15]	351	50	18.8	86.6

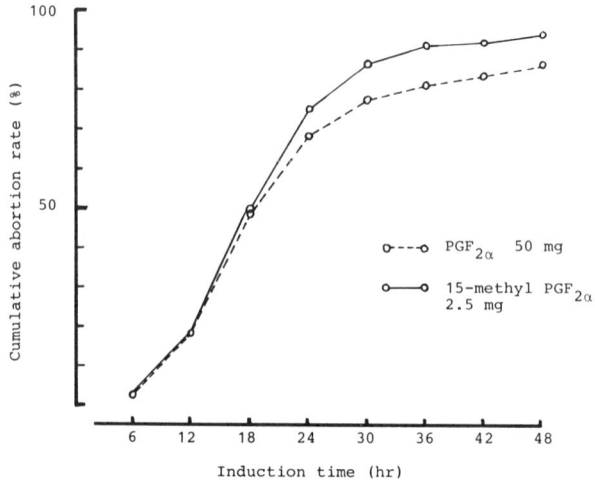

Figure 8-2 Cumulative abortion rates for 919 patients following single intraamniotic administration of $PGF_2\alpha$ or 15(S),15-methyl $PGF_2\alpha$. Source: WHO[15].

VAGINAL AND INTRAMUSCULAR ADMINISTRATION

Classical prostaglandins usually are not useful for administration by noninvasive routes. For example, intramuscular injection of these compounds often is associated with severe pain at the injection site. Gastrointestinal side effects are common following vaginal administration.

The efficacy and safety of several prostaglandin analogues administered by intramuscular injection have been evaluated. The first analogue investigated on a large scale was 15-methyl $PGF_2\alpha$. In a multicenter study performed by the WHO Prostaglandin Task Force, it was found that repeated intramuscular injections of 15-methyl $PGF_2\alpha$ were effective in terminating pregnancy in the second trimester. Abortion occurred within 30 hours in 84.9% of patients (437 out of 515) (Figure 8-3).[19] Treatment, however, was associated with a high frequency of gastrointestinal side effects. Therefore, it was concluded that this method had limited value as a primary method for induction of abortion, but might be of value to terminate pregnancy process when another primary abortion method had failed.

More recent studies have shown that the frequency of gastrointestinal side effects is reduced significantly if another prostaglandin analogue, 16-phenoxy tetranor PGE_2 methyl sulfonylamide, is used. Karim and co-workers have reported that administration of this analogue in a dose of either 0.5 mg every fourth hour or 1.0 mg every

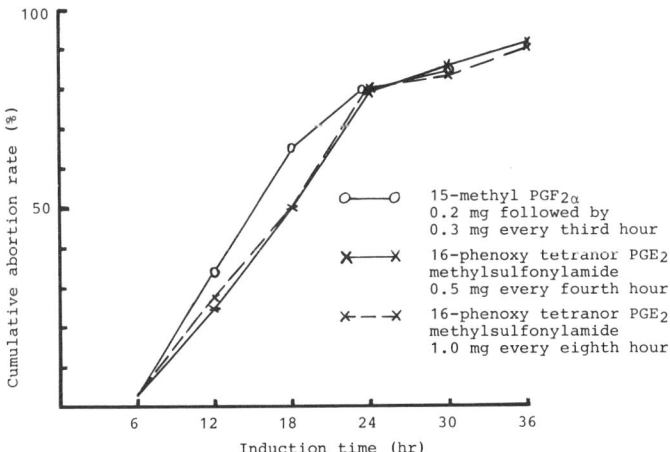

Figure 8-3 Cumulative abortion rates following intramuscular injections of prostaglandin analogues for termination of second-trimester pregnancy. Treatment: 0.2 mg followed by 0.3 mg every third hour of 15(S),15-methyl $PGF_2\alpha$ up to 30 hours—515 patients (Source: WHO[19]); 0.5 mg every fourth hour of 16-phenoxy w 17,18,19,20 tetranor PGE_2 up to 36 hours—118 patients; 1.0 mg every eighth hour of 16-phenoxy w 17,18,19,20 tetranor PGE_2 methylsulphonylamide—80 patients. Source: Karim et al.[20]

eighth hour by the intramuscular route resulted in a success rate of approximately 90% (Figure 8-3).[20] The overall incidence of diarrhea and vomiting was low (one episode per patient). This frequency is only slightly higher than that reported for intraamniotic administration of hypertonic saline (Figure 8-4). Intramuscular injection of the analogue 15-methyl PGE_2 methyl ester also is associated with a lower frequency of vomiting and diarrhea than with 15-methyl $PGE_2\alpha$. With this analogue, however, the side effects of fever and shivering are common.[21]

Tests to determine the levels of 15-methyl $PGF_2\alpha$ in the plasma after intramuscular injection have shown that the drug is absorbed very rapidly. The peak plasma concentration usually occurs 20 to 30 minutes after injection; this then falls rapidly (Figure 8-5).[22] If

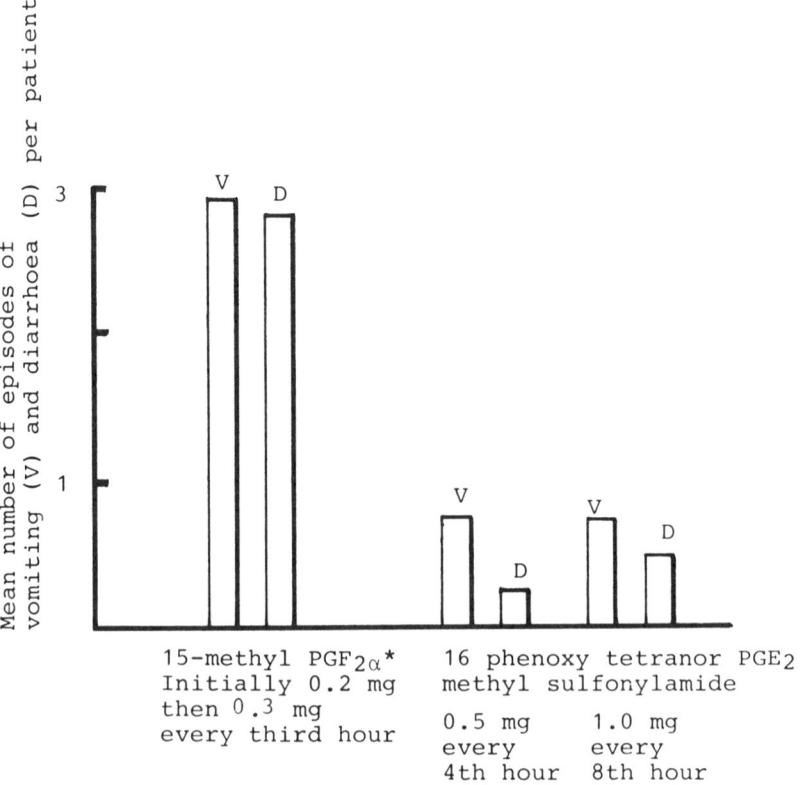

Figure 8-4 Gastrointestinal side effects following intramuscular injections of prostaglandin analogues for termination of second-trimester pregnancy. Treatment: 0.2 mg followed by 0.3 mg every third hour of 15(S),15-methyl $PGF_2\alpha$ up to 30 hours—515 patients (Source: WHO[19]); 0.5 mg every fourth hour of 16-phenoxy w 17,18,19,20 tetranor PGE_2 up to 36 hours—118 patients; 1.0 mg every eighth hour of 16-phenoxy w 17,18,19,20 tetranor PGE_2 methylsulphonylamide—80 patients. Source: Karim et al.[20]

15-methyl PGF$_2\alpha$ is administered by the vaginal route (Figure 8-6), on the other hand, these high peaks (and subsequent falls) can be avoided.[23] Since the frequency of gastrointestinal side effects is related directly to the plasma levels of most prostaglandins, it is likely that vomiting and diarrhea will occur less frequently if the same analogue is administered by the vaginal instead of the intramuscular route.

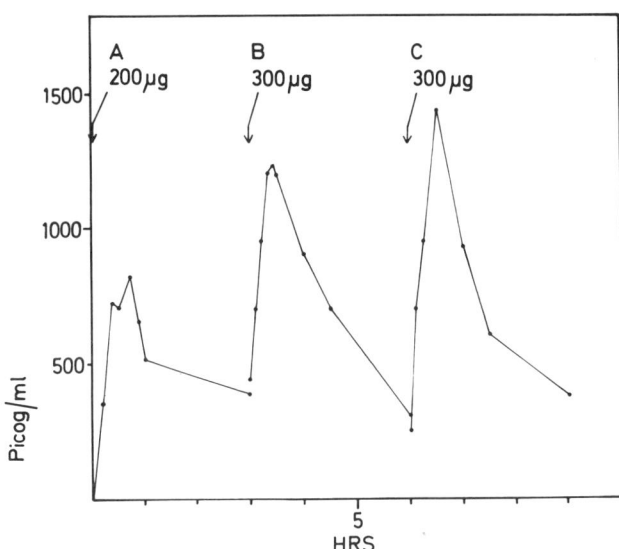

Figure 8-5 Plasma levels of 15(S),15-methyl PGF$_2\alpha$ following repeated intramuscular injections. The initial injection of 0.2 mg was followed by 0.3 mg every third hour. Source: Green et al.[22]

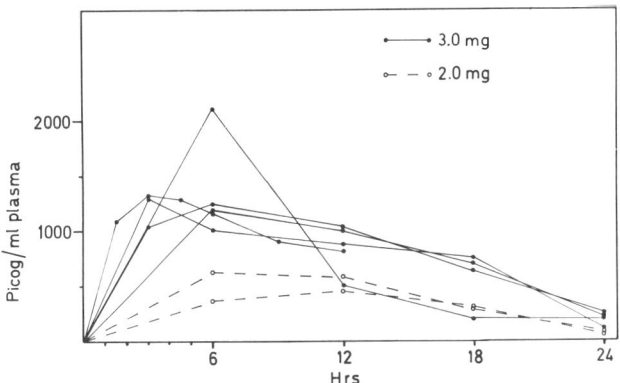

Figure 8-6 Plasma levels of 15-methyl PGF$_2\alpha$ free acid and methyl ester following one single vaginal administration of a slow releasing vaginal suppository containing either 3 mg or 2 mg of 15(S),15-methyl PGF$_2\alpha$ methyl ester. Source: Green and Bygdeman.[23]

Several prostaglandin analogues also stimulate uterine contractility following vaginal administration. Only 15-methyl PGF$_2\alpha$ methyl ester, however, has been investigated on a large scale, since most of the other analogues are unstable in suppository form. Either repeated vaginal administration of 1.5 mg or a single vaginal treatment of 3.0 mg in a slow-releasing suppository is highly effective in terminating second-trimester pregnancy.[24,25] If repeated intramuscular injections of 15-methyl PGF$_2\alpha$ were added 24 hours after administration of the long-acting suppository, almost all patients aborted within 36 hours following start of therapy (Figure 8-7). Although gastrointestinal side effects are less frequent following vaginal administration of 15-methyl PGF$_2\alpha$ methyl ester than following intramuscular administration of 15-methyl PGF$_2\alpha$, especially if the long-acting suppository is used, the rate is still higher than with instillation of intraamniotic saline.

The best results so far have been reported with the use of 16,16 dimethyl PGE$_2$ free acid and its esters administered at three-hourly intervals in suppositories containing 400–1200 µg of the free acid in triglyceride base.[26] Twenty-nine out of 30 patients aborted within 30

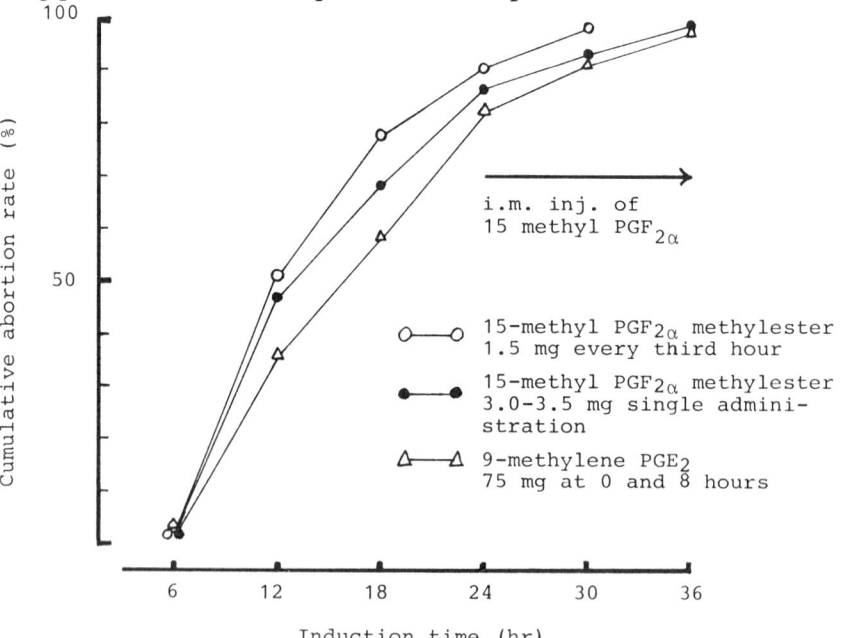

Figure 8-7 Cumulative abortion rates following vaginal administration of prostaglandin analogues. Treatment: 75 mg repeated after 8 hours of 9-deoxo-16,16 dimethyl-9-methylene PGE$_2$—50 patients; 1.5 mg every third hour of 15(S),15-methyl PGF$_2\alpha$ methyl ester up to 30 hours—75 patients; 3.0–3.5 mg 15(S),15-methyl PGF$_2\alpha$ methyl ester in a slow-releasing suppository—175 patients. Source: Bygdeman et al.[24,25,27]

hours. Karim, and Karim and Ratnam[8,9] used glycerine base suppositories containing 16,16 dimethyl PGE_2 p-benzaldehyde semicarbazone ester administered every four hours. All 30 patients aborted within 36 hours. Side effects with both compounds were low. The routine clinical use of this analogue will not be possible until the problem of instability in the suppository base is solved.

Preliminary results indicate that a new prostaglandin analogue, 9-deoxo-16,16 dimethyl-9-methylene PGE_2, may be a better alternative. This analogue has an enhanced chemical stability and is equally effective as 15-methyl $PGF_2\alpha$ methyl ester for termination of second-trimester pregnancy after vaginal administration (Figure 8-7).[27] The frequency of gastrointestinal side effects was significantly lower than that found with 15-methyl $PGF_2\alpha$ methyl ester, and averaged only one episode of vomiting and diarrhea per patient (Figure 8-8).

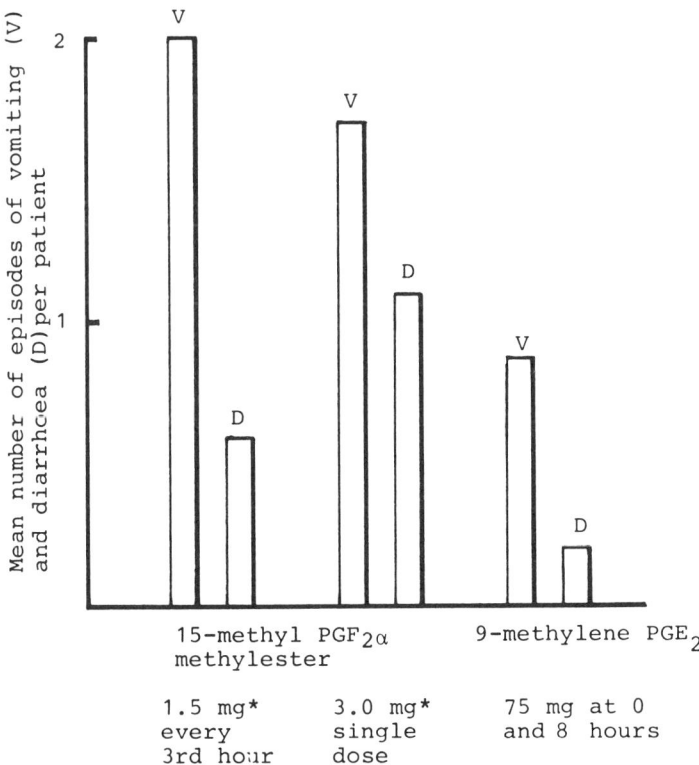

Figure 8-8 Gastrointestinal side effects following vaginal administration of prostaglandin analogues. Treatment: 75 mg repeated after 8 hours of 9-deoxo-16,16 dimethyl-9-methylene PGE_2—50 patients; 1.5 mg every third hour of 15(S),15-methyl $PGF_2\alpha$ methyl ester up to 30 hours—75 patients; 3.0–3.5 mg 15(S),15-methyl $PGF_2\alpha$ methyl ester in a slow-releasing suppository—175 patients. Source: Bygdeman et al.[24,25,27]

PREOPERATIVE DILATATION OF THE CERVIX

It is generally agreed that the frequency of complications with vacuum aspiration or dilatation and evacuation (D&E) increases with increasing gestational age.[28] Some complications, such as cervical laceration and uterine perforation, are directly related to mechanical trauma. Others, such as hemorrhage and incomplete evacuation, may be due to an inadequate or difficult dilatation. If D&E is performed after the 12th week of gestation, cervical injury is twice as frequent and uterine perforation more than six times as frequent as with saline infusion techniques.[29]

Several studies have shown that pretreatment with prostaglandin is an effective method to ease the process of dilatation of the cervical canal and make vacuum aspiration a simpler and more uneventful procedure. The drawbacks of prostaglandin pretreatment are: 1) a long pretreatment time, 2) uterine contractions which sometimes are painful, and 3) the occurrence of gastrointestinal side effects.

Studies on the efficacy and safety of pretreatment with prostaglandin prior to vacuum aspiration or D&E during the second trimester are sparse. Figure 8-9 shows the results of a pilot study which included 489 women, of whom 106 were in the second trimester of pregnancy.[30] In the majority of the patients, the degree of cervical

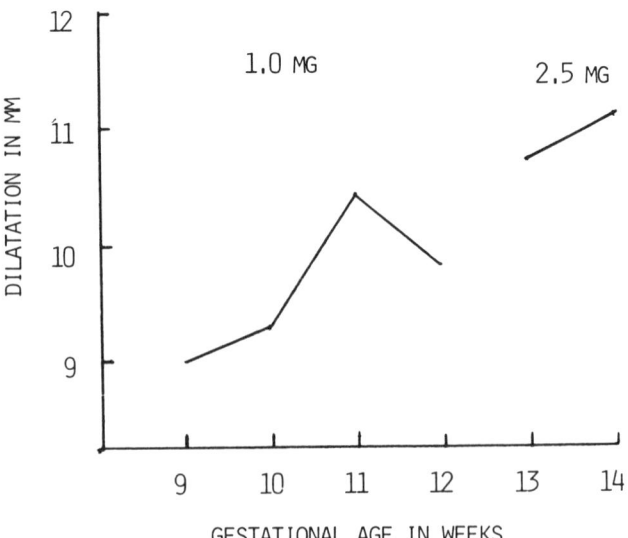

Figure 8-9 Mean cervical dilatation following pretreatment with one single vaginal suppository containing 15-methyl $PGF_{2\alpha}$ methyl ester in relation to gestational age. Patients in the 9th to 12th week received 1.0 mg and those in the 13th to 14th week 2.5 mg. Source: Frankman et al.[30]

dilatation was sufficient to allow evacuation without further treatment. In the remaining patients the cervix had become soft, and additional dilatation was not regarded as difficult. No cervical lacerations were observed, and no perforation of the uterus occurred; nonetheless, further studies are needed to establish if pretreatment with prostaglandin analogues will result in a significant reduction in the complications specific to mechanical dilatation of the cervix.

COMPARISON WITH OTHER METHODS

Hypertonic saline, hypertonic glucose, and urea in combination with $PGF_2\alpha$ or PGE_2 are among the various compounds which have been used for termination of second-trimester pregnancy by intraamniotic administration. Large-scale randomized comparative studies of these different methods are few, however. Those which are available compare intraamniotic administration of hypertonic saline with $PGF_2\alpha$ given by the same route.[14,16] It is clear that $PGF_2\alpha$, administered intraamniotically, is more effective, with a higher success rate and a shorter induction-to-abortion interval than is unaugmented hypertonic saline. The differences are reduced, however, if intravenous infusion of oxytocin is added. Unfortunately, intravenous oxytocin infusion is inconvenient and difficult to maintain; water intoxication can also occur. $PGF_2\alpha$ is easier to administer since the volume to be injected (8 ml to 10 ml) is much smaller than that of hypertonic saline (200 ml). For a number of theoretical reasons, intraamniotic $PGF_2\alpha$ may be a less dangerous abortifacient than hypertonic saline:

- Hypernatremia is not a risk
- Inadvertent intravascular or intraperitoneal injection of $PGF_2\alpha$ appears to be less dangerous, since $PGF_2\alpha$ is rapidly metabolized
- There is less tissue damage from intramyometrial administration of $PGF_2\alpha$
- Consumptive coagulopathies appear to be less frequent with $PGF_2\alpha$ [31]

Although the prostaglandins may be regarded as theoretically safer in practice than hypertonic saline for amnioinfusion, comparative studies indicate that when hypertonic saline is used by skilled physicians, there are few differences in complication rates.

The frequency of gastrointestinal side effects is higher following $PGF_2\alpha$ therapy. The incidence of cervical laceration or cervicovaginal fistula (especially if prostaglandin therapy is augmented with intravenous oxytocin when significant amounts of intraamniotic $PGF_2\alpha$

still are stimulating the uterus) may also be higher following $PGF_2\alpha$ therapy.[32]

A large surveillance study by Grimes et al. has evaluated the risks of $PGF_2\alpha$ and saline as they have been used in the United States.[33] The selection of the treatment was not randomized, however. Furthermore, the treatment schedule varied from one center to another. In most cases both saline and $PGF_2\alpha$ were augmented with continuous intravenous oxytocin. The total number of complications and the number of women with major complications were higher for the $PGF_2\alpha$ group; hemorrhage requiring transfusion, infection, fever, retained products of conception, the need for operative intervention, and hospital readmissions were more frequent with $PGF_2\alpha$ plus oxytocin. The death rate, however, was higher with saline plus oxytocin.[34] These results differ from the WHO studies. A higher frequency of bleeding probably is not a general feature of prostaglandin treatment, since rates comparable to or lower than the rates for hypertonic saline are obtained if a dose of prostaglandin analogues with a prolonged stimulatory effect on uterine contractility is used.[5] Higher rates of fever (over 38°C) have been reported for patients aborted with saline compared to patients aborted with prostaglandin in a study by Edelman et al.,[16] in contrast to that of Grimes et al.[33]

The results of both these latter studies indicate that the rate of incomplete abortion was higher following $PGF_2\alpha$ than following hypertonic saline treatment, but the influence of gestational age was not considered in either of these two studies. Our analysis of a large number of prostaglandin-induced abortions in both the first and second trimester of pregnancy indicates that the lowest rate of complete abortions is found around the 12th week. With advancing gestational age, the frequency of complete abortion increases (Figure 8-10).

The most important advantage of certain prostaglandin analogues compared to hypertonic saline and other compounds presently in use for termination of second-trimester pregnancy is the possibility of administering these analogues by noninvasive routes. The promising results reported in pilot studies with intramuscular injection of 16 phenoxy tetranor PGE_2 methyl sulfonylamide and vaginal administration of 9-deoxo-16,16 dimethyl-9-methylene PGE_2 indicate that abortion methods based on noninvasive administration and associated with a low rate of gastrointestinal side effects soon may be available.

Some of the major complications associated with second-trimester abortion are due to inadvertent injections of the compound in areas other than the intraamniotic space. If the vaginal or intramuscular route is used, such complications can be avoided. The simplicity of the treatment hopefully will facilitate large abortion programs in countries with shortages of trained medical personnel. The noninvasive route offers the additional advantage of the treatment being equally useful during the early and the late part of the second trimester. Delaying the abortion from the 13th to 15th week of pregnancy to after the 15th week, when intraamniotic puncture can be performed, therefore is not necessary.

Surveillance studies from the United States indicate that the frequency of immediate complications if the pregnancy is terminated by D&E in the 13th to 15th weeks' gestation is equal to, or even lower than if hypertonic saline is used at 16th to 18th weeks' gestation.[29] Future studies may show noninvasive administration of prostaglandin analogues to be an alternative to D&E for termination of early second-trimester pregnancy. In general, methods which best ensure the safety of the patient and require the least reliance on the skill of the physician are preferred.

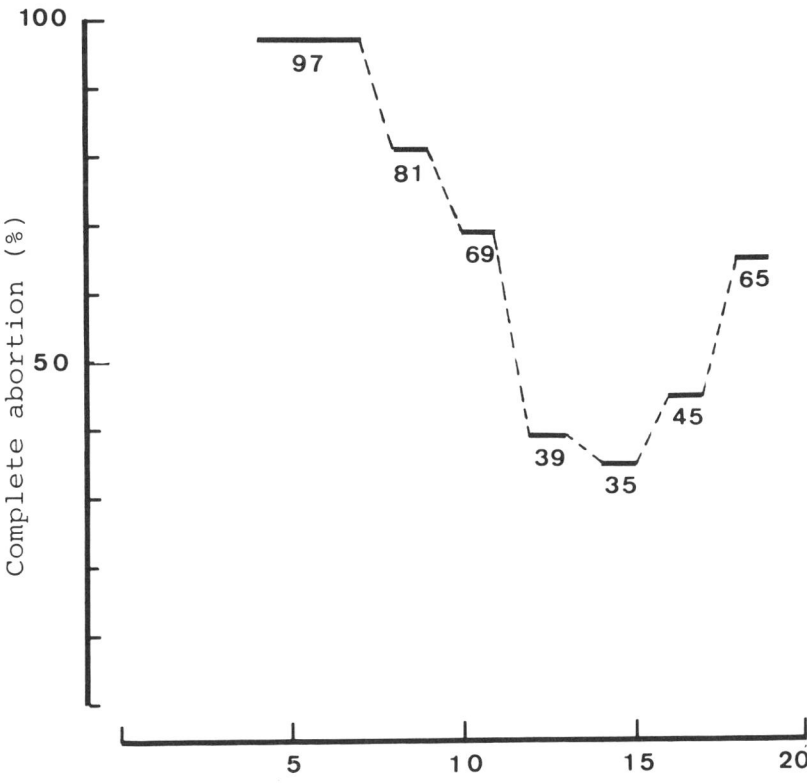

Figure 8-10 Frequency of complete abortions in relation to gestational age following termination of pregnancy by prostaglandins.

SUMMARY

Intrauterine administration of $PGF_2\alpha$ has a well-established place among the compounds currently in use for termination of second-trimester pregnancy. There is little doubt that $PGF_2\alpha$ is a more effective primary abortifacient than hypertonic saline. Although the prostaglandins may be regarded as theoretically safer, comparative studies indicate that, in practice, when hypertonic saline and $PGF_2\alpha$ are used by skilled physicians, there are few differences in complication rates.

Both experimental data and comparative studies show that 15(S), 15-methyl $PGF_2\alpha$ is more effective than $PGF_2\alpha$ administered intraamniotically as a single treatment procedure.

The most important advantage with prostaglandin therapy is the possibility of using noninvasive routes of administration. The continuous development of new analogues has resulted in compounds which are highly effective in stimulating uterine contractility, associated with a low frequency of gastrointestinal side effects, suitable for both intramuscular and vaginal administration, and applicable for termination of pregnancy during both the early and late part of the second trimester.

This work was supported by grants from the World Health Organization.

REFERENCES

1. Embrey MP, Hillier K, Mahendran P: Termination of pregnancy by extra-amniotic prostaglandins and the synergistic effect of oxytocin. *Adv Biosciences* 9:507, 1973.
2. Bygdeman M, Beguin F, Toppozada M, et al: Intrauterine administration of prostaglandin $F_2\alpha$ for induction of abortion. *Adv Biosciences* 9:525, 1973.
3. Lauersen NH, Wilson KH: Continuous extraovular administration of prostaglandin $F_2\alpha$ for midtrimester abortions. *Am J Obstet Gynecol.* 120:273, 1974.
4. Lange AP, Secher NJ, Thomsen-Pedersen G: Induction of therapeutic abortion using either extra-amniotic prostaglandin $F_2\alpha$ or hypertonic saline followed by oxytocin. *Prostaglandins* 6:149, 1974.
5. Bygdeman M: Comparison of prostaglandin and hypertonic saline for termination of pregnancy. *Obstet Gynecol.* 52:424, 1978.
6. Mackenzie IZ, Hillier K, Embrey MP: Single extra-amniotic injection of prostaglandin E_2 in viscous gel to induce midtrimester abortion. *Br Med J* 1:240, 1975.
7. WHO Prostaglandin Task Force: Single extraamniotic administration of 0.92 mg 15-methyl $PGF_2\alpha$ in hyscon for termination of pregnancy in the 10th to 20th week of gestation. An international multicentre study. *Am J Obstet Gynecol.* 129:597, 1977.

8. Karim SMM: Singapore experience with prostaglandin. Routine use and recent advances, in *Obstetrical and Gynecological Uses of Prostaglandin*, vol 1. Lancaster, England, MTP, 1976, p 127.

9. Karim SMM, Ratnam SS: Newer aspects of practical applications of prostaglandins in obstetrics and gynecology, in Kharasch N, Fried J (eds): *Biochemical Aspects of Prostaglandins and Thromboxanes*. New York, Academic Press, 1977.

10. Corson SL, Bolognese RJ: Use of intramuscular 15(S), 15-methyl prostaglandin $F_2\alpha$ in failed abortions. *Am J Obstet Gynecol.* 133:145, 1979.

11. Lauersen NH, Wilson KH: The effects of intra-muscular injections of 15(S), 15-methyl prostaglandin $F_2\alpha$ in failed abortion. *Fertil Steril.* 28:381, 1977.

12. Anderson GG, Steege J: Clinical experience using intra-amniotic prostaglandin $F_2\alpha$ for midtrimester abortion in 600 patients. *Obstet Gynecol.* 46:591, 1975.

13. Kajanoja P, Jungner G, Seppala M, et al: Prostaglandin induction of 424 midtrimester abortions. *Int J Gynaecol Obstet.* 12:198, 1974.

14. WHO Prostaglandin Task Force: Comparison of intraamniotic prostaglandin $F_2\alpha$ and hypertonic saline for induction of second trimester abortion. *Br Med J.* 1:1370, 1976.

15. WHO Prostaglandin Task Force: Comparison of single intraamniotic injections of 15-methyl prostaglandin $F_2\alpha$ and $PGF_2\alpha$ for termination of second trimester pregnancy. An international multicentre study. *Am J Obstet Gynecol.* 129:601, 1977.

16. Edelman DA, Brenner WE, Mehta AC, et al: A comparative study of intra-amniotic saline and two prostaglandin $F_2\alpha$ dose schedules for midtrimester abortion. *Am J Obstet Gynecol.* 125:188, 1976.

17. Toppozada M, Beguin F, Bygdeman M, et al: Response of the midpregnant human uterus to systemic administration of 15(S), 15-methyl prostaglandin $F_2\alpha$. *Prostaglandins* 2:239, 1972.

18. Green K, Granstrom E, Bygdeman M, et al: Kinetic and metabolic studies of 15-methyl prostaglandin $F_2\alpha$ administered intra-amniotically for induction of abortion. *Prostaglandins* 11:699, 1976.

19. WHO Prostaglandin Task Force: Intramuscular administration of 15-methyl $PGF_2\alpha$ for induction of abortion in the 10th to 20th week of pregnancy. *Am J Obstet Gynecol.* 129:593, 1977.

20. Karim SMM, Choo HT, Lim AL, et al: Termination of second trimester pregnancy with intramuscular administration of 16-phenoxy w 17,18,19,20-tetranor PGE_2 methyl-sulphonylamide. *Prostaglandins* 15:1063, 1978.

21. Brenner WE, Gruber W, Staurovsky LG, et al: Induction of artificial abortion with intramuscular administration of 15(S), 15-methyl PGE_2 and 15(S), 15-methyl $PGF_2\alpha$, in *Obstetrical and Gynecological Uses of Prostaglandins*, vol 1. Lancaster, England, MTP, 1976, p 175.

22. Green K, Bygdeman M, Leader A, et al: Pharmacokinetic studies on 15-methyl prostaglandin $F_2\alpha$ and its methylester after administration to the human via various routes for induction of abortion, in *Advances in Prostaglandin and Thromboxane Research*, vol 2. New York, Raven Press, 1976, p 719.

23. Green K, Bygdeman M: Plasma levels of 15(S), 15-methyl $PGF_2\alpha$ following administration in various routes for induction of abortion. *Prostaglandins* 14:1013, 1977.

24. Bygdeman M, Borell U, Leader A, et al: Induction of first and second trimester abortion by the vaginal administration, in *Advances in Prostaglandin and Thromboxane Research*, vol 2. New York, Raven Press, 1976, p 693.

25. Bygdeman M, Ganguli A, Kinoshita K, et al: Development of vaginal suppository suitable for single administration of interruption of second trimester pregnancy. *Contraception* 15:129, 1977.

26. Martin JN, Bygdeman M, Ramadan M, et al: Vaginally administered 16,16-dimethyl PGE$_2$ for the induction of midtrimester abortion. *Prostaglandins* 11:123, 1976.

27. Bygdeman M, Green K, Bergstrom S, et al: New prostaglandin E$_2$ analogue for pregnancy termination. *Lancet* 1:1136, 1979.

28. Edelman DA, Brenner WE, Berger GS: The effectiveness and complications of abortions by dilatation and vacuum aspiration versus dilatation and rigid metal curettage. *Am J Obstet Gynecol.* 119:473, 1974.

29. Grimes DA, Schultz KF, Cates W, et al: Midtrimester abortion by dilatation and evacuation: A safe and practical alternative. *N Engl J Med.* 296:1141, 1977.

30. Frankman O, Bygdeman M, Green K, et al: Dilatation of the cervix prior to vacuum aspiration by single vaginal administration of 15-methyl PGF$_2\alpha$ methyl ester. *Contraception* 21:571, 1980.

31. Brenner WE, Berger GS: Pharmacologic methods of inducing midtrimester abortion: Risks and benefits, in Sciarra J, Zatuchni GI, Speidel JJ (eds): *Risks, Benefits, and Controversies in Fertility Control.* Hagerstown, Md., Harper & Row, 1978.

32. Kajanoja P, Jungner G, Widholm O, et al: Rupture of the cervix in prostaglandin abortion. *J Obstet Gynaecol Br Commonw.* 81:242, 1974.

33. Grimes DA, Schulz KF, Cates W, et al: Midtrimester abortion by intraamniotic prostaglandin F$_2\alpha$. Safer than saline? *Obstet Gynecol.* 49:612, 1977.

34. Cates W, Grimes DA, Haber RH, et al: Abortion deaths associated with the use of prostaglandin F$_2\alpha$. *Am J Obstet Gynecol.* 127:219, 1977.

9 Hyperosmolar Urea

Ronald T. Burkman
Theodore M. King
Milagros F. Atienza

The ideal method of managing patients requesting second-trimester abortion is still a matter of controversy. The most widely used regimens at this time include intraamniotic administration of hypertonic saline, hyperosmolar urea, prostaglandin $F_2\alpha$ ($PGF_2\alpha$), and dilatation and evacuation. This chapter reviews the administration of hyperosmolar urea for the induction of elective second-trimester abortion as practiced at the Fertility Control Center of the Johns Hopkins Hospital.

METHOD OF ADMINISTRATION

Before the instillation procedure, all patients undergo a careful history and physical examination and a thorough discussion of the procedure, including its risks. A detailed, informed consent form is signed. Routine laboratory testing includes a hematocrit, urinalysis, Pap smear, gonorrhea culture, Rh determination, serologic test for syphilis, and pregnancy test. If the duration of gestation is between 16 and 22 weeks from the first day of the last menstrual period, patients are considered candidates for urea instillation. Sonography is utilized for evaluation of those patients who either are close to these limits or have abnormalities on physical examination, such as uterine size which is inconsistent with estimated gestational age or uterine myomas. To date, an absolute contraindication to the procedure has not been encountered in our clinic. Hyperosmolar urea is prepared before the installation by mixing 40 ml of 5% dextrose and water with 40 g of lyophilized urea salt. Two bottles or 80 g are utilized for each patient. The 80 g dose constitutes a final volume of about 135 ml or a 59.7% concentration. Each patient undergoes an immediate preoperative abdominal and pelvic examination, and confirmation of the presence of fetal heart tones with a Doppler device. Laminaria tents are inserted for a minimum of six hours prior to instillation. Between one and five laminaria tents (5 mm in size) are inserted under antiseptic conditions, and the patients are kept at bedrest. No further vaginal examinations are routinely performed until the time of abortion or until at least 24 hours have elapsed after the instillation of urea. All laminaria still in place in unaborted patients are removed at the 24-hour examination.

Before the urea instillation is begun, the patient is requested to empty her bladder; her abdomen then is cleansed with antiseptic and draped with sterile towels. The usual site for amniocentesis is in the midline, 2 to 3 cm above the pubic hair line. About 5 to 10 ml of 1% lidocaine is injected around the site of amniocentesis. A 3.5 inch No. 16 Touhy epidural needle is used. After a free flow of clear fluid is obtained, at least 100 ml and usually 200 ml of amniotic fluid is removed through a disposable extension tube with a three-way stopcock. If the fluid cannot be removed readily by a syringe, it is removed by syphoning with the help of gentle pressure on the uterine fundus. If the tap is bloody and does not clear immediately, the Touhy needle is either repositioned or a second amniocentesis is performed. Urea is not instilled until a free flow of amniotic fluid is obtained. The usual causes for failed amniocentesis or bloody taps are large anterior placentae, gestational ages less than 16 weeks and, occasionally, abnormal pregnancies with oligohydramnios. No preoperative medications such as tranquilizers or analgesics are utilized.

Following the removal of amniotic fluid, the previously prepared urea is infused slowly via gravity. Currently, all patients receive an additional 5 mg $PGF_2\alpha$ intraamniotically following the urea infusion. A 2.5 mg test dose is given slowly and, if no untoward reactions occur, the 2.5 mg dose is repeated after five minutes. $PGF_2\alpha$ is not utilized, however, for patients with a history of asthma or known sensitivity to $PGF_2\alpha$. For such patients, intravenous oxytocin at 322 mU/min is started immediately following urea infusion. This dose is prepared by mixing 200 units of oxytocin with 500 ml of 5% dextrose and 0.2% sodium chloride; it is administered at a rate of 50 ml/hr with an electronic pump.

Routine postinjection care includes the frequent monitoring of vital signs, careful recording of fluid intake and output, and ascertainment of membrane rupture, bleeding, labor, and abortion. Oxytocin given intravenously in the dose described above is indicated if labor has not begun approximately four hours after rupture of membranes, or 24 hours after injection, or after fetal expulsion to control bleeding and assist in placental expulsion. Serum electrolytes are monitored at least every 12 hours when oxytocin is administered at this dose. The oxytocin infusion is stopped for 2 to 4 hours if there is clinical evidence of water intoxication, if the serum sodium is less than 132 mEq/liter, if intake exceeds output by more than 1500 ml, or urinary output becomes inadequate, or if there has been a suspected intravascular injection of urea. More recently, along with the routine use of laminaria tents, most patients who remain unaborted by 24 hours no longer receive intravenous oxytocin, but rather are given a vaginal suppository of 10 mg prostaglandin E_2 (PGE_2) every 3 to 4 hours if active labor does not commence. Patients who have risk factors for coronary vascular disease are not given PGE_2, but receive intravenous oxytocin instead. If, on the other hand, fetal expulsion has not occurred within 48 hours and is not believed to be imminent, vaginal evacuation of the uterus is undertaken with intravenous analgesia of 50 mg meperidine and 10 mg diazepam. Furthermore, if hemorrhage or evidence of chorioamnionitis occurs prior to 48 hours, the pregnancy is terminated vaginally.

If the placenta has not been passed after two hours, curettage with ring forceps is carried out using intravenous analgesia. After observation for at least four hours following completion of the abortion, patients are given detailed instructions regarding potential complications, provided with contraception or contraceptive advice, and given follow-up appointments four weeks later. Follow-up information has been obtained on about 80% of the abortion patients at the Fertility Control Center in the past five years.

SUMMARY OF RESULTS

A number of clinical studies have been completed at the Fertility Control Center to evaluate the efficacy and safety of hyperosmolar urea as an abortifacient. Studies from our center[1] and elsewhere[2,3] have shown that it is necessary to supplement the actions of urea with other agents, such as intravenous oxytocin or intraamniotic $PGF_2\alpha$, in order to obtain mean injection-abortion intervals of less than 24 hours. Although the initial experience with intravenous oxytocin for augmentation at a rate of 332 mU/min yielded satisfactory injection-abortion intervals,[4] the antidiuretic action of oxytocin and the potential risk of water intoxication led to the evaluation of other approaches. Accordingly, studies evaluating the intraamniotic use of $PGF_2\alpha$ in doses of 20 mg,[5] 10 mg,[6] and 5 mg[1,7] were completed in a sequential fashion in an effort to determine a minimally effective dose. Finally, in an effort to reduce the possibility of cervical injury, the use of laminaria tents is being evaluated at present.

The clinical characteristics of the patients for the various groups studied are shown in Table 9-1. Over 20% had a coexisting medical condition, including asthma, gonorrhea, obesity, anemia, heart disease, urinary tract infection, and hypertension. About 60% of the patients were teenagers, with over one-third aged 17 or less.

The injection-to-abortion intervals are summaried in Table 9-2. All mean injection-to-abortion intervals are consistently less than 24 hours. Lengthier times usually are reported for nulliparous patients compared to parous patients. The percentage of patients who received $PGF_2\alpha$ augmentation and in whom abortion had not taken place after 24 hours ranged from 10% to 20%. There have been no instances of live fetal abortion in our program.

Table 9-1
Clinical Characteristics of Urea Patients

	No.	Mean Age (years)	Para 0	Para 1 or greater	Mean Duration of Gestation (weeks)*
Urea + oxytocin (332 mU/min)	650	20.7	355	295	17.0 (13–22)
Urea + $PGF_2\alpha$ (20 mg)	30	20.4	17	13	19.3 (13–22)
Urea + $PGF_2\alpha$ (10 mg)	1083	20.3	624	459	19.9 (13–24)
Urea + $PGF_2\alpha$ (5 mg) (No laminaria tents)	349	20.0	216	133	19.6 (14–24)
Urea + $PGF_2\alpha$ (5 mg) (One laminaria tent)	197	19.5	160	37	19.9 (16–22)

*Ranges in parentheses.

Table 9-2
Injection-Abortion Intervals of Urea Patients

	No.	Injection-Abortion Interval (hours)*	
		Mean	Range
Parity: 0			
Urea + Oxytocin	341	21.5	3–61
Urea + PGF$_2\alpha$ (20 mg)	16	18.2	4–36
Urea + PGF$_2\alpha$ (10 mg)	632	15.9	2–60
Urea + PGF$_2\alpha$ (5 mg) (No laminaria)	213	17.0	6–45
Urea + PGF$_2\alpha$ (5 mg) (One laminaria)	160	12.0	4–46
Parity: 1 or greater			
Urea + Oxytocin	289	16.6	4–54
Urea + PGF$_2\alpha$ (20 mg)	12	13.7	3–30
Urea + PGF$_2\alpha$ (10 mg)	434	13.9	1–47
Urea + PGF$_2\alpha$ (5 mg) (No laminaria)	133	16.3	3–46
Urea + PGF$_2\alpha$ (mg) (One laminaria)	37	13.9	4–44
Total Groups			
Urea + Oxytocin	630	19.2	3–61
Urea + PGF$_2\alpha$ (20 mg)	28	16.3	3–36
Urea + PGF$_2\alpha$ (10 mg)	1066	15.1	1–60
Urea + PGF$_2\alpha$ (5 mg) (No laminaria)	346	16.7	3–46
Urea + PGF$_2\alpha$ (5 mg) (One laminaria)	197	12.3	4–46

*From intraamniotic injection of medication to abortion of fetus.

Table 9-3 shows the clinical course. Incomplete abortion remains an important problem, although failed abortion has become quite uncommon. As has been reported previously,[7] the need for oxytocin augmentation has been reduced.

Table 9-3
Clinical Outcome of Urea Patients

	No.	Complete Abortion		Incomplete Abortion		Failure	
		No.	%	No.	%	No.	%
Urea + Oxytocin	650	385	59.2	245	37.7	20	3.1
Urea + PGF$_2\alpha$ (20 mg)	30	16	53.3	12	40.0	2	6.7
Urea + PGF$_2\alpha$ (10 mg)	1083	566	52.2	500	46.2	17	1.6
Urea + PGF$_2\alpha$ (5 mg) (No laminaria)	349	222	63.6	124	35.5	3	0.9
Urea + PGF$_2\alpha$ (5 mg) (One laminaria)	197	140	71.1	55	27.9	2	1.0

The more frequent complications of the procedure are presented in Table 9-4. In addition to those listed, there have been two instances of coagulopathy, three cases of intravascular urea spill, and one case of subacute bacterial endocarditis. One patient required hysterectomy due to *Clostridia perfringens* sepsis.

DISCUSSION AND REVIEW

Each of the currently available methods of inducing second-trimester abortion has advantages and disadvantages. Intravascular injection of hypertonic sodium chloride has been associated with hemolysis, seizures, coma, cardiac arrest, and death.[8] Furthermore, clinical coagulopathy may occur in up to 1% of these patients, particularly if oxytocin augmentation is begun immediately following hypertonic sodium chloride injection.[9,10]

The use of $PGF_2\alpha$ alone is associated with increased failure rates and a need for frequent re-injection. Moreover, the drug is expensive and, when it is utilized for gestations greater than 18 weeks, live fetal birth occasionally can occur.[11] Finally, all intraamniotic methods require hospital back-up and a support staff that is knowledgeable in the management of incomplete and failed abortion, hemorrhage, infection, and cervical laceration.

Dilatation and evacuation for second-trimester pregnancies recently has received a great deal of support in the literature.[12,13] In some hands this approach requires multiple patient visits or even hospitalization for pre-evacuation treatment of the cervix with laminaria tents.[14] In addition, greater skill is needed in order to carry out these procedures compared to suction curettage in the first trimester. Although the short duration of the evacuation procedure has obvious psychological advantages for the patient as compared to instillation techniques, a considerable degree of psychological adjustment may be required for the operator.[15] Finally, the safety and efficacy of this technique for gestations beyond 18 weeks have not yet been evaluated in series involving large numbers of patients.

Unfortunately, the utilization of intraamniotic urea for second-trimester abortion has not provided a solution to all the disadvantages and problems listed with other methods. The remaining discussion will briefly review the mechanism of action and the hematological and biochemical changes as well as the complications associated with urea, and contrast them with second-trimester techniques.

One possible mechanism of action of urea is decidual or placental damage which leads to synthesis and release of prostaglandins.

Table 9-4
Common Complications of Urea Patients

	Urea + Oxytocin (650 Cases)		Urea + PGF$_2\alpha$ (20 mg) (30 Cases)		Urea + PGF$_2\alpha$ (10 mg) (1083 Cases)		Urea + PGF$_2\alpha$ (5 mg) (No laminaria) (349 Cases)		Urea + PGF$_2\alpha$ (5 mg) (One laminaria) (197 Cases)	
	No.	%	No.	%	No.	%	No.	%	No.	%
Hemorrhage (500 ml or need for curettage)*	35	5.4	3	10.0	102	9.4	31	8.9	7	3.6
Endometritis										
Hospitalization	29	4.5	1	3.3	54	5.0	6	1.7	2	1.0
Outpatient	30	4.6	1	3.3	66	6.1	11	3.2	2	1.0
Cervical laceration										
Transverse	6†	0.9	1	3.3	4	0.4	3	0.9	1	1.0
Vertical	0	...	0	...	31	2.9	5	1.4	2	0.5
Gastrointestinal‡										
Nausea-vomiting	347	53.4	22	73.3	788	72.8	213	61.0	...	...
Diarrhea	5	0.8	1	3.3	51	4.7	9	2.6	...	...

*Five patients required blood transfusion.
†Postabortal examinations not routine for this entire group.
‡Gastrointestinal sequelae not analyzed for Urea + PGF$_2\alpha$ (5 mg), one laminaria group.

Hyperosmolar urea produces varying types of "coagulation necrosis" and other damage to the placenta.[16] Presumably this is secondary to the hyperosmolarity of the urea and possibly leads to prostaglandin release. A study by Niebyl and co-workers[17] is supportive of this theory. Patients undergoing urea abortion who were pretreated with aspirin, a known prostaglandin inhibitor, had longer injection-to-abortion intervals than patients pretreated with placebos. In another study completed at the Fertility Control Center, however, isolated rat uterine strips were pre-incubated in baths containing indomethacin, another prostaglandin inhibitor. Prostaglandin release was reduced, but contractile force was not changed.[18] Thus, at least in the rat, prostaglandin did not appear to be an obligatory factor in hyperosmolar urea-induced contractions. Finally, when levels of prostaglandin E and F and their metabolites were measured serially in the blood and amniotic fluid of patients undergoing a urea-induced abortion, it appeared that uterine contractions could occur independent of the rise in prostaglandin production.[19]

In addition to producing uterine contractions, hyperosmolar urea apparently is toxic to the fetus. Studies in Rhesus monkeys have shown that urea is taken up rapidly by the fetus from the surrounding amniotic fluid and that the fetus plays a role in distributing the drug to the placenta.[20] Fetal heart beat ceases in approximately two hours.[1] Passage of hyperosmolar solute into the fetus possibly results in a loss of cardiac function when a certain critical fetal osmolarity is exceeded.

The hematologic and coagulation factor changes following urea instillation have been evaluated in two studies by our group.[4,5] Hematocrit levels do not vary significantly over the first 24 hours, but leukocyte counts show a gradual rise for the first 16 hours. This latter change is seen when second-trimester abortion is induced by other agents as well, however. Measurements of fibrinogen and platelets show some variation over 24 hours, but no consistent pattern. In 18% to 36% of patients, a significant increase in fibrinogen-fibrin degradation products occurs within 24 hours following injection. The frequency and degree of such changes, however, are less than those of the changes observed after hypertonic saline instillation.[8] Despite the observed changes in coagulation factors, clinical evidence of a disseminated intravascular coagulopathy is quite rare. For example, among 2500 cases at the Fertility Control Center, there have been only two instances of clinical coagulopathy.[9] In contrast, almost 1% of patients undergoing instillation of hypertonic saline followed by oxytocin augmentation experienced a clinically significant coagulation disorder.

A number of biochemical changes occur following urea instillation in the second trimester. Characteristically, serum urea nitrogen levels rise to a peak of 25–30 mg% four hours after instillation; this is followed by a gradual return to normal levels within 24 hours.[5] These changes are more pronounced when oxytocin is utilized for augmentation. In addition, there are some variations in levels of serum electrolytes; however, none exceed the normal range expected for patients. Serum bilirubin, serum glutamic oxalacetic transaminase, lactic dehydrogenase, and alkaline phosphatase all show some elevation for the first 24 hours following urea instillation; this is probably due to destruction of the fetal-placental unit. Finally, uric acid, calcium, phosphate, cholesterol, total protein, and albumin levels do not vary significantly when measured serially during the first 24 hours after urea instillation.

Investigators at several other centers have demonstrated the efficacy of hyperosmolar urea as a second-trimester abortifacient.[21-24] In reviewing these studies, as well as the results at the Fertility Control Center, it is clear that the injection-to-abortion interval is influenced by a number of factors. First, nulliparous patients usually experience greater delays than do multiparous patients. Second, shortly after injection with either intravenous oxytocin or intraamniotic prostaglandin augmentation is necessary in order to achieve mean injection-to-abortion intervals less than 24 hours. Third, the final intraamniotic concentration of urea also appears to be important, in that shorter intervals are achieved when the final infused urea concentration approaches 60% and when the amount of amniotic fluid removed at amniocentesis is 100 ml or greater. Finally, the utilization of preinjection laminaria tents shortens the injection-to-abortion interval.

In reviewing the problems and complications that occur with urea, a number of points should be made. Incomplete abortion remains a problem; about 30% to 40% of patients require curettage if one uses the authors' definition for incomplete abortion. Failure of the primary procedure still remains an occasional problem, but can be managed readily with vaginal evacuation.[25] Such evacuations are carried out easily, since labor already has effaced and dilated the cervix to some extent, and the products of conception are situated in the lower uterine segment. Furthermore, the fetal products are macerated. Operators should have considerable experience with curettage for incomplete second-trimester abortion before attempting such procedures, however.

Hemorrhage requiring transfusion is quite uncommon. The most frequent causes are retained placental tissue and uterine atony. The former can be managed by curettage, while the latter may require repeated bimanual uterine massage for several minutes. Coagulopathy, as discussed previously, is extremely rare.

Between 1% to 2% of patients require hospitalization for treatment of endometritis. These rates for infection are quite similar to those reported in other series of second-trimester terminations.[22,23]

The most frequently encountered organisms include *E. coli, Staphylococcus aureus,* Group B *beta streptococci,* and *Bacteroides.*[26] The postabortal endometrial flora is quite similar to the flora of the vagina and cervix prior to abortion.[27] Standard treatment for inpatients has included broad spectrum parenteral antibiotics such as ampicillin or penicillin plus an aminoglycoside. Early curettage also is an important part of the therapy.

Cervical injury remains a problem with second-trimester abortion procedures. Injuries range from small vertical lacerations to complete detachments of the posterior or anterior cervix.[28] With the use of laminaria tents, however, the frequency and severity of such injuries are decreased.[23,24] For example, all three lacerations occurring with laminaria in this series were small and required only two to three interrupted sutures to close. When large lacerations are encountered, treatment consists of immediate debridement followed by closure in layers. Despite careful repair, breakdown is common; to date, there is no information available regarding the future reproductive capacity of such patients. Unless careful speculum and digital examinations are routinely performed after the abortion, such lacerations can be easily missed, since they do not usually lead to extensive bleeding.

Gastrointestinal side effects, particularly nausea and vomiting, are frequent, but diarrhea is rare when low doses of intraamniotic $PGF_2\alpha$ are utilized for augmentation. In general, the gastrointestinal side effects do not present a difficult management problem, although intravenous hydration occasionally is needed.

Intravascular injection of hyperosmolar urea is uncommon if amniocentesis is carefully performed.[29] Symptoms include nausea, headache, sensations of warmth, and intense uterine cramping. In addition, abnormal blood pigments occasionally may be noted in the urine. Treatment includes monitoring of fluid intake and output as well as renal function, avoidance of oxytocics, and intravenous hydration. Urea probably poses less concern after such spills than does hypertonic saline because of its action as an osmotic diuretic and because of its ability to cross cell membranes readily.

SUMMARY

The advantages of urea include: predictable injection-abortion intervals; ease of mastering the technique; limited hematologic, coagulation, and biochemical changes; and a relatively low frequency of life-threatening complications. To date, controlled clinical trials testing hyperosmolar urea versus other modalities such as hypertonic saline and dilatation and evacuation have not been carried out. Therefore, it is impossible to state whether or not the utilization of this approach is the safest and most efficacious means of accomplishing second-trimester abortion, particularly for later gestations.

REFERENCES

1. King TM, Dubin NH, Atienza MF, et al: Intraamniotic urea and prostaglandin $F_2\alpha$ for midtrimester abortion: clinical and laboratory evaluation. *Am J Obstet Gynecol.* 129:817, 1977.
2. Raud HR, Balsdon MJ, Collins JA: Serum human chorionic gonadotropin, human chorionic somatomammotropin, and progesterone following intraamniotic injection of hypertonic urea. *Am J Obstet Gynecol.* 113:887, 1972.
3. Greenhalf JO: Termination of pregnancy during the midtrimester by intraamniotic injection of urea. *Br J Clin Pract.* 26:24, 1972.
4. Burnett LS, King TM, Atienza MF, et al: Intraamniotic urea as a midtrimester abortifacient: clinical results and serum and urinary changes. *Am J Obstet Gynecol.* 121:7, 1975.
5. King TM, Atienza MF, Burkman RT, et al: The synergistic activity of intraamniotic prostaglandin $F_2\alpha$ and urea in the midtrimester elective abortion. *Am J Obstet Gynecol.* 120:704, 1974.
6. Burkman RT, Atienza MF, King TM, et al: Intraamniotic urea and prostaglandin $F_2\alpha$ for midtrimester abortion: a modified regimen. *Am J Obstet Gynecol.* 126:328, 1976.
7. Burkman RT, Atienza MF, King TM, et al: Hyperosmolar urea for elective midtrimester abortion. *Am J Obstet Gynecol.* 131:10, 1978.
8. Burnett LS, Wentz AC, King TM: Techniques of pregnancy termination—Part II. *Obstet Gynecol Surv.* 29:6, 1974.
9. Burkman RT, Bell WR, Atienza MF, et al: Coagulopathy with midtrimester induced abortion: association with hyperosmolar urea administration. *Am J Obstet Gynecol.* 127:533, 1977.
10. Cohen E, Ballard CA: Consumption coagulopathy associated with intraamniotic saline instillation and the effect of intravenous oxytocin. *Obstet Gynecol.* 43:300, 1974.
11. King TM, Burkman RT, Burnett LS, et al: Abortion: practice and promise. *Adv Plann Parent.* 10:204, 1975.
12. Grimes DA, Schulz KF, Cates W, et al: Midtrimester abortion by dilatation and evacuation: a safe and practical alternative. *N Engl J Med.* 296:1141, 1977.
13. Hodari AA, Peralta J, Quiroga PJ, et al: Dilatation and curettage for second-trimester abortions. *Am J Obstet Gynecol.* 127:850, 1977.
14. Hern WM, Oakes AG: Multiple laminaria treatment in early midtrimester outpatient suction abortion: a preliminary report. *Adv Plann Parent.* 12:93, 1977.
15. Goldsmith S, Kaltreider NB, Margolis AJ: Second trimester abortion by dilatation and extraction (D&E): surgical techniques and psychological reactions. Presented at the annual meeting of the Association of Planned Parenthood Physicians, Atlanta, October 13, 1977.
16. Babaknia A, Parmley TH, Burkman RT, et al: The histopathology of the placenta following second-trimester pregnancy termination. *Obstet Gynecol.* 53:583, 1979.

17. Niebyl JR, Blake DA, Burnett LS, et al: The influence of aspirin on the course of induced midtrimester abortion. *Am J Obstet Gynecol.* 124:607, 1976.

18. Dubin NH, Ghodgaonkar RB, Blake DA, et al: Hyperosmolar urea induced uterine contractions following prostaglandin inhibition. *Biol Reprod.* 16:661, 1977.

19. Dubin NH, Ghodgaonkar RB, Baros NA, et al: Uterine activity and prostaglandin production following intraamniotic hyperosmolar urea. *Prostaglandins* 14:753, 1977.

20. Blake DA, Burnett LS, Miyasaki BL, et al: Pharmacokinetics of intraamniotically administered hyperosmolar urea in Rhesus monkeys. *Am J Obstet Gynecol.* 124:245, 1976.

21. Craft IL: Intraamniotic urea and low dose prostaglandin E_2 for midtrimester termination. *Lancet* 1:1115, 1975.

22. Greenhalf JO: Termination of pregnancy during the midtrimester by intraamniotic injection of urea. *Br J Clin Pract.* 26:24, 1972.

23. Golditch IM, Solberg N: Induction of midtrimester abortion with intraamniotic urea, intravenous oxytocin and laminaria. *J Reprod Med.* 15:225, 1975.

24. Strauss JH, Wilson M, Caldwell D, et al: Laminaria use in midtrimester abortions induced by intra-amniotic prostaglandin $F_{2\alpha}$ with urea and intravenous oxytocin. *Am J Obstet Gynecol.* 134:260, 1979.

25. Burkman RT, Atienza MF, King TM, et al: The management of midtrimester abortion failures by vaginal evacuation. *Obstet Gynecol.* 49:233, 1977.

26. Burkman RT, Atienza MF, King TM: Culture and treatment results in endometritis following elective abortion. *Am J Obstet Gynecol.* 128:556, 1977.

27. Burkman RT, Spence MR, Atienza MF, et al: Bacteriologic culture results obtained before and after elective midtrimester urea abortion. *Contraception* 17:513, 1978.

28. Burkman RT, Atienza MF, King TM: Detachment of the uterine cervix in association with induced midtrimester abortion. *Am J Obstet Gynecol.* 129:585, 1977.

29. Kovasznay BM, Burkman RT, Atienza MF, et al: Intravascular spill of hyperosmolar urea during induced midtrimester abortion. *Obstet Gynecol.* 53:127, 1979.

10 Dilatation and Evacuation

David A. Grimes
Willard Cates, Jr.

Three general approaches exist for emptying the uterus during the second trimester of pregnancy: hysterotomy, induction of labor, and dilatation and evacuation (D&E). Each of these methods of abortion shares two features: 1) a portal of exit, and 2) expulsive or tractile force on extraction to evacuate the uterine contents.

With hysterotomy, the physician creates a surgical opening in the uterus, manually empties the cavity, and repairs the wound. Because of high morbidity and mortality, prohibitive cost, and prolonged recuperation, hysterotomy has been virtually abandoned as a primary abortion method in the United States.[1]

Induction of premature labor attempts to generate expulsive forces which enlarge the natural anatomic opening of the uterus as well as expel the products of conception. Chemical insults to the fetoplacental unit or administration of prostaglandins initiate uterine contractility in the second trimester. Teleologically, however, the uterus has evolved to retain its contents tenaciously at this stage of pregnancy, while reserving the capacity to expel defective pregnancies in the first trimester and viable fetuses later on in the third. Thus, the second trimester is the least physiologic time during pregnancy for the uterus to empty itself.

Induction of labor in the second trimester often is slow, unpredictable, and painful. In addition to the side effects and hazards associated with the abortifacient agents themselves, women undergoing second-trimester abortion by labor induction also incur risks generally associated with parturition, such as amniotic fluid embolism.[2]

Dilatation and evacuation incorporates certain advantages of hysterotomy and labor induction. The principal advantage D&E shares with hysterotomy is that the evacuation procedure is brief and definitive; like abortion by labor induction, D&E uses the dilated cervix as the portal of egress. Traction (rather than expulsion) is the means by which the cavity is evacuated. D&E thus provides a faster, safer, and more comfortable abortion than alternative methods. This chapter will document the use of second-trimester D&E in the United States, describe current techniques, review the safety of the method, and then compare D&E with its alternatives.

USE OF SECOND-TRIMESTER DILATATION AND EVACUATION IN THE UNITED STATES

Dilatation and evacuation has become one of the two most frequently used methods of abortion in the second trimester. According to data provided to the Center for Disease Control (CDC) by 28 states,[1] D&E accounted for 38.7% of all abortions in 1977 at ≥ 13 weeks' gestation (Table 10-1). Intrauterine saline instillation accounted for 38.3%, while intrauterine prostaglandin $F_2\alpha$ ($PGF_2\alpha$) administration accounted for 16.6%.

Table 10-1
Reported Legal Abortions at ≥ 13 Weeks' Gestation by Type of Procedure,* United States, 1977

Type of Procedure	Number	%
Dilatation and evacuation	17,590	38.7
Intrauterine saline instillation	17,441	38.3
Intrauterine prostaglandin instillation	7534	16.6
Hysterotomy/hysterectomy	399	0.9
Other	2170	4.8
Unknown	367	0.8
Total	45,501	100.0

*Based on data from 28 states; excludes abortions with gestational age not specified.
Source: Center for Disease Control, *Abortion Surveillance 1977*, Atlanta, issued September, 1979, Table 18.

In 1977, D&E was the predominant method of abortion in the 13- to 15-week interval (73.3%). Both saline and PGF$_2\alpha$ instillation were used more frequently in the 16- to 20-week interval (50.1% and 25.7%, respectively), with D&E accounting for only 16.7% of cases. At 21 weeks' gestation, saline instillation remained the predominant method (64.3%), with D&E and PGF$_2\alpha$ responsible for nearly equal proportions (12.7% and 12.6%, respectively). The predominance of D&E in the 13- to 15-week interval may be due in large part to the technical difficulty of performing an amniocentesis for instillation of abortifacients until the uterus is approximately 16 weeks in size.

CURRENT TECHNIQUES OF SECOND-TRIMESTER DILATATION AND EVACUATION

Although the upper gestational age limit for D&E abortions may be as high as 24 weeks (Table 10-2), the majority of these operations take place earlier in the second trimester (Table 10-3). The predominance of earlier second-trimester D&E abortions reflects the gestational ages at which women request abortion (Figure 10-1). Adherence to a 12-week limit for curettage abortions artifactually skews the gestational age distribution of women obtaining second-trimester abortions.[3] For women requesting abortion at 13- to 15-weeks' gestation, use of D&E obviates the need for costly and hazardous delays until 16 weeks or later for amnioinfusion abortion.[4] In general, the incidence of second-trimester abortion should be inversely proportional to gestational age, with the exception of small but important numbers of abortions which occur late because of the need to obtain antenatal diagnoses of fetal defects.

Second-trimester D&E abortions are performed on an outpatient basis in both hospitals and free-standing clinics (Table 10-2). Low morbidity rates have been reported from both types of facilities, and no presently available data support the suggestion to limit performance of such abortions to hospitals (Table 10-3). One clinic[5] has challenged a state regulation restricting abortions beyond 12 weeks' gestation to hospitals. In 1979 the National Medical Committee of Planned Parenthood Federation of America authorized performance of second-trimester D&E abortions in nonhospital facilities of selected affiliates.

Many physicians performing second-trimester D&E abortions do not routinely obtain ultrasound estimates of gestational age. Rather, ultrasonography is reserved for clinical indications such as marked discrepancies between menstrual history and estimated uterine size. Other physicians routinely use ultrasound to corroborate gestational age for those women near the upper gestational age limit for D&E abortions. Still others use this diagnostic examination for all

Table 10-2
Differences in Technique of Dilatation and Evacuation Among Reported Single Institution Studies, United States

Study	Latest Gestation (wks)	Facility	Routine Sonography	Dilatation Method	Dilatation Duration (hrs)	Anesthesia	Equipment (Forceps)
Barr[14]	21	Hospital	No	Laminaria	12–24	Local	Sopher
Burnhill[25]	16	Clinic	Yes	Laminaria	4–24	Local	Heavy
DeLee[26]	24	Hospital	No	Repeat Laminaria	48	General	Ring
Glick and Sacks[27]	24	Hospital	No	Laminaria	12–24	General	Special
Goodman[28]	19	Hospital	No	Laminaria	15–20	Either	Sponge
Grimes, et al[22]	21	Hospital	No	Laminaria	12	Local	Bierer
Hanson[8]	20	Hospital	No	Laminaria	12–14	Local	Sponge
Hern and Oakes[9]	19	Clinic	Yes	Repeat Laminaria	48	Local	Bierer
Hodari, et al[29]	20	Hospital	No	Pratt	0	General	Ring
Kaltreider, et al[16]	20	Hospital	No	Laminaria	12–24	General	Sopher
Koplik[30]	16	Clinic	No	Laminaria	12–24	Local	Special
Livingston[5]	16	Clinic	No	Hanks	0	General	Sponge
Meadowbrook[31]	20	Clinic through 18 weeks	No	Laminaria	12–24	Local	Special
Berry and Peterson[32]	19	Hospital	For gestations ≥ 18 weeks	Pratt	0	Local	Peterson
Stubblefield, et al[12]	18	Hospital	No	Laminaria	12	Either	Large Cannula, Foerester

122

Table 10-3
Studies of Dilatation and Evacuation Procedures, United States

Study	Date	Type Study	No. of Patients (Weeks' Gestation)	Findings
Tietze and Lewit[17,33]	1972 (D&E) 1973 (saline)	Multicenter, prospective, cohort, nonrandomized	N = 2734 2317 (13-14) 417 (15+)	Complication rates increase with increasing gestational age. Total complications for D&E fewer than saline at all gestations.
Stewart and Goldstein[34]	1972	Case series	N = 195 180 (13-14) 15 (15-16)	Complication rates increase with gestational age. No comparison of D&E and saline complications.
Brenner and Edelman[18] (includes data from US, England, India, and Singapore)	1974	Multicenter, prospective, cohort, nonrandomized	N = 338 (13-15)	Complication rates with sharp curettage through 15 weeks similar to saline at later gestations. Suction curettage alone had higher complication rates than sharp curettage alone.
Koplik[30]	1975	Case series	N = 141 95 (13-14) 46 (> 14)	No significant difference in complications by gestational age.
DeLee[26]	1976	Case series	N = 47 28 (14-16) 12 (17-19) 6 (20-22) 1 (23-24)	No major complications. One minor complication of fever.
Grimes, et al[20]	1977	Multicenter, prospective, cohort, nonrandomized	N = 6213 5632 (13-16) 581 (17-20)	Major complications for D&E 60% lower than for saline instillation.

Table 10-3 *(continued)*
Studies of Dilatation and Evacuation Procedures, United States

Study	Date	Type Study	No. of Patients (Weeks' Gestation)	Findings
Smith, Steinhoff and Palmore[19]	1978	Multicenter, prospective, cohort, nonrandomized	N = 721 696 (13–16) 25 (17–20)	Complication rates with D&E in 13 to 16-week range less than instillation procedures later.
Stubblefield, et al[12]	1978	Case series	N = 73 21 (13) 20 (14) 20 (15–16) 12 (17–18)	No major complications. Larger cannula had greater blood loss at lower gestational ages, but faster and more complete uterine evacuation.
Barr[14]	1978	Case series	N = 900 48.3% (18–20)	Major complication rate 0.44/100 D&E procedures. Two uterine perforations.
Glick and Sacks[27]	1978	Case series	N = 1074 334 (< 15) 289 (16) 267 (17–18) 156 (19–20) 23 (21–22) 5 (23–24)	Major complication rate 0.55/100 D&E procedures. Five cases of DIC, 1 recognized perforation.
Hanson[8]	1978	Case series	N = 3123 819 (14) 673 (15) 465 (16) 281 (17)	Major complication rate of 0.2%.

Study	Date	Type Study	No. of Patients (Weeks' Gestation)	Findings
Hanson[8] (continued)			332 (18) 246 (19) 200 (20) 21 (21)	
Berry and Peterson[32]	1978	Case series	N = >5000	Rate of uterine perforation < 0.4/100, transfusion < 0.1/100, infection 0.3/100.
Hodari, et al[29]	1977	Case series	N = 2490 1144 (15) 1012 (16) 267 (17) 57 (18) 7 (19) 3 (20)	Major complication rate of 1.65/100 D&E procedures. Total complication rate of 2.77/100 D&E procedures.
Hern and Oakes[9]	1977	Case series	N = 150 45 (13) 35 (14) 44 (15) 16 (16) 5 (17) 4 (18) 1 (19)	Mean blood loss 117 ml, mean operative time 10 minutes, one suspected uterine perforation, no major complications.
Goldsmith, Kaltreider, and Margolis[35]	1977	Case series	N = 130 24 (14–15) 59 (16–17) 36 (18–19) 11 (20)	Complication rates with D&E similar to those found in JPSA/CDC. Slightly higher rates for infection and retained tissue than JPSA/CDC.

Table 10-3 *(continued)*
Studies of Dilatation and Evacuation Procedures, United States

Study	Date	Type Study	No. of Patients (Weeks' Gestation)	Findings
Goodman[28]	1977	Case series	N = 50 17 (14–15) 22 (16–17) 11 (18–19)	No major complications. One case of febrile morbidity.
Livingston[5]	1977	Case series	N = 6168 5896 (13–14) 272 (15–16)	Major complication rate of 0.58/100 D&E procedures. Total complication rate of 7.4/100 D&E.
Burnhill[25]	1978	Case series	N = 568 207 (15) 348 (16) 6 (17) 6 (18) 1 (19)	Total complication rate of 10.2/100 D&E procedures. Perforations 14 times more frequent with D&E after 14 menstrual weeks than before. Series based on underestimated gestations.
Kaltreider, Goldsmith and Margolis[16]	1979	Cohort, nonrandomized	N = 250 52 (14–15) 106 (16–17) 72 (18–19) 20 (≥ 20)	D&E was associated with greater comfort and less guilt, anger, and depression than $PGF_2\alpha$.
Grimes, Hulka, and McCutchen[22]	In press	Randomized clinical trial	N = 94 8 (≤ 12) 16 (13–14) 34 (15–16) 27 (17–18) 6 (19–20) 3 (≥ 21)	Total complication rate 6/100 D&E procedures; 34/100 $PGF_2\alpha$ procedures. Significantly better compliance with D&E regimen, shorter hospital stay, fewer gastrointestinal side effects.

patients whose fetuses are judged to be of a gestational age greater than 12 weeks.

Predilatation by laminaria appears to have considerable support in the current practice of second-trimester D&E. Acute mechanical dilatation of the cervix to large diameters can be technically difficult, traumatic, and potentially deleterious to a woman's subsequent childbearing capacity.[6,7] Most physicians who use laminaria leave them in place from 8 to 12 hours to as long as 24 hours. An occasional physician uses laminaria for less than 12 hours for pregnancies ≤ 16 weeks,[8] while others use repetitive packings of multiple laminaria over 48 hours.[9]

Although local and general anesthesia are used for second-trimester D&E abortions, the former is more popular. While the risks of major complications associated with local or general anesthesia for first-trimester suction curettage are comparable,[10] several studies have documented significantly greater blood loss with general anesthesia.[11] This observation may be applicable to second-trimester D&E as well. Halothane and other agents which relax the uterus should be avoided.[12]

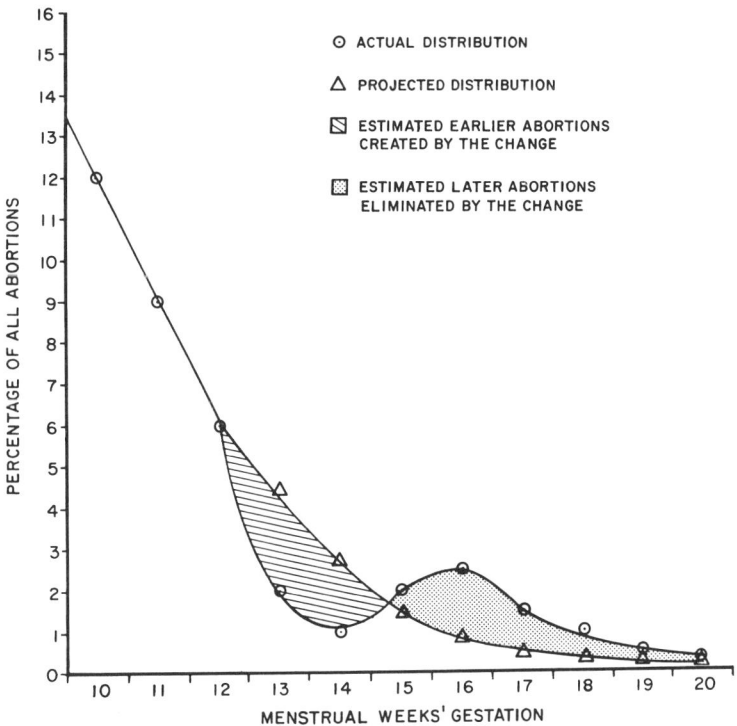

Figure 10-1 Actual distribution of abortions and projected distribution without any delay in the 13- to 16-week interval, by gestational age, US, 1975.

In addition to the smaller blood loss associated with local anesthesia, *intracervical* injection with anesthetics to which vasoconstrictors have been added may result in even less bleeding. As described by Finks, this procedure entails injecting a local anesthetic such as lidocaine with epinephrine deeply into the cervix and lower uterine segment.[13] Uptake of the solution in the uterus may be responsible for the effective hemostasis which is achieved in most cases. Extensive experience in the United States[14] as well as overseas[13,15] attests to the usefulness of this technique.

Most surgeons rely on large forceps to evacuate the products of conception. The commercially available Bierer, Sopher, Clemeston, or Peterson forceps feature heavy construction, long shanks, and reverse serrations on the grasping surfaces to provide a more secure grip. Large bore suction cannulae present an alternative to such forceps. Stubblefield and associates found that a 15.9 mm diameter suction cannula obviated the need for crushing forceps in the 15- to 16-week interval and earlier.[12] They also observed that the elimination of fetal dismemberment makes second-trimester D&E more acceptable to physicians. For later pregnancies, forceps were required, however.

Administration of oxytocic agents and prophylactic antibiotics varies from institution to institution. Many physicians give oxytocics to decrease intraoperative bleeding and to provide a firmer uterine wall. Others avoid them in hopes of avoiding entrapment of the fetal calvarium. Prophylactic antibiotics, usually tetracycline or doxycycline, commonly are given postoperatively.

Morbidity and Mortality

Dilatation and evacuation appears to be the safest available method of abortion through 20 weeks' gestation. As summarized in Table 10-3, numerous case series have documented major complication rates ranging from 0.4 to 1.7 per 100 abortions. Total complication rates have varied from 2.8 to 10.2 per 100 abortions.

Comparative studies are more illuminating, however. For example, Kaltreider, Goldsmith, and Margolis focused on the psychologic morbidity of D&E compared to intraamniotic $PGF_2\alpha$.[16] They found that D&E was associated with greater patient comfort and less guilt, anger, and depression than instillation of $PGF_2\alpha$. They also noted that much of the emotional burden of the abortion was shifted from the woman to the physician in these cases.

The initial report of the Joint Program for the Study of Abortion demonstrated that the major complication rate for D&E at 13 to 14 weeks' gestation (0.8 per 100 abortions) was less than that for saline instillation at any gestational age (1.4 to 2.5 per 100 abortions).[17] In addition, the total complication rate for D&E at ≥ 15 weeks' gestation (7.9 per 100 abortions) was less than that for saline instillation at any gestational age (21.0 to 29.5 per 100 abortions).

Brenner and Edelman observed that performing a D&E abortion in the 13- to 15-week interval may be preferable to delaying until the woman is at ≥ 16 weeks' gestation for saline instillation.[18] The total complication rate associated with D&E at 13 to 15 weeks' gestation was 12.5 per 100 abortions, while that observed with saline instillation at 16 to 18 weeks was 10.6. However, "the saline method appeared to be associated with higher rates of serious or potentially serious complications—infections, pulmonary complications and death."[18]

Examining Hawaiian data, Smith and associates reached similar conclusions.[19] In the 13- to 16-week interval, D&E and suction curettage (alone or with sharp curettage) had total complication rates of 12.3 and 13.9 per 100 abortions, respectively. In contrast, saline abortion in this interval had a complication rate of 33.5. Smith et al. concluded that instrumental evacuation was the method of choice in the 13- to 16-week interval; they further advised that waiting to perform amnioinfusion was not justifiable in an attempt to reduce medical risks.

The second phase of the Joint Program for the Study of Abortion, incorporating an even larger sample size, corroborated the earlier findings.[20] In a comparison of 6213 abortions by D&E and 8662 by saline instillation at 13 to 20 weeks' gestation, D&E was found to be significantly safer. Major complication rates associated with the two methods were 0.69 and 1.78 per 100 abortions, respectively. Total complication rates paralleled major complication rates, although the differences were even greater. Women receiving saline required treatments for their complications significantly more often.

Critics of such nonrandomized studies have challenged their findings and have called for a randomized clinical trial to resolve the question of safety.[21] In response, a study was conducted at the University of North Carolina of 100 patients estimated to be 13 to 18 weeks' pregnant.[22] Fifty were allocated randomly to abortion by outpatient D&E and 50 to instillation of $PGF_2\alpha$. There were no significant differences in the demographic characteristics of the patients in either subgroup.

Patients assigned to abortion by $PGF_2\alpha$ waited significantly longer to obtain an abortion. The total complication rate for D&E was 6 per 100 abortions, while that for $PGF_2\alpha$ was 34. No major complications occurred in the D&E group in contrast to three in the $PGF_2\alpha$-treated group.[22] In addition, all but two women assigned to D&E underwent abortion as outpatients, while all women receiving $PGF_2\alpha$ spent at least one night in the hospital.

The mortality statistics for second-trimester D&E confirm its safety relative to abortion by instillation of abortifacients (see Chapter 12). The risk of dying from a D&E abortion at ≥ 13 weeks is greater than that from curettage abortion earlier in pregnancy; nevertheless, the risk of dying appears to be less than that from instillation of either saline or prostaglandin $F_2\alpha$. From 1972 to 1977, D&E had an overall death-to-case rate of 8.3 per 100,000 abortions, compared with 20.6 for instillation of prostaglandin $F_2\alpha$ (and other agents), and 15.5 for saline. Thus, in terms of both morbidity and mortality, D&E appears to be the safest available method of second-trimester abortion.

CLINICAL COMPARISON OF DILATATION AND EVACUATION WITH INSTILLATION ABORTION

The optimal method of second-trimester abortion should be simple, convenient, inexpensive, and safe. Although no current method for second-trimester abortion fulfills all of these criteria, D&E satisfies more of them than do present day alternatives.

Performing a second-trimester D&E is more complex technically than performing an amnioinfusion. However, this disadvantage is balanced by a significantly higher success rate than that generally obtained with instillation abortions,[20] and the dilemma of a live fetus is eliminated. Clearly, either failed abortion or delivery of a live fetus substantially complicates the abortion process for all concerned.

How technically difficult is a second-trimester D&E? The operation appears to be simpler than a vaginal hysterectomy, an operation all gynecologists have learned to perform. Nonetheless, appropriate training and equipment are prerequisites for safe performance of D&E abortions. Residents in obstetrics and gynecology at Harvard University, for example, learn to perform such procedures under faculty supervision.[12] It is questionable whether this educational activity is widespread.

From the physician's perspective, second-trimester D&E is not only more complex technically but emotionally as well. To perform an amnioinfusion and then to leave the woman in the care of nurses is simpler indeed than confronting the destruction of the fetus during a D&E abortion. Many activities in medicine are stressful to physicians. Overall concern should be focused primarily on the emotional burden of the woman requesting second-trimester abortion, and secondarily on that of the medical staff which cares for her. This statement notwithstanding, it is possible to design programs which attempt to address the concerns of the staff as well as of the patient.[16,23]

Second-trimester D&E is more convenient than abortion by instillation of abortifacients. The woman can be scheduled immediately for surgery at a specific date and time rather than having to wait for a hospital bed to become available. Absences from work or school and arrangements for child care can be made with certainty. Delays are openly discouraged. Some clinics performing D&E abortions use a graduated fee scale which increases with advancing gestational age.[24] Women undergoing D&E as outpatients avoid the inconvenience of admission and discharge from a hospital as well.

The medical staff also may find D&E more convenient than instillation abortions. Physicians can schedule D&E procedures. In contrast, with instillation abortions, a physician must remain available to attend to problems during labor and to complete the abortion in a high percentage of cases.[20] Nursing care for a woman undergoing D&E abortion is abbreviated and more convenient as well.

A second-trimester D&E is less expensive than an instillation abortion. The principal reason is that D&E abortions usually are performed on an outpatient basis. Although this is not necessarily representative of fees throughout the United States in 1979, the Director of the National Abortion Federation reveals that instillation abortions may cost as much as $275 more than a second-trimester D&E abortion provided at the same facility.

Abortion by second-trimester D&E is generally faster than by instillation of abortifacients. Although intervals for cervical predilatation by laminaria vary, most authors report a surgical evacuation time of less than 20 minutes. Both with laminaria pretreatment[22] and without,[20] D&E has had a significantly shorter duration than instillation abortions. Repetitive packing of laminaria,[9] however, entails a longer interval for predilatation and, hence, a total time which may exceed the induction-to-abortion times obtained with current instillation regimens.

As noted previously, D&E appears to be the safest available method of second-trimester abortion. Case series, prospective single and multicenter cohort studies, a randomized clinical trial, and nationwide surveillance of abortion-related deaths, all support this conclusion. The potential late complications of second-trimester D&E, as well as of other second-trimester techniques, remain largely speculative. Clearly, additional study is needed in this area. Until such information is available, however, the choice of abortion methods should be based on currently known information rather than on speculation.

CONCLUSION

D&E is a leading method of second-trimester abortion in the United

States today in spite of allegations to the contrary.[21] The technique commonly consists of dilatation by laminaria followed by evacuation with special forceps, combined with sharp and suction curettage. More than 15 publications in the United States have documented low morbidity rates for the procedure, and nationwide surveillance of abortion deaths has demonstrated a low mortality rate as well.

Although D&E is technically and emotionally more complex for the physician, it is simpler, more convenient, less expensive, faster, and safer for the woman. It is emotionally less traumatic from the patient's point of view.[16] Existing data suggest that D&E should be considered against which all new methods of second-trimester abortion should be compared.

REFERENCES

1. Center for Disease Control: *Abortion Surveillance 1977*, Atlanta, issued September, 1979.
2. Grimes DA, Cates W Jr: Fatal amniotic fluid embolism during induced abortion, 1972–1975, *South Med J.* 70:1325, 1977.
3. Cates W Jr: D&E after 12 weeks: safe or hazardous? *Contemp Ob/Gyn.* 13:23, 1979.
4. Cates W Jr, Schulz KF, Grimes DA, et al: The effects of delay and method of choice on the risk of abortion morbidity. *Fam Plann Perspect.* 9:266, 1977.
5. Livingston FM: Affidavit to the Superior Court of the New Jersey Appellate Division, Bergen County, October 21, 1977.
6. Hulka J, Higgins G: Tears of the internal cervical os during dilatation for routine curettage. *Am J Obstet Gynecol.* 82:913, 1961.
7. Harlap S, Shino P, Ramcharan S, et al: A prospective study of spontaneous fetal losses after induced abortions: *N Engl J Med.* 301:677, 1979.
8. Hanson MS: D&E midtrimester abortion. Presented at the 16th annual meeting, Association of Planned Parenthood Physicians, San Diego, October 25–27, 1977.
9. Hern WM, Oakes AG: Multiple laminaria treatment in early midtrimester outpatient suction abortion: a preliminary report. *Adv Plann Parent.* 12:93, 1977.
10. Grimes DA, Schulz KF, Cates W Jr, et al: Local versus general anesthesia: which is safer for performing suction curettage abortions? *Am J Obstet Gynecol.* (in press).
11. Grimes DA, Cates W Jr: Complications from legally-induced abortion: a review. *Obstet Gynecol Surv.* 34:177, 1979.
12. Stubblefield PG, Albrecht BH, Koos E, et al: A randomized study of 12 mm and 15.9 mm cannulas in midtrimester abortion by laminaria and vacuum curettage. *Fertil Steril.* 29:512, 1978.
13. Finks AA: Midtrimester abortion. *Lancet* 1:263, 1973.
14. Barr MM: Midtrimester abortions—12 to 20 weeks by dilatation and evacuation method under local anesthesia. *Adv Plann Parent.* 13:16, 1978.
15. Van Den Bergh AS: Abortion procured in the second trimester of pregnancy. *Medisch Contact* 29:1555, 1974.

16. Kaltreider NB, Goldsmith S, Margolis AJ: The impact of midtrimester abortion techniques on patients and staff. *Am J Obstet Gynecol.* 135:235, 1979.

17. Tietze C, Lewit S: Early medical complications of abortion by saline: Joint Program for the Study of Abortion (JPSA). *Stud Fam Plann.* 4:133, 1973.

18. Brenner WE, Edelman DA: Dilatation and evacuation of 13 to 15 weeks' gestation versus intraamniotic saline after 15 weeks' gestation. *Contraception* 10:171, 1974.

19. Smith RG, Steinhoff PG, Palmore JA: Potential reduction of medical complications from induced abortions. *Int J Obstet Gynecol.* 15:337, 1978.

20. Grimes DA, Schulz KF, Cates W Jr, et al: Midtrimester abortion by dilatation and evacuation. A safe and practical alternative. *N Engl J Med.* 296:1141, 1977.

21. Borell U, Embrey MP, Bygdeman M, et al: Midtrimester abortion by dilatation and evacuation. (Letter). *Am J Obstet Gynecol.* 131:232, 1978.

22. Grimes DA, Hulka JF, McCutchen MF: Midtrimester abortion by dilatation and evacuation versus intraamniotic instillation of prostaglandin $F_2\alpha$: a randomized clinical trial. *Am J Obstet Gynecol.* 137:785, 1980.

23. Rooks JB, Cates W Jr: Emotional impact of D&E versus instillation. *Fam Plann Perspect.* 9:276, 1977.

24. *1979 Membership Directory,* New York, National Abortion Federation, 1979.

25. Burnhill MS: Vaginal second trimester abortion, in Sciarra JJ, Speidel JJ, Zatuchni G (eds): *Risks, Benefits, and Controversies in Fertility Control.* Hagerstown, Md., Harper & Row, 1978, p 331.

26. DeLee ST: Termination of pregnancy in the midtrimester using a new technique: preliminary report. *Int Surg.* 61:545, 1976.

27. Glick E, Sacks M: Public health aspects of dilatation and evacuation. Presented at the 106th annual meeting of the American Public Health Association, Los Angeles, October 14, 1978.

28. Goodman MP: Vacuum dilatation and evacuation for midtrimester abortion. *J Reprod Med.* (in press).

29. Hodari AA, Peralta J, Quiroga PJ, et al: Dilatation and curettage for second-trimester abortions. *Am J Obstet Gynecol.* 127:850, 1977.

30. Koplik L: Early midtrimester abortion by curettage. Presented at the 13th annual meeting, Association of Planned Parenthood Physicians, Los Angeles, April 7, 1975.

31. Meadowbrook Women's Clinic: D&E procedures. *Meadowbrook Memo* 3:1, 1978.

32. Berry FN, Peterson WF: D&E plus suction in midtrimester abortion. *The Female Patient* 3:86, November 1978.

33. Tietze C, Lewit S: Joint Program for the Study of Abortion: early medical complications of legal abortion. *Stud Fam Plann.* 3:97, 1972.

34. Stewart GK, Goldstein P: Medical and surgical complications of therapeutic abortions. *Obstet Gynecol.* 40:539, 1972.

35. Goldsmith S, Kaltreider NB, Margolis AJ: Second trimester abortion by dilatation and evacuation (D&E); surgical techniques and psychological reactions. Presented at the 15th annual meeting, Association of Planned Parenthood Physicians, Atlanta, October 13, 1977.

11 Laminaria and Other Adjunctive Methods

Phillip G. Stubblefield

Pieces of seaweed stems of the laminaria species often were used by nineteenth century practitioners to produce gradual dilatation of the uterine cervix, and were described in obstetric writings of the times. Early in the twentieth century, this practice ceased in England, Europe, and the United States because of associated sepsis and because abortion had become illegal in many countries. Subsequent legalization of abortion in the United States resulted in the reintroduction of laminaria by physicians who had seen them used in Asia. In 1970, the Danish obstetricians Olsen, Nielsen and Ostergaard reported a series of 2159 patients treated with laminaria prior to curettage abortion.[1] In 1971, Manabe of the University of Kyoto, Japan, described the use of laminaria with first- and second-trimester abortions as well as the technique of their insertion and common problems associated with their use.[2] In the same year, Newton described 500 cases of first-trimester abortion with laminaria dilatation.[3] Shortly thereafter, Eaton et al. reported a series of 250 patients similarly treated[4] and, in 1972, Hale and Pion published a report from the

Kapiolani Hospital in Honolulu, Hawaii, which remains to this day a definitive statement on the use of laminaria in obstetric practice.[5]

In subsequent years, laminaria have been used more widely in first-trimester abortion, as an adjunct to abortion by curettage in the second trimester, and to augment the efficacy of intraamniotic prostaglandin, combinations of urea and prostaglandin, and prostaglandin analogues administered by various routes. Most recently, laminaria once again have been used for cervical dilatation before the induction of labor at term. In spite of the recent resurgence of interest in the use of laminaria, controversy still exists as to whether the advantages of their use are outweighed by various possible complications.

This chapter will describe laminaria and their use, as well as briefly discuss recent efforts to develop alternative means of nontraumatic cervical dilatation in conjunction with second-trimester abortion.

LAMINARIA CHARACTERISTICS

Description

Laminaria tents of 5.5 to 6.0 cm length are sold in the United States in packages containing one presterilized laminaria. Two species are available: *Laminaria japonica,* laminaria from Japan, and *Laminaria digitata,* laminaria from Scandinavia (Table 11-1). *Laminaria japonica* are smaller and are composed of finer fibers than the *Laminaria digitata.* Both types have a hole at one end through which a

Table 11-1
Suppliers of Laminaria Tents in the United States

Laminaria digitata Tents	
Berkeley Bio-Engineering	Rocket of London, Inc.
600 McCormick Street	P.O. Box 407
San Leandro, CA 94577	Branford, CT 06405

Laminaria japonica Tents*	
British Marketing Enterprise, Ltd.	Medical Aids
589 First Street, West	6308 Knoll Drive
Sonoma, CA 95476	Minneapolis, MN 55436
Medi-Spec	Milex Products, Inc.
3483 Golden Gate Way	5915 Northwest
P.O. Box 53	Chicago, IL 60631
Lafayette, CA 94549	

*Mizutani Brand.

string is placed for removal after use. Japanese laminaria are tapered and retain this shape when wet. The Scandinavian products, on the other hand, are of uniform diameter when dry, and when wet they swell more at each end than in the middle. Both types soften as they swell, and frequently demonstrate a marked indentation approximately 1 cm from the end that was situated inside the cervical canal, thereby indicating a degree of constriction at the region of the internal cervical os. Occasionally, swelling of the laminaria above the internal os results in entrapment. This is said to occur more frequently with Scandinavian laminaria, which also are said to fragment more easily with attempts at removal than is the case with the Japanese product. For these reasons, authorities in the United States who have commented on both types of laminaria advise the use of *Laminaria japonica*.[6,7]

Small-sized tents swell proportionally more than do larger sizes of the same type. Whether one or the other type of laminaria swells more rapidly or produces more dilatation in vivo is not known.

Sterilization of Tents

Laminaria can be sterilized either by ethylene oxide gas, as reported by Newton,[3] or by gamma irradiation, as is practiced commercially. Sterilization by soaking in 99% ethanol is not satisfactory. Newton reported culturing *E. coli* from the interstices of laminaria so treated.[3]

Technique of Insertion

After bimanual examination to determine the size and position of the uterus, the cervix is exposed with a vaginal speculum and wiped with an antiseptic, such as povidone-iodine. A gentle probing of the cervical canal with a cotton applicator stick dipped in antiseptic, and an application of an antiseptic ointment to the laminaria are preferred. If only one small or medium laminaria is to be used, as in the case of first-trimester abortion, then the laminaria can be inserted gently without the aid of a tenaculum. If more than one laminaria is needed, however, then countertraction with a tenaculum is essential in order to straighten the cervicouterine axis, facilitate insertion, and, most importantly, avoid perforation with the laminaria. In most cases, if the laminaria are inserted so that only 2 to 3 mm of the distal stringed end protrudes from the external os, the proximal end will be situated properly just above the internal os. Two 10 × 10 cm gauze sponges dipped in antiseptic solution and placed over the cervix and into the vaginal fornices, prevent explusion of the laminaria.

Pressure is maintained against the sponges with a forcep while the speculum is removed.

The patient should be kept recumbent for several minutes after insertion to avoid vasovagal syncope. Insertion of one laminaria generally produces minimal, if any, pain. Insertion of three or four tents consistently produces pain which resolves in a few minutes, however, but which frequently becomes bothersome once again several hours later as the laminaria swell. Oral analgesic agents are prescribed routinely when multiple laminaria are inserted.

Removal of Laminaria

The gauze sponges and laminaria can be removed blindly with the fingers, but the preferred method is to remove the sponges, then visualize the cervix with a speculum, and remove the laminaria by gentle traction on the strings with forceps. A forceful pull should be avoided, as this can break the string, and forceful traction on the end of the laminaria with forceps may cause them to crumble. Attempts to slide a small metal dilator alongside the entrapped laminaria may result in perforation. Some physicians have advocated trachelorrhaphy for removal of trapped laminaria,[6] while others have resorted to hysterotomy. The wisest course is prolonged, gentle traction on the string for several minutes. If this fails, the patient should be asked to wait an additional 4 to 6 hours. By this time, additional dilatation and softening of the cervix usually permits removal.

LAMINARIA AND CERVICAL DILATATION

Mechanism of Dilatation

When exposed to water, laminaria slowly swell to a size two to four times their dry diameter. It generally has been assumed that dilatation is accomplished because of gentle prolonged pressure upon the cervix. Two inert devices have been reported to produce cervical dilatation comparable to that achieved by laminaria tents: the Anker dilator, a hairpin-shaped loop of spring steel,[8] and the rubber balloon dilator developed by Gutnick.[9]

Our own observations cast some light upon the mechanism of dilatation by laminaria. We measured the diameter of the laminaria when wet and at the time of removal from the cervical canal of women in the early second trimester of pregnancy. At the same time we calibrated the internal diameter of the cervical canal by noting the largest metal dilator that could be inserted past the internal os without resistance.[10] When a single laminaria was used, the cervical canal was always larger than the laminaria. The difference between cervical canal diameter and laminaria diameter (dilatation difference) was greatest for the smallest laminaria (Table 11-2). This finding suggests that the laminaria must trigger an active process within the cervix causing it to dilate away from the laminaria.

Table 11-2
Wet Diameter of *Laminaria japonica* Tents, Cervical Calibration, and Difference Between the Two Diameters in Patients Treated Overnight

Diameter (mm)	Calibration		Dilatation Difference
	Pratt Units	*mm*	
5	31	9.9	4.9
7	33	10.5	3.5
7	33	10.5	3.5
7	35	11.1	4.1
7	35	11.1	4.1
7	39	12.4	5.4
8	31	9.9	1.9
8	33	10.5	2.5
8	35	11.1	3.1
8	37	11.8	3.8
8	41	13.1	5.1
8.5	35	11.1	2.6
8.5	41	13.1	4.6
9	35	11.1	2.1
9	37	11.8	2.8
9	37	11.8	2.8
10	39	12.4	2.4

Mean dilatation difference: 3.24 ± 1.1 mm (SD).
Mean gestational age of patients: 13.1 ± 2.6 weeks.
Source: Stubblefield and Bentov.[10] By permission. From Zatuchni GI, Sciarra JJ, Speidel JJ (eds): *Pregnancy Termination: Procedures, Safety and New Developments.* Hagerstown, Md, Harper & Row Publishers, 1979. © Northwestern University, Chicago, Illinois, USA.

Measurements during forcible dilatation in vitro by Liu et al.,[11] in vivo by Hulka et al.[12] and more recently by Atienza et al.[13] suggest that when dilatation is carried out by insertion of metal rods which provide force only for a few seconds at a time, increased force is needed at 9 to 10 mm, with a decrease in force being required thereafter. This suggests a disruption or tearing of cervical fibers. In our studies with an expanding metal dilator,[14] we found that a progressive increase in force was required as dilatation proceeded. No sudden giving way or decrease in force was required that would suggest tearing when dilatation was accomplished with application of force over 5 to 10 minutes. The still more prolonged process of dilatation accomplished by laminaria with very weak forces remains to be studied. This process appears in many ways to mimic the gross changes that occur late in normal pregnancy, in that softening of the cervix accompanies dilatation. Atienza et al. clearly demonstrated this with a force-monitoring device.[13] Women treated with a single laminaria tent for just three hours required less force for subsequent forcible dilatation than did women not treated with laminaria.

Several authors have reported the results of cervical calibration with metal dilators after treatment with laminaria tents.[1,2,5,13,15,16]

Eaton treated 250 women 4 to 14 weeks pregnant with a single small- or medium-sized *Laminaria digitata* tent left in situ overnight.[4] In 8% of patients, the tent was expelled and no dilatation was accomplished; 1.2% of patients had such severe pain that the tent had to be removed within three hours of insertion. Of the remaining patients, dilatation of 8 to 9 mm was achieved in 5%, 10 to 11 mm in 68%, and 12 mm in 27%.[4]

Newton treated 500 patients from 2 to 18 weeks pregnant with a single, small-sized *Laminaria digitata* tent, left in place overnight in most cases. In all but two instances, sufficient dilatation was accomplished for insertion of a 9- to 12-mm vacuum cannula.[3]

In Hale and Pion's series of first-trimester abortion patients, a single medium laminaria tent of unspecified type produced sufficient dilatation to allow insertion of a 13-mm dilator in 25% of cases where the laminaria was in place for 4 to 5 hours, while the same size dilator could be inserted without resistance in 90% of cases where the laminaria was left in place for more than 16 hours.[5]

Niswander related gestational age to dilatation by overnight placement of medium-sized tents of either type in 327 patients.[15] A cervical calibration of 11 mm or more was achieved in 20% of patients pregnant 10 or fewer weeks, and 44% of those at 13 or more weeks; it was at least 9 mm in 70% of the cases.

In the 1000 cases reported by Golditch and Glasser,[16] a medium-sized tent of either type was reported to produce a 12 mm calibration after overnight placement in 36.8% of cases. Eleven millimeters was achieved in 28.4%, 10 mm in 18.4%, 9 mm in 8.9%, 8 mm in 4.8%, and less than 8 mm in only 2.7%.

The author and his colleagues have calibrated the cervical canal at the time of removal of different sizes and numbers of *Laminaria japonica* tents in patients thought to be 13 to 16½ weeks pregnant at preoperative examination.[9,10] In general, increasing the number of tents increases the dilatation, although the increment of dilatation for each additional laminaria decreases progressively (Table 11-3). Within the two sizes tested, the larger laminaria produced more dilatation than the smaller ones. Gestational age affected the amount of dilatation in patients who had two medium tents placed overnight only in that patients less than 12 weeks pregnant by postoperative assessment of the aspirated tissue had less dilatation than those with more advanced pregnancies (Table 11-4). In our series with two medium *Laminaria japonica* tents, previous pregnancy experience did not affect dilatation in any consistent way (Table 11-5).

The author's present routine for patients presumed to be 13 to 16½ weeks' pregnant is overnight placement of three to four medium Japanese laminaria tents. In almost all cases, a 16 mm vacuum curette can be inserted without additional dilatation unless there is an error in the estimation of gestational age.

Laminaria must not be left in place longer than 24 hours because of risk of infection.[17] To achieve wider dilatation necessary for late second-trimester abortion, the original laminaria can be replaced with a larger number of fresh, dry laminaria until 2 cm or more of dilatation is achieved,[18,19] Bierer and Steiner have reported using forcible dilatation to 15 to 16 mm, insertion of laminaria for

Table 11-3
Cervical Dilatation Achieved by Different Sizes* and Numbers of *Laminaria japonica* Tents

Sizes, Numbers, and Time in Situ	N	Dilatation ± SD (mm)
2-5 small and medium laminaria for 3-5 hours	5	11.1 ± 1.9
Laminaria for 16-22 hours		
1 small	5	11.0 ± 1.0
2 small	3	10.6 ± 1.0
3 small	18	14.5 ± 0.9
4 small	12	15.3 ± 2.5
1 medium	18	12.1 ± 1.1
2 medium	55	14.1 ± 1.6
3 medium	23	15.5 ± 1.0

Effect of Numbers	T	P	Effect of Size	T	P
1 or 2 vs 3 small	10.3	< 0.001	1 small vs 1 medium	2.1	= 0.02
3 small vs 4 small	1.3	0.11	2 small vs 2 medium	3.7	< 0.001
1 medium vs 2 medium	4.9	< 0.001	3 small vs 3 medium	3.3	< 0.001
2 medium vs 3 medium	3.9	< 0.001			

*Dry sizes: small 1-3 mm; medium 3-5 mm.
Source: Stubblefield and Bentov.[10] By permission. From Zatuchni GI, Sciarra JJ and Speidel JJ (eds): *Pregnancy Termination: Procedures, Safety and New Developments.* Hagerstown, Md, Harper & Row Publishers, 1979. © Northwestern University, Chicago.

24 hours, and subsequent forcible dilatation to 30 to 40 mm, all apparently without cervical injury.[20] Unfortunately, detailed data as to the relationship between uterine size, number of laminaria, and time required have not been reported.

Table 11-4
Effect of Gestational Age* on Cervical Dilatation Achieved by Two Medium (3-5 mm, dry) *Laminara japonica*

Gestational Age*	N	Dilatation ± SD (mm)
Fewer than 12 weeks	6	12.3 ± 2.9
12 and 13 weeks	12	14.0 ± 1.5
14 weeks	11	14.5 ± 1.2
15 weeks	11	14.5 ± 1.2
16 and 17 weeks	15	15.7 ± 1.3

One-way analysis of variance, $F = 2.8$, $P = 0.36$
Fewer than 12 weeks compared to 12 and 13 weeks, $T = 1.69$, $P = 0.055$
*As determined by fetal foot measurement after abortion
Source: Stubblefield and Bentov.[10] By permission. From Zatuchni GI, Sciarra JJ and Speidel JJ (eds): *Pregnancy Termination: Procedures, Safety and New Developments*. Hagerstown, Md, Harper & Row Publishers, 1979. © Northwestern University, Chicago.

Table 11-5
Effect of Parity on Cervical Dilatation Achieved by Two Medium (3 to 5 mm, dry) *Laminaria japonica*

Parity	N	Dilatation ± SD (mm)
Para 0, gravida 1	26	14.2 ± 1.4
Para 0, gravida 2	6	14.8 ± 1.1
Para 1, gravida 2	12	14.2 ± 1.6
Para 1, gravida 3, abortus 1	11	13.6 ± 2.4

One-way analysis of variance, $F = 0.72$, $P = 0.545$
Source: Stubblefield and Bentov.[10] By permission. From Zatuchni GI, Sciarra JJ and Speidel JJ (eds): *Pregnancy Termination: Procedures, Safety and New Developments*. Hagerstown, Md, Harper & Row Publishers, 1979. © Northwestern University, Chicago.

Laminaria and the Complications of Vacuum Curettage Abortion

Gentle dilatation with laminaria tents instead of forcible dilatation might be expected to reduce the risk for cervical trauma and for uterine perforation. On the other hand, the use of laminaria also might be expected to add to the risk of infectious complications of abortion. Other factors, such as operator skill, the type of rigid dilator used, parity of the patient, and whether or not the uterus is emptied completely, may profoundly affect any assessment of the apparent benefit or risk associated with laminaria use. The early comparative studies by Olsen et al.[1] and by Hale and Pion[5] reported fewer perforations and less cervical trauma when laminaria were used, compared with full-sized Hegar dilators. Several authors have reported large series of laminaria-treated cases which support these findings.[3,4,15-17] The series of 1000 patients reported by Golditch and Glasser[16] and the 1368 patients reported by Hern[17] without a single perforation are especially impressive. On the other hand, not all present-day practitioners use full-sized Hegar dilators. When Pratt tapered dilators were used, Wulff and Freiman[21] had a rate of only 0.158% documented perforations and 0.048% suspected perforations of 16,410 first-trimester abortions. Even more impressive is Bozorgi's reported series of 12,219 cases with use of half-sized Hegar dilators and only two perforations (0.02%).[22] The authors cited above described their rates of infection as being low. By today's standard, however, they are not. For example, Golditch and Glasser's 1974 report of endometritis in 2.4% of 1000 patients treated with laminaria[16] does not compare favorably to the 0.097% rate for all infectious complications reported by Wulff and Freiman in 1976 for 16,410 patients who had dilatation with metal dilators.[21]

Table 11-6
Rates and Relative Risks of Aggregated Major and Selected Minor Complications Associated with Laminaria and Rigid Dilators for Suction Curettage at 12 Weeks' Gestation

Complication	Rate* Rigid Dilators	Laminaria	RR†	95% CL§
Aggregated major complications‡	0.41	0.28	1.5	0.8–2.9
Selected minor complications:				
Febrile (> 1 day)	0.89	0.52	1.7	1.1–2.8
Uterine perforation	0.30	0.09	3.2	1.1–9.6
Uterine hemorrhage	0.34	0.22	1.6	0.7–3.4
Cervical injury	1.48	1.81	0.8	0.6–1.1
Retained products of conception	0.63	0.77	0.8	0.5–1.2

*Complications per 100 abortions.
†Relative Risk = Risk of rigid dilators compared to laminaria.
‡As defined in Grimes DA et al: Methods of midtrimester abortion: which is safest? *Int J Gynaecol Obstet.* 15:184, 1977.
§Confidence limit.
Source: Gold J, Schulz KF, Cates W Jr et al.[23] By permission.

Ideally, the controversy regarding the benefit of laminaria use before first-trimester curettage should be resolved in a randomized, controlled clinical trial. Unfortunately, with the low rates of complications now expected in either group, several thousand cases would be necessary. An alternative approach has been followed by the Joint Program for the Study of Abortion at the Center for Disease Control. A series of 29,760 first-trimester abortions performed in several participating hospitals has been studied with reference to type of dilatation and associated complications.[23] The data, summarized in Table 11-6, demonstrate a statistically significant reduction in rates of uterine perforation, but a slight increase in the rate of cervical injury when laminaria were used. The latter may have resulted from a selection bias that resulted in younger patients, with cervices thought to be more difficult to dilate, having been chosen to receive laminaria. Febrile morbidity was *less* common with laminaria than when rigid dilators were used. Choice of laminaria or rigid dilatation appeared less important as a determinant of complication rates than other factors such as the operator's experience and type of anesthesia.

In the author's experience, cervical perforation, although rare, is the most common site of uterine injury during first-trimester abortion.[24] This is especially true if forcible dilatation is required. The injury can result in fatal hemorrhage. Laminaria dilatation would be expected to reduce the risk of such injury.

Laminaria with Second-Trimester Curettage

Several different techniques for uterine curettage in the second trimester have been described. These include forcible dilatation followed by morcellation and extraction of the fetus with forceps,[25,26] overnight treatment with multiple laminaria followed by forceps extraction and vacuum curettage,[7,27] vacuum extraction with a large bore cannula after laminaria treatment,[28] and the use of successive sets of laminaria prior to curettage.[17,19,20] No reports compare patients treated with forcible dilatation to those treated with laminaria before second-trimester curettage. Reported rates of complications have been low with all of the methods noted above. The lowest reported rate of complications of late second-trimester curettage abortions for a large number of patients is that of Hanson, who describes only five major complications among 3123 procedures performed after laminaria dilatation.[29]

At 13 to 14 weeks from last menses, fetal parts can be evacuated with a 12 mm vacuum cannula,[28] and 12 mm dilatation usually is easily accomplished mechanically. Beyond 14 weeks, however, extraction of the fetus is more difficult, and the procedure is prolonged unless greater cervical dilatation is provided. Johnstone et al.[30] reported that the cervical canal remained abnormally large when calibrated at six weeks after abortion in women who had forcible dilatation beyond 10 mm. Richardson and Dixon[31] and, more recently, Petersen[26] have reported second-trimester spontaneous abortion in subsequent pregnancy that might have been attributed to previous induced abortion with forcible dilatation. It is reasonable to assume that the gentle dilatation by laminaria achieved over a prolonged time would be less likely to result in cervical injury than would forcible dilatation to large diameters, but this assumption has not yet been adequately studied. Apparently, the only report of pregnancies subsequent to laminaria use for second-trimester abortion is that of Hanson, who described eight patients who had term pregnancies.[29]

Although there are no comparative data that clearly demonstrate the advantages of laminaria over forcible dilatation in the second trimester, the benefits of laminaria in clinical practice seem obvious. With the wide cervical dilatation achieved by multiple laminaria placed overnight, the surgeon can introduce instruments into the uterine cavity without force. This greatly facilitates the extraction of the larger second-trimester fetus.

LAMINARIA TO AUGMENT MEDICAL MEANS OF SECOND-TRIMESTER ABORTION

Laminaria and Uterine Contractility

Insertion of laminaria or similar foreign bodies into the cervical canal eventually results in some degree of uterine contractile activity. Such methods apparently have been used in diverse cultures for the purpose of provoking abortion since ancient times.

A standard method of second-trimester abortion in Japan is cervical dilatation with multiple laminaria followed by the insertion of a large balloon (metreurynter) directly into the uterine cavity. The device then is filled with fluid and attached by its vaginal extension to a weight hung over a pulley at the end of the patient's bed. Generally, intravenous oxytocin is used as well, and fetal expulsion is said to occur within 24 hours. To demonstrate the efficacy of mechanical stimulation in producing uterine contraction, Manabe et al. recorded intrauterine pressure in a series of seven cases where oxytocin was not used.[32] Measurable uterine contractions were noted within six hours of laminaria insertion; within 24 hours regular contractions of 30 to 40 mm Hg were recorded at three-minute intervals. The metreurynter was then inserted, and the patients went on to abort between 7 and 28 hours later.

In this country Robbins et al. treated 15 patients with a single medium-sized *Laminaria digitata* followed immediately by intravenous oxytocin at 100 IU per 12 hours.[33] Only four patients aborted within 48 hours, two aborted at 9 and 11 days, and the others were aborted by saline infusion or curettage. Clearly, a single laminaria tent combined with oxytocin provides a slow and ineffective method for abortion, while the more intense stimulation of the uterus as supplied by multiple laminaria and metreurynter is effective.

Laminaria to Augment Abortion by Hypertonic Saline

Hale and Pion's report included a discussion of laminaria used to augment intraamniotic saline. The mean saline instillation-to-abortion time was reduced from 28.5 hours in the control group to 22 hours in cases where laminaria were inserted after saline infusion, and to 20.7 hours when laminaria were inserted prior to saline instillation.[5] These findings were confirmed by Lischke and Goodlin in two papers in 1972 and 1973.[34,35] They routinely began high-dose oxytocin six hours after saline instillation and reported a still further reduction in the mean interval from instillation to abortion.

In contrast, Hanson et al. found that primigravid patients treated with laminaria and intravenous oxytocin did not abort significantly faster than a similar group of primigravid women aborted with saline and oxytocin without laminaria.[36] Moreover, their laminaria-treated patients had a significantly higher incidence of fever (22%) than did their other patients. Horowitz and Barr in 1974,[37] Robbins in 1978[38] and, most recently, Hachamovitch et al.[39] have reported large series of patients aborted with laminaria and high-dose intravenous oxytocin in conjunction with hypertonic saline in which there were excellent results and few complications. The incidence of complications with saline abortion is influenced by the precise details of the instillation procedure, the use of pyrogen-free saline, the timeliness and dosage of oxytocin used for augmentation and, unquestionably, physician skill in management of the procedure and its sequelae. A large study with randomization of patients would be required to resolve the issue as to whether the benefit of laminaria outweighs any increased risk from infection. This issue has not been resolved, probably because much of the scientific interest in abortion has shifted from saline to prostaglandins.

Laminaria to Augment Intraamniotic Prostaglandin $F_2\alpha$ ($PGF_2\alpha$)

Engel et al.[40] and Brenner et al.[41] in 1973 were the first to demonstrate that treatment with laminaria could reduce the interval from injection of $PGF_2\alpha$ to abortion. The following year, our group,[42] Berman et al.[43] and Golbus[44] confirmed these findings. Subsequently, more extensive series utilizing laminaria tents have been published by our group in 1975,[45] Golbus et al.,[46] Robbins et al.,[33] Duenhoelter et al.[47] in 1976, Horowitz,[48] and Robbins[38] in 1978. The only authors who did not report a benefit of laminaria treatment with intraamniotic $PGF_2\alpha$ were Corson and Bolognese.[49]

In the author's experience, laminaria placed in the cervix the day before $PGF_2\alpha$ infusion were more efficacious than if placed immediately before the procedure.[45] This is demonstrable by changes in the mean times from injection of $PGF_2\alpha$ to abortion but is shown most convincingly by a shift of the cumulative percentage of patients' abortion vs time curves (Figure 11-1). Prior pregnancy appears to affect the time from injection to abortion in patients treated with $PGF_2\alpha$;

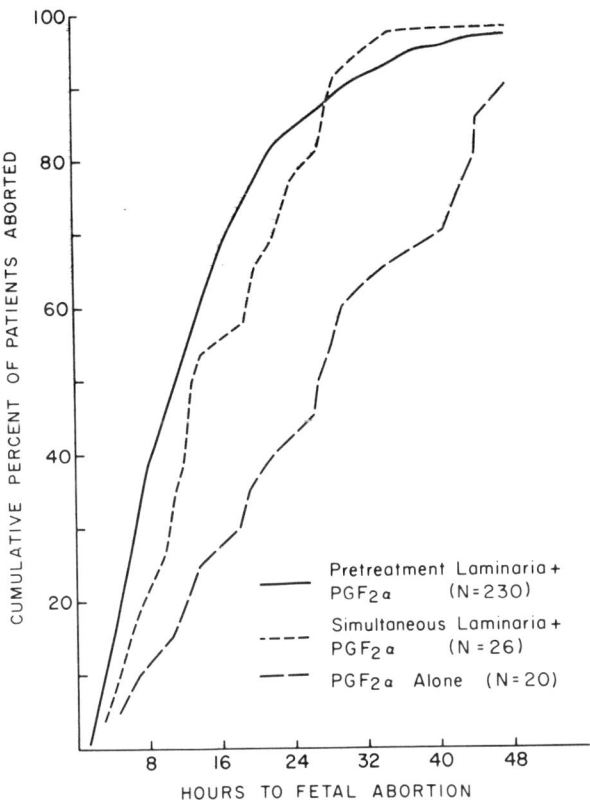

Figure 11-1 Cumulative percentage of patients aborted vs time to fetal abortion: $PGF_2\alpha$ alone, pretreatment with overnight placement of laminaria tents, and simultaneous placement of laminaria tents. Source: Stubblefield PG et al.[45] By permission.

primigravidas need a longer time to abort than multigravidas. This same observation has been made in some series where laminaria were used at the same time as the $PGF_2\alpha$. In the author's experience, however, when laminaria are inserted 14 to 18 hours before the $PGF_2\alpha$ is given, any difference between primigravid and parous women is abolished, at least insofar as it is reflected in the cumulative percentage of patients aborted over time (Figure 11-2).

The author also has studied the effect of numbers of small or medium *Laminaria digitata* tents upon the cumulative percentage of patients aborted over time and upon mean time to abortion of patients treated with $PGF_2\alpha$ after overnight placement of the tents. It was possible to demonstrate a shortened time to abortion when more tents could be inserted.

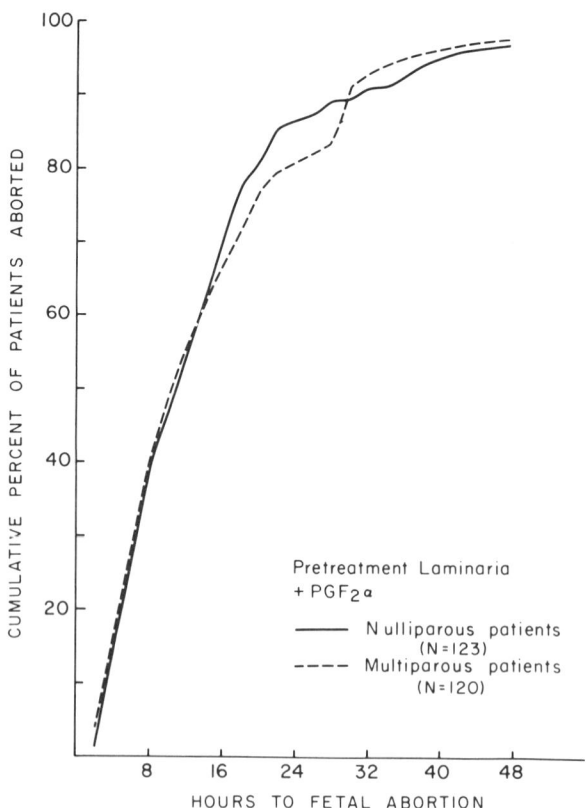

Figure 11-2 Effect of parity on cumulative percentage of patients aborted vs time with laminaria pretreatment before $PGF_2\alpha$: nulliparous vs parous patients. Source: Stubblefield PG et al.[45] By permission.

Laminaria and Complications of $PGF_2\alpha$ Abortion

An unexpected major hazard of intraamniotic $PGF_2\alpha$ has been cervical rupture with expulsion of the fetus and placenta through a cervicovaginal fistula.[50] This injury, which is quite rare for abortion induced by hypertonic saline alone, also has been described when saline was augmented with high doses of oxytocin. Young, primigravid women, especially those who require increasing doses of $PGF_2\alpha$, appear prone to the problem.[51] It has not been reported with PGE_2 unless $PGF_2\alpha$ was used as well. The risk of cervicovaginal fistula is reduced but not abolished by laminaria treatment. Lischke and Gordon reported a case of cervicovaginal fistula when two laminaria were inserted just prior to abortion by saline and high-dose oxytocin.[52] Duenhoelter and Gant[53] noted three cervicovaginal fistulae and one lateral cervical tear in their initial series of 122 patients treated with intraamniotic $PGF_2\alpha$ and none in the subsequent series where laminaria were used.[47] At Boston Hospital for Women, cervicovaginal fistula is seen approximately once in each 1000 cases when laminaria are inserted the day before $PGF_2\alpha$ infusion.

Uterine rupture apparently is not prevented by laminaria pretreatment. At Boston Hospital for Women there have been two such cases; both were multiparas who received high-dose oxytocin stimulation after failure of $PGF_2\alpha$ to produce abortion.[54]

Febrile morbidity and serious pelvic infection have not been reported more frequently in laminaria series than in those where laminaria were not used. Other details of management are probably more important in determining the incidence of infection, and these vary from series to series. Patients with prolonged abortion times and those who abort incompletely are at greatest risk. The author's regimen has been modified to include early use of oxytocin or, more recently, parenteral or vaginal prostaglandin when the membranes rupture after intraamniotic instillation of $PGF_2\alpha$ and uterine activity is lost. In all cases, the retained placenta is promptly removed, and the uterus is routinely explored. These modifications have resulted in a low rate of infectious complications in our hands. This statement notwithstanding, Green and Brenner have reported a case of serious clostridial sepsis in association with abortion by laminaria and prostaglandin.[55]

Laminaria to Augment Second-Trimester Abortion by Intramuscular Prostaglandin Analogues

In 1974, Bieniarz et al. reported that primigravid women treated overnight with one to four tents of *Laminaria digitata* before abortion by intramuscular 15-methyl prostaglandin E_2 (methyl PGE_2) had a marked reduction in abortion time compared with primigravid women not so treated.[56] In the author's experience with the same prostaglandin analogue, patients who had laminaria placed the night prior to start of the methyl PGE_2 also had significantly reduced mean abortion times, and all laminaria-treated patients aborted by 24 hours (Figure 11-3). The author has constructed a dose-response curve which demonstrates an increased cumulative percentage of patients aborting for a given dose of methyl PGE_2 when laminaria pretreatment was used (Figure 11-4).[57] Gastrointestinal side effects and temperature elevations were less frequent in the laminaria-treated patients, presumably because they required less 15-methyl PGE_2.

Sharma et al. in 1975 inserted laminaria the night before start of therapy with a different intramuscularly administered analogue, 15-(S),15-methyl prostaglandin $F_2\alpha$.[58] They noted a significant

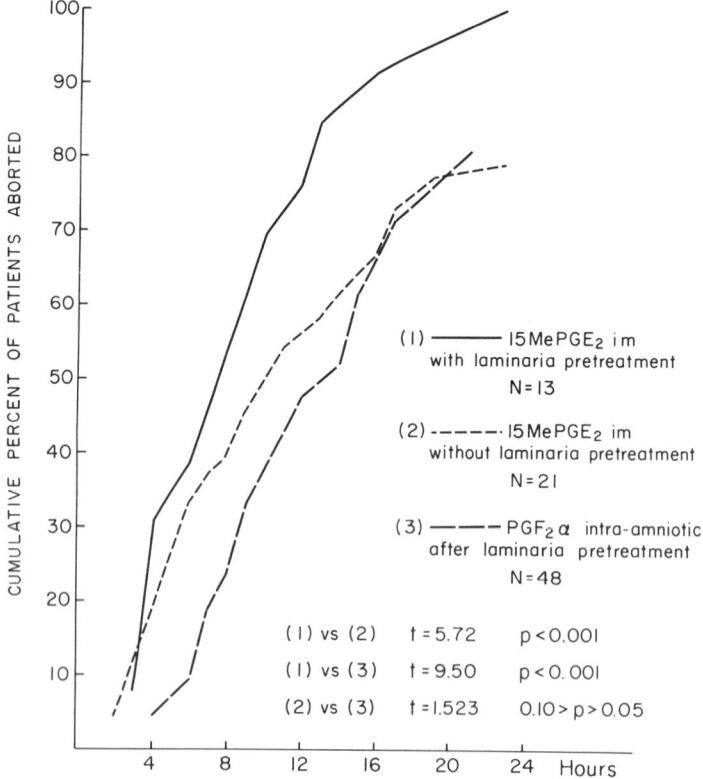

Figure 11-3 Comparison of cumulative percent of patients aborted vs time curves for patients pretreated with laminaria tents before IM 15 Me PGE_2, the same drug without laminaria, and laminaria pretreatment before intraamniotic $PGF_2\alpha$.

reduction in abortion time in the laminaria-treated group. This was confirmed in 1976 by Robbins and Mann who also documented the association of overnight pretreatment with laminaria, a reduction in gastrointestinal side effects, a decreased need for analgesia, and a greater proportion of patients aborting within 24 hours.[59] No increase in febrile morbidity or infection was attributed to laminaria use. In contrast, Gruber and Brenner inserted laminaria tents only 30 minutes before start of methyl $PGF_2\alpha$ therapy. They noted no improvement in efficacy, but endometritis was diagnosed in 20% of the laminaria-treated cases, in contrast to only 5% of the patients not so treated.[60]

With the prostaglandin analogues, as with intraamniotic PGF_2, the benefit of laminaria is much more easily demonstrated when the laminaria are left in the cervix overnight than when they are inserted at the start of prostaglandin treatment.

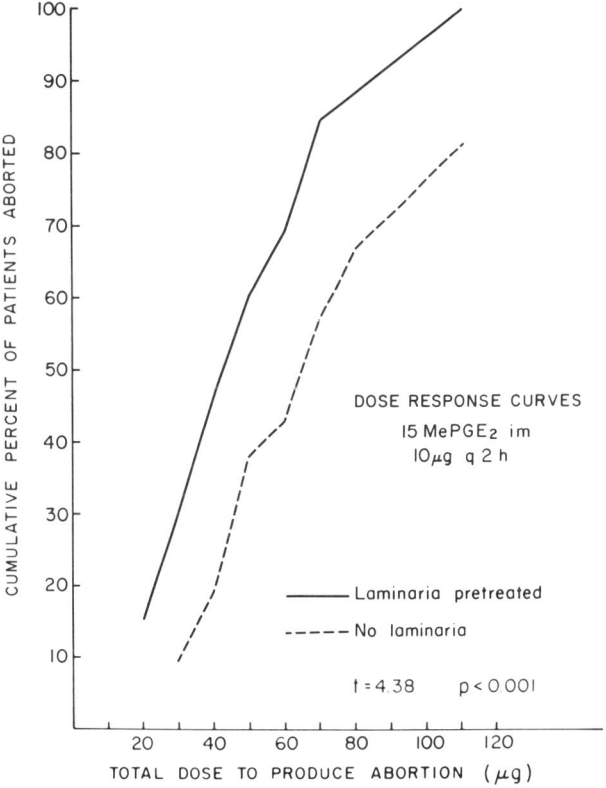

Figure 11-4 Cumulative percentage of patients aborted vs time curves as a function of dose of 15 Me PGE_2 required to produce abortion in patients who did or did not receive laminaria pretreatment. Source: Stubblefield PG et al.[57] By permission.

Laminaria with Urea-oxytocin, Urea-prostaglandin, Calcium-prostaglandin, and Extraamniotic Prostaglandin

Golditch and Solberg compared patients treated with 80 g of intraamniotic urea and intravenous oxytocin to patients treated with the same combination plus laminaria inserted at the time of urea infusion.[61] A significant reduction in the injection-to-abortion interval was accomplished by use of laminaria without any increase in complications.

Wellman and Jacobson studied the effect of placement of two laminaria tents at the time of infusion upon efficacy of 5, 10, or 15 mg doses of $PGF_2\alpha$ in combination with intraamniotic urea, 80 g.[62] No benefit was observed from laminaria use, but neither was infection increased by their use. Wilson used overnight treatment with laminaria for all of his patients when comparing three different urea, prostaglandin, and oxytocin regimens.[63] He reported the shortest mean injection-to-abortion time for second-trimester amnioinfusion yet recorded: 8 hours, 42 minutes for 113 patients treated by laminaria, 20 mg of $PGF_2\alpha$ and 40 g urea with intravenous oxytocin. No cervical trauma was observed in this group.

Laminaria inserted at the time of intraamniotic instillation of a combination of 50 ml hypertonic saline with 40 mg of $PGF_2\alpha$ have been shown to reduce the mean abortion time and to provide a method for second-trimester abortion of great efficacy, as demonstrated in 1033 cases by Pahl and Lundy.[64]

In a pilot study of combinations of intraamniotic calcium and reduced doses of $PGF_2\alpha$, Weinstein et al.[65] reported a short mean abortion time in second-trimester patients who had overnight treatment with laminaria followed by intraamniotic calcium and 20 mg $PGF_2\alpha$. On the other hand, patients who received laminaria overnight followed by 20 mg $PGF_2\alpha$ alone had very prolonged abortion times.

Hodgson and Van Gorp followed overnight treatment with laminaria with placement of a transcervical catheter for administration of extraamniotic $PGF_2\alpha$ in combination with intravenous oxytocin. Excellent abortifacient efficacy resulted, with few side effects or complications.[66]

Laminaria and Induction of Labor

Cross and Pitkin[67] demonstrated in a randomized study that two to five "thick" *Laminaria japonica* inserted the night before planned induction of labor, produced a significant improvement in the Bishop Score, resulted in the onset of spontaneous labor in 6 of 35 patients, and reduced the length of subsequent labor in comparison with the control group. There were no differences in febrile morbidity between laminaria-treated and control groups. Similar findings were reported in a smaller series by Lackritz et al. from our institution.[68] They used 6 to 10 medium-sized *Laminaria japonica* placed overnight.

ALTERNATIVES TO LAMINARIA

Ott recently has traced the development of methods for dilatation of the uterine cervix from the fifth century BC through modern times.[69] Nineteenth century physicians described expanding tents made from sponge, laminaria, tupelo *(Nyssa aquatica)* and slippery elm bark, hydrostatic dilators of rubber, graduated metal or rubber rods, and expanding steel dilators. With the renewed interest in safer means for induced abortion, older devices have been reevaluated and several approaches to cervical dilatation are being studied.

The Anker Dilator

In 1973, Von Friesen[8] reported the clinical evaluation of a metal dilator previously described by Herman Anker in 1958. The Anker dilator is a hairpin-shaped loop of spring steel, held compressed by a retaining clip until it is placed in the cervical canal (Figure 11-5). After

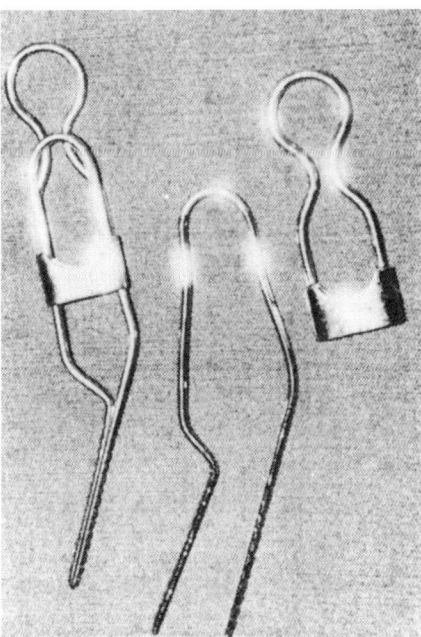

Figure 11-5 Anker dilator in compressed, open, and closed positions.

overnight treatment with the device, 14 mm dilatation was achieved in 85% of a group of 115 parous women, and 72% of a group of 46 nulliparous women. No complications were attributed to the dilator in this series. The Anker dilator should be inexpensive to produce, could be resterilized for reuse indefinitely, and certainly merits further study. As yet, no subsequent reports of its use have been forthcoming.

The Gutnick Device

This inflatable dilator was designed by Dr. Morton Gutnick of Philadelphia. It consists of a modified Foley urinary catheter (Figure 11-6). It has a central lumen with a removable, semirigid stylet for

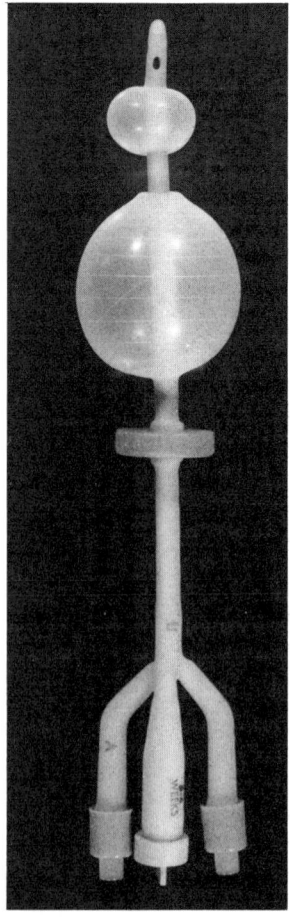

Figure 11-6 The balloon dilator developed by Morton Gutnick. Source: Stubblefield PG, Bentov I.[10] By permission.

insertion, a small anchor balloon close to the tip, a proximal larger dilator balloon, and a hard rubber disc fixed to the shaft to limit inward migration of the device into the uterus. After insertion into the cervical canal, the balloons are inflated with sterile saline and the device left in situ for the desired time, i.e., from a few minutes to overnight or longer. Borten et al. inserted the Gutnick device just after amnioinfusion of hypertonic saline and $PGF_2\alpha$ for second-trimester abortion, and reported a reduced interval from injection to abortion when only the dilator balloon was inflated, but no reduction in time to abortion when the anchor balloon was inflated as well.[70] In a different study by Hanson, the cervical canal was calibrated after placement of the Gutnick device and before curettage abortion in the early second-trimester.[29] Seven patients who had the device in situ for 2 to 5 hours had a mean cervical calibration of 10.4 mm, while 43 patients who had the device in situ overnight had a mean dilatation of 12.3 mm. In this trial, the Gutnick device was comparable to one medium Japanese laminaria in the amount of dilatation achieved. Pain with inflation of the device was a problem when a 60 ml volume was instilled. There was only minimal discomfort when 45 ml was used. The Gutnick device is an effective dilator and, with subsequent modification to reduce its diameter and facilitate insertion, it may offer a useful alternative to laminaria.

The Preterm Device

The author has completed a preliminary trial of a four-bladed expanding dilator designed by the late Itzhak Bentov[14] (Figures 11-7, 11-8). This device allows the operator to control precisely the amount of force exerted upon the cervix and to read the amount of expansion of the dilator as dilation is occurring. In a small series of first-trimester patients, dilatation to a maximum of 11 mm was consistently achieved. The time interval required was 5 to 10 minutes. From a practical point of view, this expanding dilator could be used in a clinical setting without the delay required by laminaria. A larger clinical trial of the device is indicated.

Expanding Polymers

Chemical systems have the potential of providing expansion in association with uniform and controllable rates of swelling. Whether or not any can be found that will provide sufficient force upon the internal os to effect dilatation comparable to laminaria remains to be demonstrated; however, Zeller and Scholz have reported development of laminaria-like tents made of formaldehyde-gelatin, and the preliminary trial of these tents in excised uteri.[71]

Plant Products Other Than Laminaria

Indian physicians recently have reported the manufacture of tents from the seed husk of *Plantago ovata* (Isapgol), a plant grown

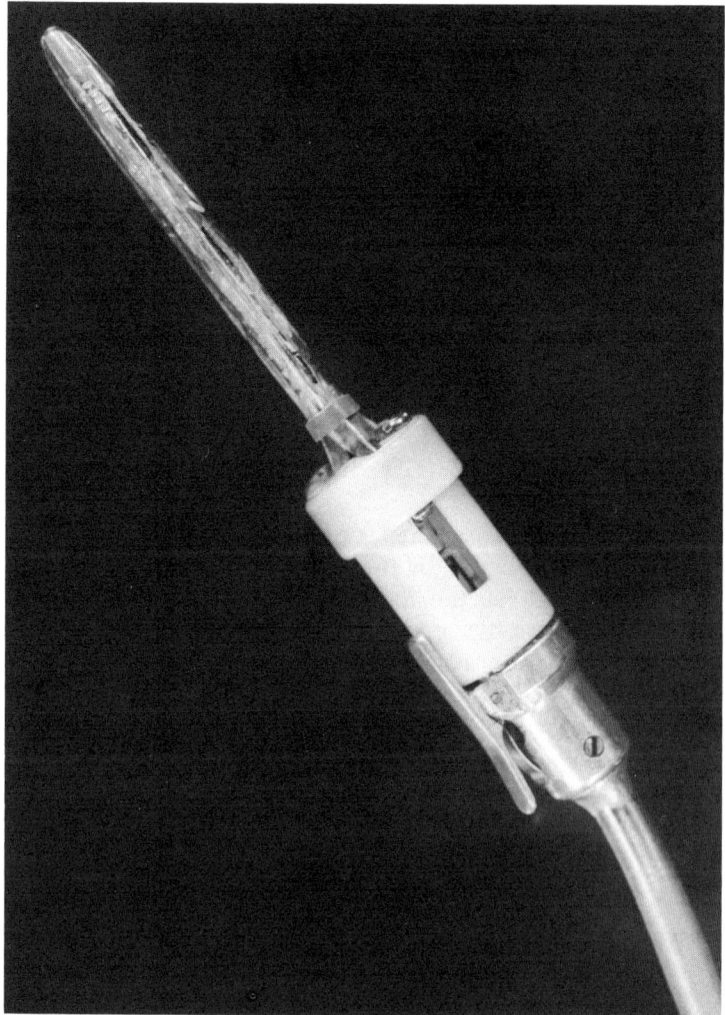

Figure 11-7 The preterm dilator in closed position. The covering sterile latex sheath has been removed for clarity. Source: Stubblefield PG, Bentov I.[10] By permission.

widely in India.[72] In a trial involving 322 first-trimester abortion patients and 111 second-trimester abortion patients, satisfactory dilatation was achieved in 94% of patients with one tent, and in all cases where two or three were used. Tents were left in situ for 8 to 12 hours.

COMMENT

Our forefathers used laminaria tents, tupelo, and sponge tents, but these have been generally abandoned as they were apt to shut up the

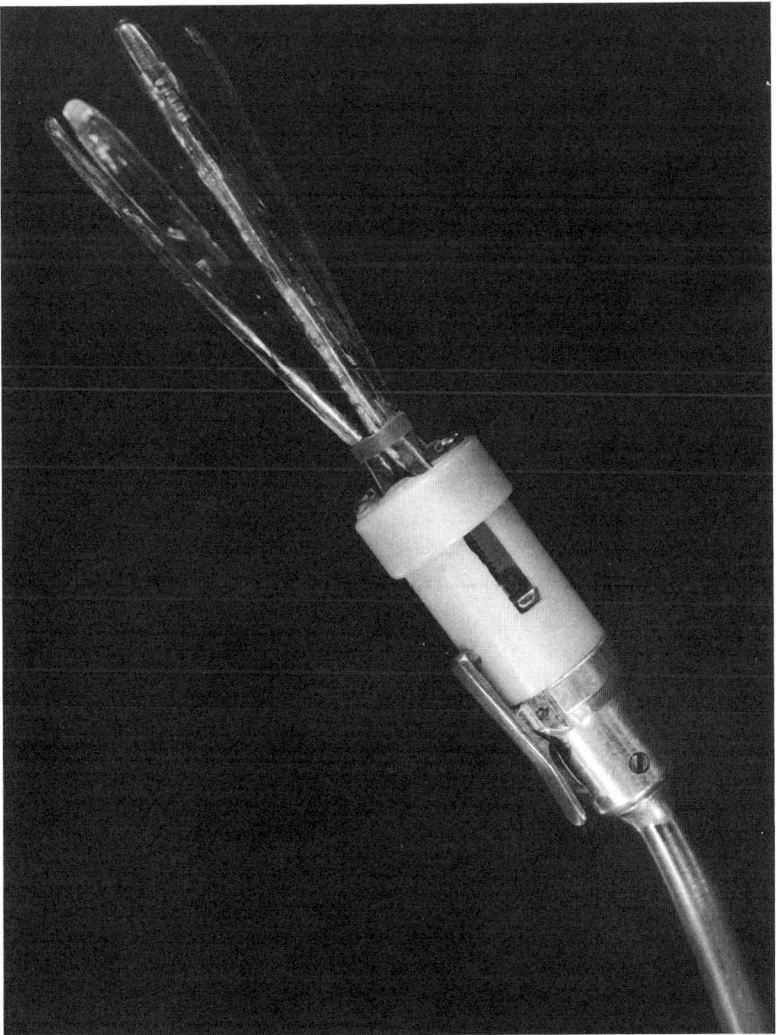

Figure 11-8 The preterm dilator in fully opened position. Source: Stubblefield PG, Bentov I.[10] By permission.

secretions and force infection out into the tissues and, undoubtedly, sometimes actually introduced infection. Sometimes, too, in unskilled hands, a laminaria tent perforated a uterus at the cervical junction or at the fundus. The accessibility of the uterine cavity secured by means of tents was superior to that by our present day methods, especially when larger and larger tents were introduced in succession, and with better precautions we may be driven to revert to them sooner or later.

These words, written by Howard Kelly 50 years ago, were indeed prophetic. With the "better precautions" of reliable sterilization and with the need for legal abortion, we have returned once again to laminaria.

REFERENCES

1. Olsen CE, Nielsen HB, Ostergaard E: Complications in therapeutic abortions. *Int J Gynecol Obstet.* 8:823, 1970.
2. Manabe Y: Laminaria tent for gradual and safe cervical dilatation. *Am J Obstet Gynecol.* 110:743, 1971.
3. Newton BW: Laminaria tent: relic of the past or modern medical device? *Am J Obstet Gynecol.* 113:442, 1972.
4. Eaton CG, Cohn F, Bollinger CC: Laminaria tent as a cervical dilator prior to aspiration-type therapeutic abortion. *Obstet Gynecol.* 39:553, 1972.
5. Hale RW, Pion RJ: Laminaria: An underutilized clinical adjunct. *Clin Obstet Gynecol.* 15:829, 1972.
6. Hanson FW, Niswander KR, Trelford JD: Cervical migration of laminaria tents. *Am J Obstet Gynecol.* 114:385, 1972.
7. Hanson MS: Abortion in teenagers. *Clin Obstet Gynecol.* 21:1175, 1978.
8. Von Friesen B: The Anker dilator in therapeutic abortion. *Acta Obstet Gynecol Scand.* 52:191, 1973.
9. Stubblefield PG, Frederiksen MC, Berek JS, et al: Evaluation of a balloon dilator before second-trimester abortion by vacuum curettage. *Am J Obstet Gynecol.* 135:199, 1979.
10. Stubblefield PG, Bentov I: Alternatives for cervical dilatation, in Zatuchni GI, Sciarra JJ, Speidel JJ (eds): *Pregnancy Termination: Procedures, Safety, and New Developments.* Hagerstown, Md, Harper & Row, 1979. © Northwestern University, Chicago.
11. Liu DTY, Black MM, Melcher DH, et al: Dilatation of the parous nonpregnant cervix. *Br J Obstet Gynecol.* 82:246, 1975.
12. Hulka JR, Lefler HT, Anlone A, et al: A new electronic force monitor to measure factors influencing cervical dilatation for vacuum curettage. *Am J Obstet Gynecol.* 120:166, 1974.
13. Atienza MF, Burkman RT, King TM: Forces associated with cervical dilatation at suction abortion: Qualitative and quantitative data in studies completed with a force-sensing instrument, in Naftolin F, Stubblefield PG (eds): *Dilatation of the Uterine Cervix.* New York, Raven Press, 1979.
14. Bentov I, Stubblefield PG: Measurement of the tangential forces required for dilatation of the human cervix for abortion: studies with a new mechanical dilator, in Naftolin F, Stubblefield PG (eds): *Dilatation of the Uterine Cervix.* New York, Raven Press, 1979.

15. Niswander KR: Laminaria tents as an aid in suction abortion. *Calif Med.* 119:11, 1973.

16. Golditch IM, Glasser MH: The use of laminaria tents for cervical dilatation prior to vacuum aspiration abortion. *Am J Obstet Gynecol.* 119:481, 1974.

17. Hern WM: Laminaria in abortion: Use in 1,368 patients in first trimester. *Rocky Mt Med J.* 72:390, 1975.

18. Hern WM, Oakes AG: Multiple laminaria treatment in early midtrimester outpatient suction abortion: A preliminary report. *Adv Plann Parent.* 12:93, 1977.

19. DeLee ST: Termination of pregnancy in the midtrimester using a new technic. *Int Surg.* 61:545, 1976.

20. Bierer I, Steiner V: Termination of pregnancy in the second trimester with the aid of laminaria tents. *Med Gynecol Sociol.* 6:9, 1971.

21. Wulff GJL, Freiman SM: Elective abortion: Complications seen in a free-standing clinic. *Obstet Gynecol.* 49:351, 1977.

22. Bozorgi N: Statistical analysis of first trimester pregnancy terminations in an ambulatory surgical center. *Am J Obstet Gynecol.* 127:763, 1977.

23. Gold J, Schulz KF, Cates W Jr, et al: The relative safety of laminaria and rigid cervical dilators used before suction curettage abortions performed in the first trimester of pregnancy, in Naftolin F, Stubblefield PG (eds): *Dilatation of the Uterine Cervix.* New York, Raven Press, 1979.

24. Berek SJ, Stubblefield PG: Anatomical and clinical correlations of uterine perforation. *Am J Obstet Gynecol.* 135:181, 1979.

25. Finks AA: Midtrimester abortion. *Lancet* 1:263, 2973.

26. Petersen W: Dilatation and evacuation. Patient evaluation and surgical techniques, in Zatuchni GI, Sciarra JJ, Speidel JJ (eds): *Pregnancy Termination: Procedures, Safety and New Developments.* Hagerstown, Md, Harper & Row, 1979. © Northwestern University, Chicago.

27. Barr MM: Mid-trimester abortion at 12 to 20 weeks by dilatation and evacuation method under local anesthesia. *Adv Plann Parent.* 13:16, 1978.

28. Stubblefield PG, Albrecht BH, Koos B, et al: A randomized study of 12 mm and 15.9 mm cannulas in midtrimester abortion by laminaria and vacuum curettage. *Fertil Steril.* 29:512, 1978.

29. Hanson MS: D&E midtrimester abortion preceded by laminaria. Presented at the 16th Annual Meeting of the Association of Planned Parenthood Physicians, San Diego, October 25–27, 1978.

30. Johnstone FD, Beard RJ, Boyd IE, et al: Cervical diameter after suction termination of pregnancy. *Br Med J.* 1:68, 1976.

31. Richardson JA, Dixon G: Effects of legal termination on subsequent pregnancy. *Br Med J.* 1:1303, 1976.

32. Manabe Y, Nakajima A, Griggs JF: Uterine contractility and placental histology in abortion by laminaria and metreurynter. *Obstet Gynecol.* 41:753, 1973.

33. Robbins J, Nathanson HG, Fox RL, et al: Midtrimester abortion with laminaria, prostaglandin, and oxytocin. *Adv Plann Parent.* 11:12, 1976.

34. Lischke JH, Goodlin RC: Use of laminaria tents with saline abortion. *Lancet* 1:49, 1972.

35. Lischke JH, Goodlin RC: Use of laminaria tents with hypertonic saline amnioinfusion. *Am J Obstet Gynecol.* 116:586, 1973.

36. Hanson FW, Haslett EO, Sacks DA: *Laminaria digitata* in saline abortions. *Obstet Gynecol.* 43:761, 1974.

37. Horowitz AJ, Barr MM: Adjunctive use of laminaria tents with hypertonic saline induced mid-trimester abortion. *Contraception* 9:409, 1974.

38. Robbins J: A clinical comparison of intra-amniotic prostaglandin F_2 alpha and intra-amniotic hypertonic saline for midtrimester pregnancy termination. *Adv Plann Parent.* 13:27, 1978.

39. Hachamovitch M, Bracken MB, Simons H: Saline instillation abortion with laminaria and megadose oxytocin. *Am J Obstet Gynecol.* 135:327, 1979.

40. Engel T, Greer B, Kochenour N, et al: Midtrimester abortion using prostaglandin $F_2\alpha$, oxytocin, and laminaria. *Fertil Steril.* 24:565, 1973.

41. Brenner WE, Hendricks CH, Dingfelder J, et al: Laminaria augmentation of intra-amniotic prostaglandin $F_2\alpha$ for the induction of mid-trimester abortion. *Prostaglandins* 3:879, 1973.

42. Stubblefield PG, Naftolin F, Frigoletto F, et al: Pretreatment with laminaria tents before midtrimester abortion with intra-amniotic prostaglandin $F_2\alpha$. *Am J Obstet Gynecol.* 118:284, 1974.

43. Berman R, Hale RW, Reich LA, et al: Intraamniotic prostaglandin $PGF_2\alpha$ (Tham Salt) and the laminaria tent in midtrimester termination of pregnancy. *Contraception* 9:635, 1974.

44. Golbus MS: Laminaria and intra-amniotic prostaglandin $F_2\alpha$ for induction of midtrimester abortions. *Am J Obstet Gynecol.* 110:569, 1974.

45. Stubblefield PG, Naftolin F, Frigoletto F, et al: Laminaria augmentation of intra-amniotic $PGF_2\alpha$ for midtrimester pregnancy termination. *Prostaglandins* 10:413, 1975.

46. Golbus MS, Morgolis AJ, Sweet RL, et al: Experience with 276 intra-amniotic prostaglandin $F_2\alpha$ induced midtrimester abortions. *Prostaglandins* 11:841, 1976.

47. Duenhoelter JH, Gant NF, Jimenez JM: Concurrent use of prostaglandin F_2 and laminaria tents for induction of midtrimester abortion. *Obstet Gynecol.* 47:469, 1976.

48. Horowitz AJ: Midtrimester abortion utilizing intraamniotic prostaglandin $F_2\alpha$ laminaria and oxytocin. *J Reprod Med.* 21:236, 1978.

49. Corson SL, Bolognese RJ: Intra-amniotic prostaglandin $F_2\alpha$ as a midtrimester abortifacient: Effect of oxytocin and laminara. *J Reprod Med.* 14:47, 1975.

50. Wentz AC, Thompson BH, King TM: Posterior cervical rupture following prostaglandin induced midtrimester abortion. *Am J Obstet Gynecol.* 115:1107, 1973.

51. Kajanoja P, Junger G, Seppala M, et al: Prostaglandin induction of 424 midtrimester abortions. *Int J Gynecol Obstet.* 12:198, 1974.

52. Lischke JH, Gordon HR: Cervicovaginal fistula complicating induced midtrimester abortion despite laminaria tent insertion. *Am J Obstet Gynecol.* 120:852, 1974.

53. Duenhoelter JH, Gant NR: Complications following prostaglandin $F_2\alpha$ induced midtrimester abortion. *Obstet Gynecol.* 46:247, 1975.

54. Propping D, Stubblefield PG, Golub J, et al: Uterine rupture following midtrimester abortion by laminaria, prostaglandin $F_2\alpha$ and oxytocin: Report of two cases. *Am J Obstet Gynecol.* 128:689, 1977.

55. Green SL, Brenner WE: Clostridial sepsis after abortion with $PGF_2\alpha$ and intracervical laminaria tents—a case report. *Int J Gynecol Obstet.* 15:322, 1978.

56. Bieniarz J, Hunter G, Scommegna A: Efficacy and acceptability of 15(S)-15-methyl prostaglandin E_2 methyl ester for midtrimester pregnancy termination. *Am J Obstet Gynecol.* 120:840, 1974.

57. Stubblefield PG, Naftolin F, Lee EY, et al: Combination therapy for midtrimester abortion: laminaria and analogues of prostaglandin. *Contraception* 13:723, 1976.

58. Sharma SD, Hale RW, Sato NE: Intramuscular 15-(S),15 methyl prostaglandin $F_2\alpha$ for midtrimester and missed abortions. *Obstet Gynecol.* 46:468, 1975.

59. Robbins J, Mann LE: Laminaria augmentation of midtrimester pregnancy termination by intramuscular prostaglandin 15-(S),15 methyl F_2 alpha. *J Reprod Med.* 16:334, 1976.

60. Gruber W, Brenner WE, Staurovsky LG, et al: Evaluation of intramuscular 15-(S)-15 methyl prostaglandin $F_2\alpha$ tromethamine salt for induction of abortion, medications to attenuate side effects, and intracervical laminaria tents. *Fertil Steril.* 27:1009, 1976.

61. Golditch IM, Solberg N: Induction of midtrimester abortion with intraamniotic urea, intravenous oxytocin and laminaria. *J Reprod Med.* 15:225, 1975.

62. Wellman L, Jacobson A: Intraamniotic prostaglandin $F_2\alpha$ and urea for midtrimester abortion. *Fertil Steril.* 27:1374, 1976.

63. Wilson WB: Midtrimester abortion with urea, prostaglandin $F_2\alpha$, laminaria, and oxytocin. *Obstet Gynecol.* 51:699, 1978.

64. Pahl IR, Lundy LE: Experience with midtrimester abortion. *Obstet Gynecol.* 53:587, 1979.

65. Weinstein L, Droegemueller W, Greer B: The synergistic effect of calcium and prostaglandin $F_2\alpha$ in second trimester abortion. *Obstet Gynecol.* 48:469, 1976.

66. Hodgson JE, Van Gorp PE: Induction of midtrimester abortion by the combined method of continuous extraovular infusion of prostaglandin $F_2\alpha$ and intracervical laminaria tents. *Fertil Steril.* 27:1359, 1976.

67. Cross WG, Pitkin RM: Laminaria as an adjunct in induction of labor. *Obstet Gynecol.* 51:606, 1978.

68. Lackritz R, Gibson M, Frigoletto FD, Jr: Preinduction use of laminaria for the unripe cervix. *Am J Obstet Gynecol.* 134:349, 1979.

69. Ott ER: Cervical dilatation—a review. *Popul Rep.* [F]85, 1977.

70. Borten M, Stubblefield PG, Friedman E: Evaluation of a balloon dilator to augment midtrimester abortion. *Am J Obstet Gynecol.* 130:156, 1978.

71. Zeller VR, Scholz C: Erfahrungsbericht mit den neuentwickelten Formaldehyd-gelatine-stiften zur Zervixdilatation. *Zentralbl Gynaekol.* 98:1372, 1976.

72. Khanna NM, Sarin JPS, Nandi RC, et al: Isaptent—a new aid for cervical dilatation. *IPPF Med Bull.* June 1979.

PART IV
Evaluation

12 Morbidity and Mortality

Willard Cates, Jr.
David A. Grimes

Over the past decade, the availability of legal abortion in the United States has permitted compilation of data necessary to evaluate the relative safety of different methods of second-trimester abortion. Prior to this time, clinical recommendations regarding various abortion methods were based largely on foreign data. American reports on abortion were based either on the large numbers of complications observed after illegal abortions or from small series of legally induced "therapeutic" abortions performed on high-risk patients in hospitals. This situation often resulted in clinical recommendations which were based upon uncontrolled impressions rather than on rigorous scientific observations. For example, as recently as the 1960s, a standard textbook of gynecology advised hysterotomy for all abortions at $\geq$ 13 weeks' gestation, bedrest for four to seven days after abortion by curettage, and delay "for as long as possible" before a second attempt to empty a uterus completely.[1]

Once abortion became legal, however, scientific studies could be undertaken to determine the safest methods of inducing either first- or second-trimester abortion. Recently, the results of several comparative studies have challenged prior clinical impressions and have caused vigorous debate among physicians regarding the safest methods for second-trimester abortion.

This chapter reviews the data on the morbidity and mortality from second-trimester abortion methods used during the past decade. Methodologic considerations in evaluating the safety of second-trimester abortion methods are briefly described first. Then, the largest comparative studies on abortion morbidity are presented and, finally, the trends in abortion mortality for the most frequently used methods of second-trimester abortion are discussed.

METHODOLOGIC CONSIDERATIONS

Several research approaches are available to assess the safety of second-trimester abortion methods: descriptive (anecdotal, case series), analytic, and experimental. Anecdotal descriptions of new techniques usually provide little, if any, quantification of the complications associated with these methods; rather, they are intended to stimulate the further use of innovative though often untested, modalities. Case series report aggregate anecdotal experience and often have elaborate research designs to evaluate the outcomes of their technique. As such, they provide systematic quantification of complication rates occurring with the technique; however, no comparison populations are provided in the case series format. Without appropriate comparison groups, the scientific value of such observations is limited. These studies simply describe what some clinicians can achieve with certain techniques.

Analytic studies are those which provide comparison groups; at the same time, they are observational in nature and do not follow a predetermined experimental protocol involving randomization. Rather, women have abortions performed by the usual clinicial practices of the institutions, and complications are managed at the discretion of the clinician. The outcomes from different abortion techniques can be compared systematically by using identical questionnaire forms, similar data collection techniques, and standardized definitions of abortion complications. Differences among population groups undergoing the procedures being compared can be overcome after completion of the study by using the analytic techniques of stratification or standardization.

When clinicians are allowed to use their customary procedures, results from observational studies may be more representative of current clinical practice than those in which an experimental protocol is rigorously defined. Moreover, analytic studies allow for evaluation of refinements in clinical methods as they occur during the study interval. Unfortunately, observational studies are subject to sources of potential bias—including selection of the study population, ascertainment of subtle complications, and distortion in characteristics between the comparison groups—any or all of which may limit the possibilities for drawing valid inferences.

Experimental studies (clinical trials) usually involve randomized patient allocation in the treatment groups being compared. Such studies frequently include "blinded" ascertainment of outcomes to overcome the possibility of observer bias. Finally, protocols for defining and managing complications usually are part of an experimental research design. Results gained from experimental studies often provide a stronger foundation for making scientifically valid inferences than studies of an observational nature.

In spite of the inherent advantages of randomized clinical trials, the results from such studies should be subject to a critical review similar to that which is given to results derived from observational investigations.[2] This is because randomization does not guarantee comparability, nor does it justify ignoring evidence of noncomparability. For example, in the World Health Organization's clinical trial comparing saline and prostaglandin $F_2\alpha$ ($PGF_2\alpha$), patients were supposed to be randomly assigned to either a $PGF_2\alpha$ or a saline group.[3] However, the numbers in each group—717 for $PGF_2\alpha$, 796 for saline—differed by 11%. A difference of this magnitude is unlikely to be due to chance.

Use of experimental protocols to compare surgical procedures also suffers because of variations in operator skill and changes in surgical technique during the study interval.[4] Differences in operator skill obviously influence the results of any surgical procedure involving more than one surgeon. In a recent clinical trial of two abortion methods, different operators using the same two procedures had different complication rates.[5] Because operator skill may be of critical importance in performing D&E procedures at later stages of gestation, experimental designs may not be the best approach to evaluate their safety. Many surgeons will resist accepting the inferences that could be drawn from the results of the clinical trials. For example, if the study showed D&E to be safer than other methods under comparison, some would argue that the study surgeons were more skilled than average. If the results showed the opposite, some would assert the surgeons were less skilled.

Experimental designs to study second-trimester abortion

methods have other practical limitations as well. Because of the low rate of severe complications observed even with later abortions, large numbers of observations usually are required to obtain the statistical power necessary to measure real differences among the various methods. Ethical considerations of informed consent prior to randomization inhibit the recruitment of patients, and design complexities of experimental studies raise the costs of the investigation. Therefore, randomized clinical trials are not the most timely or cost-efficient way to compare two methods. Finally, if more than one center is used, observer variability is possible even with the most carefully designed experimental research protocols.[6]

The choice of the most appropriate research design to evaluate the comparative safety of different second-trimester abortion methods thus is unsettled. At present, the use of carefully designed observational studies repeated in different locales and analyzed with appropriate statistical techniques may be the most valuable approach to evaluating the rapidly changing technology of second-trimester abortions.

COMPARATIVE STUDIES OF ABORTION MORBIDITY

Several large-scale comparative studies have evaluated the safety of different abortion methods during the past decade. Some have compared surgical techniques with instillation methods; others have compared different instillation procedures. To avoid the problems of drawing inferences from small numbers, comparative mortality data are drawn primarily from those investigations with a minimum of 100 patients in each of the cited study groups.

Dilatation and Evacuation Vs Instillation Agents

All six comparative studies conducted in the United States to evaluate the safety of D&E vs intraamniotic abortifacients determened that D&E consistently had lower complication rates (Table 12-1). In 1971 and 1972, under the auspices of the Population Council the Joint Program for the Study of Abortion found that the complication rates for women undergoing abortion by D&E at 13 weeks' gestation or later were lower than those for patients undergoing abortion by saline instillation at comparable gestational ages.[7] Unfortunately, the appropriate inferences from this study were not recognized for several years, possibly because of the attention given to the increasing risk of complications associated with advancing gestational age. Few authorities considered the risks of uterine evacuation after 12 weeks, compared to those of the available alternative methods of abortion at this later gestational age.

Vs Intraamniotic Agents for Second-Trimester Abortion

Authors	Year of Publication	Type of Study	No. of Patients	Findings
Tietze and Lewit[7]	1972 (D&E) 1973 (saline)	Multicenter, observational (prospective)	D&E = 2734 S = 14,690	Total complications for D&E through 15 weeks less than for saline at later gestations.
Brenner and Edelman[8]	1974	Multicenter, observational (prospective)	D&E = 338 S = 442	Complication rates with sharp curettage through 15 weeks similar to saline at later gestations. Suction curettage alone had higher complication rates than sharp curettage alone.
Grimes, et al[15]	1977	Multicenter, observational (prospective)	D&E = 6213 S = 8662	Major complications for D&E 60% lower than for saline instillation. D&E had lower rates of fever, endometritis, hemorrhage, and retained products of conception, but higher rates of cervical injury and uterine perforation.
Smith, et al[10]	1978	Multicenter, observational (prospective)	D&E = 721 S = 1069	Complication rates with D&E in 13-16 week interval less than instillation procedures thereafter.
Stubblefield, et al[11]	1978	Single center, observational (prospective)	D&E = 406 P = 623	Complication rates with D&E from 13-18 weeks lower than with prostaglandin instillation. D&E had lower rates of fever, anemia, pain, endometritis, cervicitis, and hemorrhage after discharge. D&E had higher rates of hemorrhage during the procedure.
Grimes, et al[33]	1980	Single center, experimental	D&E = 50 P = 50	D&E had lower rates of total complications than prostaglandin instillation.

D&E = Dilatation and Evacuation.
S = Saline.
P = Prostaglandin $F_2\alpha$.

In 1974, the International Fertility Research Program determined that the complication rates from sharp curettage through 15 weeks were similar to those of saline at later gestational ages.[8] In the 13- to 15-week interval, however, suction curettage used without special forceps had higher complication rates than sharp curettage alone. The authors advocated controlled studies to determine whether their findings could be replicated elsewhere.

In 1977, the Joint Program for the Study of Abortion, now under the auspices of the Center for Disease Control, reported a comprehensive investigation of D&E and compared this procedure with saline instillation.[9] JPSA/CDC found D&E a significantly safer procedure. The relative risk of sustaining one or more major complications was 2.6 times higher for saline than D&E, even after adjusting for gestational age, patient age, patient follow-up, pre-existing conditions, prophylactic antibiotic administration, and level of operator training. Also, significantly more frequent among the patients treated with saline were fever, endometritis, hemorrhage, retained products of conception, and urinary tract infections. On the other hand, cervical injuries and uterine perforations occurred significantly more often in the D&E group.

Results of two smaller, though unique, observational studies have been consistent with the results of JPSA/CDC. In Hawaii, a study of all induced abortions performed between 1970 and 1974 showed that complication rates for D&E procedures performed during 13 to 16 weeks' gestation were lower than those for instillation procedures performed thereafter.[10] This study, unlike JPSA/CDC, was not based on a selected sample but rather on all procedures performed in Hawaii during the four-year study interval. Thus, it is less likely that either patient or physician selection biases influenced the outcome. Similarly, at Boston Hospital for Women, D&E from 13 to 18 weeks' gestation was found to have lower complication rates than prostaglandin instillation at 16 or more weeks.[11] This latter study focused on results obtained in a single institution. Because the definitions and management of different complications were uniform, it is unlikely that the method of diagnosis of complications or their treatment affected these results.

The University of North Carolina sponsored the only experimental protocol which evaluated D&E and prostaglandin instillation. Patients were randomly assigned to one of the two treatment groups. All abortions, whether D&E or prostaglandin instillation, were performed by one clinician in order to eliminate operator variability. Women who underwent D&E procedures had lower rates of total complications than those who had prostaglandin instillation abortions (see Chapter 10).

The results of these comparative studies of D&E vs instillation procedures are remarkedly consistent. Although the complication rates have varied from study to study, they show that D&E can be performed more safely than the instillation of abortifacients. Much of the advantage of D&E over instillation procedures is gained because it can be performed early in the second trimester, during the 13- to 16-week gestational age interval.[12] On the other hand, if one considers women requesting abortions at 17 weeks' gestation or later, the choice is less certain and depends on such factors as staff acceptance of and experience with the D&E procedure. Future comparative studies should focus on those D&E procedures performed at this later gestational age, rather than aggregating them with the earlier second-trimester D&E procedures which now are known to have lower complication rates.

Prostaglandin $F_2\alpha$ Vs Hypertonic Saline

Preliminary investigations of $PGF_2\alpha$ led to an initial enthusiasm regarding its theoretical, relative safety compared to hypertonic saline as a second-trimester intraamniotic abortifacient.[13] Recently published comparative studies, however, do not support this alleged greater safety of $PGF_2\alpha$ over saline (Table 12-2).[14] The three largest studies reported to date have come from JPSA/CDC,[15] the WHO,[3] and the Indian Council of Medical Research (ICMR).[16] JPSA/CDC and ICMR were observational studies; the WHO investigation was of an experimental design. Nonetheless, the results of these three studies were very similar. The prostaglandin agents had shorter instillation-to-abortion times but were associated with significantly higher rates of major complications. Indeed, the agreement on the magnitude of the increased risk associated with use of prostaglandin agents was striking. For example, the relative risk of hemorrhage for prostaglandin was 3.1 in the CDC study, 3.0 in the WHO study, and 3.5 in the ICMR study. This consistency among the three largest studies, performed with different research designs in different parts of the world, strongly suggests that prostaglandin agents are causally related to the higher rates of the more serious, though less frequent, complications.

Additional, smaller comparative studies generally have agreed with the results of the larger studies. $PGF_2\alpha$ was faster than saline in inducing abortion but caused more frequent minor complications such as nausea, vomiting, diarrhea, and retained products of conception. Two investigations by the International Fertility Research Program found $PGF_2\alpha$ had lower rates of febrile morbidity than saline.[17,18] The larger investigations found the opposite.

Comparative studies in New York and Massachusetts have

Table 12-2
Comparative Studies of Intraamniotic Prostaglandin $F_{2\alpha}$ Vs Hypertonic Saline

Authors	Year of Publication	Type of Study	No. of Patients	Findings
Edelman, et al[29]	1976	Multicenter, experimental	P = 242 S = 130	$PGF_{2\alpha}$ had higher rates of gastrointestinal side effects but lower rates of fever.
World Health Organization[3]	1976	Multicenter, experimental	P = 717 S = 796	$PGF_{2\alpha}$ had higher rates for hemorrhage, blood transfusion, surgical re-evacuation, dyspnea, flushing, and chest pain.
Berger and Edelman[17]	1977	Single center, observational (retrospective)	P = 100 S = 100	$PGF_{2\alpha}$ had a lower rate for fever.
Grimes, et al[15]	1977	Multicenter, observational (prospective)	P = 1241 S = 10,013	$PGF_{2\alpha}$ had higher rates for fever, endometrial hemorrhage, convulsions, antibiotic administration, major and minor operative treatments of complications, and readmission to a hospital.
Robins[19]	1978	Multicenter, observational (retrospective)	P = 700 S = 170	$PGF_{2\alpha}$ had higher rates of liveborn fetuses.
Bhatt, et al[30]	1978	Single center, experimental	P = 100 S = 100	$PGF_{2\alpha}$ had higher rates of excessive blood loss.
Pahl and Lundy[20]	1979	Single center, observational (retrospective)	P = 324 S = 439	$PGF_{2\alpha}$ had higher rates of liveborn fetuses, nausea, and vomiting.
Indian Council for Medical Research[31,32]	1979, 1980	Multicenter, observational (prospective)	P = 1295 S = 507	$PGF_{2\alpha}$ had higher rates of minor complications, hemorrhage, post-abortion bleeding, wound sepsis, and cervical injury.

S = Saline.
P = Prostaglandin $F_{2\alpha}$.

highlighted another of the problems associated with using $PGF_2\alpha$ as the primary abortifacient—the liveborn fetus.[19,20] $PGF_2\alpha$ is about 40 times more likely to produce a liveborn fetus than is hypertonic saline. While delivery of a living fetus is not life-threatening to the patient who previously had requested an abortion, it has disturbing social and medicolegal ramifications. It is possible that the higher rates of liveborn fetuses, as much as the increased rates of complications to the woman, have convinced many practitioners that $PGF_2\alpha$ should not be used as a primary abortifacient alone, but rather in combination with other agents.

Combination Methods

Recently, attention has focused on instillation methods which use combinations of abortifacient agents in the hope that each medication would potentiate the beneficial effects of the other. Combinations usually involve a primary fetocidal agent (hypertonic saline or hyperosmolar urea), an augmenting oxytocic agent ($PGF_2\alpha$, PGE_2, or oxytocin), and/or a dilating agent (laminaria or PGE_2). At least one authority has speculated that such combinations would lead to potentiation of the risks as well as the benefits.[21] To date, the reported comparative studies have not supported this contention.[20,22,23]

Investigators in New York City found that a combination of intraamniotic hypertonic saline and $PGF_2\alpha$ reduced the instillation-to-abortion time.[22] At Johns Hopkins Hospital, combinations of hyperosmolar urea and $PGF_2\alpha$ shortened the instillation-to-abortion time and reduced risks when compared to urea-oxytocin or saline-oxytocin protocols.[23] Moreover, it was found that a 5 mg dose of $PGF_2\alpha$ given to augment the urea had better effects than either a 10 mg or 20 mg dose of $PGF_2\alpha$, thus decreasing the costs and risks of the prostaglandin agents. A combination of hypertonic saline, $PGF_2\alpha$, and laminaria had significantly faster induction-to-abortion times and statistically similar rates of hemorrhage and fever than the use of either saline or $PGF_2\alpha$ alone.[20]

Mortality from Second-Trimester Abortion

During the past decade, abortion-related mortality has served as a major index of the national trends in abortion morbidity. Vital statistics data clearly have shown that the overall number of abortion-related deaths (including the combined categories of legal, illegal, and spontaneous) has declined dramatically. This decline has been related temporally to the increasing availability of legal abortions.[24] Some of this change presumably represents the substitution of the safer legal abortions in pregnancies that formerly would have been terminated through less safe, illegal channels.

Another factor affecting the decline of the overall abortion mortality rate has been the decrease in the death-to-case rate for legally induced abortions over the past decade.[25] From 1970 to 1972, Berger and his colleagues conducted an extensive study of deaths related to legally-induced abortions performed in New York State.[26] During these two years, approximately 50% of all legally induced abortions in the United States were performed in New York State. The total death-to-case rate for legal abortion at that time was 6.5 per 100,000 procedures.

In 1972, the Center for Disease Control began to monitor all deaths from legally-induced abortions throughout the nation. During the past six years, the total death-to-case rate has declined from 4.1 per 100,000 procedures in 1972 and 1973, to 3.3 in 1974 and 1975, to 1.3 in 1976 and 1977 (Table 12-3). This dramatic decline from 6.5 to 1.3 deaths per 100,000 can be explained by at least four factors:

- The increasing percentage of abortions being performed during the earlier, safer gestational ages.
- Increasing experience with abortion by practicing physicians, including greater experience in the management of complications.

Table 12-3
Death-to-Case Rate and Number of Deaths from Legal Abortions, by Type of Procedure, New York State, 1970–1972, and United States, 1972–1973, 1974–1975, 1976–1977

	Death-to-Case Rate† (number of deaths in parentheses)				
	NY State	United States			
Type of Procedure	1970–72[26]	1972–73‡	1974–75‡	1976–77‡	1972–77 Total‡
Uterine evacuation	2.7 (10)	1.9 (20)	1.9 (28)	0.9 (18)	1.5 (66)
Curettage (≤12 weeks)	—	1.8 (18)	1.6 (23)	0.5 (10)	1.2 (51)
D&E (≥13 weeks)	—	*	*	*	8.3 (15)
Instillation					
Saline	19.5 (11)	16.9 (20)	16.0 (14)	3.5 (3)	15.5 (37)
Prostaglandin and others	—	*	*	*	20.6 (11)
Hysterotomy/hysterectomy	271.1 (8)	*	*	*	45.3 (9)
Total	6.5 (29)	4.1 (49)	3.3 (54)	1.3 (26)	2.6 (129)

*Small number of deaths makes rate unreliable.
†Deaths per 100,000 procedures.
‡Source: Epidemiologic surveillance of abortion-related deaths, Center for Disease Control, 1972 to 1977.

- Increasing percentage of safer curettage procedures, including dilatation and evacuation.
- Under-reporting of legal abortion deaths during the most recent years.

Comparative death-to-case rates do not provide as convincing a basis for distinguishing among the different methods of second-trimester abortion as do comparative morbidity data. Mortality data on uterine evacuation, saline instillation, and hysterotomy/hysterectomy procedures are available from New York State from 1970 to 1972, and from the United States from 1972 to 1977. The relatively small number of deaths reported for each method in any particular year unfortunately subjects these rates to wide statistical variation.

In addition to the small numbers, the absence of reliable denominator data—especially for prostaglandin instillations—limits the usefulness of comparative mortality data. This chapter presents a slightly different basis for calculating denominators than was used in our previous publications.[27] In prior reports, data from 1974 and 1975 distributions of method and gestational age were used to estimate the number and type of procedures performed in 1972 and 1973. This approach tends to exaggerate the number of procedures performed by the instillation of prostaglandins; $PGF_2\alpha$ was not available for general distribution before it was licensed in November 1973. The calculations for this chapter include an estimate of the number of prostaglandin abortions performed prior to 1973 based on data supplied by the Upjohn Company to the Food and Drug Administration. This provides a more realistic projection of the number of abortions performed using prostaglandin and other agents, and accounts for the higher death-to-case rates for the years 1972 to 1977 than previously reported.

In the United States for the six years 1972 to 1977, D&E methods had a crude death-to-case rate of 8.3 deaths per 100,000 procedures ⩾ 13 weeks' gestation, compared to 15.5 for the instillation of hypertonic saline, 20.6 for the instillation of prostaglandins and other agents, and 45.3 for hysterotomy/hysterectomy procedures (Table 12-3). A similar mortality rate for D&E was reported from Britain between 1968 and 1973. During those six years, D&E had a death-to-case rate of 6.6 per 100,000 procedures.[28] In Britain, national surveillance of maternal mortality, including abortion-related deaths, is based on a well-established system of confidential inquiries into all deaths among women of reproductive age. Data ascertainment generally is considered complete. The consistency between the American and the British death-to-case rates for D&E procedures provides evidence that these rates are an accurate portrayal of the mortality risks from the procedures.

The 95% confidence interval for the death-to-case rates for second-trimester D&E (4 to 14/1000) does not overlap that for the instillation agents. Chance is thus an unlikely explanation for these observed differences. Because the risk of dying increases with gestational age, however, the death-to-case rate for D&E is less (6.7/100,000) in the 13- to 15-week gestational age interval than at 16 weeks' gestation or later (13.4/100,000). As with the morbidity data, the comparative advantage of D&E in the mortality data lies largely in the "grey zone." After 15 weeks, the death-to-case rates between D&E and instillation agents are quite similar.

In the United States, the total number of deaths following D&E has been increasing over each of the three two-year intervals from 1972 to 1977; two deaths from D&E occurred in 1972 and 1973, five in 1974 and 1975, and eight in 1976 and 1977. Because the death-to-case rates from curettage procedures performed at earlier gestations have been declining during the same intervals, this trend is of concern. Several factors may account for this finding:

- The number of D&E procedures *has* increased
- Because of the relatively small number of deaths involved, the variations could represent chance fluctuation of rare events
- As new operators learn this surgical technique, there may be more complications
- D&E might be used in higher-risk women
- The mean gestational age of D&E may have increased

Further surveillance of deaths from D&E will be necessary in order to differentiate the extent to which each of these factors may account for the increasing number of deaths following D&E.

Unlike the secular trends for deaths from D&E, deaths from instillation procedures have been decreasing over the past six years. Moreover, the death-to-case rate for hypertonic saline has decreased during the entire decade. Data from New York State show that the mortality rate for hypertonic saline declined from 19.5/100,000 procedures in 1970 to 1972, leveled at 16 to 17 between 1972 and 1975, and then fell markedly in the years 1976 and 1977. Possible reasons for the sharp decline during the last two years in the death-to-case rate for hypertonic saline may be:

- Improvements in the management of common complications related to hypertonic saline
- More selective use of hypertonic saline among low-risk women

- Under-reporting of deaths associated with hypertonic saline in more recent years
- Over-counting the proportion of hypertonic saline instillation procedures being performed in more recent years

The number of deaths from prostaglandin and other instillation agents has remained at a low level between 1972 and 1977, and followed no trend in each of the two-year intervals. Three deaths occurred in 1972 and 1977, five in 1974 and 1975, and three in 1976 and 1977. Our aggregation of deaths from other instillation procedures (one each from hyperosmolar urea, oxytocin, and Luenbach's paste) with those from $PGF_2\alpha$ was intended both to provide more power to the comparative rates and to allow the estimation of more accurate denominators for combination procedures. Even with this aggregation, however, the total number of deaths (11) in the six-year interval is so small that random statistical variation could account for the observed differences in death-to-case rates between saline and other instillation agents. Moreover, disagreement over the most accurate estimate of the number of procedures actually performed during the interval also limits any inferences that can be drawn about the mortality risks from prostaglandin and other instillation agents. Finally, the use of prostaglandin and other agents has been recommended specifically for high-risk women. Analysis of the deaths in which $PGF_2\alpha$ was used indicates that several women who died had underlying preexisting conditions which contributed to the cause of their death.[28] For these reasons, we are cautious not to overstate the implications of the mortality data in providing a basis for differentiating between the safety of available instillation methods.

Hysterotomy and hysterectomy procedures continue to have higher death-to-case rates than alternative second-trimester methods, although the risk of dying from hysterotomy and hysterectomy apparently decreased during the decade from 271 per 100,000 procedures observed in New York from 1970 to 1972, to 45 per 100,000 procedures in the United States between 1972 and 1977. In the latter interval, however, the death-to-case rate for hysterotomy and hysterectomy still was more than two times higher than that for either D&E or instillation procedures. The small number of deaths from these major surgical procedures produces wide statistical variation in their death-to-case rates. Nonetheless, the 95% confidence interval for the death-to-case rate for hysterotomy and hysterectomy (20 to 86/100,000) is higher than the rates of other second-trimester procedures, making chance an unlikely explanation for these differences.

To summarize, the comparative mortality data do not provide so strong a foundation to differentiate among D&E, hypertonic saline, prostaglandin, and other agents as do the comparative morbidity data. Nonetheless, they do emphasize the preferability of any of these methods over hysterotomy or hysterectomy. These major surgical procedures, especially when used after failed instillation procedures, have a sufficiently high death-to-case rate that they should be reserved for only the most specific indications.

CONCLUSION

Over the past decade, the morbidity and mortality from second-trimester abortion has decreased. Removal of the 12-week gestational age barrier for curettage procedures, thus allowing D&E abortions to be performed in 13- to 16-week interval, has contributed to this decline. In a similar manner, the recognition that hysterotomy/hysterectomy procedures are more dangerous than other available alternatives has led to a decline in their utilization. Finally, improvements in management of complications from hypertonic saline, hyperosmolar urea, and prostaglandin agents have lowered the risks from these procedures.

While abortions performed in the second trimester probably will always be more dangerous than those performed at earlier gestational ages, continued developments in this field can be expected to reduce further the number of deaths and complications.

REFERENCES

1. TeLinde RW: *Operative Gynecology*, 3rd ed, Philadelphia, JB Lippincott, 1962, p 567.
2. Rothman KJ: Epidemiologic methods in clinical trials. *Cancer* 39:1771, 1977.
3. World Health Organization Task Force on the Use of Prostaglandins for the Regulation of Fertility: Comparison of intraamniotic prostaglandin $F_2\alpha$ and hypertonic saline for induction of second-trimester abortion. *Br Med J.* 1:1373, 1976.
4. Bonchek LI: Are randomized trials appropriate for evaluating new operations? *N Engl J Med.* 301:44, 1979.
5. Miller ER, Wood JL, Andolsek L, et al: First trimester abortion by vacuum aspiration: interphysician variability. *Int J Gynaecol Obstet.* 16:144, 1978.
6. Andolsek L, Cheng M, Hren M, et al: The safety of local anesthesia and outpatient treatments: a controlled study of induced abortion by vacuum aspiration. *Stud Fam Plann.* 8:118, 1977.
7. Tietze C, Lewit S: Joint Program for the Study of Abortion (JPSA): Early medical complications of legal abortion. *Stud Fam Plann.* 3:97, 1972.
8. Brenner WE, Edelman DA: Dilatation and evacuation at 13 to 15

weeks' gestation versus intraamniotic saline after 15 weeks' gestation. *Contraception* 10:171, 1974.

9. Grimes DA, Schulz KF, Cates W Jr, et al: Midtrimester abortion by dilatation and evacuation: a safe and practical alternative. *N Engl J Med.* 296:1141, 1977.

10. Smith RG, Steinhoff PG, Palmore JA: Potential reduction of medical complications from induced abortions. *Int J Gynaecol Obstet.* 15:337, 1978.

11. Stubblefield PG, Kayman DJ, Osorio-Burns L: Midtrimester abortion by dilatation and evacuation and by laminaria and prostaglandin $F_2\alpha$: Experience in a teaching hospital. Presented at the Postgraduate Course on Abortion, 16th annual meeting of the Association for Planned Parenthood Physicians, San Diego, October 24, 1978.

12. Cates W Jr, Schulz KF, Gold J, et al: Complications of surgical evacuation procedures for abortions after 12 weeks' gestation, in Zatuchni GI, Sciarra JJ, Speidel JJ (eds): *Pregnancy Termination: Procedures, Safety and New Developments* Hagerstown, Md, Harper & Row, 1979, p 206.

13. Bygdeman M: Comparison of efficacy and complications following administration of prostaglandin or hypertonic saline for termination of second trimester pregnancy. *Obstet Gynecol.* 52:424, 1978.

14. Grimes DA, Cates W Jr: The comparative efficacy and safety of intraamniotic prostaglandin $F_2\alpha$ and hypertonic saline for second-trimester abortion: a review and critique. *J Reprod Med.* 22:248, 1979.

15. Grimes DA, Schulz KF, Cates W Jr, et al: Midtrimester abortion by intraamniotic prostaglandin $F_2\alpha$. Safer than saline? *Obstet Gynecol.* 49:612, 1977.

16. Tejuja S, Choudhury SD, Manchanda PK: Use of intra- and extraamniotic prostaglandins for the termination of pregnancies—report of multicentric trial in India. *Contraception* 18:641, 1978.

17. Berger GS, Edelman DA: A clinical comparison of prostaglandin $F_2\alpha$ and intraamniotic saline for induction of midtrimester abortion. *Ann Chir Gynaecol.* 66:55, 1977.

18. Kee SH, Lean TH, Vengadasalam D, et al: The safety and efficacy of intraamniotic instillation of saline and 2 prostaglandin $F_2\alpha$ dose schedules for midtrimester abortion. Presented at the VII Asian Congress of Obstetrics and Gynaecology, Bangkok, Thailand, November 20–25, 1977.

19. Robins J: A clinical comparison of intra-amniotic prostaglandin $F_2\alpha$ and intra-amniotic hypertonic saline for mid-trimester pregnancy termination. *Adv Plann Parent.* 13:27, 1978.

20. Pahl IR, Lundy LE: Experience with midtrimester abortion. *Obstet Gynecol.* 53:587, 1979.

21. Shulman H: Biologic obstacles to abortion, in Zatuchni GI, Sciarra JJ, Speidel JJ (eds): *Pregnancy Termination: Procedures, Safety and New Developments.* Hagerstown, Md, Harper & Row, 1979, p 2.

22. Kerenyi T, Den T: Intraamniotic instillation of saline and prostaglandin for midtrimester abortion, in Zatuchni GI, Sciarra JJ, Speidel JJ (eds): *Pregnancy Termination: Procedures, Safety and New Developments.* Hagerstown, Md, Harper & Row, 1979, p 254.

23. Burkman RT Jr, Dubin N, King T: Use of hyperosmolar urea for elective abortion of midtrimester pregnancy, in Zatuchni GI, Sciarra JJ, Speidel JJ (eds): *Pregnancy Termination: Procedures, Safety and New Developments.* Hagerstown, Md, Harper & Row, 1979, p 261.

24. Cates W Jr, Rochat RW, Grimes DA, et al: Legalized abortion: effect on national trends of maternal and abortion-related mortality (1940–1976). *Am J Obstet Gynecol.* 132:211, 1978.

25. Cates W Jr, Tietze C: Standardized mortality rates associated with legal abortion: United States, 1972-1975. *Fam Plann Perspect.* 10:109, 1978.

26. Berger GS, Tietze C, Pakter J, et al: Maternal mortality associated with legal abortion in New York State: July 1, 1970-June 30, 1972. *Obstet Gynecol.* 43:315, 1974.

27. Cates W Jr, Grimes DA, Smith JC, et al: The risk of dying from legal abortion, United States, 1972-1975. *Int J Gynaecol Obstet.* 15:172, 1977.

28. Cates W Jr, Grimes DA, Haber RJ, et al: Abortion deaths associated with the use of prostaglandin $F_2\alpha$. *Am J Obstet. Gynecol.* 127:219, 1977.

29. Edelman DA, Brenner WE, Mehta AC, et al: A comparative study of intra-amniotic saline and 2 prostaglandin $F_2\alpha$ dose schedules for midtrimester abortion. *Am J Obstet. Gynecol.* 125:188, 1976.

30. Bhatt RV, Pachauri S, Koshy E, et al: Midtrimester abortion with prostaglandin and hypertonic saline: A comparative study. *Int J Gynaecol Obstet.* 16:254, 1979.

31. Prema K: Studies on sequelae of induced abortion. *ICMR Bull.* 9(5):1, 1979.

32. Cates W Jr, Grimes DA, Schulz KF, et al: Response to Indian Council of Medical Research studies of the safety of prostaglandin abortions. *Contraception* 22:103, 1980.

33. Grimes DA, Hulka JF, McCutchen ME: Midtrimester abortion by dilatation and evacuation versus intra-amniotic instillation of prostaglandin $F_2\alpha$: A randomized clinical trial. *Am J Obstet Gynecol.* 137:785, 1980.

13 Future Reproduction

Carol J. Rowland Hogue

FUTURE REPRODUCTION AFTER SECOND-TRIMESTER INDUCED ABORTION

Any discussion of reproduction after second-trimester abortion should consider that the aborted pregnancy may have been at risk of complications and/or malformations, and that future pregnancies in the same woman might be subject to the same risk factors which led her to seek a second-trimester termination of the current pregnancy. Women who abort in the first trimester represent a heterogeneous mixture of low-risk and high-risk pregnancies. Those who obtain a second-trimester abortion are generally quite different; many are avoiding immediate, potentially severe reproductive risks. Delay in diagnosis of a serious health problem such as rubella, diabetes, Down's syndrome, etc., usually dictates that the abortion must occur after the 12th week of pregnancy. Even abortions for nonmedical reasons in the second trimester often represent terminations of high-risk pregnancies because of sociodemographic problems such as maternal age, parity, economic status, marital status, and failure to seek care in the first trimester.

The question which logically must be raised is: Are these women trading the alleviation of an immediate problem pregnancy for still greater, future reproductive risks? The answer clearly is "no" when there are medical reasons such as rubella for the aborted pregnancy. The answer also is "no" when women abort their last pregnancy and never become pregnant again because of advanced age or major health problems. For the very young, nulliparous and unmarried women who face this question, however, the answer to this question is unknown. After a decade of experience with second-trimester abortion, very little is known about subsequent reproductive risks.

In some instances, future reproduction actually may be less risky because the aborted pregnancy was terminated when the patient was very young, and her future pregnancies will occur when she is more mature. Moreover, teenagers are known to experience greater rates of adverse pregnancy outcomes for second births as compared with first births.[1,2] Therefore, if investigation reveals no difference in rates of adverse outcomes between primigravid teens and post-abortion nulliparous teens matched for age at delivery, this result actually may signal lower risk to those who are experiencing their first term birth instead of their second at that age.[3]

In addition to maternal age and parity, other factors may affect the relationship between second-trimester abortion and later reproduction. Chief among these, perhaps, is the technical method of the termination procedure. For example, dilatation of 12 mm or more has been associated with enlarged cervical diameter on follow-up examinations.[4] In contrast, procedures not requiring great amounts of mechanical dilatation may not carry the risks to future offspring associated with a potentially weakened or possibly incompetent cervix.

Neither of these hypotheses has been tested adequately. Although numerous studies of long-term fertility complications following first-trimester procedures have been reported, little information exists regarding the effects of second-trimester procedures.[5,6] One classic, carefully performed study of vaginal hysterotomy was published 20 years ago, but its usefulness is minimal because that procedure is no longer commonly performed.[7] More recent and better designed research has focused on procedures performed during the first trimester, since most investigations have involved too few cases of second-trimester abortion to justify analysis,[8,9] or have lacked the necessary information to analyze the effect of the abortion procedure on subsequent pregnancy outcomes.[6,10] An exception to this general statement is one center in the WHO collaborative study, which recently has reported on the outcome of subsequent pregnancies for previously aborted women by trimester of abortion, classified by gestation periods of 12 weeks or less, and 13 weeks or more.[11]

REPRODUCTION AFTER INTRAAMNIOTIC SALINE PROCEDURES

Only one follow-up study of reproduction following saline procedures has been reported.[12] Of 213 women who had a saline-induced pregnancy termination from 1955 to 1976 at the Kaplan Hospital in Rehovot, Israel, 103 were contacted. Thirty-four percent of the terminations had been performed for "social" indications; the remainder were performed because of death in utero or maternal rubella. Almost one-fourth of the pregnancies were past the 26th week of gestation when terminated. The termination was induced by intraamniotic administration of 30% saline. No oxytocin was administered. More than 80% of the cases were completed by curettage.[12] Conditions which could have affected future reproduction were detected among three patients at follow-up: one woman had hydrosalpinx, one had cervical incompetence, and one had intrauterine adhesions. Two of 70 women who had desired future pregnancies had not been able to conceive; one case was thought to be due to older age and the other potentially a result of the procedure. The outcomes of the remaining 68 pregnancies are shown in Table 13-1. The spontaneous abortion rate was 3%. It is not known what rates to expect from a comparable series of women living in that area who had not previously had abortions.

Another study shown in Table 13-1 was a record review of pregnancies occurring over a four-year period in Seattle, Washington,

Table 13-1
Pregnancies Following Saline Abortions

	No. of Pregnancies	Spontaneous Abortions	Low Birth Weight or Pre-term Deliveries	Full-term Deliveries
Borenstein et al. (1979)[12]	68	2	66*	
Daling and Emanuel (1977)[3]	30		3	27
Slater, Davies and Harlap (1979)[13]	18		1	17

*Information unavailable.

beginning in 1972.[3] Among the total series of 4806 pregnancies reported by Daling and Emanuel, 590 women reported a prior induced abortion. Only 30 of the pregnancies followed saline instillation. Three (10%) of these resulted in a premature infant. The rate of prematurity in this small sample was not significantly different from that observed among all women with prior induced abortion, or from the rate derived for the control group.

Slater, Davies, and Harlap also reported (Table 13-1) that the rate of low birth weight among the 18 women who had saline abortions was not significantly different from the rate experienced by all previously aborted women who were followed through record linkage at the Hebrew University-Hadassah Medical School from 1967 to 1976.[13] This finding might be interpreted as indicating an increased risk following saline terminations in Israel, since all pregnancies preceded by abortion had a significantly higher rate of low birth weight than did the matched control pregnancies. Nevertheless, the low birth weight rate of 5.5% following saline terminations was actually lower than the control group's rate of 6.3%. This finding points out the danger of drawing conclusions from very small samples. An additional problem with both of these studies from Israel was the sizeable number of pregnancies for which the nature of the previous termination procedure could not be determined.

REPRODUCTION AFTER PROCEDURES REQUIRING DILATATION AND SHARP OR SUCTION CURETTAGE

Peterson[14] and Hanson[15] both have reported on the subsequent reproduction of a series of postabortal patients followed for several years. Combining these two published studies, as shown in Table 13-2, there was a total of 253 pregnancies, with a spontaneous abortion rate of more than 13% and a prematurity rate of nearly 16%. The latter appears to be high, but in the absence of an appropriate control group, it is not possible to determine whether it is higher than expected.

A study of abortions performed in Singapore between 1970 and 1974 found similar rates of spontaneous abortions and low birth weight deliveries among a small number of women after abortions which had been performed by D&C or by D&E. Among these 34 pregnancies (also shown in Table 13-2), five (15%) aborted spontaneously, and four (14%) of the deliveries weighed 2500 g or less. These later series of patients differ from those in the American studies in terms of racial, ethnic, and socioeconomic status. The small number of women studied presents as great a problem as it does in the studies of pregnancies following saline instillation.

The primary concern about second-trimester procedures requiring dilatation is that the large degree of dilatation necessitated by advanced gestational age may adversely affect a subsequent pregnancy. Some evidence for this was reported in studies by Johnstone et al.[4] and by Slater et al.[13] In the former study, there was information on degree of dilatation for a small subset of the pregnancies following

Table 13-2
Pregnancies Following Dilatation and Evacuation

	No. of Pregnancies	Spontaneous Abortions	Low Birth Weight or Pre-term Deliveries	Full-term Deliveries
Peterson (1978)[14]	242	34	35	173
Hanson (1978)[15]	11	*	0	11
Hogue et al.[19] (unpub.)				
D&C	18	3	3	12
D&E	16	2	1	13

*Information unavailable.

abortion. For these 63 women, dilatation of 12 mm or more was associated, albeit insignificantly, with increased rates of low birth weight. No other complications were significantly associated with extent of dilatation. A larger study by Obel[11] found a significant (2.9-fold) risk of low birth weight for 67 pregnancies following suction abortion with dilatation greater than 12 mm, as compared to 337 pregnancies following suction with dilatation of less than 12 mm. Johnstone and associates[4] discovered that when cervical diameters were measured six weeks postabortion and compared with cervical diameters of pregnant, primigravid women, significant correlation was found between cervical dilatation at abortion and cervical diameter six weeks later. Furthermore, patients whose cervices had been dilated more than 10 mm had significantly greater cervical diameter than the mean for the entire group.

REPRODUCTION AFTER PROSTAGLANDIN PROCEDURES

Reproduction following prostaglandin-induced abortions has been studied.[16] Most (82%) of the procedures used to terminate the pregnancies were performed by extraamniotic administration of prostaglandins. PGE_2 was administered in 77% of the cases and $PGF_2\alpha$ or an analogue was administered to the remainder.

The results are summarized in Table 13-3. In this study, the controls were of similar social class, but of lower average parity and higher average age. Only crude rates of adverse outcomes were compared. For these, the overall spontaneous abortion rate was significantly higher in the series of women with prior induced abortion (13%) than in the control group (7.5%). On the other hand, the controls had higher rates of preterm deliveries, although the difference was not statistically significant. First-trimester spontaneous abortions probably were underreported in the control group because they were determined from maternity records, whereas for the abortion series pregnancy histories were obtained by means of a follow-up questionnaire.

Table 13-3
Singleton Pregnancies Following Prostaglandin*
Induction of Abortion

	No. of Pregnancies	Spontaneous Abortions ≤ 13 wks	Spontaneous Abortions ≥ 12 wks	Pre-term Deliveries	Full-term Deliveries
Following PGE$_2$ or PGF$_2\alpha$	144	12	7	4	121
Controls	517	30	9	31	447

*92% of abortions were performed after the twelfth week of gestation.
Source: Mackenzie and Hillier (1977).[16]

FUTURE DIRECTIONS

At present there is intense interest in the relative safety of different abortion procedures performed in the early second trimester. This interest has been generated by a comparison of immediate and short-term complications caused by each procedure. Before deciding which method is the safest, however, it would seem advisable to complete the picture of complications by comparing the long-term effects of all potential procedures. Unfortunately, the presently available evidence does not allow such a comparison to be made. Furthermore, it may be quite difficult to obtain the necessary data because of several problems which are inherent in any study of the question. For example, Cates lists 14 categories of factors which should be considered in addition to the type of abortifacient when late effects are analyzed.[17] An additional consideration to any interpretation of these data is the epidemiologic methodology selected to evaluate the results.[5]

Four points are particularly relevant to the study of reproduction subsequent to second-trimester procedures:

- The women should be classified according to reason for

requesting the abortion procedure. Several studies reviewed above include abortions performed for therapeutic reasons.[12,3,16] Because prior pregnancy wastage and complications may affect future reproductive potential, it is crucial that abortions performed because of complications of pregnancy be analyzed separately from those performed for nonmedical reasons.

- It is very important to ascertain precisely the type of abortion for all or nearly all women in the study. Retrospective analyses of medical records, especially those based on maternity records which include only a pregnancy history, usually do not include sufficient information to enable classification of the prior abortion experience according to procedure used. Investigators who based studies on such retrospective methodology routinely have been able to analyze only a portion of their series—Daling and Emanuel,[3] 49%; Koller and Eikhom,[18] 70%; Slater et al.,[13] 65% for abortion type, 55% of D&C abortions for degree of dilatation. It seems, therefore, that it is probably not possible to use this methodologic approach successfully in order to determine the effect of the abortion procedure.
- When a prospective methodology is chosen to circumvent the second problem, the problem of loss to follow-up becomes an important issue. In the early 1950s Lindahl was able to follow 90% of the women he had identified.[7] More recent studies, however, have not experienced that high a follow-up rate; for example, Peterson[14] reported 51%, while Borenstein[13] found 76% and Hogue et al[19] also had relatively few.
- Compounding this problem is that many of the women who respond may not have experienced a subsequent pregnancy at the time of the study, and many of the pregnancies which did occur also may have been terminated by induced abortion. For example, the yield of pregnancies for which outcomes could be determined in Peterson's study was only 17%, or 8.5% of the original number of aborted women.[14] What this means is that very large populations of women undergoing second-trimester procedures must be followed in order to provide adequate numbers of subsequent pregnancies for analysis. Also, one must be concerned with the representativeness of results whenever the percentage of subjects lost to follow-up is large.

- It is crucial that an appropriate comparison be made to determine expected rates of adverse outcomes. Probably several comparison groups should be used: one composed of first-trimester aborters, one composed of women matched for age and gravidity who present themselves for prenatal care at the time of the index series' abortions; and one composed of women matched for age and parity at the time of the aborters' subsequent deliveries. Each of these comparison groups is necessary because a different question is answerable for each one, and all three questions are important: 1) Is the risk to future reproduction the same for first-trimester aborters as for second-trimester aborters? 2) Is the risk to future reproduction the same for second-trimester aborters as if they had carried these pregnancies to term? 3) Is the risk to future reproduction the same for the second-trimester aborters as if they had never been pregnant at all? Of course, for all comparison groups it is necessary to identify factors associated with risk status, such as smoking, educational attainment, parity, and age, and control for these factors through design or analysis.

These four methodologic points, in addition to the other difficulties of studying induced abortion which all studies encounter, make worthwhile investigations difficult. Nonetheless, it is possible to carry out a good study of long-term complications, and it is exceedingly important that such studies be undertaken.

REFERENCES

1. Jekel JF, Harrison JT, Bancroft DRE, et al: A comparison of the health of index and subsequent babies born to school age mothers. *Am J Public Health* 65:370, 1975.
2. United States Department of Health, Education, and Welfare: Weight at birth and survival of the newborn: by age of mother and total-birth order. *Vital Health Stat.* 21:33, 1965.
3. Daling JT, Emanuel I: Induced abortion and subsequent outcome of pregnancy in a series of American women. *N Engl J Med.* 297:1241, 1977.
4. Johnstone FD, Beard RJ, Boyd IE, et al: Cervical diameter after suction termination of pregnancy. *Br Med J.* 1:68, 1976.
5. Hogue CJR: Review of postulated fertility complications subsequent to pregnancy termination, in Sciarra JJ, Zatuchni GI, Speidel JJ (eds): *Risks, Benefits, and Controversies in Fertility Control.* Hagerstown, Md, Harper & Row, 1978.
6. Maine D: Does abortion affect later pregnancies? *Int Fam Plann Perspect.* 5:22, 1979.

7. Lindahl J: *Somatic Complications Following Legal Abortions.* Stockholm, Scandinavian University Books, 1959.

8. Hogue CJR: Low birth weight subsequent to induced abortion: a historical prospective study of 948 women in Skopje, Yugoslavia. *Am J Obstet Gynecol.* 123:675, 1975.

9. World Health Organization Task Force on the Sequelae of Abortion: Gestation, birthweight, and spontaneous abortion in pregnancy after induced abortion. *Lancet* 1:142, 1979.

10. Harlap S, Shiono P, Ramcharan S, et al: A prospective study of spontaneous fetal losses following induced abortions. *N Engl J Med.* 301:677, 1979.

11. Obel E: Pregnancy complications following legally induced abortion with special reference to abortion technique. *Acta Obstet Gynecol Scand.* 58:147, 1979.

12. Borenstein R, Ashkenazy M, Lancet M: Early complications and late sequelae of hypertonic saline induction. Presented at the 5th European Congress on Sterility and Fertility, Venice, Italy, 1979. Reported in *Ob/Gyn News,* March 1, 1979, p 46.

13. Slater PE, Davies AM, Harlap S: The effect of method of abortion on the outcome of subsequent pregnancy. *J Reprod Med.* (in press).

14. Peterson WF: Dilatation and evacuation: patient evaluation and surgical techniques. Presented at the Workshop and Postgraduate Course on Pregnancy Termination Procedures, Safety and New Developments, Nassau, Bahamas, May 23-26, 1978.

15. Hanson M: D&E midtrimester abortion. Presented at the 16th annual meeting of the Association of Planned Parenthood Physicians, San Diego, Ca, October 26, 1978.

16. Mackenzie IZ, Hillier K: Prostaglandin-induced abortion and outcome of subsequent pregnancies: a prospective controlled study. *Br Med J.* 2:1114, 1977.

17. Cates W Jr: Late effects of induced abortion: hypothesis or knowledge? *J Reprod Med.* 22:207, 1979.

18. Koller O, Eikhom SN: Late sequellae of induced abortion in primigravidae: the outcome of subsequent pregnancies. *Acta Obstet Gynecol Scand.* 56:311, 1977.

19. Hogue C: Unpublished data, 1979.

14 The Role of Health Agencies

Jean Pakter
Julian Gold

The role of public health agencies in the evaluation of abortions can be discussed from the local or the national point of view.

A state or city agency usually has the responsibility of implementing legislative decisions regarding the availability and performance of legal abortions. This responsibility may include collecting data on the number and characteristics of women having legal abortions, promulgating guidelines for the performance of abortions and evaluating the public health consequences of the available abortion services. In a prime example of such activity, despite limitations of time and a lack of prior experience in abortion surveillance and abortion epidemiology, in July 1970 the New York City Health Department established a system of abortion reporting, medical standards, and evaluation methodology that subsequently became models for state and national legislation.[1]

In order that individual state or city experiences with abortion could be put into perspective, the Center for Disease Control, through its Family Planning Division, initiated a program of abortion surveillance in 1969. CDC's objective was twofold: first, to report the number and characteristics of American women who chose abortion, and second, to identify and eliminate preventable abortion-related morbidity and mortality.

This chapter discusses the roles of the New York City Health Department and the Center for Disease Control as public health agencies in the surveillance and evaluation of induced abortions. With the recent implementation of restrictive abortion regulations by numerous city and state legislative bodies, the withdrawal of federal (Medicaid and other) funds for abortions, and the changing practices of abortion, continued evaluation of the public health consequences of abortion by responsible health agencies must be regarded as an essential public health service.

THE ROLE OF A LOCAL HEALTH DEPARTMENT: NEW YORK CITY

In April 1970, the New York State Legislature passed a bill, effective July 1, 1970, which legalized abortion of gestations up to 24 weeks. It was obvious to members of the New York City Health Department that rapid action was needed to set up an appropriate plan to ensure the accessibility of legal abortions, with the primary considerations of safety and availability. Knowledge of the potential risks associated with induced abortion was relatively limited at that time, and most physicians were frank to admit that they lacked experience in this area of medical practice. The few individuals who operated clandestinely in the prelegal period were not publicly reporting of their activities.

Accordingly, the Department's Obstetric Advisory Committee, consisting of the leading obstetricians and gynecologists in the community, was convened on an emergency basis. After a number of sessions, guidelines which embodied what were thought to be realistic and necessary safeguards were developed for the performance of abortions. After much deliberation and disagreement on the part of a minority of the Committee members who believed that during the first year all abortions (first- and second-trimester) should be performed in hospitals, it was decided to permit first-trimester procedures to be done on an ambulatory basis. If clinics were to be free standing, they were expected to have proper and adequate facilities, equipment, and staff, as well as necessary safeguards, including arrangements with a nearby hospital in case of emergency.

Although the Committee members agreed that surveillance and reporting of abortions would have been simpler if all could have been performed in hospitals, it also was apparent that no one could foresee how many women would soon be utilizing the abortion services which were about to become functional. It was obvious that many nonresidents would come into the city for pregnancy termination. On that basis alone, there was a legitimate concern that hospitals might not be able to accommodate the potential demand. Indeed, the Committee's estimates of the demand ranged from 50,000 to more than 200,000 procedures per year. The latter estimate turned out to be more accurate.

The guidelines developed by the Obstetric Advisory Committee were adopted by the Health Department in September 1970 and added to the New York City Health Code as Article 42. An additional mandate was a reporting system which entailed submission of a weekly form by all facilities. This form contained information about the numbers of abortions by trimester, the method of abortion employed, and the complications experienced. A confidential certificate of termination of pregnancy was required for every case. This certificate was and still remains confidential and not subject to subpoena. By means of these certificates, the Department was able to collect rapidly data on the demographic characteristics of the population being served, the length of pregnancy, the method of termination, and any complications. The current certificates also yield information on Medicaid and other third-party payment.

According to these guidelines, every fatality associated with abortion must be reported to the Medical Examiner's office, and a death certificate filed for each case. The number of deaths associated with abortions in the prelegal era (i.e., prior to July 1970) stands in marked contrast to the few which have occurred since the present law has been in effect. For example, in 1958 there were 45 abortion-related deaths; in 1968, 21 deaths. By 1978, however, the number was down to three (one following a legal abortion and two following "illegal" abortions). Since "illegal" abortions had constituted a leading cause of pregnancy-related deaths in the prelegal period and had motivated many individuals in public health to strive for the legalization of abortions, this striking decline is testimony to the correctness of their assumptions (Table 14-1).

From the outset it became evident that the Health Department, with its commitment to achieve and maintain high standards of care for women and their families, had an obligation to assume a major role in evaluating abortion services.

The components of evaluation included:

1. Guidelines and standards
2. Data collection, as obtained through the weekly clinic

Table 14-1
Impact of Legal Abortions on Selected New York Vital Statistics, 1968–1978

	1968	1969	1970	1971	1972	1973	1974	1975	1976	1977	1978
Birth rates (per 100,000 pop.)	18.0	18.5	18.9	16.7	14.8	14.0	14.0	13.9	14.4§	14.5§	14.0§
Infant mortality rates/1000 birth (≥ 1000 g)	23.1	24.4	21.6	20.9	19.8	19.9	19.7	19.3	19.0	17.8	17.1
All deaths associated with pregnancy	66	77	68	37	54	36	28	26	32	24	18
Puerperal mortality rate (per 10,000 pregnancies)	4.7	5.3	4.6	2.8	4.6	3.3	2.5	2.4	2.9	2.2	1.7
All Abortion Assoc. Deaths	21	24	22	12	14	7	1	3	1	1	3
(Rate per 10,000 pregnancies)	1.5	1.6	1.5	0.9	1.2	0.6	0.1	0.3	0.1	0.1	0.3
Number of deaths following illegal abortion	21	24	16	4	9	1	0	0	0	0	2
Number of deaths following legal abortion	...	...	6	8	5	6	1	3	1	1	1
Births to teenagers*											
under 15	438	489	492	376	404	388	356	395	388	345	314
15–17	6334	6709	6986	6136	6136	6187	6100	5992	5915	5934	5571
18–19	12,376	12,942	12,725	10,700	9860	9285	9316	9320	8994	9172	8802
TOTAL	19,148	20,140	20,203†	17,212	16,400	15,860	15,772	15,507	15,297	15,451	14,687

Table 14-1 *(continued)*
Impact of Legal Abortions on Selected New York Vital Statistics, 1968–1978

	6 Mos. 1970	1971	1972	1973	1974	1975	1976	1977	1978
Abortions to teenagers*									
Under 15	48†	565	638	761	778	788	738	790	604
15–17	1108†	3827	4470	5561	6317	6385	6719	6643	6900
18–19	1957†	7203	7728	9316	10,045	9953	10,284	10,345	10,834
TOTAL	3113†	11,595	12,836	15,638	17,140	17,126	17,741	17,778	18,338
Induced abortions (legal)									
Residents	19,349	67,032	70,837	81,200	85,898	81,426	83,652	86,676	89,729
Nonresidents	24,610	139,641	132,410	68,555	34,931	24,891	18,364	15,783	16,108
TOTAL	43,959	206,673	203,247	149,775	120,829	106,317	102,016	102,459	105,837

*Teenage female population increased 20.8% from 1960 to 1970 (15–19 years).
†Last half of 1970.
‡July 1970—Legalization of abortions.
§New population figure—if used, old rates would be 13.9, 14.0, 13.5.

reports and individual patient certificates (Table 14-2)
3. Special data analysis and tabulation (Tables 14-3, 14-4)

Table 14-2
Number of Legal Abortions Recorded in New York City by Residence Status, Gestation, and Method, 1971–1979

Residence Status Gestation and Method	Three-Year Periods		1977 thru Aug. 1979
	1971–1973	*1974–1976*	
Residents of New York City			
TOTAL	219,069	250,976	236,225
12 weeks or under	181,471	222,558	213,309
Over 12 weeks	37,598	28,418	22,916
Suction	153,766	212,093	209,502
D&C*	38,689	17,642	10,000
Saline	24,103	17,477	13,650
Hysterotomy	1543	476	
Hysterectomy	130	132	
Mechanical	112	3	3073
Other	726	3153	
Nonresidents			
TOTAL	340,606	78,186	42,629
12 weeks or under	272,554	59,643	32,266
Over 12 weeks	68,052	18,543	10,363
Suction	251,008	59,387	31,238
D&C*	40,657	1784	1674
Saline	46,835	16,397	9020
Hysterotomy	489	51	
Hysterectomy	23	21	
Mechanical	1193	1	697
Other	401	545	
Residents and Nonresidents			
TOTAL	559,675	329,162	278,854
12 weeks or under	454,025	282,201	245,575
Over 12 weeks	105,650	46,961	33,279
Suction	404,774	271,480	240,740
D&C*	79,346	19,426	11,674
Saline	70,938	33,874	22,670
Hysterotomy	2032	527	
Hysterectomy	153	153	
Mechanical	1305	4	3770
Other	1127	3698	

*Sharp curettage in 1978 and 1979.
Source: Vital records.

Table 14-3
Number of Deaths Recorded in New York City Associated with Legal Abortions Performed in New York City by Residence Status, Gestation, and Method, 1971–1979

Residence Status, Gestation and Method	Three-Year Periods		
	1971–1973	1974–1976	1977 thru Aug. 1979
Residents of New York City			
TOTAL	13	4	3
12 weeks or under	3	1	2
Over 12 weeks	10	3	1
Suction	2	1	2
D&C	0	0	0
Saline	6	3*	1
Hysterotomy	4	0	0
Hysterectomy	1	0	0
Mechanical	0	0	0
Other	0	0	0
Nonresidents			
TOTAL	4	1	1
12 weeks or under	0	0	0
Over 12 weeks	4	1	1
Suction	0	0	0
D&C	0	0	0
Saline	3	1	1
Hysterotomy	0	0	0
Hysterectomy	0	0	0
Mechanical	1	0	0
Other	0	0	0
Residents and Nonresidents			
TOTAL	17	5	4
12 weeks or under	3	1	2
Over 12 weeks	14	4	2
Suction	2	1	2
D&C	0	0	0
Saline	9	4*	2
Hysterotomy	4	0	0
Hysterectomy	1	0	0
Mechanical	1	0	0
Other	0	0	0

*Includes 1 saline with prostaglandin.
Note: This table does not include deaths occurring outside New York City.
Source: Vital Records.

4. Issuance of reports and bulletins based on these data—monthly and periodically in publications

Table 14-4
Legal Abortion Deaths, Ratio per 100,000 Abortions: by Residence Status, Gestation, and Method
New York City, 1971–1979

Residence Status, Gestation and Method	Three-Year Periods		
	1971–1973	*1974–1976*	*1977 thru Aug. 1979*
Residents of New York City			
TOTAL	5.9	1.6	1.3
12 weeks or under	1.7	0.4	0.9
Over 12 weeks	26.6	10.6	4.4
Suction	1.3	0.5	1.0
D&C			
Saline	24.9	17.2	7.3
Hysterotomy			
Hysterectomy	199.1		
Mechanical			
Other			
Nonresidents			
TOTAL	1.2	1.3	2.3
12 weeks or under			
Over 12 weeks	5.9	5.4	9.6
Suction			
D&C			
Saline	6.4	6.1	11.1
Hysterotomy			
Hysterectomy	47.5		
Mechanical			
Other			
Residents and Nonresidents			
TOTAL	3.0	1.5	1.4
12 weeks or under	0.7	0.4	0.8
Over 12 weeks	13.3	8.5	6.0
Suction	0.5	0.4	0.8
D&C			
Saline	12.7	11.8	8.8
Hysterotomy			
Hysterectomy	130.0		
Mechanical			
Other			

Source: Vital Records.

5. Surveillance—on-site visits and review by professional teams
6. Periodic reviews and reevaluation to assess need for change in standards or focus on emergency problems with issuance of advisories, such as: "Guidelines for Termination of Pregnancy by Saline Instillation," "Standards for Rh (D) Immune Globulin Administration," "Pathologic Examination of Tissue "
7. Working with related agencies—state, federal, and voluntary groups, especially with the Center for Disease Control
8. Investigation of complaints by patients, professionals (physicians, nurses and social workers), and citizens
9. Ascertaining reasons for patients' delay in obtaining early terminations to refuce further the number of second-trimester abortions

A published report, based on a nine-month experience in New York City, was the basis of an editorial in the *New York Times* on August 21, 1971, entitled "Year of Legal Abortion."[1] In recognition of the important role of the report, the editorial stated:

> The first year of legalized abortion in New York City has brought a substantial decline in maternal mortality. Also down significantly are the city's total birth rate and its rate of illegitimate births. Equally important in social terms, the year's experience shows that women of all ethnic and racial groups have availed themselves of the opportunity to prevent unwanted births legally—and, in many cases, at little or no cost. One happy incidental result is that all this city's shelters caring for unmarried pregnant girls have reported this year a sizeable drop in admission applications.
>
> The implications of this analysis go well beyond New York City or even New York State. The authors pointed out that New York City had been performing a national function in this initial period, since roughly 60% of the 164,300 abortions performed were obtained by women from outside the city. On the basis of their data, Pakter and Nelson estimated that there would be a national "demand" for about 1.7 million abortions annually if such operations were legal throughout the country. If this estimate is correct, New York City, which has less than 4% of the nation's population, had received almost 10% of the national "demand" for abortions. New York City's initial experience proved that large numbers of abortions can be done safely and relatively cheaply once the legal barriers are lifted. That demonstration further strengthened the case for similar liberalization of existing laws throughout the nation. While family planning remains the best way to guard against unwanted children, it is no service to society to keep on the statute books prohibitions that condemn American women to grim risks in abortion mills.

The Supreme Court's decision to liberalize abortion for the entire United States in January 1973, two and a half years after New York State's legalization, was in great measure influenced by the data gathered in New York City and cited as a reference in *Roe v. Wade*.[2] A number of other publications concerning the New York City abortion program included two-year, three-year, and five-year experiences,[3-5] evaluation of abortion-related mortality,[6-8] saline instillation risks,[9] and economic aspects related to Medicaid coverage.[10] Also investigated was the impact of the abortion program on teenage pregnancy and "repeaters."[11]

Comments

On-site visits by a team of obstetric, nursing, and social service consultants are invaluable in assessing the quality of care provided to women seeking abortions. The reports of these teams are sent to the administrators of the respective clinics and have resulted in many improvements in patient care.

With the passage of time, standards may need alteration, deletion, and/or additions. Changes in techniques and the use of new abortion modalities call for continued, ongoing evaluation. The collaboration of the medical community, especially the Obstetric Advisory Committee to the Department of Health, is essential for meaningful evaluation. In addition, data-sharing with other agencies, in particular CDC, has enhanced the evaluation process. The experience from areas outside New York City has been of value in enabling us to compare our results with those of others. The Population Council report as conducted by Tietze, a document now known as the JPSA study, was important in determining complication rates for abortions, since the trends noted in our data were comparable. This study, presently being conducted by CDC for the nation as a whole, includes New York data and is expected to continue in the future.

Periodic review and evaluation of results are indicated to establish risk vs benefits. For example, if prostaglandin appears to have lower risk than saline instillation, promotion of the former is indicated. Furthermore, if D&E is considered safer than amnioinfusion, data supporting this procedure have to be evaluated carefully before changes in techniques are recommended. If the best procedure is not yet determined, the benefits and risks of each procedure need to be presented to the public.

The local health department is an appropriate agency to receive complaints pertaining to abortion services and to investigate not only medical but also social and economic problems. Overcharging, inaccessibility of services for the poor, and lack of follow-up services after discharge are all programmatic components which must be reviewed. Complaints and inquiries may be initiated by a patient, her family, a friend, or a professional person (physician, nurse or social worker). Cases which involve a series of delays in accepting a woman for termination of pregnancy are not unknown. As a result, the gestation may proceed beyond 24 weeks, and the applicant then refused care because she is too "advanced." In other instances, delays have resulted in first-trimester pregnancies being carried over into the second trimester. Such problems merit concern by the health agency and call for corrective measures to minimize their incidence, since the risks associated with second-trimester abortions are about ten times greater than those associated with first-trimester abortions.

Some delays in obtaining abortions are attributable to patients themselves—especially among the young—because of fear, ignorance, or lack of funds. Although the percentage of second-trimester abortions has declined in the past decade from 20.7% to 10% among residents, the numbers are still too high, as are the relative risks compared to earlier terminations.

Conclusion

The roles of a local health agency, such as the New York City Department of Health, and a national health agency, such as the Center for Disease Control, in evaluation of abortion services are significant. With the transition from illegal to legal abortions, it is incumbent on a health agency, working in cooperation with the medical community, to promote and maintain high standards of care, minimize risks to the public, and preserve necessary patient safeguards while assuring accessibility of the abortion procedure. The remarkable record of decline in abortion-related deaths is evidence of such achievement.

An epidemiologic approach in collecting information as well as in data and trend analysis is essential. Information must be shared with the medical community and the public. Where revision of techniques and/or procedures is indicated, advisory groups should assist in developing effective methods of implementation. In the final analysis, however, the goal should be the reduction of the need for abortion, particularly in the second trimester.

EVALUATION OF ABORTIONS AT THE NATIONAL LEVEL

The year 1967 saw the beginning of a rapid change in the availability of legal abortion. By the end of 1969, nine states had enacted laws which permitted abortion on grounds other than for preservation of the life of the mother. Between 1967 and 1971, 17 additional states either reformed or repealed their previously restrictive laws (Table 14-5).

Table 14-5
Chronological Record of the Status of Abortion Law Changes, Abortion Reporting, and Abortion Ratios in the United States 1969, 1972, 1974, 1977

	1969	1972	1974	1977
Cumulative No. of states with reform abortion laws enacted since 1967	9	17	...*	...*
No. of states from which statewide abortion data are reported†	8	20	36	45
Additional states from which abortion data are reported from individual hospitals or facilities	2	8	15	6
Total No. of states from which partial or complete abortion data are reported†	10	28	51	51
Total No. of abortions reported to CDC	22,670	586,760	763,476§	1,079,430
National abortion ratio (abortions per 1000 live births)‡	6.3	180.1	241.6	324.5

*On January 22, 1973, the U.S. Court ruled that the Texas and Georgia abortion laws were unconstitutional, thereby nullifying all restrictive abortion laws. Interpretation of, and legislative response to, the Supreme Court decision varied from state to state.
†Beginning 1970 includes District of Columbia.
‡Live birth data are total United States births by year as reported by the National Center for Health Statistics, Monthly Vital Statistics Reports.
§Does not include 17,348 abortions for 1974 reported to the CDC after publication of the 1974 Abortion Surveillance Report.

In recognition of the national need to coordinate the surveillance of legal abortions, CDC's Family Planning Division established an Abortion Surveillance Branch in 1969. This action represented the first time the United States Public Health Service was able to deal with abortion as a public health issue and establish a unit to provide accurate and impartial data to the public, interested legislative bodies, and the medical profession. During this same year, the Center for Disease Control published its first annual Abortion Surveillance report.[12] Fewer than 25,000 legal abortions were reported by eight states that already had established centralized reporting, and by two states from which some incomplete data were available. By the end of

1972, however, 28 states reported almost 600,000 procedures. Following the Supreme Court decision in January 1973,[13] all states began to report to CDC the number and selected characteristics of women having legal abortions. By 1977, over one million abortions were reported annually (Table 14-5).

In general, CDC relies on the central health agency in each state to collect data on abortions performed within that jurisdiction. For the states that currently have no statewide data collecting system tied into a central health agency, CDC receives voluntarily reported abortion data directly from hospitals and other health facilities. The history of state abortion reporting to CDC is summarized in Table 14-5. CDC and the National Center for Health Statistics (NCHS) presently are working toward having abortion data collected as a part of the vital statistics component of the Cooperative Health Statistics System (CHSS). When this is accomplished, CDC will begin to receive statistical information from NCHS rather than directly from the states.

In addition to monitoring the number of abortions performed, CDC reports selected characteristics of women who obtain abortions. Interpretations of the temporal trends of some of these characteristics have provided invaluable reference data for evaluation of the availability and utilization of abortion services (Table 14-6). For example, in 1972, 44% of women having abortions had to travel out of their state of residence. In contrast, in 1977 only 10% had out-of-state procedures. This trend reflects the increasing availability of services and continuing community acceptance of abortion. When local and national demographic data on abortion are compared, New York City has shown the greatest change in the proportion of abortions performed on out-of-state residents. In the earlier years, especially prior to 1973, the proportion of nonresidents coming to New York City for abortions exceeded that of residents. At present, even though that proportion has dropped because most women are now able to obtain abortions in their own states, about 15% of women receiving abortions in New York City are nonresidents. Of these, a significant number come to New York City in order to have late abortions which are not available where they live.

One of the most beneficial effects of the increasing national availability of abortion services has been that abortions are now being performed at earlier gestational ages than was previously the case. In 1977, 89% of abortions were performed at less than 13 weeks' gestation, compared to 87% in 1974 and 82% in 1972. Thirty-six states and the District of Columbia report information on gestation at the time of abortion. This includes 65% of all reported abortions. Presently, national data on the characteristics of all women who obtain abortions at various gestational ages are not available. This informational deficit

Table 14-6
Selected Characteristics of Women Receiving Abortions: United States and New York City 1972, 1974, 1977

	Percent Distribution*					
	1972		1974		1977	
Characteristics	US†	NYC‡	US†	NYC‡	US†	NYC‡
Residence						
Abortion in-state	56.2	34.9	86.6	71.1	90.0	84.6
Abortion out-of-state	43.8	65.1	13.4	28.9	10.0	15.4
Age						
≤ 19	32.6	29.6	32.7	24.6	30.8	21.7
20–24	32.5	33.7	31.8	31.3	34.5	32.7
≥ 25	34.9	36.7	35.6	44.1	34.7	45.6
Race						
White	77.0	73.2	69.7	59.4	66.4	54.4
Black and other	23.0	26.8	30.3	40.6	33.6	45.6
Type of Procedure						
Curettage	88.6	87.9	89.7	87.3	93.8	90.3
Intrauterine instillation	10.4	11.7	7.8	11.9	5.4	8.6
Hysterotomy/hysterectomy	0.6	0.2	0.6	0.2	0.2	0.1
Other	0.5	0.2	1.9	0.5	0.7	1.1
Weeks of Gestation						
≤ 8	34.0		42.6		51.2	
9–10	30.7	82.5§	28.7	82.0§	27.2	88.8§
11–12	17.5		15.4		13.1	
13–15	8.4	6.4	5.5	5.7	3.4	3.6
16–20	8.2	8.4	6.5	8.3	4.3	5.5
≥ 21	1.3	2.6	1.2	3.0	0.9	2.1

*Excludes unknowns.
†Percent of all women having induced abortions in NYC during the year specified.
‡Percent of all women having induced abortions in the US during the year specified.
§12 weeks or less.

has hindered public health workers in their efforts to identify those groups of women who delay having their abortions until the second trimester. Certain states and New York City do have data cross-tabulated, however, and this information will be available in future Abortion Surveillance Reports from CDC.

The main value of coordinated national abortion surveillance is that it provides a data source. Individual states and large cities can compare the characteristics of, and outcomes for, their residents with those women obtaining abortions in other areas and in the nation.

These comparisons aid public health agencies in promulgating the abortion standards which have helped to make legal abortion one of the safest surgical procedures performed in the United States.[14] In addition, national abortion statistics have been used by the Supreme Court in making its 1973 decisions of *Roe v. Wade* and *Doe v. Bolton*[13]; in subsequent decisions in November 1975, which ruled that abortions not performed by physicians are unlawful[15]; and in July 1976, when the court ruled that prohibition of saline abortion is unlawful.[16]

In isolated instances recent legislative decisions have potentially reduced the accessibility of abortion services. At the city,[17] state,[18] and federal[19] levels, such decisions may have the effect of forcing women to delay their abortions while a) fulfilling the requirements of the restrictive legislation,[20] b) raising personal funds to pay for the procedure, or c) seeking alternatives to legal abortion.

Any delay in having an abortion after the decision to terminate the pregnancy has been made is directly associated with increased risks of morbidity and mortality. An important need thus exists for collection of accurate abortion data in order to determine the public health consequences of legislative decisions which, in some cases, have been made in contradiction to available scientific evidence.

REFERENCES

1. Pakter J, Nelson F: Abortion in New York City: the first nine months. *Fam Plann Perspect.* 3:5, 1971.
2. *Roe v. Wade* Abortion Mortality and Morbidity 208, 209 7/12/71, U.S. Dept. Health, Education & Welfare, Public Health Service, New York City.
3. Pakter J, O'Hare D, Nelson F, et al: Two years' experience in New York City with the liberalized abortion law—progress and problems. *Am J Public Health* 63:524, 1973.
4. Pakter J: A review of three years' experience with legalized abortions in New York City (from inception to six months after the Supreme Court decision). *Adv Plann Parent.* 9:8, 1974.
5. Pakter J, Nelson F, Svigir M: Legal abortion, a half decade of experience. *Fam Plann Perspect.* 7:248, 1975.
6. Tietze C, Pakter J, Berger G: Mortality with legal abortion in New York City, 1970-1972, a preliminary report. *JAMA* 225:507, 1973.
7. Pakter J, O'Hare D, Helpern M, et al: Impact of the liberalized abortion law in New York City on deaths associated with pregnancy: a two-year experience. *Bull NY Acad Med.* 2nd Series 49:804, 1973.
8. Berger GS, Tietze C, Pakter J, et al: Maternal mortality associated with legal abortion in New York State: July 1, 1970-June 30, 1972. *Obstet Gynecol.* 43:315, 1974.
9. Schiffer MA, Pakter J, Clahr J: Mortality associated with hypertonic saline abortion. *Obstet Gynecol.* 42:759, 1973.
10. Robinson M, Pakter J, Svigir M: Medicaid coverage of abortions in New York City: costs and benefits. *Fam Plann Perspect.* 6:202, 1974.
11. Daily EF, Nicholas N, Nelson F, et al: Repeat abortions in New York City: 1970-1972. *Fam Plann Perspect.* 5:89, 1973.

12. Center for Disease Control: Abortion Surveillance, annual summary, 1969. Atlanta, 1970.

13. *Doe v. Bolton*, 70-74, & *Roe v. Wade*, 70-18, U.S. Supreme Court, 1973.

14. Cates W Jr, et al: Legal abortion mortality in the United States. Epidemiologic surveillance, 1972-1974. *JAMA* 237:452, 1977.

15. *Connecticut v. Menillo*, 44 USLW 3271 (U.S. Supreme Court, 11/11/75).

16. *Planned Parenthood of Central Missouri v. Danforth* (U.S. Supreme Court, 7/1/76).

17. City of Akron (Ohio) City Council: Regulation of Abortions. Ordinance passed February 28, 1978.

18. State of Pennsylvania: The Abortion Control Act. Act No. 209 of 1974, Harrisburg, Pa.

19. Gold J, Cates W Jr: Restriction of federal funds for abortion: 18 months later. *Am J Public Health* 69:929, 1979.

20. Cates W Jr, Gold J, Selik RM: Regulation of abortion services: for better or worse? *New Engl J Med.* 301:722, 1979.

15 Recommended Procedures for Evaluation of Abortion Techniques

David A. Edelman

Numerous reports on a variety of medical and surgical techniques of abortion have been published since the legalization of abortion in the United States in the early 1970s. It often is difficult to compare the results from different studies or to interpret the results of a given study for a number of reasons, including inadequate definitions of terms, failure to describe the abortion procedure in sufficient detail, inappropriate analyses of the data, and/or failure to include other essential information.

The essential final steps necessary for any evaluation of abortion techniques are the performance of appropriate statistical analyses and an accurate interpretation of their meaning. Relatively simple methods of statistical evaluation are described in most elementary texts on the subject. The tests should be implemented as a logical consequence of a study protocol that, among other things, specifies the study design and procedures for data collection, lists the criteria for patient selection, describes the specific abortion technique, and defines outcome events.

This chapter discusses various aspects of study design as well as some of the analytical techniques that may be used to evaluate the data obtained. Also discussed is information that investigators should include in published reports to permit an adequate evaluation of a particular abortion procedure and/or to enable comparison with results from other studies.

STUDY DESIGN

Although clinical trials in which abortion techniques are randomly assigned to subjects are considered by some as the hallmark of scientific respectability, they are not always appropriate. The particular study design should always reflect the objectives of the clinical investigation. If, for example, a comparison of the relative safety and efficacy of two abortion procedures is proposed, then a trial in which procedures are randomly assigned to subjects may well be the best study design. If, on the other hand, a comparison of abortion times for two instillation procedures is all that is required, a sequential study design may be preferable. Although the sequential study design can more quickly reveal the superiority of one procedure over the other, it has been used infrequently in the evaluation of abortion procedures, probably because investigators are usually interested in more than one outcome variable. If interest were directed toward several variables, on the other hand, then several simultaneous sequential plans would be required, and this would make the investigation quite cumbersome.

Randomized trials are not necessarily the most efficient or cost-effective study designs. A comparison of the complication rates of two or more abortion procedures routinely used in a clinic might best be conducted by a retrospective analysis of the data contained in the patients' clinic charts. However, the evaluation of two types of cannulae for performing first-trimester abortions might best be accompanied by random assignment of methods to subjects. In randomized trials, there are many different methods of assigning abortion procedures to subjects. The one most appropriate to the needs of the particular study should be selected. Assignment can be made on the basis of the patient's clinic/hospital chart number, the day of the week, or a random scheme, that is, number-generated. Recently, Zelen suggested an innovative method whereby patients are randomly assigned to the standard and the experimental treatment groups.[1] Informed consent is sought only from those patients assigned to the experimental group. Patients who refuse the experimental treatment are then treated by the standard method and become part of the control group. The value of such a trial is not necessarily negated if randomization is not feasible, but the possibility of selection biases must be recognized and kept in mind at the time of data analysis.

ESSENTIAL INFORMATION

Adequate evaluation of results and comparison of specific results with the results of other studies are possible only when all essential information is provided. This information will, of course, vary with the type of abortion procedures being evaluated but must include data on those variables that may be associated with the abortion outcome. For example, for vacuum aspiration abortions, the mean estimated amount of blood loss increases with gestational age. Even in an evaluation of first-trimester abortion procedures, it is essential to obtain data on gestational age and, if possible, to evaluate complication rates as a function of this variable.

Information considered essential to the evaluation of abortion procedures includes:

Abortion technique This should include a complete description of the abortion procedure, as well as the generic name for all drugs used (anesthetic agents, premedications, abortifacients, postmedication, etc.). The schedule of drug use should also be provided.

Abortion outcome Whether the abortion failed, was complete or was incomplete, as well as whether there were any live births, should be indicated.

Side effects and complications Since the differentiation of side effects and complications is sometimes only a matter of definition, both should be reported. The time when side effects or complications occurred should be recorded as: during the abortion procedure, after completion of the abortion but before hospital/clinic discharge, or after hospital discharge. Complications resulting from secondary procedures to augment or complete a procedure also need to be reported.

Patient follow-up Events that occur after the patient's discharge from the hospital/clinic are vital to the evaluation of abortion procedures. Information obtained at follow-up should include the occurrence of complications and the contraceptive measures used by the patient.

Pertinent medical data The contraceptive method(s) used by the patient, her gestational age, the indications for the abortion, and any preexisting medical conditions should be recorded.

Sociodemographic data The patient's age, parity, and number of previous induced abortions are essential to adequate evaluation.

It is critical that all terms be well defined. Too frequently, results reported by different investigators cannot be compared because terms either were not defined or were defined poorly. Specific definitions of complete or incomplete abortion, successful or failed abortion, and gestational age are crucial to the interpretation of the results of a study and permit comparison with the results from other studies. As far as possible, definitions should be standardized.

ANALYTICAL TECHNIQUES FOR THE REPORTING OF DATA

The intent of this section is to suggest some simple ways of presenting and analyzing the data that require only the use of a basic hand calculator.

A frequency distribution table showing the number and percentage of cases in each category is a useful and simple way to display data (Example #1). Frequency distributions of variables such as age, parity, gestational age, side effects, complications, and length of hospitalization provide essential information for the evaluation of the abortion procedure. Moreover, frequency distributions can be compared using chi-square tests of homogeneity.[2] In the event that two such distributions are compared and each has only two categories (such as is seen in a "2 by 2" table), then one should use Yates' correction for continuity to the chi-square test. At times, the mean and range (maximum and minimum) of the observations may provide additional useful information (Example #2).

EXAMPLES

Example #1

Age (year)	No.	%
1–10	22	12.4
11–20	17	9.6
21–30	93	52.2
31–40	46	25.8
Total	178	100%

Example #2

The Mean Gestational Age of the group was 14.6 weeks and ages ranged from 12 to 18 weeks' gestation.

Some investigators prefer to use mean values and their standard errors rather than frequency distributions. Even if the variables were normally distributed, this method of displaying data is not very informative. For example, stating that the parity of the patients was 1.3 ± 0.2 does not indicate how many were nulliparas, multiparas, or grand multiparas.

Complication rates, evaluated either as an overall rate or as a rate of specific complications, should be computed and compared for factors thought to be related to the rates. For example, since some investigators have reported that complication rates increase with gestational age, the relationship between these two factors should be investigated. The appropriate frequency distributions can be compared using chi-square tests of homogeneity. If, as is frequently the case, there are only a "few" complications in a category and/or the sample sizes are small, the distributions should be compared using Fischer's exact test.[2]

The interval between the initiation and the completion of the abortion process frequently is a variable of interest for nonsurgical abortion procedures. Most investigators report mean instillation-to-abortion intervals (Example #3). The principal limitation of this statistic is that it necessarily excludes those patients who fail to abort. A preferable statistic is the median time from instillation to abortion (the time by which 50% of the patients abort). The cumulative distribution of abortion times will also provide valuable information in that it gives the percentage of patients aborting within any time interval (Example #4). Comparison of two cumulative distributions can be performed using the Kolmogorov-Smisnov test.[2] Comparison of medians is made with the median test.

Example #3

With one technique, eight of ten patients aborted in 4, 6, 9, 7, 3, 9, 14, and 18 hours. Therefore, the mean time which can only be calculated on the eight who aborted was 8.75 hours.

Example #4

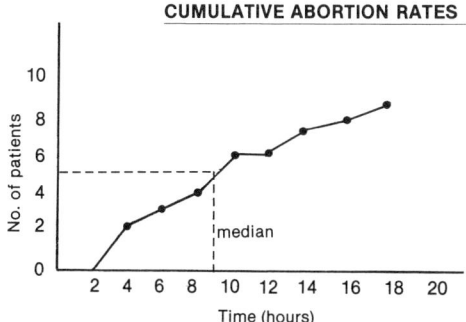

The preceding statistical tests are easy to conduct and can provide a realistic analysis of the data. When the results of any clinical tests are evaluated, however, the difference between statistical significance and clinical importance must always be considered. If a result is found to be statistically significant, it may or may not be believed to be relevant clinically.

TYPES OF ERROR

One of two types of errors can be made whenever a statistical test is performed. These errors, known as type I and type II, are illustrated in Table 15-1. The probabilities of these errors are α and β, respectively. Statistical tests are designed so that one can select α, usually chosen to be equal to or less than 0.10. The sample size (N), α, and β are interrelated. Once α and N have been specified, β is determined. For fixed N, decreasing the value of α will increase the value of β. If both α and β are to be decreased, then N must be increased. For all but simple test situations, values of β are difficult to compute. The investigator should recognize that any time the null hypothesis (the hypothesis of no difference) is accepted, there is a chance of making a type II error, namely, accepting the hypothesis when it is false. If the sample size is small, the investigator should consider performing additional evaluations before accepting this hypothesis of no effect.

Table 15-1
Types of Errors in Hypothesis Testing

Decision	Unknown State of Affairs in the Population	
	Null Hypothesis True	*Null Hypothesis* False
Reject null Hypothesis	Type I error$^\alpha$	No error
Accept null Hypothesis	No error	Type II error$^\beta$

COMMENT

Some ideas have been presented regarding the design of an abortion study, the essential information needed to evaluate the abortion procedure adequately, and the analytical techniques for the evaluation of data. The objectives of any evaluation of abortion procedures should dictate a study design leading to a trial that will provide answers to clinically important problems in a manner which is efficient, economical, and direct. The statistical procedures used for data evaluation should provide a simple presentation and clear interpretation of the study results.

This chapter was supported in part by the International Fertility Research Program and the Office of Population, United States Agency for International Development (AID pha-C-1172).

REFERENCES

1. Zelen M: A new design for randomized clinical trials. *N Engl J Med.* 300:1242, 1979.
2. Siegel S: *Nonparametric Statistics for the Behavioral Sciences.* New York, McGraw-Hill, 1956.

PART V
Related Issues

16 How Much is a Fetus Worth?

Jack W. Provonsha

The frequent association of the pro-feminist and pro-abortion movements is neither illogical nor unexpected. Both involve resistance to the traditional male-dominated social model. Men who support feministic aims often readily agree that, since women run the risk and experience the discomfort of childbearing, they should have the final say in the matter.

Unfortunately, this position raises some interesting questions. Should that final say be absolute? Does no one else have a stake in the issue—the fetus, the father, society at large? Consider the fact that society quite legitimately refuses a woman absolute rights over her newborn infant. She has no freedom to destroy it or even to abuse it at will. The *newborn* has a say, even if the rest of us temporarily must speak for it. To date, I have heard no expressions of advocacy for freedom to practice infanticide by any feminist organization with which I am familiar. Apparently, somewhere between the warm, fluid darkness of the uterus and the light of day a value transformation takes place.

A similar transformation is expressed by the thinking of those obstetricians who view the fetus, at least the early fetus, in objective or tissue terms—"the most common tumor in the female uterus." One of my medical colleagues even refuses to consider abortion as a moral issue—"It is solely a medical matter and should be left at that." However, such physicians would never allow purely medical or even preferential considerations to govern the care, or lack of it, given to the healthy newborn. Apparently for them, too, a funny thing happens on the way to the "foramen."

It is clear that much of the conflict regarding the worth of the fetus revolves around when it undergoes value metamorphosis. Does this happen:

- At conception, when supposedly it receives its human "soul" (for centuries the Church simply followed Aristotle's soul-implantation at 40 days for males and 80 days for females)?
- At implantation, when it at least has a creditable physiologic future (a consideration, by the way, legitimizing abortifacient IUDs or "morning-after injections")?
- At that mythical boundary between embryo and fetus?
- At quickening, when the fetus announces its nontumor presence (as formed the basis for Old English and Early American law)?
- At viability, with its calendar arbitrariness?
- At delivery, when most of the baby is out (as some of the older Rabbis taught)?
- At respiration, (as in Genesis where "God breathed into his nostrils the breath of life and man became a living soul")?

When does this happen ethically, not just legally? Lawyers and ethicians do not always see eye-to-eye on such matters. Law by its nature has to be precise and well-defined even if it is arbitrary—i.e., 24 weeks! Ethicians, on the other hand, lie awake at night.

The higher-level question lying behind all of this concerns the quality of humanness. What we are trying to discover is when in the course of its development does tissue come to make human claims upon us. But this question presupposes that we have decided first what it means to be human, a question that haunts most of the bioethical issues modern technology has brought forth. It even may be that, until we reach some level of consensus regarding this fundamental question, bioethics will remain the unhappy hunting ground of frustrated philosophers playing parlor games with dangling ethical questions for which there are no final answers.

The field of inquiry is divided between those who draw a qualitative distinction between man and the lesser animals and those who do not. For those who do, man usually is characterized either in terms of possessing a unique "human soul" or in terms of certain functional differences, such as the ability to make choices and to feel accountable.

On the one hand, those who choose an implanted immortal soul as that which specifically renders tissue human, have at least one advantage when it comes to the abortion issue. Conception is the only occasion in the whole course of events when something happens during a brief moment of time that is truly "momentous." Those shady gradations represented by terms like implantation, embryo/fetus, quickening, and viability are difficult to understand. Even delivery and breathing do not represent a profound modification in the fetus as much as a change in situ and an adjustment in physiology. How different is the fetus ten minutes before parturition and ten minutes after; that is, different in a way that would affect its value?

On the other hand, except for tricky theological matters such as original sin, salvation, baptism, limbo, and the like, the loss of fetal life on these terms would seem not overly important, since the little souls are immortal in any case. (Of course, to persons who hold the "soul" view, such theological matters are often crucial.)

Those who view the "soul" as referring primarily to function, who maintain that humanness signifies the ability to *do* something more than man's brute neighbors do—to reason, to choose, to become creatively accountable—are the ones in real trouble with the abortion issue. Surely embryos and fetuses do none of these things. In fact, neither do newborns, and there's the rub. Presumably it would be equally as acceptable to destroy newborns as fetuses, since both are in the same prehuman boat. Infanticide would be permissible as feticide, and feticide would be practicable ethically, if not medically, in any trimester. In this case, the human question is: "When?" When does one become accountable? At age seven? At age 12? Surely not at 24 gestational weeks. The people at U.S. Department of Health, Education, and Welfare continue to wrestle with such matters in their search for a definition of consent for experimentation. Maybe only God would know this, and unfortunately He does not seem to be talking.

The point I am trying to illustrate is that, in a pluralistic society where people's beliefs and value systems differ widely, it is difficult to achieve legal, let alone ethical, consensus. We may pass laws based upon voting majorities and may submit these laws to the scrutiny of an olympiad judiciary—which simply represents another level voting majority—but we shall experience great difficulty making everybody happy with the results, as we have all learned by now.

To achieve consensus is difficult, but we must try. What follows may be considered an attempt to bring a measure of rational tranquility into an intensifying ethical storm. It is expressed in the hope that it may even serve to promote more meaningful public practice.

I submit, the abortion issue cannot be resolved ethically by attempting to discover the precise moment when tissue becomes human. This is true, first, because a large segment of our society does not accept the old-fashioned notion of an implanted immortal "soul." In spite of the current rash of books and articles supposedly confirming the existence of life after death, I do not agree. As an unabashedly Christian believer, my conception of the hereafter is conditioned more by the Hebraic, and thus Biblical, conception of man than the platonic Greek dualism implied by the soul doctrine. But I am also tolerant of and respectful of other people's beliefs and points of view, as we all must be if we expect to live together on this troublesome planet.

Second, the abortion issue cannot be solved by finding "the moment," because all of the moments after the first are "moments" only arbitrarily. Certainly the legal definition of viability as a precise number of weeks, however necessary for a jurisprudential convenience, is nontheless artifactual.

And if one defines humanness only in terms of human function—even in terms of human function for one day, that is, in terms of choice, accountability, etc.—one opens up a host of other Pandora's boxes besides this one. We readily recoil at the prospect of legitimizing infanticide, as such a definition might. Especially would infanticide be a possibility for those individuals who, by reason of brain defect occurring in genetic or intrauterine life, can never now or in the future do any requisite human things. We have institutions overflowing with blighted persons. What would happen to such individuals if we defined humanness in these terms? These ready-made sources of nonresisting, experimental subjects and organ transplant donors have already been eyed with some eagerness. And what of *our* responsibilities toward those who can do certain things no longer—our senile, demented elderly? They, too, are "cluttering up" our institutional and financial landscape.

It is possible, of course, to grant intrinsic worth to a fetus, at whatever stage, even as an embryo, on grounds other than its "soul." Embryos and fetuses are of greater value than mere tissue largely because of what they may become. They borrow at least a part of their value from that possible future. But they also possess other "intrinsic" values to those of us who are sensitive to such things. The marvel that is the genetic code! As soon as all of those genes and chromosomes have come together, it has happened. Those fantastic, incredible things that will be taking place over the weeks, months, and years that follow are already established in that microscopic miracle of creation. Forgive the hyperbole, but one is almost tempted to bow one's head in awe and reverence at the vision. Personally, I cannot understand how molecular and cellular biologists can avoid becoming deeply religious people.

But even if fetuses and embryos have no really human future because of genetic or other defect, their value still transcends mere tissue-value because of another quality that defines humanness. And this is my main contribution to the ongoing discussion.

Genus *homo* along with his *sapiens* and *faber* qualities possesses another quality that is in a measure derived from these others. He is *Homo symbolicus*. None of these qualities is possessed in absolute degree, of course, but their relative extent is so great that we can almost speak of absolute distinctions between man and even his nearest relatives.

By *Homo symbolicus* we refer to that quality in man that enables him to posit "representative" values. The term "symbol" in this case indicates any entity, object, thing, action that "refers to," "points to," or "stands for" something else. That which serves a "representative" function may, of course, also have its own greater or lesser intrinsic non-referring value.

It is this gift in man that forms the basis of most of his "human" activities. It is the basis, for example, of his articulate speech. Sounds, or inscriptions, come to have "meaning" for those in on the secret. When one reads or listens to another talking, one does not merely see markings on the paper or hear sounds; one "sees" and "hears" ideas. The markings and sounds are thus "symbolic." They refer. This gift is also the basis for human intellect. Most of human thought, once the language structure is established, is verbal (symbolic) thought.

The use of symbols is the foundation for most of our complex social interactions, including the economic. Without the ability to attribute "representative value" to pieces of paper, bars of metal, shiny pieces of carbon, or whatever (some of which might be relatively worthless intrinsically), all of the "Wall Streets" of the world would grind to a screeching halt and we should be reduced to crude barter economics—a sack of wheat for a shirt or a pair of shoes.

Symbols are thus enormously useful to humans at all levels of life. And they are not to be taken lightly if humanness is to persist. Religious people always have understood their significance, in part because of another feature of symbols. They not only stand for and thus communicate, but they also condition attitudes, including value attitudes, toward the reality symbolized. The way one treats or regards the symbol may very greatly affect one's attitudes toward that to which the symbol points or refers. This is why religion generally has abounded with symbolic richness. Some religious structures almost overwhelm us with a sense of awe and reverence just by our stepping inside them. A holy book becomes a holy object because it "points to"; that is, it "represents" what religion is about.

It is this symbolic quality in man that is too frequently overlooked in the issue before us. To illustrate it most effectively, let us take a brief look at the opposite end of life. May I illustrate from a patient of my own? She was a lady in her late 70s who had suffered a number of small strokes which diminished her capacity in a variety of ways. She had become something of a care problem, but was still kept in the home of her daughter who loved and looked after her.

One night the daughter called in great distress, "Doctor, please come; something terrible has happened to mother." I arrived at the home a short time later to find the old lady lying in bed in a profound coma; her respiration was labored and erratic, her pulse irregular and difficult to palpate. It took no special degree of medical acumen to recognize that a serious cerebral accident had occurred and that her survival was in question.

She was taken by ambulance to the hospital, where further observation confirmed the seriousness of her condition. I tried to prepare the daughter for the obvious. Her thoughtful response after listening to my portrayal of the situation was, "Doctor, I don't think I want you to do anything for mother."

Now, of course, she did not mean that to be taken literally. What she was thinking of was all of those fancy gadgets, respirators, cardiac pacemakers, and the like, by which we can almost endlessly prolong the dying process these days. Understanding this, I replied, "There really isn't very much we can do for your mother." (This was not strictly true, either. What I meant was "to bring her back to normal mental function.") "But," I went on, "we will do all we can to keep her comfortable."

Now, whom was I treating? The daughter, of course. There was no reason for her decision to leave her with a residue of guilt. But I was also treating *me*, and the nurses and others who were responsible for her care. I obviously was not directing my remark to the patient, who by definition (deep coma) was about as "comfortable" as anyone can become.

But the facts were, and are, that I care about my attitude toward people. I want to preserve my humaneness, my compassion. The old woman was no longer "human" by any functional definition. She was already a "functional" corpse, and we probably could have kept her cadaver pulsatile for a fairly long time if we had hooked her up to the "gadgets." Nonetheless, she still *meant* human at this point in her life and thus retained human, albeit symbolic, claims upon us. And until the changes could be placed on that symbol so that she could come to mean corpse—and we have fairly well-established, even ritualistic, ways of doing this—it was important that we honored the claims of that symbolic human life for our sakes.

I submit that what was true at the end of life also speaks to life at its beginnings. Symbols are usually not consciously created, though they may be consciously, or even unconsciously, destroyed. Symbolic values can be desymbolized as when, for example, we objectify and depersonalize those individuals to whose human claims upon us we do not wish to listen. The horrors of war such as the My Lai incident with Lt. Calley and his associates come easily to mind, as do the revelations of the Nuremburg trials in Germany.

But the original claims come to us out of our traditions and collective experiences. Fetuses have always generally meant something special. One does not carry a fetus as one "carries" an appendix. One is "with child"; one is "going to have a baby." And that's one of the things that has kept human life human since time immemorial. It is this attitude that provides the open arms at parturition—and thus a sense of acceptance of and value for children without which there can be tragic deprivation.

We can "de-symbolize" fetuses, too. In fact, we seem to be doing so in some segments of our society. But we had better take a long look at the general consequences of this tendency, if what I have been suggesting about the attitude-conditioning potential of symbols is true. To "de-symbolize" may also be to "devalue," and we have enough of that going in our society to keep us all awake nights.

SUMMARY

To summarize: What is a fetus worth? The fetus may gain its value from several directions, depending upon one's beliefs and personal value system. It can be of value as one possessing a human "soul." In a pluralistic society, unfortunately for consensus, not all share that belief. It can be of value as a "miracle of creation" with profound future potential. This is a position I share with some, but I realize not with everybody. It also can be of value because of our collective concern with keeping human life human on this planet. This is one concern that I think is generally shared by us all. But to protect that concern means we must also be prepared to protect those supporting symbolic values that serve it. This includes looking after the marginal, even submarginal, individuals among us. It includes protecting our ability to feel compassion for our senile elderly. It also includes resisting fetal devaluation.

To be sure, there are times when values, even human values, compete, and ethics must also wrestle with these times. Often, in order to resolve the conflict, it is necessary to decide that one value is more important than another. What this means, in the present case, is that sometimes a fetus (as a symbol) may be sacrificed because of its threat to the humanness (not merely the life—humanness is a quality of life) of its mother. The thing symbolized always stakes a prior claim over the symbol. This must *never* be accepted unless that threat is severe enough to require it—a judgment, I suggest, involving all of the persons directly concerned. An abortion must *never* become a trivial action. The devision must *always* be carefully considered even if finally it rests in the hands of the pregnant woman. There *always* should be counseling. It ought *always* to pain our souls a little for the sake of all of us and our common humanity. We should all be prepared to share the burden, *and* we ought to be prepared to pay the bill. Providing viable alternatives to abortion could be a costly matter, but I submit that, on the above terms, a fetus is worth it.

Naturalist Edwin Way Teale once said somewhere, "It is those who have compassion for all life who will best safeguard the life of man. Those who become aroused only when man is endangered become aroused too late." Perhaps this also applies to symbolic man as well as to "endangered species." Come to think of it, man, at least moral man, may be the most endangered species of all.

17 Social Issues

Henry P. David

More papers have been published on abortion than on any other type of surgery. No elective surgical procedure has evoked as much public debate, generated such ethical and moral controversy, or received greater attention from the media.[1] Abortion is as much a social issue as it is a medical concern. It poses dilemmas for all concerned.

This chapter will attempt to place second-trimester abortion in a social perspective, because the prevention of unwanted pregnancy and early abortion both are preferable to the emotionally and financially more costly second-trimester termination procedures. Within this context, the following issues will be considered: historical trends in the United States, the incidence of delayed abortions and the social costs resulting therefrom, known sociodemographic and psychosocial characteristics of second-trimester abortion patients, service provider influences, and, finally, proposed strategies of social intervention.

HISTORICAL TRENDS

In early nineteenth century America, withdrawal or *coitus interruptus* was the most commonly practiced form of contraception. In the year 1800 not a single jurisdiction in the United States had any statute restricting the practice of abortion. Abortion early in pregnancy not only was quite common but was condoned as a means of terminating unwanted pregnancies, particularly among young unmarried or economically deprived women.[2,3] Few people at that time expressed moral qualms about the practice of abortion. It was widely assumed that the fetus was not really alive until the woman felt the first recognizable fetal movement, popularly called "quickening" in the 16th to 18th week of pregnancy, although its occurrence varies a great deal from woman to woman.[4] At that time there were no reliable tests for diagnosing pregnancy, so "quickening" was considered a sure test that a woman really was pregnant. Other early signs of pregnancy always could be explained on the assumption that something might be "blocking" normal menstrual cycles. The medical procedures for restoring menstrual flow at that time were similar to those of inducing early abortion. Potions designed to remove an obstruction to menstruation were described in home medical guides and were easily available from physicians, midwives, and pharmacists. According to Mohr, "The practice of aborting unwanted pregnancies was, if not common, almost certainly not rare in the United States during the first decades of the nineteenth century."[2] Considering the state of social development in the colonial era, there was considerable compassion for the woman involved. Indictments for abortion were seldom brought before American courts, which regularly sustained the most lenient interpretations of the "quickening" doctrine.

On the other side of the Atlantic in England, during the reign of George III in 1803, Lord Ellenborough's Act made procurement of an abortion before "quickening" a felony "to be punished by fine, imprisonment, or exposure in the pillory, or that the criminal may be publicly or privately whipped or transported beyond the sea for any term not exceeding 14 years."[5] Procuring an abortion after "quickening" was considered murder, punishable by death. This Act later was modified under George IV and supplanted during Queen Victoria's reign by the Offences Against the Person Act of 1861, which decreed surgical abortion at any stage of pregnancy a criminal offense, punishable by life imprisonment.[6,7]

Not to be outdone by the legal system held in such high esteem by the former colonies, the first law dealing specifically with the legal status of abortion in the United States was passed in 1821 by the General Assembly of Connecticut. It restricted the administration of a "noxious or destructive substance...to any woman then quick with child."[8] Surgical abortion before "quickening" was first prohibited by a section of the New York Revised Statutes of 1829 (enacted in 1828). The New York legislation was the earliest Anglo-American statute containing an express therapeutic exception, justifying abortion "if necessary to preserve the life of the mother."[9]

A review of documents contemporary with the passage of the New York State legislation demonstrates that the primary concern at the time was *not* with the unquickened fetus but rather with protecting the life and health of women who had unwanted pregnancies from damage by abortion, since every operation in this pre-Lister era of medicine entailed the possibility of life-threatening infection. The emphasis of the New York legislators on preventing unnecessary surgery is reflected in their decision to place the abortion statute in the Penal Code instead of the Medical Practices Act, where every previous or subsequent law governing medicine and surgical procedures is to be found.

The evolution of abortion legislation in the United States was linked to the evolution of medical training and practice, and remained so throughout the nineteenth century. Prior to the Civil War, most American medical schools were operated as proprietary businesses and competed for paying students. Few applicants were denied admission. By the mid-nineteenth century, medical and nonmedical abortionists flourished. Using appealing forms of advertising, it was possible to develop businesses earning more than a million dollars a year (in 1845 dollars!).

After the founding of the American Medical Association in 1847, organized efforts were gradually launched to professionalize medical training, as well as to upgrade the quality of health services, and to obtain legal and public recognition of the professional status of physicians. Early antiabortion campaigns portrayed doctors fighting the health risks associated with botched abortions and opposing the brazen advertisements of greedy abortionists. For example, in 1864 the American Medical Association offered a prize for the most popular antiabortion essay.[2]

The antiabortion movement was particularly supported by upper-class, white Anglo-Saxon Protestants who were anxious about declining birthrates among native-born married women, and concerned about the reproductive potential of new immigrants. It also was supported by feminists who counseled abstinence as the only sure protection against unwanted pregnancy and who perceived abortion as an undesirable by-product of the suppression of women. The latter supporters eventually were joined in their campaign by the antiobscenity crusaders.[10]

Somewhat curiously, the religious press maintained almost complete silence about abortion. Until 1865, Protestant churches concurred with earlier Catholic theological views that therapeutic abortion was not a sin before "quickening," the moment at which the fetus was believed to gain life and acquire a soul.[3,6,10] The reversal of this position by some Protestant clergy at the behest of the American Medical Association was strengthened in 1869 when Pope Pius IX issued his decree banning all abortion, even to save the life of the woman. However, neither the Protestant nor the Catholic religious establishments became conspicuously involved in the antiabortion stand of organized medicine. After the Civil War, more and more American states dropped traditional "quickening" doctrines and revoked common law immunities for pregnant women. By 1900, abortion was illegal in all American jurisdictions and remained so for nearly 70 years.[2] The American Medical Association was recognized as the primary arbiter of medical training and practice.

The historical context of abortion-related legislation is particularly important with regard to second-trimester abortion.[10] Most nineteenth-century women considered abortion before "quickening" as their right. Potions to stimulate late or irregular menstruation were advertised widely in family newspapers as "female regulators."[11,12] It was understood, however, that a woman's right to control her body changed the moment she felt fetal movement and became aware of another being moving within her body. That difference in a woman's perceptions continues to have importance to this day and strongly influences the ethics as well as the emotions about second-trimester abortion.[13]

INCIDENCE

Fortuitously, the proportion of second-trimester abortions has declined steadily from 17.9% of all abortions in 1972 to 8.5% in 1977. This represents a drop of more than 52% in the six years for which data are available.[14] On the basis of the 1,277,000 total abortions estimated by the Alan Guttmacher Institute to have been performed in the United States during 1977,[15] and the proportions of second-trimester procedures suggested by the Center for Disease Control's calculations, it is likely that about 118,000 abortions were performed beyond 12 weeks' gestation in 1977.[16] International comparisons suggest that the United States continues to rank high among the countries of the world in the reported proportion of second-trimester abortions.[17] Even if this statement is correct, one must recognize that few abortions are performed anywhere at more than 20 weeks' gestation, even when legally permitted. For example, only about 0.4% of all legal abortions in the United Kingdom[18] and 0.9% in the United States in 1977[14] fell into this category.

ECONOMIC AND SOCIAL COSTS

Termination of pregnancy in the second trimester is associated with higher mortality and complication rates, is more expensive, and often requires more technical skill on the part of the operator.[17,19] Indeed, the mortality rate increases by approximately 50% for each week of delay after eight weeks' gestation.[20-23] This higher risk to health is accompanied by greater financial expenditures and probabilities of psychological trauma, all of which increase direct and indirect social costs.

LIMITATIONS OF PSYCHOSOCIAL RESEARCH IN THE UNITED STATES

Psychosocial research on abortion in the United States has been handicapped by the absence of a uniform national reporting system. It thus has been difficult to obtain nationally representative population samples from public or private facilities providing second-trimester abortions. Further problems are the lack of comparability between local and regional studies, limited services available prior to the 1973 Supreme Court decision, and the absence of standardized instruments for the assessment of psychosocial determinants.[24] All of these constraints tend to make it difficult to generalize about sociodemographic characteristics and psychosocial patterns associated with abortion delay in the United States, or to develop practical health information and educational methodologies oriented either to special groups of women at risk, service providers, or community policy makers.

Most available major, published psychosocial research studies of second-trimester abortion patients were conducted during the early 1970s, in the period just before the January 1973 Supreme Court decision. At that time, second-trimester abortion procedures were legally available in only a few major metropolitan centers and often were performed amid considerable public turmoil and acrimonious debate within the medical profession.[25] Frequently, patients had to travel long distances to receive care. Two more recent studies, however, both as yet unpublished, have attempted to compare first- and second-trimester abortion patients from localities where both procedures were easily available and accessible to local residents. An interview study of 1066 first- and second-trimester abortion patients in Washington, DC, all of whom resided within 50 miles of the downtown area, was conducted in late 1974 and 1975 by Burr and Schulz.[26] In addition, a comparative analysis of 1004 medical records of first- and second-trimester abortion patients at three Boston hospitals and one outpatient facility subsequently was prepared for CDC by Cannon-Bonventre, Kahn, and Engelman.[27] These two studies will be cited in this chapter as the Washington Study and the Boston Study, respectively.

Interpretation of social and psychological findings depends, in part, on methodologic considerations.[28] For example, evidence for intrapsychic or unconscious conflict most frequently is derived from clinical case studies. These introduce the bias of self-selection, since the overwhelming majority of women report feelings of relief after abortion and do not seek psychological therapy. Nonetheless, abortion generally is experienced as a stressful event.[29,30] Much of this stress is associated with the discovery and acknowledgment of an unwanted pregnancy, the need for a decision to terminate or carry to term, and the concern (for many women) about where and how to obtain a legal abortion. Clearly, psychosocial considerations are important, not only in terms of the after-effects of an abortion but also as they relate to reactions surrounding the discovery of an unwanted pregnancy, the stress of the decision-making process, and the experience of having had and terminated an unwanted pregnancy.

SOCIODEMOGRAPHIC CHARACTERISTICS

The Joint Program for the Study of Abortion, the first major study of abortion following the liberalization of abortion statutes in several states, found the highest proportion of late abortions occurring among the youngest women.[31,32] This observation has been confirmed by nearly all other researchers.[17,27,33-43] For example, in Boston the 15- to 19-year-old age group constituted over 66% of all women aborting in the second trimester.[27] Age was not found to be a key factor in Washington,[26] but a recent report on resident New York City women indicated that 37% of all late aborters in 1978 were teenagers.[43] National data compiled by the Center for Disease Control suggest that adolescents seek and obtain about 45% of all second-trimester abortions.[44]

Because age frequently is correlated with other factors, it is not surprising that women who have second-trimester abortions are most often single, nulliparous, undereducated, and poor. Many are students with limited financial resources. Even though age is a recognized demographic variable by itself, it also often serves as an indicator of the level of psychosocial development, maturity, and experience, all of which influence the response to an unwanted pregnancy.

Presently available data suggest that black women are at greater risk for both first- and second-trimester abortions than are non-black women in the United States population. In particular, black women are overrepresented among those who seek late abortions; however, the lack of uniformity in recording ethnic groups leaves this observation open to some question.[16,27,42,45]

Religious preferences of both first- and second-trimester abortion patients tend to follow local patterns and do not seem to be associated with delayed pregnancy termination. For example, Catholics in Boston constituted the highest percentage of women seeking second-trimester abortions, followed by Protestants. Jewish women were the only group with a substantially lower proportion of abortions in the second trimester,[27] but the number of Jewish women in the general population is low. In those studies where reasonably reliable information on prior terminations was available, repeaters tended to seek subsequent abortions earlier.

Economic disadvantage has become an increasingly important determinant among the sociodemographic factors relating to abortion, especially after the December 1977 Congressional legislation banning the use of federal money for abortions except in narrowly defined, life-threatening situations, in cases where two physicians certify that continuation of pregnancy would result in severe and long-lasting physical damage, and in cases of "promptly" reported rape or incest.[46] The US Supreme Court already had ruled on June 20, 1977 that states and localities need not pay for "nontherapeutic" abortions for indigent women (even though state and local governments pay for childbearing and other pregnancy-related expenses), and that public hospitals need not provide such abortions.[46] According to Department of Health, Education, and Welfare reports, federal abortion claims were reduced by 99% following implementation of these Congressional directives.[47] Subsequently, restrictions on availability of public funds were found to be significantly associated with later gestational age at time of abortion.[48]

PSYCHOSOCIAL CHARACTERISTICS

There is probably no psychologically painless way to deal with an unwanted pregnancy, whether it be interrupted voluntarily or carried to term. Psychologic variables and emotional patterns[24,30,49-51] will be considered in greater detail in other chapters of this monograph (see Chapters 18 and 19). Among the most frequently cited problems in studies of second-trimester abortion are: ambivalence about the abortion decision, hesitation or fear of confiding in partners or parents, and late recognition or denial of pregnancy until signs and symptoms become obvious.

Very late abortions, performed after women have experienced "quickening," appear to be followed by more severe psychologic reactions than procedures performed earlier in gestation.[52] The strongest negative reactions are likely to occur in women who were persuaded or coerced into an abortion by their partners or parents.[53,54] In addition, by the time some teens finally confront their pregnancy, it may be too late to arrange termination.[55] Interviews with second-trimester abortion patients, their partners or parents, and with professional staff, all suggest a wide range of external constraints and internal conflicts impinging on abortion decision.[25,27,33,35,53,55-57] External conflicts may surround a lack of information on availability or location of services, financial difficulties, bureaucratic delays, parental notification requirements, and inaccurate medical or laboratory diagnoses. Some conservative physicians advise young patients that it is too early to tell whether they are pregnant, and foster delay by telling them to return after having missed another period. In certain communities so-called informed consent laws, currently under challenge by the American Civil Liberties Union, have made it more difficult and time-consuming to obtain an abortion.[58] Weeks pass quickly when a woman is able to come to a clinic only on specific days or when clinics operate only at certain hours.

It generally is agreed that psychological conflict is experienced more often by young, unmarried religious women.[30,51] In part, such a reaction may derive from a perceived lack of support for the abortion decision by parents or partners.[59,60] In the Washington Study, women were unusual in the sense that they were late in first suspecting their pregnancies and late in obtaining confirmations.[26]

The strongest single determinant for seeking late abortions in the Washington Study was a history of irregular menstrual periods. This finding is consistent with the idea that biological differences may play a role in determining the ease of recognizing pregnancy. At the same time, no particular constellation of sociodemographic or psychosocial characteristics differentiated between first- and second-trimester aborters. Individually oriented factors prevailed. It was recognized, however, that psychologic factors could influence menstrual cycle regularity and particularly the perception of early pregnancy.[26]

It is reasonable that "a complex behavioral outcome such as delay in seeking abortion cannot be expected to have a simple explanation."[16] While many factors impinge on the decision-making process, age appears to be of paramount importance, along with its correlates of maturity, education and socioeconomic status.

There is general agreement on the importance of psychosocial factors in abortion delay, but little consensus on the interplay of lack of information, administrative or institutional barriers, and the woman's inability to cope with conflict, feelings of powerlessness, and an environment believed to be hostile.[24] Most observers agree, however, that considerable contraceptive risk-taking has taken place among women seeking second-trimester abortions. For example, while two-thirds of first- and second-trimester abortion patients in Boston did not practice contraception before coming for their abortions, those women whose records indicated either no use of contraception or irregular use were more often in the second-trimester group.[27]

SERVICE PROVIDER INFLUENCES

Medical and allied health personnel are central to the equitable and effective provision of abortion services. As "gatekeepers," they control access to abortion and are involved in virtually every aspect of the patient's care, from early referral to postabortion counseling and follow-up. The attitudes of these individuals increasingly are the subject of psychosocial research in fertility regulation.

For many physicians and nurses, performing abortions represents an ethical and moral dilemma, presenting conflicts between a personal commitment to save lives and the recognition of a woman's right to decide to terminate her unwanted pregnancy.[61-65] Conditions of medical and nursing practice, perceptions of professional roles, and the woman's economic status seem to be interrelated. Women with greater economic resources historically have had far fewer difficulties than economically disadvantaged women in obtaining abortions from qualified physicians, regardless of whether the desired abortion was legal or illegal.[10] Non-university-affiliated physicians practicing primarily among low-income groups often tend to express more conservative attitudes.[66] Inequity is increased in those areas where private prejudice is permitted to become public policy, because physicians and hospital administrators indeed can refuse to perform or to permit the performance of legal abortions.[67]

The medical staff dilemma is particularly apparent in the choice of procedure for a second-trimester abortion. If a woman requests termination during the 14th week, should the physician wait until week 16 or 17, relying on intraamniotic instillation of either saline or prostaglandin, or proceed immediately with dilatation and evacuation.

Although the instillation technique is psychologically easier for the physician, it is more difficult for the patient, since it requires a 12 to 36 hours' hospital stay, labor, and the trauma of delivering a dead fetus with recognizable features. Recent experience with the D&E method suggests that this method is safer than either saline or prostaglandin, far less time consuming, considerably less expensive, useful in the "grey" zone of the 13 to 16 weeks' gestational interval, and associated with reduced pain and risk of psychologic trauma for the woman[19,21,44,50,68-71] (Chapter 10).

These considerations notwithstanding, fetal dismemberment is difficult to perform and to witness. The D&E procedure increases the psychologic burden for the operating room staff, who perceive themselves as more involved, thus compounding the emotional stress and distaste engendered by abortion. Second-trimester D&E requires a personal "commitment to choice, to abortion, to woman's rights and to the necessity for these procedures."[72] Larger cannulae which help to reduce the visible aspects of fetal dismemberment seem to make the procedures easier and more acceptable to staff.[73]

Within this context of personal dilemma, it is important to recall that courses in human sexuality, contraception, and abortion are relatively recent additions to training programs in medical and nursing schools.[74-76] Because physicians and nurses are protected by conscience clauses in prevailing statutes, many decline to staff abortion services. As a consequence, eight out of ten United States counties did not have a single abortion facility as late as 1976.[15] As long as obstetricians-gynecologists and allied health professionals remain ambivalent about legal/moral issues, it is not surprising that their personal feelings about abortions become major determinants of health personnel's responses to women's requests for terminating unwanted pregnancies, whether in the first or second trimester.

SOCIAL INTERVENTION STRATEGIES

A recent study in selected metropolitan Washington, DC high schools indicates that adolescent peer counselors are knowledgeable about teenage sexual behavior, can identify major reasons for wanted and unwanted pregnancies, and can make practical recommendations for a community trying to cope with teenage problem pregnancies.[77] Among their suggestions are:

- Greater parental initiative in talking about sex and pregnancy
- Revision of school sex education programs to place more

emphasis on women's needs and communication with men
- Assertiveness training for young women
- Development, marketing, and distribution of an effective nonprescription contraceptive acceptable to teenagers

A 1978-1979 national probability sample survey of 1254 American families confirms that teenagers are more prepared for and comfortable with family discussions about human sexuality than are their parents.[78] Experience with groups of parents yields innumerable examples of reluctance to talk about sexual behavior with teenagers.[79] Some parents feel threatened by their children's sophistication and allow misconceptions about contraception to persist. New community approaches must be developed and supported if the adolescent's request for parental help and understanding is to be accommodated.[80] For example, some adolescents may prefer discussions with parents of other teenagers, just as some parents may feel more at ease with other people's children. While many teenagers want to be encouraged that it is one of their prerogatives to say "no" to peer pressures for sex, they also need to be informed about responsible sexual behavior and the resolution of problem pregnancies.

To a considerable extent, ignorance about the health risks associated with second-trimester abortion is due to the timidity of schools in aggressively offering programs which provide such information. The cautious, unobtrusive, low-profile approach to teenage sexuality, contraception, and abortion frequently reflects the higher priority given to preventing hostile parental reactions than to preventing problem pregnancies.[81,82] In other words, the school system is addressing parental rather than student needs.

Among the exceptions to this statement is an adolescent peer counseling program in family planning pioneered by Planned Parenthood/Metropolitan Washington in several Washington, DC public schools in 1975. Planned Parenthood also operates a clinic one day a week at a local high school. This is the first family planning facility in the country located on the premises of a public school. Counseling and contraceptive services are easily accessible. Peer counselors learn to be sensitive to female students' needs in response to perceived male pressures. Peers also work at strengthening female assertiveness and encouraging realistic discussions of sexuality and contraception. Sometimes it can be harder to talk about sex than to do it.

Many teenagers do not know where to get help. Public and private service providers often neglect to advertise or conduct "outreach" programs in high-risk areas. As a result, too many young people find information or help only after they suspect pregnancy. Even then, they often feel threatened by professional staff, some of whom may feel equally uncomfortable about interacting with young, sexually active teenagers. Although mature minors now have the legal right to pregnancy termination, many private hospitals still refuse to perform abortions on anyone under age 18 without parental permission or notification.[55] Misinformation and myths about abortion only heighten a susceptible woman's fears and anxieties.

Few women seeking second-trimester abortions are sufficiently sophisticated to inquire about the preferred method of termination. D&E is much less painful and traumatic for the woman, as well as less costly. It is clearly in the woman's interest, as well as in society's, to choose this procedure whenever such a choice is available.[83-85] There will be a continued need for individual counseling to help a woman to anticipate and cope with the stresses so often associated with abortion. Counseling should also be available (when indicated) for the woman's sexual partner or for the woman and man together.

The continuing controversy surrounding abortion influences the way the media react to or, more often, ignore the subject. Since teenagers tend to depend on one another for information about pregnancy resolution, many inaccurate beliefs go uncorrected. Among these are the notions that abortion always requires parental consent, is a gruesome ordeal, and always results in subsequent sterility. These misconceptions and fears are aggravated by antiabortion literature, which may be the only written commentary some teenagers have read.[85] Attempts to disseminate more accurate information, and thereby reduce the incidence of postponed abortions, should be directed to teenagers.[86] Such communication should convey:

- The advantages of early decisions on pregnancy resolution
- The health benefits of early recognition of pregnancy symptoms
- The increased health risks and greater financial and emotional costs associated with second-trimester abortions

A social intervention strategy must be conspicuously aggressive if it is to succeed. Since high visibility surely will engender opposition, care must be taken from the very beginning to assure support from policy makers in the schools, selected churches, and the media.

There is a growing recognition that decisions about contraceptive risk-taking are highly individual.[87] Persons seeking advice about contraception or pregnancy resolution are usually "healthy." Their inquiries more often reflect personal anxieties rather than perceptions of "illness." Such individual perspectives easily can come into conflict with medical orientation. As noted by Potts, "A great many doctors attempt to cast decisions concerning fertility regulation in the traditional medical context...(and) will often perform abortions to save a woman's physical health, but not to preserve the economic health of the family."[88]

The process of obtaining an abortion greatly alleviates the social stigma of an unwanted pregnancy.[30,51] Perceived within that context, a physician technically implements a woman's personal choice rather than diagnoses or treats a disease. This change in the physician's role is perhaps a greater divisive influence in the abortion debate than the widely discussed moral and theological issues.[88]

Fertility regulation has been proclaimed a basic human right by the United Nations. Although individual physicians have led the fight for improved availability and accessibility of high quality services, organized medicine in the United States historically has been reluctant to support family planning services unless established and operated under strict medical controls.[2,10,89] By definition, second-trimester abortion is a medical procedure. One way to reduce its incidence is to speed the development of new and highly effective vaginal barrier methods of contraception which are acceptable to adolescents. There is also a need for a more sophisticated social marketing approach which builds on the experience of community-based distribution programs, is backed by wide dissemination of informational materials, and supported by persuasive advertising on radio and television.

It is time to recognize that our concern is with healthy human beings and to join with others in social intervention strategies designed to enhance responsible reproductive behavior, particularly among those most at risk for delayed abortion decisions.

REFERENCES

1. David HP: Abortion: a continuing debate. *Fam Plann Perspect.* 10:313, 1978.

2. Mohr JC: *Abortion in America: the origins and evolution of national policy, 1800–1900.* New York, Oxford University Press, 1978.

3. Means CC: A historian's view, in Hall R (ed): *Abortion in a Changing World.* New York, Columbia University Press, 1970, 1:16, 2:137.

4. Hellman LM, Pritchard JA, Wynn RM: *Williams' Obstetrics,* 14th ed. New York, Appleton-Century-Crofts, 1971.

5. Hodge HL: *Foeticide or Criminal Abortion.* Philadelphia, Lindsay & Blakiston, 1869.

6. Williams G: *The Sanctity of Life and the Criminal Law.* New York, Knopf, 1957.

7. Dickens BM: *Abortion and The Law.* Bristol, England, MacGibbon & Kee, 1966.

8. *The Public Statute Laws of the State of Connecticut,* 1821, p 152.

9. Means CC: The law of New York concerning abortion and the status of

the foetus, 1664-1668: a case of cessation of constitutionality. *NY Law Forum* 14:411, 1968.

10. Gordon L: *Woman's Body, Woman's Right.* New York, Grossman/Viking, 1976.

11. Callahan D: *Abortion: Law, Choice and Morality.* New York, Macmillan, 1970.

12. Davis G: *Interception of Pregnancy.* London, Angus & Robertson, 1974.

13. Rooks JB: Personal communication, 1979.

14. Center for Disease Control: *Abortion Surveillance, 1979.* Atlanta, issued 1979.

15. Forrest JD, Tietze C, Sullivan E: Abortion in the United States, 1976-1977. *Fam Plann Perspect.* 10:271, 1978.

16. Burr WA, Schulz KF, Cates W Jr: Causes and correlates of delayed abortion: a critique of the literature. Unpublished data, 1979.

17. Tietze C: *Induced Abortion: 1979*, 3rd ed. New York, Population Council, 1979.

18. Registrar General: *Supplement on Abortion.* London, HM Stationery Office, 1973.

19. Tietze C: Safety and health hazards of abortion. *J Obstet Gynaecol.* (Singapore) 9:49, 1978.

20. Cates W Jr, Schulz KF, Grimes DA, et al: The effect of delay and method choice on the risk of abortion morbidity. *Fam Plann Perspect.* 9:266, 1977.

21. Cates W Jr: Proposal: a graduated scale for the cost of legal abortions. Presented at the annual meeting of the National Abortion Federation, New York, July 1979.

22. Center for Disease Control: Abortion Surveillance. Atlanta, 1977. *Morbid Mortal Wkly Rep.* 28:381, 1979.

23. Cates W Jr, Tietze C: Standardized mortality rate associated with legal abortion: United States, 1972-1975. *Fam Plann Perspect.* 10:109, 1978.

24. David HP: Psychosocial studies of abortion in the United States, in David HP, Friedman HL, vd Tak J, Sevilla M (eds): *Abortion in Psychosocial Perspective: Trends in Transnational Research.* New York, Springer, 1978, p 77.

25. Denes M: *In Necessity and Sorrow: Life and Death in an Abortion Hospital.* New York, Basic Books, 1976.

26. Burr WA, Schulz KF: Delayed abortion in an area of easy accessibility. Presented at the annual meeting of the Association of Planned Parenthood Physicians, Atlanta, 1977.

27. Cannon-Bonventre K, Kahn J, Engelman E: Educational methodologies to decrease second trimester abortions. Unpublished report prepared for the Center for Disease Control, Atlanta, 1977.

28. Illsley R, Hall M: Psychosocial aspects of abortion: a review of and needed research. *Bull WHO*, 53:83, 1976.

29. David HP: Abortion in psychological perspective. *Am J Orthopsychiatry* 42:61, 1972.

30. Adler NE: Abortion: a social-psychological perspective. *J Soc Issues:* 35:100, 1979.

31. Tietze C, Lewit S: Joint Program for the Study of Abortion (JPSA): early medical complications of legal abortions. *Stud Fam Plann.* 3:97, 1972.

32. Tietze C, Lewit S: A national medical experience: the Joint Program for the Study of Abortion (JPSA), in Osofsky HJ, Osofsky JD (eds): *The Abortion Experience.* Hagerstown, Md, Harper & Row, 1973, p 1.

33. Steinhoff PG: Background characteristics of abortion patients, in Osofsky HJ, Osofsky JD (eds): *The Abortion Experience.* Hagerstown, Md, Harper & Row, 1973, p 206.

34. Pion RJ, Smith RG, Hale RW: The Hawaii experience, in Osofsky HJ, Osofsky JD (eds): *The Abortion Experience*. Hagerstown, Md, Harper & Row, 1973, p 177.

35. Kerenyi TD, Glascock EL, Horowitz ML: Reasons for delayed abortion: results of 400 interviews. *Am J Obstet Gynecol.* 117:299, 1973.

36. Bracken MB, Swigar ME: Factors associated with delay in seeking induced abortions. *Am J Obstet Gynecol.* 113:301, 1972.

37. Bracken MB: An epidemiological study of psychosocial correlates of delayed decisions to abort. Unpublished PhD dissertation. New Haven, Yale University, 1974.

38. Bracken MB, Kasl SV: First and repeat abortions: a study of decision making and delay. *J Biosoc Sci.* 7:473, 1975.

39. Bracken MB, Kasl SV: Denial of pregnancy, conflict, and delayed decisions to abort. *Proceedings of 4th International Congress of Psychosomatic Obstetrics and Gynecology,* Basel, Karger, 1975, p 301.

40. Bracken MB, Kasl SV: Delay in seeking induced abortion: a review and theoretical analysis. *Am J Obstet Gynecol.* 121:1008, 1975.

41. Pakter J, Nelson F, Svigir M: Legal abortion: a half-decade of experience. *Fam Plann Perspect.* 7:248, 1975.

42. Fielding LW, Sachtleben MR, Friedman LM, et al: *Comparison of Women Seeking Early and Late Abortion.*

43. Pakter J: Personal communication, September 1979.

44. Tyler CW Jr, Cates W Jr: Personal communication, September 1979.

45. Ryser PE, Laufe LE, Berg R: Racial differences in abortion seeking. *Contraception* 12:199, 1975.

46. Alan Guttmacher Institute: *Abortions and the Poor: Private Morality, Public Responsibility.* New York, 1979.

47. Rosoff JI (ed): Washington memo (W-10). July 6, 1979.

48. Center for Disease Control: Health effects of restricting federal funds for abortion. Atlanta, *Morbid Mort Wkly Rep.* 28:37, 1979.

49. Kaltreider N: Emotional patterns related to delay in decision to seek legal abortion: a pilot study. *Calif Med.* 118:23, 1973.

50. Kaltreider N, Goldsmith S, Margolis A: The impact of midtrimester abortion techniques on patients and staff. Unpublished data, 1978.

51. Adler NE: Psychosocial issues of therapeutic abortion, in Youngs D, Ehrhardt A (eds): *Psychosomatic Obstetrics and Gynecology.* New York, Appleton-Century-Crofts, 1979.

52. Bracken MB: A causal model of psychosomatic reactions to vacuum aspiration abortion. *Soc Psychiatry* 13:135, 1978.

53. Francke LB: *The Ambivalence of Abortion.* New York, Random House, 1978.

54. Senay EC: Therapeutic abortion: clinical aspects. *Arch Gen Psychiatry* 23:408, 1970.

55. Hiatt F: Mother was surprised. *The Washingtonian,* December 1976.

56. Miles P: Interviews with second-trimester abortion patients at Washington Hospital Center Women's Clinic. Unpublished data, 1973.

57. Brewer C: Induced abortion after feeling fetal movements: its causes and emotional sequences. *J Biosoc Sci.* 10:203, 1978.

58. *Akron Center for Reproductive Health v. City of Akron.* (C78-155A, n.d., Ohio, 1978).

59. Bracken MB, Hachamovitch M, Grossman G: The decision to abort and psychological sequalae. *J Nerv Ment Dis.* 158:154, 1974.

60. Bracken MB, Klerman LV, Bracken M: Coping with pregnancy resolution among never married women. *Am J Orthopsychiatry* 48:320, 1978.

61. Char WG, McDermott JF: Abortions and acute identity crisis in nurses. *Am J Psychiatry* 128:66, 1972.

62. Bourne JP: Abortion: influences on health professionals' attitudes. *Hospitals* 46:80, 1972.

63. Kessler K, Weiss T: Ward staff problems with abortion. *Int J Psychiatr Med.* 5:97, 1974.

64. Rosen RA, Werley HA, Ager JW, et al: Health professionals: attitudes toward abortion. *Public Opin Quart.* 38:158, 1974.

65. Nathanson CA, Becker MH: The influence of physicians' attitudes on abortion performance, patient management and professional fees. *Fam Plann Perspect.* 9:158, 1977.

66. LoSciuto LA, Balin H, Zahn MA: Physicians' attitudes toward abortion. *J Reprod Med.* 9:70, 1972.

67. Stewart PL: A survey of obstetrician-gynecologists' abortion attitudes and performance. *Med Care* 16:1036, 1978.

68. Center for Disease Control: Comparative risks of three methods of midtrimester abortion. *Morbid Mortal Wkly Rep.* 25:370, 1976.

69. Von Allmen SD, Cates W Jr, Schulz KF, et al: Costs of treating abortion-related complications. *Fam Plann Perspect.* 9:273, 1977.

70. Grimes DA, Schulz KF, Cates W Jr, et al: Midtrimester abortion by dilatation and evacuation: a safe and practical alternative. *N Engl J Med.* 296:1141, 1977.

71. Peterson WF: Interview in Female Health Topics and Diagnostics. *Reporter* 1:5, 1978.

72. Burnhill MS: Vaginal second-trimester abortion, in Sciarra JJ, Zatuchni GI, Speidel JJ (eds): *Risks, Benefits and Controversies in Fertility Control.* Hagerstown, Md, Harper & Row, 1978, p 331.

73. Stubblefield PG, Albrecht BH, Koos B, et al: A randomized study of 12 mm and 15.9 mm cannulas in midtrimester abortion by laminaria and vacuum curettage. *Fertil Steril.* 29:512, 1978.

74. Lief HI: What medical schools teach about sex. *Bull Tulane Univ Med Fac.* 22:161, 1963.

75. Lief HI, Karlen A (eds): *Sex Education in Medicine.* New York, Halsted, 1976.

76. Woods SM: Sex education in medical schools, in Money J, Musaph H (eds): *Handbook of Sexology.* Amsterdam, Excerpta Medica, 1977, p 1107.

77. David HP, Johnson RL: *Teen Problem Pregnancies: Peer Counselors' Perceptions About Community Concerns and Solutions.* Washington, DC, Transnational Family Research Institute/Planned Parenthood, 1979.

78. Clark R, Barron DD: *The General Mills American Family Report, 1978-79: Family Health in an Era of Stress.* Minneapolis, General Mills, 1979.

79. Scales P: The effects of sex education: a review and critique of the literature, in Gordon S, Scales P (eds): *The Sexual Adolescent: Strategies for Reducing Teenage Pregnancy and Venereal Disease.* North Scituate, Duxbury, 1978.

80. Faber E (ed): *Community Sex Education Programs for Parents.* Syracuse, NY, Institute for Family Research and Education, 1977.

81. Day N, Brady L, Faerstein M, et al: *Improving Family Planning Services for Teenagers.* San Francisco, Urban and Rural Systems Associates, 1976.

82. Furstenberg FF: *Unplanned Parenthood: The Social Consequences of Teenage Childbearing.* New York, The Free Press, 1976.

83. Rooks JB, Cates W Jr: Emotional impact of D&E vs. instillation. *Fam Plann Perspect.* 9:276, 1977.

84. Hern W: Dilatation evacuation abortion stressful for staff. *Ob/Gyn News* 14:17, 1979.

85. Margolis A: Interview cited in *Ob/Gyn News* 14:8, 1979.

86. Green LW: Should health education abandon attitude change strategies? *Health-Educ Monogr.* No. 30, 25, 1970.

87. Luker K: Contraceptive risk and abortion: results and implications of a San Francisco Bay area study. *Stud Fam Plann.* 8:190, 1977.

88. Potts M: Perspectives on fertility control. *Int J Gynaecol Obstet.* 16:449, 1979

89. Reed J: *From Private Vice to Public Virtue.* New York, Basic Books, 1978.

18 Psychological Impact on Patients and Staff

Nancy B. Kaltreider

Far more than most other medical procedures, abortion is surrounded by social considerations and poses a number of potential problems for all concerned with it. Dealing with second-trimester abortion is particularly difficult, not only because the fetus may be perceived less as a potential life at some time in the distance future (and more as a baby at that moment), but also because the woman who delays her decision to seek an abortion may be emotionally more fragile than the woman who chooses to abort early. To compound matters further, patient and staff reactions to second-trimester abortion clearly are influenced by the characteristics of the method of pregnancy termination per se. The use of dilatation and evacuation in the second trimester presents a unique situation; what may be best for the patient may be most upsetting for her physician and his/her colleagues.

BACKGROUND

Social Issues

The literature which views abortion within a sociopsychologic perspective recently has been carefully reviewed and summarized by Adler[1] (see also Chapter 17). Legal regulations, funding problems, and prevailing social attitudes, all must be considered as a part of the context within which one must view the published studies of patients' psychologic responses to abortion. The first major, well-controlled psychiatric study of legal abortion was done in Scandinavia[2]; it revealed few serious psychologic after-effects. In the United States, descriptive studies which followed this early work have confirmed that strong negative reactions are rare[3,4]; the predominant postabortion response is one of relief.[5] Nonetheless, some women do experience transient periods of regret, depression, and guilt following their abortions.[6,7]

For the purposes of this chapter, it is important to identify potential factors which could contribute to relative psychological risk, particularly those factors which have special pertinence for patients in the second trimester. Payne et al.[8] have suggested seven predictors of difficulty in working through the conflicts associated with unwanted pregnancy and abortion:

- History of mental illness
- Immature interpersonal relationships
- Unstable, conflict-laden relationship with one's partner
- History of a negative relationship with one's mother
- Ambivalence regarding abortion
- A religious or cultural background hostile to abortion
- Single status, especially if one has not borne children

Since no decision about an unwanted pregnancy is stress-free, it is appropriate to note that Payne et al. observed that even the most vulnerable women generally reported at the six-month follow-up that the decision to have an abortion was the right one.[8] Pregnancies which are desired and aborted for physical reasons[9] or which occur to the young adolescent are likely to be at particular risk of adverse psychologic sequelae.[10] Women who wait to choose abortion until the second trimester of pregnancy also may be at increased psychologic risk. During this era of relatively available abortions, a demographic study by Bracken and Swigar[11] indicated that women who waited until after the 10th week of pregnancy are significantly more likely to be:

- Under 21 years of age

- Single
- Multiparous or primaparous
- High school dropouts
- Without a private physician
- Black
- Not using contraceptives at the time of conception

Despite the enhanced medical and psychological risks, at least some of which are known to some segments of the public, second-trimester abortions constitute 11% of the procedures done in the United States in 1976[12]; this percentage possibly will increase as a result of recent limitations placed on federal funding of first-trimester procedures. The current controversy about abortion can only be expected to add to the nature and the degree of social distress and stigmatization experienced by the patient seeking abortion in the second trimester.

Patient Issues

An interview study conducted in San Francisco[13] has suggested that, despite optimal public health planning, there will continue to be women who delay their decisions to obtain abortions until the second trimester. In this survey, women seeking second-trimester abortions tended to have had more disturbed relationships with both parents before their pregnancy, as well as interpersonal relationships characterized by little meaningful communication, when compared to women who sought first-trimester abortions. One can postulate that lack of appropriate role models for sharing of the decision-making process subsequently led to attempts at coping by the use of the process of denial. While this rigid defense mechanism may be somewhat useful during rapid psychologic changes experienced in adolescence, its value with regard to an unwanted pregnancy is minimal. Examination of the educational and social histories of these patients suggested that the second-trimester group was less successful in general and that a poor self-image made it difficult for them to act to protect their egos from destructive forces. Clearly, for women with a background of emotional deprivation, it may be particularly difficult to give up the potential love of the yet unborn child. As these women allowed their pregnancies to progress into the second trimester, they became increasingly aware of an identifiable "baby." This shift in emotional orientation, so aptly described by Bibring et al.,[14] was experienced by the women who had felt quickening.

After the abortion, the first-trimester abortion patients focused on their sense of relief and their desire to take up their lives at the point where they had left off before the pregnancy. The second-trimester abortion patients, on the other hand, generally expressed mixed feelings or tried to cope by continued denial. Some described themselves as "empty" or as having lost "a child."

Several major studies since 1972 have confirmed the general impression that second-trimester abortion patients often had no previous experience with independent action,[15] were ambivalent, and had a low recognition threshold for the pregnancy. Although medical misinformation or "red tape" often is cited as a factor contributing to delay, the more mature the patient, the less likely will she be deterred by institutional barriers.[11] At the same time, it should be recognized that the patient carrying a desired but defective pregnancy is at special emotional risk.[16] Osofsky et al. noted greater reported emotional difficulty among saline patients than among first-trimester abortion patients or those aborted by dilatation and evacuation at 14 to 17 weeks.[17]

Staff Issues

The attitudes and experiences of the providers of abortion services also affect the patient's response to the procedure. Soon after voluntary abortion became a legal reality, some authorities observed an unanticipated, strong emotional reaction by the staff.[18,19] Char and McDermott noted that "an intellectual and theoretical approach to a problem is not the same as personal and emotional involvement."[18] Kane and co-workers observed staff ambivalence and further suggested that the professional identity crisis was heightened when the patient was anonymous, the medical staff was distant, the nurses were involuntary participants, and a recognizable fetus had to be handled.[19] This group's thoughtful suggestions for the psychologic management of hospitalized abortion patients were largely ignored as most early abortions shifted to outpatient clinics or the private practitioner's office. Nonetheless, emotional issues have continued to be more apparent for patients who obtained second-trimester abortions on inpatient services where nursing support was available. Similar emotional issues are now confronting the physician since the development of the D&E method. Here the gynecologist becomes an active agent in ending fetal being, while the patient is spared this emotional confrontation (as well as any pain) by general anesthesia.

Given the present choice of second-trimester procedures, it seemed important to contrast the effects of each major type on patients and staff. As a result, the differential impact on patients, nurses, and physicians between the D&E and amnioinfusion procedures was studied.[20] The following describes the methodology and results of such studies by the author and her colleagues.

STUDY METHOD

Second-trimester abortions were performed by D&E on 250 consecutive women seeking abortion with pregnancies from 14 to 20 weeks in duration. Laminaria were introduced into the cervix 12 to 24 hours in advance of vacuum aspiration and curettage, which then were carried out under general anesthesia without overnight hospitalization. Special ovum forceps were used for extraction of the fetus.

During the course of the study, 20 patients also had second-trimester abortions by amnioinfusion methods at the University of California, San Francisco. These patients were either women whose pregnancies were judged to be too far advanced for the D&E method (21 to 23 weeks from LMP), or patients of another physician who did not perform D&E abortions. The abortions were initiated by intra-amniotic prostaglandin injection and intracervical laminaria. Labor followed, and a dead fetus was expelled. The patients in this group comprised a contrast group for our psychologic study.

Our psychologic study evaluated 30 consecutive patients who were candidates for the D&E procedure and 20 consecutive patients who were to have amnioinfusion abortions (Table 18-1). Three women from each group failed to return for follow-up. All subjects completed a demographic and attitudinal questionnaire and a Profile of Mood States Scale[21] before their abortions. Three weeks after their abortions, the women filled out a second attitudinal questionnaire, a Profile of Mood States Scale, and an Impact of Event Scale[22] measuring response to a stressful event. In addition, 12 of the D&E and nine of the amnioinfusion patients were interviewed for an hour by the author at follow-up in an attempt to discuss subjective responses to the abortion. The four physicians and the nurses involved in abortion care were also interviewed.

Table 18-1
Comparison of Demographic Characteristics of Patients in Psychological Study (N = 44)

Variable (mean)	D&E Patients N=27	Amino-infusion Patients N=17	Significance
Age	21.4	21.0	NS*
Years of education	12.7	12.0	NS
Weeks since LMP	16.8	19.7	< .001
Previous pregnancies	1.0	1.0	NS
Previous abortions	0.4	0.3	NS

*NS = not significant.

RESULTS

Patients

Prior to the abortion, there were no significant demographic differences between the two groups on the questionnaire, except that the amnioinfusion patients were further along in their pregnancies (mean 19.7 weeks) than the D&E group (mean 16.8 weeks). Response patterns to subscales on the Profile of Moods Scale were similar, except that patients anticipating an amnioinfusion abortion were significantly more tense ($t = -1.9, p < .03$).

Both groups indicated generally ambivalent feelings about the pregnancy, usually included the potential father in the discussion (but not necessarily the decision about the abortion), and frequently wished that it were possible to continue the pregnancy (71%). The reasons for decisional delay were varied and included being unaware of the pregnancy (35%), indecision (22%), and hopes of working out a way to keep the baby (15%). Thirteen percent of the D&E sample and 24% of the amnioinfusion group indicated that they had felt fetal movement; an open-ended interview inquiry suggested that the true percentage was actually higher, but that denial of this fact was emotionally necessary just prior to the abortion procedure.

Three weeks after abortion, a repeat comparison between these two groups showed that the amnioinfusion and the D&E patients had had significantly different experiences. The D&E group indicated more frequently that the procedure went smoothly, and it was more likely to have been experienced as minor surgery ($p < .00005$). The amnioinfusion group, on the other hand, noted that the procedure hurt much more than they had expected ($p < .0004$), and was experienced more like a labor or loss of a child ($p < .0001$). On the Profile of Mood States Scale, using analysis of covariants to adjust for the pretest scores, the D&E patients scored significantly higher on vigor ($p < .04$), while the amnioinfusion patients noted more depression ($p < .05$) and anger ($p < .05$). A lingering sense of guilt was reported by none of the D&E patients, while it was present in 24% of the amnioinfusion patients. On the Impact of Event Scale, the mean endorsement of intrusive symptomatology was not different, but the amnioinfusion patients had a much higher spread in response levels ($p < .0001$).

In the patient interviews, the D&E often was seen as helpful in getting through a difficult situation; it tended to reinforce preexisting denial. Examples from the interviews of D&E patients included these comments:

"I'm a really inquisitive person; I like to understand things. After they removed the laminaria, they just vacuum 'all that' out. When you wake up, it's like a dream."

"I knew it was a vacuum method but more complicated—that's all I wanted to know. It felt like it was out of my hands."

The need to avoid the implications of the abortion was often conspicuous in the D&E patient; the procedure helped in the suppression of her anxiety. "I got a sonogram—I could see the baby's shape on the screen and hear its heart beat—I closed my eyes. I didn't want to relate to it as a potential developing person."

In contrast, the women who went through a prostaglandin amnioinfusion abortion often had a long and painful experience which made it impossible to turn away from the reality of their choice. The products of labor were described as a "baby," and parous women found the unremitting quality of the pains more difficult than childbirth. Anger at the attending physician for being unavailable was prominent. The amnioinfusion patients had the sense of having confronted the true issues, even if mourning was the result. The quality of such experiences more clearly raises the issues of possible impact on future pregnancies. Two of the women's comments speak to this:

"When I was in labor I thought, if a fetus does this, a real baby would snap my spinal cord."

"After the abortion I thought, imagine what a seven-pound child would do to you. It will be a long time before I consider having a baby."

Nurses

The experience of participating in any abortion procedure contrasts directly with the general medical emphasis on the preservation of life. On the gynecology hospital floor, the amnioinfusion abortions were viewed by nurses not only as upsetting experiences, but also as a symbol of abandonment by the medical staff. The ward nurses' comments reflected frustration at being left to cope with upset patients delivering late at night. The house staff, although technically available, were quite clear in preferring to be in the delivery rooms where "live births" occur. Nurses found physical contact with the fetus particularly difficult; it reminded them of the "preemies" just down the hall and made them uncomfortable as they thought about their own potential future pregnancies. Light staffing on the night shift made a totally voluntary system of participation impossible.

One nurse said, "I dream about it. They bother me the most of any of the patients. Pelvic exenterations are terrible, but the abortions affect me personally. I know some day I will deliver and think of that. It's changed my ideas. I used to be intellectually very positive about the subject of abortion, but the part of me that has to do it feels really resentful."

The operating room nurses involved in the D&E procedure had, on the other hand, not only more freedom of choice about participation, but also more support from the physician who was present and bore the primary responsibility. The D&E procedure often was described as distasteful, and many nurses preferred noninvolvement. Both sides experienced conflict.

"I chose not to participate. Life is life, at eight or 25 weeks. It's not good for a patient to have a negative nurse. There was some implication by others that I was trying to get out of work."

"I felt the procedure was gross. Now I make an effort to get to know the patients. It makes it better. The first time I left the OR and vomited."

"When I was the first one to assist, the other nurses nicknamed me 'killer.'"

Prior to the open discussion meetings, none of the nurses who were involved directly had felt able to share her feelings with her coworkers. Other nurses on the staff knew there was a new abortion method but had hesitated to inquire about the details. The discussion meetings generated a plan of active support for the patients before and after the procedure, as well as open acceptance of the right of individual choice about participation.

Physicians

Physicians often tend to find the emotionally defensive second-trimester abortion patients difficult to deal with, and may welcome the relative noninvolvement that the amnioinfusion procedure offers them. A physician who performed amnioinfusions but declined to perform D&Es stated, "Killing a baby is not a way I want to think about myself." The two physicians who performed the D&E procedures in our study supported each other and relied on a strong sense of social conscience which focused on the health and desires of the women. They felt technically competent, but noted strong emotional reactions during or following the procedures, and occasional disquieting dreams.

COMMENTS

Our experience with the D&E method for second-trimester abortion contrasts favorably to the earlier reported results with a similar number of intraamniotic prostaglandin cases in Langley Porter Institute, University of California, San Francisco Hospital.[13] In that institution, 11% of amnioinfusion abortions resulted in blood loss exceeding 500 ml, while 34% were considered incomplete and required instrumental placental removal. The staff there are personally convinced that the D&E technique is safer and less painful.

Despite these advantages, however, physicians are slow to accept the D&E method. It is quite possible that their hesitation may be related to difficulty with the psychologic problems raised by fetal dismemberment. Also, the technique requires the invasion of the uterus at a time when conventional medical teaching has suggested that serious complications could ensue. For these reasons, only a small number of physicians (from the group supporting abortion on demand) has been willing to perform D&E abortions.

Physicians who do D&E abortions should be very familiar with abortion procedures. They should have special instruments for fetal removal and should have received instruction in the D&E technique from an experienced operator. In addition, they should have support and understanding from the medical community wherein they practice, as well as emotional support from members of their surgical team. Given the potentially stressful nature of second-trimester D&E procedures, the physician who feels isolated or condemned, or who is not familiar with each patient's story, may experience increased emotional distress and fear of technical problems.

Women who delay their decisions to obtain an abortion tend to have a background of greater psychopathology and to have difficulty with decision making.[23] They often lack social supports and have chronic difficulty with contraception. They represent the two ends of the age spectrum—young adolescents overwhelmed by a first pregnancy, and older women who are ambivalent about the emotional and economic costs of an additional child. The D&E procedure allows the patient to continue her characteristic pattern of denial and still have a smooth psychologic course. By contrast, the amnioinfusion procedure often is a frightening experience accompanied by pain, fetal expulsion, and medical complications; it is far more likely to engender a reaction of hostility and depression.

D&E procedures in the operating room are usually rapid and allow for a spirit of cooperation in the care of the patient by all involved, if the surgical team is thoroughly oriented and participation is voluntary for all members. Amnioinfusion abortions often require protracted and intense nursing care, while physician involvement often takes place only during emergencies. The floor nurse must deal with the expelled fetus; even nurses in favor of abortion find this a lonely and difficult task. Timing of labors for the day shift and greater attention to adequate analgesia can be helpful to the nursing service as well as to the patient.

It is hoped that the number of second-trimester abortions in the United States will continue to decrease. As yet, it is not clear if the recent suspension of federal funding for abortions will mean that more women are unable to obtain abortions in the first trimester and will need more difficult and more expensive second-trimester procedures. Such women may have more anxiety about finances as well as the social stigma associated with a late decision. The D&E procedure presents a number of advantages; under appropriate circumstances, in comparison with amnioinfusion abortion, it is of clear benefit to the patient. Since the psychologic studies described in this chapter have been based on relatively few subjects and the interview material is not quantified, further studies would do well to utilize a semistructured interview for both patients and staff to sample attitudes and experiences of each group.

Once the difficult decision is made to terminate a pregnancy in the second trimester, the most important concerns should be the safety and comfort of the patient; nonetheless, the reactions experienced by health professionals must also be taken into account. It is evident that further research is required to determine the best ways to perform this stressful task.

Thanks are due to Drs. Sadja Goldsmith and Alan Margolis for their support during this work and to Dr. Nancy E. Adler for her helpful comments.

REFERENCES

1. Adler NE: Abortion: a social-psychological perspective. *J Soc Issues* 35:100, 1979.
2. Ekblad M: Induced abortion on psychiatric grounds: a follow-up study of 479 women. *Acta Psychiatr Neurol Scand.* (suppl)99:3, 1955.
3. Patt SL, Rappaport RG, Barglow P: Follow-up of therapeutic interruption of pregnancy. *Arch Gen Psychiatry* 20:408, 1969.
4. Osofsky JD, Osofsky HJ: The psychological reaction of patients to legalized abortion. *Am J Orthopsychiatry* 42:48, 1972.
5. Ewin JA, Rouse BA: Therapeutic abortion and a prior psychiatric history. *Am J Psychiatry* 130:37, 1976.
6. Peck A, Marcus H: Psychiatric sequelae of therapeutic interruption of pregnancy. *J Nerv Ment Dis.* 143:417, 1966.
7. Smith EM: A follow-up study of women who request abortion. *Am J Orthopsychiatry* 43:574, 1973.
8. Payne EC, Kravitz AR, Notman MT, et al: Outcome following therapeutic abortion. *Arch Gen Psychiatry* 33:725, 1976.
9. Niswander K, Patterson R: Psychological reaction to a therapeutic abortion. *Obstet Gynecol.* 29:702, 1967.
10. Schaeffer C, Pine F: Pregnancy, abortion and the developmental tasks of adolescence. *J Am Acad Child Psychiatry* 11:511, 1972.

11. Bracken M, Swigar M: Factors associated with delay in seeking induced abortions. *Am J Obstet Gynecol.* 113:301, 1972.

12. Center for Disease Control: Abortion surveillance—United States, 1976. *Morb Mort Wkly Rep.* 27:175, 1978.

13. Kaltreider N: Psychological factors in midtrimester abortion. *Psychiatry Med.* 4:129, 1973.

14. Bibring GL, Dwyer TF, Huntington DS, et al: A study of the psychological processes in pregnancy and of the earliest mother-child relationship. *Psychoanal Study Child* 16:9, 1961.

15. Kerenyi TD, Glascock EL, Horowitz ML: Reasons for delayed abortion: results of four hundred interviews. *Am J Obstet Gynecol.* 117:299, 1973.

16. Blumberg B, Golbus M, Hanson K: Psychological sequelae of abortion performed for a genetic indication. *Am J Obstet Gynecol.* 122:799, 1975.

17. Osofsky JD, Osofsky HJ, Rajan R, et al: Psychosocial aspects of abortion in the United States. *Mt. Sinai J Med.* 42:456, 1975.

18. Char WF, McDermott JF: Abortions and acute identity crises in nurses. *Am J Psychiatry.* 128:952, 1972.

19. Kane FJ, Feldman M, Jain S, et al: Emotional reactions of abortion services personnel. *Arch Gen Psychiatry* 28:409–411, 1973.

20. Kaltreider N, Goldsmith S, Margolis A: The impact of midtrimester abortion techniques on patients and staff. *Am J Obstet Gynecol.* 28:409, 1973.

21. McNair D, Lorr M, Doppleman L: *Profile of Mood States Manual.* San Diego, Educational and Industrial Testing Service, 1971.

22. Horowitz MJ, Wilner N, Alvarez W: Impact of Event Scale: a measure of subjective stress. *Psychosom Med.* 41:209, 1979.

23. Bracken MB, Kasl SV: Delay in seeking induced abortion. *Am J Obstet Gynecol.* 121:1008, 1975.

19 Emotional Issues for Professionals*

Judith P. Rooks

This chapter discusses the emotional factors related to stress among professional staff who participate in the performance of second-trimester abortions. The opinions presented herein are based on unstructured interviews with physicians and nurses in special abortion services and general hospitals in various parts of the country, as well as upon a review of published literature and unpublished research reports.

SIX FACTORS WHICH AFFECT THE EMOTIONAL RESPONSES OF PROFESSIONAL STAFF

Gestational Age

The later in pregnancy that an abortion is performed, the more difficult it becomes for the staff as well as for the patient. While it is

---

*The opinions or assertions contained herein are the author's and are not to be construed as official policy of the Department of Health, Education, and Welfare.

apparent that the distinction between first- and second-trimester abortions is somewhat arbitrary, it is clear that neither the physical nor the emotional problems associated with induced abortion escalate rapidly between the 12th and 13th weeks. There is, in reality, far less difference between an abortion performed in the 12th week or the 13th week than there is between an abortion performed at 13 weeks and one performed at 20 weeks or more. All other things being equal, it is more stressful for staff to participate in one very late abortion involving a large or mature fetus (especially if the fetus shows even fleeting signs of life) than it is to participate in many abortions at 13 or 14 weeks' gestation. It therefore is almost paradoxical that the great majority of women who request second-trimester abortion do so during the early part of that trimester,[1] and that the general inability to provide an appropriate procedure at this gestational stage often results in considerable delays before the abortion can be obtained. For example, if one relies completely on instillation procedures, many abortions must be performed weeks, if not months, later in gestation than would have been the case had they been terminated by D&E. It has been estimated that if every woman who requested an abortion at 13 to 15 weeks' gestation had had access to a D&E procedure, there would be 80% to 90% fewer abortions performed at 16 weeks or later.[2]

Staff Perceptions of the Patient's Reason for Needing an Abortion and for Obtaining It so Late

Physicians and nurses who perform or assist with second-trimester abortions confront the reality of dead fetuses. They need to feel that the abortions are necessary and justifiable in a way that makes sense to them personally. They want to be able to approve of their patient's decision to seek a late abortion. Unfortunately, the medical staff often does not know the patient's story—her life situation and why she chose an abortion—and when they do know it, they cannot always approve of it. Several points related to this problem are noted below.

To begin with, it is hard for many second-trimester patients to tell their stories, especially to a professional in a clinic setting. More than half of these patients are teenagers. Many of them are from social and economic backgrounds considerably dissimilar to those of the professionals they meet in the process of obtaining an abortion. In addition, second-trimester abortion patients are likely to have had poor relationships and little communication with their parents as well as weaker ego strengths than patients who seek earlier abortions.[3] Although the following characteristics do not describe all second-trimester abortion patients, some are found so frequently among women who have second-trimester abortions that they must be recognized as risk factors at the very outset. They are: being teenagers, coming from low-income families, feeling insecure, being passive, and having weak communication skills and poor relationships with parents. Such characteristics make it harder for many patients to communicate adequately the complexity of their situations and of their feelings to a physician, counselor, or nurse.[4] Ambivalence—wishing they could continue their pregnancies and have their babies even while choosing to have abortions—also may make it harder for many patients to discuss their reasons for deciding to abort.

Another reason why many staff members do not understand their patients' reasons for needing later abortions is that they (the staff members) are not told those reasons, since usually only one member of the professional team has had an in-depth interview with each patient. Unless a specific effort is directed toward every individual who will be in the operating room during the D&E abortion or who will tend to the patient during the long process following an instillation procedure, staff members may have little basis for understanding why a given patient chose an abortion and why it took her so long to do it.

Central to this problem is the fact that it is human nature for people to judge each other. Granted that professional training has as one of its goals a degree of objectivity toward patients, in reality it is not yet possible to prevent professionals from making personal judgments and having feelings based on them. An abortion performed at 19 weeks because the fetus is malformed or affected with a genetic disease evokes different emotions from the staff than an abortion done at the same gestational age because the pregnancy was unplanned and is unwanted. It is far easier to empathize with a woman having a late abortion because of a fetal defect.[5] After all, it is not her fault either that the abortion has been advised or that it must take place so late. Unfortunately, it is less easy for nurses and physicians to empathize with a woman who has a late abortion to end a pregnancy which is normal but unwanted.

Nonetheless, the professionals who serve these women are asked to perform tasks which are not very gratifying and are sometimes extremely stressful, in order to help a woman out of a situation created either because she and her partner failed to use contraception or because she took longer than most women to discover that she was pregnant and to decide upon and arrange for an abortion. Four of 15 abortion clinic staffs studied by Hern and Corrigan[6] and 26 of 35 nurses interviewed by Effman and Rosenbloom[7] reported that they sometimes felt resentment, anger, or hostility toward second-trimester patients. Tendencies to feel angry at patients may be reinforced by the D&E procedure, which makes the abortion experience so much less painful for the patient. Kaltreider correctly has observed that the D&E procedure allows the patient to continue her characteristic pattern of denial and to have a smooth psychologic course[3] (see also Chapter 18). From the staff point of view, there may be feeling that the patient is getting off too easily and is not really forced, as are the physician and nurse, to face the reality of the destruction of her fetus.

Degree of Contact with the Fetus

Counselors have the least problems in this regard, because they have the greatest opportunity to understand fully and empathize with patients, and are least likely to see aborted fetuses. Physicians who perform amnioinfusions but leave the patient in the care of nurses for labor and fetal delivery also have a relatively unstressful role, since they can avoid the fetus altogether. On the other hand, nurses who assist during a late D&E see fetal parts and have to handle the container in which they are placed. Nurses are probably more stressed by the role they play in instillation procedures, however, in which they generally attend and assist the woman during delivery of the fetus and handle it directly in order to remove it from the bed. Physicians performing late D&E procedures have the most stressful role, because they directly and physically affect fetal life. Use of suction applied through a 16 mm cannula, for D&E procedures performed between 13 and 15 weeks, makes it possible for the surgeon and the assistants to avoid viewing the fetal parts.[8]

Fear of Complications

Several authors cite fear of complications as an important contributing factor to the reluctance of American gynecologists to perform second-trimester D&E procedures.[6,8,9] How much of this fear may be related to the potential for litigation, should a complication arise, cannot be stated with certainty. Nonetheless, this fear persists, despite strong evidence that the rates of morbidity and mortality from D&E procedures are lower than those associated with amnioinfusion.[10] The emotional impact of deaths and nonfatal complications of D&E seems to be greater than the fear associated with a higher incidence of serious complications and death from amnioinfusion. This is not surprising in light of longstanding clinical admonitions against this approach to abortion after the first trimester, and consideration of the nature of the complications associated with each of these procedures. Most of the serious complications and deaths associated with amnioinfusions occur after the procedure itself has been completed. Although some may result from operator error, most seem attributable to some idiosyncratic response of the patient to the instilled drug—disseminated intravascular coagulation associated with hypertonic saline, for instance, or ventricular fibrillation following prostaglandin administration.[11] In contrast, serious complications of D&E usually occur during the procedure or, in any case, seem more directly related to the surgeon's skills. It is not surprising that surgeons may perceive these procedures as more risky since, at the time the complications occur, the operator may feel personally at fault or responsible, whereas complications with instillation procedures are usually not attributed to the surgeon.

Willingness to Participate

Staff members who prefer not to participate in late abortions or in the care of these patients, but do so because they feel they cannot refuse, are very likely to have strong negative reactions. Physicians in internship or residency training programs or those who are employed by hospitals may be placed in this position. Nurses probably are more likely than physicians to find themselves in these situations. Large, organized abortion services may take care to see that this never occurs, but in general hospitals where second-trimester abortions are performed relatively infrequently, or in hospitals with organized abortion services at the time of an unanticipated absence of a regular nurse or during an evening or night shift, this indeed may be the case. Even nurses who voluntarily accept positions in settings specifically organized to care for abortion patients often indicate that they do not really want to be involved with all aspects of the procedures or with certain patients (repeat patients or those having very late abortions), even though they feel that they cannot refuse. Half of the nurses queried by Effman and Rosenbloom indicated that they felt ill-at-ease when attempting to do certain tasks connected with abortion care.[7]

Nurses are more vulnerable than physicians to involuntary participation in the care of abortion patients, not only on the basis of their having less power within hospital staffs, but also because of other, more subtle factors. If a physician refuses to do an abortion, either another physician will do it or it will not be scheduled. In contrast, physicians who schedule operative procedures do not necessarily check to make sure that a totally sympathetic operating room crew is available, or that the saline injection planned for 8:00 AM the next day has been approved by the 11:00 PM to 7:00 AM shift nurse who must provide care the night before surgery. As a result, nurses with negative feelings about second-trimester abortions may be confronted with a patient whose abortion already has been irreversibly initiated and who needs nursing care.

The Social Environment of the Work Group

The society of one's colleagues and co-workers is an important factor in the emotional response to work. It is especially important for people in the abortion movement. Characteristics of a work environment which make it easier for staff to withstand the emotional stress associated with second-trimester abortions include the following:

- A cohesive group with a shared and openly verbalized consensus that abortion is a necessary and beneficial health service
- Open communication up, down, and across lines of authority
- Acceptance and understanding of verbalized negative feelings
- Mutual respect
- Strong, positive leadership, which features high visibility as well as sensitivity to and concern for people, and a recognition that staff as well as patients have needs

COMMENT

The emotional stress experienced by physicians and nurses who work with second-trimester abortion patients reflects the basic problem which unwanted pregnancy continues to pose for our society. On the one hand, abortion is accepted because society gives greater weight to women's health and well-being than it gives to the fetus in early pregnancy. As the fetus grows and matures, however, it becomes valued more, and the dilemma becomes more difficult to resolve. Most of society deals with it on only an intellectual basis, if at all. The people who directly provide second-trimester abortion services must confront the dilemma in a much more personal manner. An understanding of the various factors which relate to the stresses placed upon the professional staff providing care for patients in the second trimester helps professionals to provide optimal patient care.

REFERENCES

1. Cates W Jr, Schulz KF, Grimes DA, et al: The effect of delay and method choice on the risk of abortion morbidity. *Fam Plann Perspect.* 9:266, 1977.
2. Cates W Jr: D&E after 12 weeks: safe or hazardous? *Contemp Ob/Gyn.* 13:23, 1979.
3. Kaltreider N: Psychological factors in midtrimester abortion. *Psychiatr Neurol Med Psychol.* 4:129, 1973.
4. Kerenyi TD, Glascock EL, Horowitz ML: Reasons for delayed abortion: results of 400 interviews. *Am J Obstet Gynecol.* 117:299, 1973.
5. McIntosh W, Alston H: Review of the polls: acceptance of abortion among white Catholics and Protestants, 1962, 1975. *J Sci Religion* 16:295, 1977.
6. Hern WM, Corrigan B: What about us? Staff reactions to the D&E procedure. Presented at the annual meeting of the Association of Planned Parenthood Physicians, Atlanta, 1977.
7. Effman B, Rosenbloom A: Nurses who are involved in second-trimester abortion. University of Illinois, unpublished thesis.
8. Stubblefield PG, Albrecht BH, Koos B, et al: A randomized study of 12 mm and 15.9 mm cannulas in midtrimester abortion by laminaria and vacuum curettage. *Fertil Steril.* 29:512, 1978.
9. Rooks JB, Cates W Jr: Emotional impact of D&E vs instillation. *Fam Plann Perspect.* 9:276, 1977.
10. Grimes DA, Schulz KF, Cates W Jr, et al: Midtrimester abortion by dilatation and evacuation: a safe and practical alternative. *N Engl J Med.* 296:1141, 1977.
11. Center for Disease Control: *Abortion Surveillance 1976.* Issued August 1978.

20 Counseling Issues

Judith A. Widdicombe

Counseling is a process which facilitates the expression of feelings. When counseling takes place in the context of abortion services, a number of related issues must be discussed. They include: pregnancy, motherhood, interpersonal relationships, and the means by which a thorough consideration of these issues results in a decision. The therapeutic model used most commonly to facilitate counseling is crisis intervention. This process is intended to be of short duration as well as to assume an advocative role for the patient. Proper counseling also should highlight issues that can be confronted in more traditional therapeutic settings after the current crisis is resolved.

Informed consent, on the other hand, is a process by which information relevant to the contemplated medical or surgical intervention is imparted to the patient. As such, it should discuss the benefits, risks, and alternatives to the proposed procedures, as well as encourage questions on the part of the patient and, finally, inform her of her right to change her mind at the last minute.

In some clinical settings, the distinction between these two processes is blurred, but they are indeed two separate functions which should take place prior to any abortion. From a decision-making standpoint, as well as from the educational perspective, informed consent becomes part of the counseling process because it represents information giving that can influence decision making.

Since many second-trimester abortions are performed in a hospital, the process of counseling often is performed by hospital personnel. Two factors are important in this regard. First, hospital employees may have little say about where they will be assigned. If they are assigned to an abortion unit and harbor strong negative feelings toward pregnancy termination, these individuals may assume an adversary position rather than one of advocacy from the patient's perspective. Second, many nurses have little experience with abortion procedures, and in-service training may not be available to help them develop those skills. During amnioinfusion procedures, the physician often delegates the bulk of patient care to the nursing personnel, especially for labor and delivery. If the patient is young and/or frightened, she has a great need to be taken care of and supported throughout the entire abortion process. This requires individuals who are capable of providing emotional as well as medical skills that help to reduce the risk of complication.

THE PREABORTION COUNSELING PROCESS

There are four major steps in the counseling process for second-trimester patients:

1. Decision making, including informed consent
2. Support/advocacy related to the procedure
3. Immediate medical follow-up
4. Longitudinal psychologic follow-up

The most crucial point in the entire abortion process is the decision-making process. It involves recognizing a number of feelings and responses to pregnancy, in addition to confronting the only two alternatives available: termination or continuance until term. Bracken et al. have observed that responses to this basic question of whether or not to terminate a given pregnancy often are based more upon the woman's situation at that point in time than upon a basic attitude for or against abortion.[1] Frequently, a woman's life situation at the time the pregnancy commences is complex; stresses may derive equally from her primary relationship, pressures from family members, goal objectives that may or may not be interfered with and, finally, the woman's general feeling of self-worth. The process of making a decision may be particularly difficult for certain women because, in some segments of our society, women are unaccustomed to making their own decisions. Furthermore, it may become even more difficult to separate the responsibilities that are assumed when an individual chooses not to abort from the need to be validated as a female, because strong efforts are made in our culture to foster maternal instincts.

Parenthood is a major responsibility. The role of the counselor lies mainly in being able to listen, to facilitate discussion, to be supportive, and to be nonjudgmental. If one encourages patients to identify feelings, one must also accept the fact that counselors respond to events on an emotional basis. As an example, a counselor encountered a young couple choosing abortion because they were still in college and not prepared for parenthood. The counselor found herself feeling somewhat impatient and judgmental of them because she herself had had a baby while still in college and had survived. She wondered: Why couldn't they? Later, in reflecting upon her own feelings, the counselor realized that although she had been supportive and responsive, there was a need to separate her personal feelings from her professional responsibility. Identifying those feelings was an important step in her own growth as a counselor.

Training programs are a must for counselors as well as for staff. Working with people in crisis is stressful, and professionals need an outlet to deal with that stress. The counselor must have up-to-date factual material. Abortion is a rapidly evolving medical service, and information changes frequently. Ten years ago, instillation procedures were considered the best option in the second trimester; now D&E is gaining acceptance due to an enhanced awareness of its safety.

Although it is important to allow the patient enough time to make her decision, it is equally important to remember that with each week of pregnancy the mortality rate from induced abortion rises.[2] Clarifying this from the beginning is important to the decision-making process. Objective professional consultants should be available for the ambivalent patient. Supportive clergy are helpful for those patients who have moral or ethical concerns. For the young patient who is considering single parenthood, discussions with single parents about the costs vs the benefits of rearing a child should be encouraged.

THE COUNSELING PROCESS DURING THE ABORTION

Once the decision to have an abortion has been made, the needs of the patient change. She may be afraid of pain, needles, or doctors, and the focus of her concern may become anxiety laden. The presence of a warm, nurturing counselor during the operation can be invaluable. The patient may have exposed her vulnerabilities during the decision-making process and once again may need a supportive, nonjudgmental advocate. If the abortion procedure takes place in the hospital, help is needed to guide the patient through the system and to provide individualized care. Concern for others involved in the pregnancy may be present, and communication through the counselor is advisable. Often the male partner is not involved in the decision-making process, as many relationships falter or end with the recognition that pregnancy exists.[3] For many young women, the parents can provide a major support system; great care is needed to try to make the abortion experience positive for them as well. Although many young women despair of involving their parents, when they do so it often becomes a growth experience for everyone, and new lines of communication can be established.

THE COUNSELING PROCESS AFTER THE ABORTION

Immediate postabortion follow-up may be medical in nature and is not always an integral part of counseling. However, it is often the counselor who is the contact person for questions and concerns. If the advocacy role has been a positive one, the patient will frequently initiate a return to the health care system through the counselor. Not to follow a patient or provide a means for follow-up is to abandon the patient. Since most 24-hour answering services are not staffed by medical people, there is a need to provide answering-service personnel with counseling as well as medical information.

The follow-up process often also aids the patient in becoming integrated into the health care system; the counselor can provide an advocacy role there also. Since not all health care personnel are supportive of abortion, the counselor can help the patient avoid unnecessary psychic trauma by assisting with selected referrals. A definite plan to obtain birth control or gynecological services may reduce the patient's chances of future unplanned pregnancies and increase her positive feelings about her recent decision and her future life. Many women have knowledge about contraceptive methods but do not integrate this into their lives. Risk-taking is a phenomenon of our culture, and unprotected intercourse is no exception.[4] For the older, parous woman, sterilization may be a reasonable option to consider after an abortion, and appropriate information must be available for both the woman and her partner.

LATE COUNSELING

Although longitudinal follow-up is difficult, it is useful and significant when it does take place. The patients who obtain abortions often belong to mobile elements of society, thus making attempts at follow-up frustrating. If the process of follow-up is preplanned and is presented to the patient as an integral part of the abortion procedure, the rate of long-term contacts will increase. Since many questions remain about the medical aspects of repeat abortions or future pregnancies, patients need to understand that their long-term fertility patterns may depend a great deal upon the totality of services which were provided for them.

Research over the last two decades has shown that there are few long-term psychiatric sequelae to abortion. To be sure, for some women there are functional upheavals that are limited in duration, but these, too, merit concern from the health care system. As professionals, we must help women make decisions that are best for them, and we must support those decisions after they have been made. As a health care community, we should foster the understanding that everybody does not feel good about everything at all times and that human responses, including grieving, are normal.

REFERENCES

1. Bracken MB, Klerman LV, Bracken M: Abortion, adoption, or motherhood: an empirical study of decision making during pregnancy. *Am J Obstet Gynecol.* 130:251, 1978.
2. Center for Disease Control: *Abortion Surveillance, 1976.* Atlanta, issued August, 1978.
3. Smith EM: A follow-up study of women who request abortion. *Am J Orthopsychiatry* 43:4, 1973.
4. Luker K: *Taking Chances: Abortion and the Decision Not to Contracept.* Berkeley, University of California Press, 1975.

21 Postabortal Contraception*†

Louis G. Keith
Gary S. Berger

Women who obtain abortions in the second trimester clearly should receive thorough contraceptive counseling, whether their abortion has been requested for medical or for social reasons. Since second-trimester abortions take place in specialized clinics or in hospitals, these institutions are in an ideal position to direct the patient's attention to contraception. They also can serve as an appropriate setting for the patient to receive family planning services as well as long-term follow-up and reexamination.

Among the advantages of using the abortion process as the starting point to receive contraceptive services are the following:

- Proven fertile women are easily reached.

---

*Supported in part by the Charles A. Fields Medical Foundation, Ltd., Chicago, Illinois.
†Portions of this chapter have been presented previously in the monograph *Postpartum and Postabortal Contraception* by Keith LG, Petty J, Labbock M, Berger GS, Synapse Publications, Pittsburgh, 1979, and in the chapter *Control of Reproduction in the Purperal State* by Keith LG, Berger GS, in the textbook *Obstetric Practice* edited by Aladjem S, St. Louis,CV Mosby, 1980.

- Little or no self-motivation is required to request contraceptive information
- Active contraceptive intervention reduces the risk of immediate postabortal conception, since most women normally resume fecundity after each natal event
- Family planning advice may be more acceptable if given by the institution which has just supervised the successful care of a woman
- Proper contraception after abortion may be helpful in providing a higher standard of maternal and infant health at a later date [1]

Health workers desiring to provide contraceptive services to women who have undergone abortion must realize that the patterns of contraceptive behavior which preceded the abortion (either a lack of desire to use contraception or poor compliance in proper contraceptive utilization), may recur once the immediacy of the unwanted pregnancy has been solved. This is particularly true with selected second-trimester abortions when the patients have denied needing an abortion until after the first trimester, or when they have had prior abortions.

In clinical practice, women may readily agree to accept an effective contraceptive method prior to obtaining their abortions. Afterwards, however, the fact that the abortion procedure has been safe and relatively comfortable may adversely affect any newly found enthusiasm for following through on contraceptive plans. Moreover, because some patients are able to obtain their abortions free through a system of social welfare or self insurance, enthusiastic contraceptive efforts may not be instigated. Such individuals may be inclined to evade any serious or meaningful discussions of contraception. Especially at risk are young, unmarried women or those who are unable to pay for continuing follow-up care.

Whether the primary focus in the abortion procedure has been medical or social in nature, there is no room for complacency with regard to future contraception. Patients must be led to understand that even though the presently available contraceptives are not "perfect," their proper and continued utilization poses less of a threat to health than when no method is used. In some circumstances, the use of contraceptives represents a substantial reduction in the risk to health compared to the use of abortion as the sole method of contraception.[2] The patient also must clearly understand that the likelihood of an unplanned pregnancy depends not only on the effectiveness of the contraceptive method selected and her natural level of fertility (which can be expected to decline with advancing age), but also on her adherence to the prescribed contraceptive routine.

DEMOGRAPHIC FACTORS AFFECTING CONTRACEPTIVE USE AND ABORTION

Contraceptive use and abortion are associated phenomena in sexually active women. According to Moore-Cavar,[3] international surveys of women who have had abortions found that these individuals were more likely to have used contraception at some prior time than women who had not had abortions. Similarly, women who had used contraception at some time were more likely to have had an abortion than women who never used contraception.

In spite of this association, contraceptive use in the months prior to conception among women hospitalized for complications of abortion often is low. On the other hand, contraceptive use increases markedly after abortion. This is true for developed as well as for developing countries where access to effective contraceptives may be difficult.[4] Perhaps more importantly, the use of effective methods increases after legal and illegal abortion and after medically complicated and uncomplicated abortions (Table 21-1). In the hospital setting, the postabortal selection of a contraceptive clearly is influenced as much by selected personal characteristics such as marital status, age, parity, and education, as by the general availability of contraceptives and the quality of the associated counseling programs.[4]

PHYSIOLOGIC CHANGES ASSOCIATED WITH THE POSTABORTAL STATE

While there are considerable data available regarding the physiological changes observed in the puerperium, similar data are almost totally lacking regarding the changes which take place after interruption of pregnancy in the second trimester. Most studies of changes in postabortal patients have been concerned with pregnancies which were interrupted during the first trimester. In this circumstance, ovulation often returns more rapidly than after term delivery, frequently within the first month.[5] It has been inferred that the physiologic changes observed after second-trimester abortion might differ somewhat, particularly with regard to the time required for involution of the uterus. Since the second trimester extends for a full 12 weeks, there is opportunity for wide variation in the involution process.

Involution of the Uterus

By the 14th day postpartum, the uterus generally has involuted

Table 21-1
Contraceptive Use Before and After Hospital Treatment for Abortion Complications, Selected Studies 1972 to 1979

Country	Author and Year	Before Abortion			After Abortion		
		No. Interviewed	% Using Any Method	% Using Effective Method	No. Interviewed	% Using Any Method	% Using Effective Method
India	Brenner et al. 1973	2230	25	23	2230	88	86
Indonesia	Bernard et al. 1975	1072	19	15	1057	30	24
Thailand	Bernard et al. 1975	1613	4	2	1463	47	44
Sudan	Rushwan et al. 1976	3263	10	10	2739	47	46
USA	Miller 1977	5883	48	45	3518	93	85

Adapted from Population Reports, Series F. No. 7. Table II, 1980.[4]

from an organ which weighs 1000 or more grams to one which weighs about 350 grams. Similarly, by the 14th day postabortion, most uteri also have greatly diminished in size. Some return to their approximate prepregnancy size; others, however, remain increased in bulk for the rest of the patient's life. In all probability, the specific anatomic findings in a given patient are as dependent on individual biologic characteristics as they are on the duration of gestation.

As is the case after term delivery, three major complications may interfere with the postabortal involutionary process and the restoration of the prepregnancy state of health:

1. Hemorrhage from retained products of conception
2. Infection, generally related to either retained products of conception or improper abortion techniques
3. Subinvolution, related to hemorrhage and/or infection, or without apparent cause

Should one or more of these complications interfere with the postabortal involution of the uterus, the provision of adequate therapy for the complication permits the continuation of the involutionary process in the vast majority of cases.

Lactation

In contrast to the situation observed after first-trimester abortion, patients who are farther along in pregnancy (especially after 16 gestational weeks) are more likely to experience some degree of breast engorgement and possibly even lactation. The normal physiology of lactation is based upon a gradual clearing of the steroids produced by the placenta, coincident with the appearance of spontaneous lactation triggered by pituitary hormones. During a pregnancy which continues to term, estrogen and progesterone stimulate the development of the ducts and secretory alveoli. After the postpartum removal of the placental tissue, the hormones derived from it are cleared rapidly from the maternal circulation, and prolactin begins to influence milk secretion. With the diminished influence of the placental hormones, breast sensitivity increases dramatically (Figure 21-1). Variations in breast sensitivity are demonstrable at other times of a woman's life as well, including during the menstrual cycles of women taking oral contraceptives (Figure 21-2). It has been postulated that this phenomenon may have a key role in the initiation of the feedback cycles which maintain lactation.

It is precisely because lactation is not maintained after second-trimester abortion, except in rare pathological circumstances, that prolactin begins to decline, thus permitting the appearance of LH in increasing quantities as an antecedent to the next ovulation (Figure 21-3).

The duration and degree of the lactational process after second-trimester abortion varies from patient to patient, depending to some

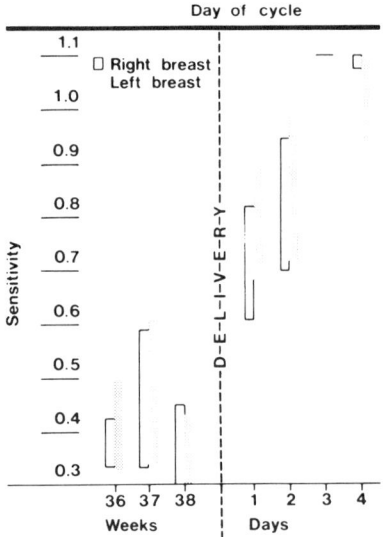

Figure 21-1 Changes in tactile sensitivity of cutaneous breast tissue in perinatal period.

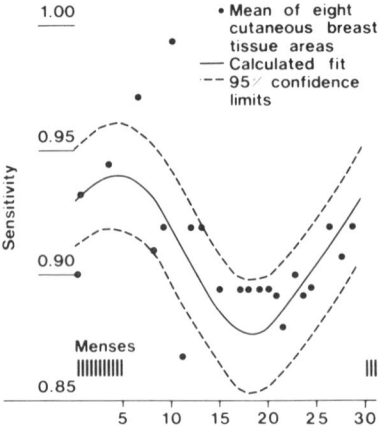

Figure 21-2 Changes in tactile sensitivity of cutaneous breast tissue in a nulliparous woman during menstrual cycle when taking oral contraceptives.

extent on the presence or absence of prior lactational experience and the gestational age of the pregnancy at the time of the abortion. The question of whether or not it is advisable to attempt to suppress the lactational process after late second-trimester abortion is beyond the scope of this presentation.

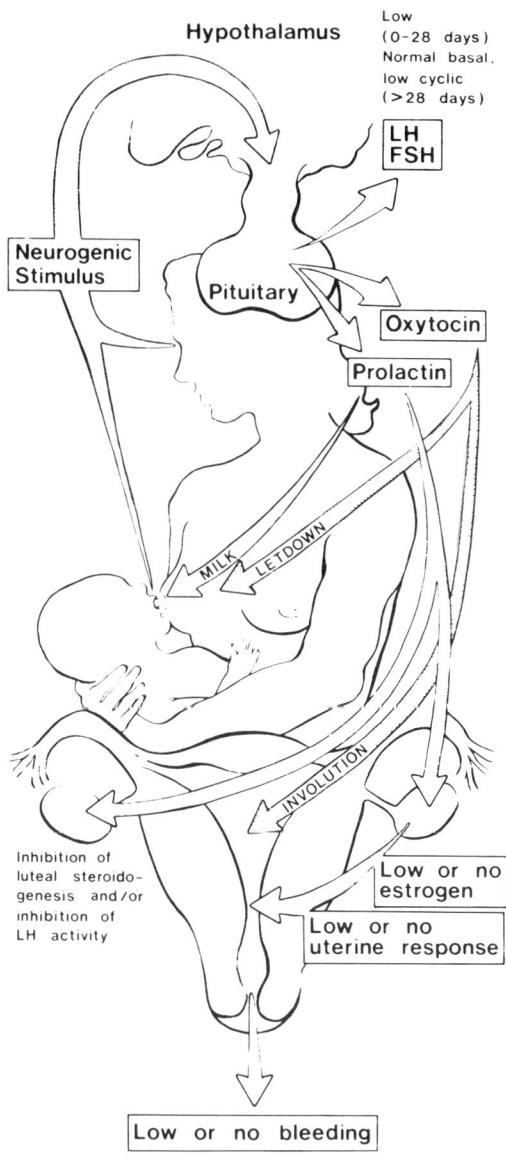

Figure 21-3 A possible mechanism for the maintenance of lactational amenorrhea.

IMMEDIATE CONTRACEPTIVE POSSIBILITIES

The four methods of contraception commonly utilized after second-trimester abortion are: a) sterilization, b) intrauterine devices, c) oral contraceptives, and d) barrier methods.

Sterilization

Before 1969, most second-trimester abortion procedures which were associated with sterilization utilized hysterectomy or hysterotomy combined with tubal ligation, since the traditional abdominal and vaginal approaches to the Fallopian tube were not practical. Since 1969, however, refinements in laparoscopic techniques have made the combination of abortion (first- or second-trimester) with sterilization a practical reality. The basic question which must be answered is whether complications accompanying the combined procedure of sterilization and abortion are more serious or frequent than those accompanying either procedure alone. A recent review of the world literature suggests that the question is far from settled.[4] Many of the studies used different methodologies and thus are difficult to compare directly. Patients who undergo the combined procedure, however, should be aware of the increased likelihood of ectopic pregnancy in those cases in which the sterilization operation fails and the woman becomes pregnant again.[6]

Abdominal approach *Conventional laparotomy plus hysterotomy* When hysterotomy is used, then the approach to the Fallopian tubes is solved, and the only decision remaining is the choice of surgical technique to achieve sterilization. The Pomeroy method of ligation is the easiest to accomplish. As such, it is used most frequently. The failure rate (subsequent pregnancies), however, is greater when the procedure is associated with the gravid state, as opposed to the nongravid state.[7] Partial or total salpingectomy has as low a failure rate as is possible, but the operating time is longer and the risk of intraoperative bleeding from incised or excised varices is greater than with the Pomeroy ligation alone. Complication rates secondary to the actual sterilization should be negligible and should be almost directly related to the laparotomy or hysterotomy alone.

Minilaparotomy Minilaparotomy incision can be made after second-trimester abortion. The major difference in the incision after second-trimester abortion and the incision in the nongravid state is its location, which varies due to the height of the fundus following uterine evacuation. Depending on operator skill and experience, incision size may vary. The advantages and disadvantages of minilaparotomy after second-trimester abortion are not dissimilar to those which exist after either a first-trimester abortion or an interval operation. These include the fact that minilaparotomy:

- Requires no extra equipment
- Requires no extra training in the use of specialized equipment
- Requires no large capital outlay for specialized equipment
- May be performed under local anesthesia
- May be performed on an outpatient basis
- May incorporate any method of tubal occlusion

Disadvantages are that:

- It is more difficult to perform in the obese patient
- The remaining pelvic and abdominal anatomy cannot be visualized

A good uterine manipulator is essential for minilaparotomy to antevert the uterus adequately against the anterior abdominal wall. By palpating the mechanically elevated uterine fundus suprapubically, the physician can choose the exact site for the incision. This is facilitated by the degree of uterine enlargement following second-trimester abortion. The tubes should then be easily accessible. The sterilization is performed by any of the ligation or mechanical occlusive techniques listed in Table 21-2. Hospitalization much beyond the time necessary to induce the abortion is unnecessary.

Endoscopic approach *Laparoscopy* The laparoscopic approach to second-trimester sterilization is possible and in many ways similar to postpartum laparoscopic sterilization.[8] In the hands of the experienced laparoscopist, it carries no appreciably greater risk of complications, provided that reasonable standards of care are followed for the procedure.

- The left subcostal or the cul-de-sac site can be used for the Verres needle if the fundus is still high [9]
- Superficial penetration by the pneumoperitoneum needle and trocar(s) is sufficient
- If the double puncture technique is chosen, the second puncture site must be in a position which enables adequate mobility, i.e., a higher and/or lateral site than usual
- Electrocoagulation without cutting or resecting is preferable
- Bipolar forceps should always be used, since the bowel will generally be in closer proximity to the enlarged uterus than when interval procedures are used

Table 21-2
Comparison of Tubal Occlusion Methods

Method	Part of Tube Treated	Approaches	Degree of Skill Required	Range of Failure Rate	Incidence of Morbidity
LIGATION					
Pomeroy	isthmus	minilaparotomy	average	0–0.4	low
		laparotomy	average	(higher when	low
		colpotomy	above average	performed by	moderate
		culdoscopy	high	culdoscopy)	low
		laparoscopy	high		low
Fimbriectomy	fimbria (distal)	minilaparotomy	average	nil	low
		laparotomy	average		low
		colpotomy	above average	(higher when	moderate
		culdoscopy	high	performed postpartum)	low
Uchida	ampulla	minilaparotomy	above average	nil	low
		laparotomy	above average		low
Madlener	isthmus	minilaparotomy	average	0.3–2	low
		laparotomy	average	(higher–30,	low
		colpotomy	above average	when performed	moderate
		culdoscopy	high	by colpotomy)	low
Irving	ampulla	minilaparotomy	average	nil	low
Cornual resection	cornual (proximal)	laparotomy	average	2.8–3.2	moderate

274

Method	Part of Tube Treated	Approaches	Degree of Skill Required	Range of Failure Rate	Incidence of Morbidity
Salpingectomy	lateral	minilaparotomy laparotomy	average average	0–1.9	moderate
Simple ligation	isthmus	minilaparotomy laparotomy colpotomy	average average above average	20	low low moderate
FULGURATION					
Coagulate only	isthmus	laparoscopy	high	1–2	moderate
Coagulate and divide	isthmus		high	0.1–2	high
Coagulate and excise	isthmus		high		high
CLIPS					
Spring-loaded	isthmus	laparoscopy (other routes possible)	high	0.2–0.6	low
BANDS					
Falope Ring	isthmus	laparoscopy	high	nil	low

Adapted from Wortman J: Tubal sterilization—review of methods, Population Reports C-7. *Sterilization.* May 1976.

- The choice of a mechanical occlusion technique can be made only after the tubes have been visualized
- If the tube appears too thick or edematous, the tubal ring or the tubal clip should not be used
- If suction curettage is employed to ensure that the uterus is completely evacuated, the suction curette may be used to manipulate the uterus without trauma. Otherwise, a sufficiently long intrauterine cannula must be employed

Failure rates following laparoscopic sterilization combined with second-trimester abortion are not available from the current literature. Theoretically, however, they should parallel those for the combined procedures in the first trimester.[6,10] Primarily because of the enlarged second-trimester uterus, many physicians have avoided adding sterilization to second-trimester procedures. While uterine injury due to trauma from the pneumoperitoneum needle and/or a trocar theoretically could be a major hazard, this potential problem can be largely alleviated by the use of the "open laparoscopy" technique developed by Hasson.[11] The marked vascularity of the mesosalpinx and broad ligament remain, nonetheless, the other potential major hazard.

Culdoscopy The popularity of this procedure has declined considerably since the development of laparoscopy. The Fallopian tubes can be fairly well visualized by means of this technique following uterine evacuation. The advantages as well as the hazards are similar to those in the first trimester.

Vaginal approach The major difficulty encountered with posterior colpotomy after second-trimester abortion procedures is the inability to visualize the Fallopian tubes if they lie either high or out of the true pelvis. When indeed they are visualized, excessive traction must be avoided as they are brought into the surgical field in order to carry out the sterilization procedure. Accessibility to the tubes may be enhanced by mechanically retroverting the fundus. In general, this approach is not recommended.

Hysterectomy for combined abortion and sterilization Few physicians favor vaginal hysterectomy as the definitive procedure for combined sterilization and abortion.[12,13] In Ballard's series of 200 cases of vaginal hysterectomy for abortion and sterilization, 22 women (10%) had specific gynecologic pathology that required immediate or possible future hysterectomy. In an additional 35%, indications for hysterectomy included mental retardation as well as psychiatric and medical indications. The remaining 55% had hysterectomy on the basis of their request for abortion and sterilization.[13] Scott justified hysterectomy combined with abortion by noting that, in many series where sterilization had been done by tubal occlusion, a high proportion of these patients eventually needed hysterectomy.[14]

Practicing physicians must ask themselves in every instance whether the risk of therapy is justified by the proposed benefit to the patient. Can equal benefit be achieved by lesser surgical procedures that carry lower morbidity and mortality rates? The indications for hysterectomy for sterilization in combination with abortion are as follows:

- Preexisting gynecologic pathology requiring major surgery
- Previous failed sterilization—fear of recurrence
- Cancer phobia—strong family history
- Desire to avoid continued menstruation or any of its disorders, such as menometrorrhagia or dysmenorrhea

In these situations, the risk/benefit ratio appears to be valid.

Intrauterine Devices (IUDs)

Although modern IUDs have been available for two decades, their use in the postabortal state has been advocated only recently. Prior to that, clinicians feared that they would be associated with increased rates of perforation and infection. This fear of infection undoubtedly influenced the 1977 U.S.Food and Drug Administration recommendation, which listed prior septic abortion as a contraindication to IUD use and recommended a delay of at least three months from the time of the abortion to the insertion of the IUD. These assumptions and clinical impressions have been challenged by recent research.[4] Numerous studies from a variety of locations now demonstrate that normal postabortal IUD insertion does not lead to increased complications or decreased continuation rates, and that the insertion of an IUD into an infected or potentially infected uterus does not lead to more morbidity or hospitalization. Clearly, the potential risks of an IUD insertion after a septic or illegal abortion must be weighed against the dangers of delaying contraception. Since a high percentage (75%) of postabortal women ovulate within three weeks after their abortion, the possibility of rapid return to the pregnant state is real. About 6% of women conceive within four to six weeks after an abortion unless they are using effective contraception. If a woman is to be protected from another pregnancy, contraception must be available prior to discharge from the clinic or hospital. Immediate protection from another pregnancy is the most important benefit of postabortal IUD insertion.

Although the exact mechanism of action of intrauterine devices is unknown, it is presently believed that they act either by interfering with fertilization or subsequent blastocyst implantation. Most IUDs are made of an "inert" plastic. Some, however, are medicated, either with copper or the hormone progesterone, both of which tend to increase the effectiveness of the device.

IUDs must be inserted by trained clinicians. They are highly effective contraceptives but, like oral contraception, they also have predictable side effects. Some of these are minor but, on occasion, they can be of a serious or even fatal nature. Clinicians who prescribe intrauterine devices must recognize these facts and bring them to the attention of their patients.

Regular reexamination of patients with intrauterine devices is mandatory. Careful attention must be directed to specific complaints which may point to signs of serious problems. The first reexamination should take place within four to six weeks after the insertion. Subsequently, the patient should be seen at least once annually. While frequent examinations do not prevent complications, they do lead to the opportunity for total reevaluation of the patient's contraceptive choice. A complete discussion of the complications of intrauterine devices, as well as practical suggestions to enhance their use, has been presented by Edelman et al.[15]

Oral Contraceptives

Extensive commentary on oral contraceptives is not possible in this chapter. Nonetheless, two points clearly must be considered as guiding principles in the prescription of these medications:

- Properly taken, the effectiveness of oral contraceptives is unquestionably very high (virtually 100%).
- Even under the best of circumstances, side effects occur to many users of oral contraceptives. Fortunately, the majority of side effects are not of a serious medical nature, though they may be the cause of pill discontinuation (i.e., Cloasma). For a small number of women, however, the complications associated with oral contraceptive use may be serious and can include disability or death.

The main question facing clinicians who prescribe oral contraceptives after second-trimester abortion is when to start. Three possibilities exist: the same day, five days later, or after the first normal menstruation. The latter approach unfortunately exposes the patient to another pregnancy. The problem with the early start (first or fifth day) is more theoretical than real. Clinicians fear that early use of the pill after abortion would predispose the patient to thrombophlebitis in a manner similar to that of the postpartum period. According to Ory[16] and Cates,[17] however, no studies have ever demonstrated that pill use after abortion increases the incidence of thrombophlebitis.

Initial Contraceptive Pill Selection

Certain present or historical contraindications to pill use are recognized. These are:

- Deep vein thrombophlebitis or thromboembolic disorders
- Cerebral vascular or coronary artery disease
- Known or suspected carcinoma of the breast
- Known or suspected estrogen-dependent neoplasia
- Undiagnosed abnormal genital bleeding

In addition, oral contraceptives are contraindicated when there is a known or suspected pregnancy.

Most of the serious side effects associated with pill use, with the possible exception of hypertension and altered glucose metabolism, are thought to be related to the estrogen content. Consequently, when feasible, all women initiating the use of oral contraceptives should be started on pills containing 50 µg or less of estrogen, and, with thorough counseling, those women who have already taken more than 50 µg should be prescribed a lower dosage. Side effects can be minimized by choosing a pill with the correct type and amount of progestogen. Of the 25 pills currently manufactured in the United States, 20 contain 50 µg or less of ethinyl estradiol, or 80 µg or less of mestranol.

OTHER TEMPORARY METHODS*

Barrier Methods

Vaginal methods of contraception can be used immediately after abortion. They offer the possibility of serving either as an

---

*A complete discussion of all barrier methods may be found in *Vaginal Contraception* by Jackson M, Berger GS, Keith LG; Boston, GK Hall and Co., 1980.

interim contraceptive method until a decision is made regarding medical contraception or sterilization, or as a long-term method. In either case, their effectiveness has been documented in a number of recent studies, and the rate of serious side effects is almost nil.[18] For many patients, the role of the barrier methods in protecting against infection with *N. gonorrhoeae* represents an added attraction.[19]

Barrier methods of contraception act by preventing direct access of live sperm to the cervical os. The majority (diaphragms, foams, creams, jellies) are applied by the female. The condom is the only barrier contraceptive utilized by the male.

Barrier methods are particularly advantageous for highly motivated individuals, for those who do not have frequent coitus, and for partners who have no objection to the slight inconvenience caused by these products. Of all the available contraceptive methods, only the barrier type consistently has been shown to reduce the chance of acquiring a venereal disease at the time of intercourse.[20]

Vaginal Spermicides

A variety of contraceptive products may be placed into the vagina prior to coitus. While their physical form and consistency differ greatly, the active spermicidal ingredient (nonoxynol-9) is similar. Products differ primarily in the selection of the carrier base of inert chemical. When properly applied, vaginal spermicides provide contraception by physically covering the external cervical os as well as by killing sperm on contact.

Statistical data regarding the effectiveness of vaginal contraceptive products vary widely (Table 21-3). A more recent epidemiologic review of these data, however, has noted several possible reasons for these differences, not the least of which is study design.[18] As a class of agents, the currently available vaginal spermicides are probably only slightly less effective than other barrier methods (diaphragm or condom) in which a mechanical barrier is always present and the contraceptive effect can be enhanced by the addition of a spermicidal cream or jelly.[18]

The application of vaginal spermicides is generally easy. In the case of the suppository, intravaginal insertion is made by either partner, as high in the vagina as possible. Foams, jellies, and creams all require the use of an applicator or plunger-like tube which permits deposition of the contraceptive material at or about the level of the cervical os (Figure 21-4). Coital movements disperse these agents around the cervix and vagina.

Table 21-3
Pregnancy Rate per 100 Woman-years, (Calculated by the Pearl Method) by Contraceptive Method

Method	Pregnancy Rate	
	Selected Clinical Trial	*Literature*
Condoms	4.10	6–29
Creams and jellies	6.33	5–36
Diaphragm	3.54	3–34
Foam	1.55	2–28
Suppositories	2.41	8–42

Source: Derman, Keith and Berger.[19]

Even among individuals who prescribe vaginal contraceptive methods routinely to their patients, there is no agreement as to how long prior to intercourse these agents should be inserted. Users of vaginal products are cautioned to read the consumer directions. In some instances, up to one hour is permissible but, presumably, the more recent the application, the more effective the spermicide. In the case of the currently available suppositories, there must actually be a delay of ten or more minutes before coitus, to allow the suppository to melt and diffuse.[21] If coitus is repeated, a reapplication of the preparation is not only desirable, but necessary. Postcoital douching, if practiced, should be delayed for six to eight hours. Controlled studies, however, are lacking to justify the validity of this clinical advice.

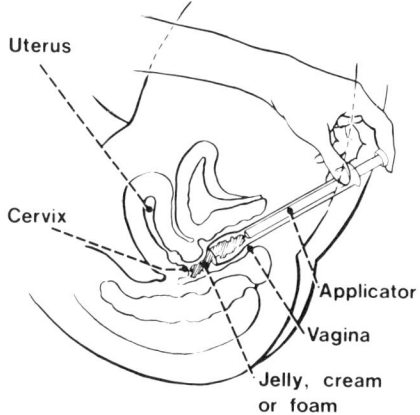

Figure 21-4 Proper insertion of vaginal foam.

Diaphragm

The diaphragm is a prescription barrier contraceptive method. It requires a fitting by a trained clinician and thus cannot be bought "over-the-counter" as can condoms and vaginal spermicides. Perhaps more importantly, its use in the immediate period after second-trimester abortion is probably quite limited because the fitting of a diaphragm should ideally take place when involution is complete and the vaginal canal has regained tonus. Each woman must be individually fitted for her diaphragm. Fitting should be rechecked every two years in the absence of childbirth, second-trimester abortion, vaginal surgery, or a weight gain or loss of greater than ten pounds. If positioned correctly, the diaphragm cannot be felt by either sexual partner during coitus.

SUMMARY

The patient who has had a second-trimester abortion clearly needs to be provided with a contraceptive method she can understand and use. A wide variety of contraceptives can be used after second-trimester abortion; these include sterilization, IUDs, pills, and vaginal barrier methods. Patients should understand that, while none of these methods is perfect, consistent and proper use of any one of them will greatly reduce the chance of another unwanted pregnancy.

REFERENCES

1. Keith L, Labbock M, Petty J, et al: *Postpartum and Postabortal Contraception*. Philadelphia, Synapse Publications, 1979.
2. Tietze C, Lewit S: Mortality associated with reversible methods of fertility regulation, in Keith L, Kent DR, Berger GS, et al (eds): *The Safety of Fertility Control*. New York, Springer, 1979, pp 42–48.
3. Moore-Cavar EC: *International Inventory of Information on Induced Abortion*. New York, Columbia University, International Institute for Human Reproduction, 1974, p 654.
4. Population Reports. Series F, No. 7. *Abortion in Developing Countries, April 1980*. Population Information Program, Johns Hopkins University, Baltimore, Md.
5. Lahteenmake P, Luukkainen T: Immediate postabortal contraception with a microdose combined preparation: Suppression of pituitary and ovarian function and elimination of HCG. *Contraception* 17:169, 1978.
6. Courey N, Horowitz A, Cunanan R: Sterilization combined with abortion, in Phillips JM, et al (ed): *Laparoscopy*. Baltimore, Md, Williams and Wilkins, 1977, pp 182–186.
7. Garb AE: A review of tubal sterilization failures. *Obstet Gynecol Surv.* 12:291, 1957.

8. Keith L, Houser KT: Puerperal sterilization, in Phillips JM, et al (ed): *Laparoscopy*. Baltimore, Md, Williams and Wilkins, 1977, pp 187-190.

9. van Lith DAF, Beekhuizen W, van Schie KJ: Complications of aspirotomy (AT): A modified dilatation and curettage procedure for terminating early second trimester pregnancies, in Zatuchni GI, Sciarra JJ, Speidel JJ (eds): *Pregnancy Termination: Procedures, Safety, and New Developments*. Hagerstown, Md, Harper & Row, 1979, pp 193-205. © Northwestern University, Chicago.

10. Cunanan RG, Courey NG, Lippes J: Complications of laparoscopic tubal sterilization. *Obstet Gynecol*. 55:501, 1980.

11. Hasson H: Open laparoscopy, in Phillips JM, et al (ed): *Laparoscopy*. Baltimore, Md, Williams and Wilkins, 1977, pp 145-149.

12. Atkinson SM Jr: Vaginal hysterectomy: The ideal abortion in multiparous patients. *South Med J*. 67:134, 1974.

13. Ballard CA: Therapeutic abortion and sterilization by vaginal hysterectomy. *Am J Obstet Gynecol*. 118:891, 1974.

14. Scott JS: Sterilization by hysterectomy. *Int Plann Parent Fed Med Bull*. 12:1, Feb 1978.

15. Edelman D, Berger GS, Keith LG: *IUDs and Their Complications*. Boston, GK Hall, 1979.

16. Ory H: Personal communication, 1979, in ref. 4.

17. Cates W Jr: Personal communication, 1979, in ref. 4.

18. Berger GS, Jackson M: The effectiveness of over-the-counter vaginal contraceptives, in Keith L, Kent DR, Berger GS, et al (eds): *The Safety of Fertility Control*. New York, Springer, 1979, pp 159-166.

19. Derman R, Keith LG, Berger GS: The role of vaginal contraceptives in preventing venereal disease and pregnancy, in Keith L, Kent DR, Berger GS, et al (eds): *The Safety of Fertility Control*. New York, Springer, 1979, pp 167-173.

20. Keith LG, Berger GS, Moss W: Cervical gonorrhea in women using different methods of contraception. *J Am Ven Dis Assoc*. 3:17, 1976.

21. Querido L, Schnabel P: Evaluating the clinical effectiveness of patentex oval, in Zatuchni GI, Sobrero AJ, Speidel JJ, et al (eds): *Vaginal Contraception*. Hagerstown, Md, Harper & Row, 1979, pp 146-153.

PART VI
International Considerations: The Dutch Abortion Experience

22 Second-Trimester Abortion Services In the Netherlands

Evert Ketting

During each of the past few years, between 80,000 and 100,000 pregnant women underwent voluntary, induced abortion in the Netherlands. The majority (about 85%) of them came from abroad. The large number of foreign women requesting abortion assistance was a logical consequence of the slow pace at which safe and easily accessible abortion facilities were being created in other Western European countries. The Dutch abortion clinics, which came into existence in the early 1970s, thus began to assume an international medical role for all of Western Europe. In the liberal situation which presently exists in the Netherlands, these clinics have been able to develop into specialized institutions with vast experience. As a result of regular communication among the various clinics, as well as a continuing exchange of points of view and experiences with regard to various aspects of treatment, both of which have been conducted within the framework of a sociomedical research organization designated as "Stimezo-Nederland," a high level of uniform quality of medical care has been reached in less than one decade.

Initially, the Dutch clinics provided only first-trimester abortion services. By the late 1970s, however, second-trimester experience, as well, had developed in the Netherlands, and these clinics became real international refuges. At the time of this writing, as a result of the politico-legal situation in neighboring countries, it appears that the Dutch clinics will have to continue to assume this responsibility for second-trimester assistance to an international group of patients in the foreseeable future.

THE PARADOXICAL LEGAL POSITION OF INDUCED ABORTION IN THE NETHERLANDS

According to the letter of the Dutch law, which dates from 1886 and is still officially in force, induced abortion is forbidden in almost every case. Nevertheless, the 18 presently existing abortion clinics have been tolerated by the responsible authorities for several years.[1] In reality, there is probably no other European country where the practice of abortion meets fewer obstacles than it does in the Netherlands.

The fact that the practice of abortion is possible in spite of its legal prohibition relates to the fact that the existing legislation has always left room to allow an abortion when medically indicated. Since the phrase "medical indication" is not defined by law, this has meant that the decision whether an induced abortion is medically indicated or not has always been left to physicians as a professional group. In any abortion action, the judge makes his judgment based upon the leading opinion among the physicians. Until the middle of the 1960s, the very restrictive character of this Dutch professional opinion meant that induced abortions were hardly ever carried out. As a result of numerous social changes, however, professional attitudes also began to change, especially in the late 1960s.

Between 1967 and 1971, a liberal attitude toward induced abortion developed among a group of leading Dutch gynecologists who themselves had started practicing induced abortion. Because of this, abortion at the pregnant woman's request slowly became possible. Prior to 1971, however, induced abortions almost always had taken place in the hospitals, which never had been able or willing to provide physically for more than 25% of the total abortions needed in the Netherlands.

As a result of this situation, several independent clinics were founded where, in principle, induced abortion could be performed upon request. Because the great majority of the leading Dutch gynecologists (e.g., the university professors) acknowledge the necessity of a liberal abortion assistance program,[2] and because the hospitals do not have the physical space to provide for large numbers of abortions, the legal position of these clinics is relatively safe. Similarly, since most practicing Dutch gynecologists are not disposed personally to practice this operation on a large scale, the existence of outpatient abortion facilities is welcomed and supported.

INDUCED ABORTION AS A NEW MEDICAL SPECIALTY

The abortion clinics in the Netherlands have been set up by ordinary general practitioners. No gynecologists are involved at present. This may seem a strange situation to some, but it is understandable in the context of Dutch medicine because the training of the general practitioners in the field of gynecology and obstetrics is more extensive than in most other countries. Moreover, without exception the gynecologists work only in hospitals. Birth control, pregnancy care, and delivery, generally speaking, are considered proper tasks of the family doctor. Only in special cases is a woman referred to a gynecologist.

For this reason, the practice of abortion became one of the general practitioner's tasks. In most clinics, these physicians work part-time and continue to maintain their own practices as family doctors. Only a few physicians, particularly those who have specialized in second-trimester abortion, work full-time in the abortion clinics. Physicians in training receive their instruction at the clinics from their more experienced colleagues. In this way, the practice of abortion has become a new medical specialty in the Netherlands, distinct from the official gynecology. Besides our own Dutch doctors, several physicians from Germany, Belgium, France, and other countries have learned to perform abortions in one of the Dutch clinics which fulfills this training function.

ASSISTANCE TO DUTCH AND FOREIGN WOMEN

Immediately after the development of the Dutch abortion clinics, large numbers of foreign women came to the Netherlands in order to obtain an induced abortion. The Dutch clinics took over England's role as an international abortion provider, especially for patients from Belgium and Western Germany and, to a certain extent, also from

France.[3] During 1977, a total of 16,000 Dutch and approximately 75,500 foreign women were treated in the Netherlands abortion clinics (Table 22-1).

Table 22-1
Induced Abortions in the United Kingdom and the Netherlands, by Nationalities

	United Kingdom		Netherlands
	1972	1977	1977
United Kingdom	108,600	102,700	...
Netherlands	200	...	16,000*
Belgium	2500	400	12,000
France	25,200	4200	1500
Western Germany	17,500	1700	60,000
Other countries	5900	24,500	2000
Total	159,900	133,500	91,500

*4000 in hospitals and 12,000 in abortion clinics.
Source: Ketting and Schnabel, 1978.[6]

Since 1975, however, the total number of foreign women treated in the Netherlands has declined slowly because of some changes which have occurred in the surrounding countries. This statement does not apply to second-trimester abortions, however. The reasons which make women from abroad apply for abortion assistance in the Netherlands are the lack of adequate abortion facilities, as well as obstacles to obtaining the procedure in their homelands. Moreover, Belgian and German women prefer to come to the Netherlands rather than to go to England for three reasons:

1. The shorter distance enables Belgian and many of the German women to come to a Dutch clinic and return to their homes the same day.
2. In the Dutch clinics, the patient's native language is spoken, as more than half of the Belgian women speak Dutch, and the staff of every clinic is able to speak German quite well.
3. In general, the cost of the treatment in the Dutch clinics is not high ($150–$200 for a first-trimester abortion and $300–$750 for a second-trimester abortion).

SECOND-TRIMESTER ABORTION IN THE NETHERLANDS

Until 1973, most women who were more than 12 weeks' pregnant were referred to clinics in the United Kingdom. In 1973, the first Dutch second-trimester abortion clinic was opened; it was called the "Bloemhovekliniek." In 1976, a second clinic was founded in Leiden: the "Medisch Centrum voor Geboortenregeling" or "Center for Human Reproduction." In the first clinic, women were treated by means of dilatation and evacuation, or prostaglandins. In principle, prostaglandins were used exclusively for pregnancies of more than 18 weeks. The women remained in the clinic for one or two nights.[4] In the Medisch Centrum voor Geboortenregeling, on the other hand, abortions are carried out up to the 19th week of pregnancy by means of a modified dilatation and evacuation procedure called aspirotomy. The treatment is ambulatory and the women leave the clinic after a short rest.[5] (See also Chapter 23 and Chapter 24.)

Both of these second-trimester clinics are highly attuned to assist foreign women for two reasons. First, the proportion of foreign women coming to the Netherlands in the second trimester of pregnancy is comparatively high. Second, the proportion of second-trimester abortions among Dutch women is rather low, because, in general, the need for abortion in the Netherlands is low. In fact, the 1.2 abortions per 1000 inhabitants make our abortion rate the lowest in the Western world.[6] Only 8% of the induced abortions among Dutch women take place after the 12th week of pregnancy. In 1977, second-trimester abortions were distributed by nationality as shown in Table 22-2.

Table 22-2
Second-Trimester Abortions
in the Netherlands, by Nationalities (%), 1977

Netherlands	14
Germany	69
Belgium and Luxembourg	10
France	4
Other countries	3
Total	100

Source: Ketting and Schnabel, 1978.[6]

THE ABORTION SITUATION IN THE NEIGHBORING COUNTRIES

The situation with regard to abortion legislation and practice in the different European countries is still in evolution. Although previously existing abortion legislation has been revised in many countries by now, establishing adequate abortion facilities often is hampered by a number of obstacles. The Dutch abortion clinics historically have played the role of a temporary refuge for the solution of urgent problem cases until the other countries were able to organize adequately their domestic abortion facilities. They do not desire or intend to maintain the present situation as a permanent one. This situation in the neighboring countries of Western Germany, Belgium, and France, is as follows.

Western Germany

In Western Germany, a new but very complicated abortion act came into existence in 1976, implying a partial liberalization. Up to the 12th week from conception (i.e., ± 14 weeks from the last menstrual period), abortion is allowed when socially indicated. After this time, however, a medical, eugenic, or psychiatric indication is legally required.

In practice, this act does not yet function very well. According to the official records, more than 65,000 German women had abortions in their own country in 1977, while some 60,000[7] were treated in the Dutch clinics in the same year. In addition, 1700 German women went to England[8] and an unknown number to Austria and Yugoslavia. By 1978, the number of domestic abortions in Germany reached 73,500, while the number of abortions performed on German women in the Netherlands decreased to about 48,000.[9]

The following problems arise in West German medical practice:

- The procedure to determine the indication for second-trimester abortion is long and difficult, and its result is uncertain. Because of this, many German women prefer to travel to Holland, where they are treated within one day after one simple phone call.
- Among West German gynecologists, the general attitude with regard to induced abortion is still very restrictive. Even those women who obtain the required certificate of indication for abortion often have difficulty in finding a practitioner who is disposed to carry out the procedure.
- Among West German physicians, the number with sufficient skill and experience in the practice of induced abortion is still small.

The problems for German patients with regard to second-trimester abortion are even greater:

- The difficult and slow procedure of obtaining the indication certificate often makes women come after the first trimester.[10]
- The negative medical attitude toward induced abortion, which is even stronger in the second trimester, makes it extremely difficult for the pregnant woman to find a physician willing to help her.
- In West Germany, as in the Netherlands and several other countries, it is difficult to increase the number of abortions carried out in hospitals. Therefore the excess of abortion procedures must be carried out in the private offices of the gynecologists. In 1977, only 8200 patients were treated in private practices (15%); in 1978 this rose to 17,000 (23%).[7] This problem is compounded by the fact that, outside the hospital, induced abortion is allowed only up to the eighth week after the conception (about tenth week from the last menstrual period).

As a result of these problems, the number of second-trimester abortions presently being performed in West Germany is rather low and cannot be expected to increase. In 1977, the number of abortions performed after more than 12 weeks from conception totalled 1440; in 1978, this number was only 1520, i.e., 2.6% and 2.1%, respectively, of the total number of abortions.[7] As a result of this situation, women presently are highly dependent on the Dutch clinics, especially after the 14th week from the last menstrual period. In 1978, approximately 2400 abortions after 14 weeks were performed on German women in the Netherlands, a number considerably larger than the number performed in Germany itself.

Belgium

Belgium is one of the few Western European countries where the abortion legislation has not been changed in recent years. The old legislation is very restrictive, and it does not seem likely that a new law will be enacted soon. Nevertheless, there are a few possibilities for abortion in Belgium. Located mostly in the French-speaking, southern part of the country, several very small clinics are quietly tolerated by the authorities. In the Dutch-speaking, northern part of the country, where the existing legislation is more strictly enforced, it is difficult to obtain an abortion. One of the major problems here is the lack of motivation among physicians and other responsible persons to create domestic abortion facilities in view of the existence of excellent facilities just across the Dutch frontier. Many Belgian doctors refer their patients directly to a Dutch clinic, a fact which causes few problems on either side of the frontier because the same language is spoken and the distance is short. According to a quite reliable estimate, about half of all Belgian women who presently seek abortion are treated in the Netherlands, i.e., 10,000 to 20,000.[11]

As to second-trimester abortion, the situation for Belgian women is very much the same as it is for West German women. Second-trimester cases are even more dependent on Dutch facilities than are the early cases. However, the proportion of second-trimester abortions among Belgian patients is not extremely high (10% in 1977). This is probably due to the fact that a certain number of Belgian women with second-trimester pregnancies still find their way to England.

France

Early in 1975, a new abortion law was passed in France. This permitted induced abortion at the woman's request up to the tenth week of gestation (from conception, ie, about 12th week from the last menstrual period). After this time, a medical indication is required. In the latter case, preliminary procedural requirements are rather complicated, and there are important local differences as to the available facilities. The development of an adequate abortion program in France is hampered primarily by the legal restriction that no medical institution is allowed to perform abortions in excess of 25% of all its treatments. This prevents the development of specialized abortion clinics. Nevertheless, abortion assistance has developed rapidly in France, as the decline in the number of French women treated abroad since 1974 proves. In 1974, 36,400 French women went to the United Kingdom for assistance, and approximately 10,000 to the Netherlands; in 1977, these numbers had decreased to 4200 and 1500, respectively.[8]

Among the French women still coming to the Netherlands, a comparatively high proportion are second-trimester cases (25% in 1977 and 33% in 1978). Probably the same proportion applies to French women who have an abortion performed in England. For the rest, the abortion situation in France is not encouraging, because the compulsory registration does not function adequately.[12] Ever since the legal modification in 1975, illegal abortion practices have continued in France, especially with regard to second-trimester cases. Because second-trimester abortion without a medical indication is forbidden, these abortions sometimes are exceedingly costly.[13]

Other Countries

Besides the women from West Germany, Belgium, and France, approximately 2000 women from Southern European countries, especially Spain and Italy, come to the Netherlands each year for abortions. But much larger numbers of women from these countries go to the United Kingdom. In Italy, abortion legislation was liberalized in 1978, but the practical result remains uncertain for the time being. The situation in Spain, where very restrictive legislation also is in force, remains equally uncertain. It is difficult to forecast how the abortion situation in these countries is going to develop in the near future.

DISCUSSION

In spite of the fact that a modification of the existing and restrictive abortion legislation has not yet taken place, a well functioning system of abortion facilities has been built up in the Netherlands. As an analogous development did not take place in neighboring countries, the Dutch abortion services soon began to assume an international function.

This situation, characterized by a large influx of patients and an actual absence of legal limitations, has made it possible to achieve a high level of specialization in the field of abortion techniques and procedures.

Because of a gradual improvement of abortion legislation and abortion practices in the neighboring countries, the need for abortion assistance in the Netherlands is now gradually diminishing. This is true only for first-trimester abortions, however. During the next few years, the Dutch abortion clinics will very probably have to continue fulfilling an international function in the field of second-trimester abortion.

REFERENCES

1. Schnabel P: *Abortus in Nederland, Hulpverlenen zonder de wet te veranderen.* Den Haag, Stimezo, 1977.
2. Ketting E: *Van misdrijf tot hulpverlening* (Een analyse van de maatschappelijke betekenis van abortus provocatus in Nederland). Alphen a/d Rijn, 1978.
3. Schnabel P: Schwangerschaftsunterbrechung in den Niederlanden. *Sexual-medizin,* 1979.

4. Van den Bergh AS: *De 'methode Finks'* (en alternatieve technieken voor therapeutische zwangerschapsafbreking in het 2e trimester van de graviditeit). Den Haag, Stimezo, 1977.

5. Van Lith DAF, Beekhuizen W, Schie KJ: Complications of aspirotomy (AT). A modified dilatation and curettage procedure for terminating early second-trimester pregnancies, in Zatuchni GI (ed): *Pregnancy Termination: Procedures, Safety and New Developments*. New York, Harper & Row, 1979.

6. Ketting E, Schnabel P: *De abortushulpverlening in 1977*. Den Haag, Stimezo, 1978.

7. Deutsches Statistisches Bundesamt, Wiesbaden, unpublished data, 1976–1978.

8. Tietze C: *Induced Abortion: 1979*. Third edition. New York, The Population Council, 1979.

9. Ketting E: *Abortus in 1978*. Den Haag, Stimezo, 1979.

10. World Health Organization: Induced Abortion. Report of a WHO Scientific Group. Technical Report Series 623, Geneva, WHO, 1978.

11. Praag Ph v: Poliklinische abortering van belgische vrouwen in Nederland. *Tijdschrift voor Geneeskunde* 34:1443–1448, 1978.

12. Blayo C: Les intérruptions volontaires de grossesse en France en 1976. *Population* 2:307, 1979.

13. Janaud A: L'intérruption des grossesses en France en 1977. *Contraception, fertilité, sexualité* 5:343, 1977.

23 Aspirotomy

Dirk A.F. van Lith
Willem Beekhuizen
Kees J. van Schie
Marijke du Plessis-Alblas

Among the useful methods for termination of second-trimester pregnancies are D&E, hypertonic saline instillation, and prostaglandin administration. In contrast to outpatient D&E, however, the use of saline or prostaglandins generally requires hospitalization and is therefore less practical and more expensive. Perhaps more important, these latter procedures often are more distressing to the patient, because they are more painful.

An increasing awareness of the potential dangers resulting from extensive cervical dilatation in second-trimester vaginal operations led to the development of aspirotomy.[1,2] This technique combines the classical D&E method with suction curettage (Figure 23-1) and adds the following favorable therapeutic points (Figure 23-2):

1. An ergotrate preparation is given intramuscularly or intravenously at the onset. This causes sustained contraction of the uterine wall, decreases the chance of perforation, and accelerates the emptying of the uterine cavity.

2. Epinephrine 1:200,000 in 1% lidocaine is used as a local anesthetic solution. This results in a reduction of immediate operative blood loss while permitting an increase of the maximum dose of lidocaine which can be administered safely. Similarly, the incidence of vasovagal reactions is minimized.

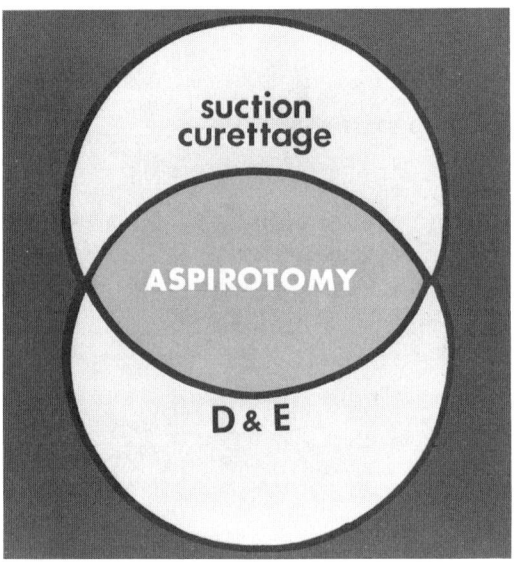

Figure 23-1 The relationship of aspirotomy to suction curettage and D&E.

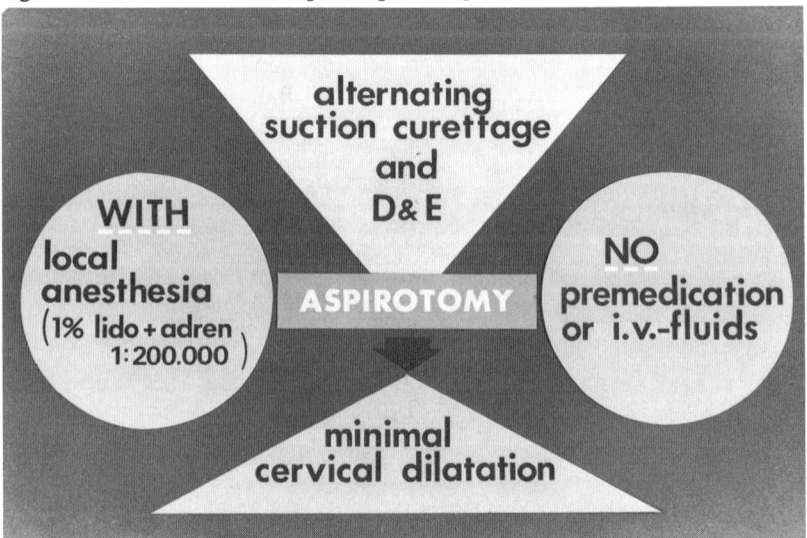

Figure 23-2 The essentials of aspirotomy.

During 1977 and 1978, 2136 patients underwent second-trimester pregnancy termination by aspirotomy at the Center for Human Reproduction in Leiden, Holland. Evacuation was achieved by alternating suction with a crushing technique. A specially designed crushing forceps limited the required cervical dilatation (Table 23-1).

Table 23-1
Dilatation Schedule for Surgical Pregnancy Termination[2]

Weeks' Gestation	Required Dilatation	Procedure
6 to 9	6 mm	Aspiration
10 to 12	8 mm	Aspiration
13 to 14	10 mm	Aspiration
14 to 16	10 mm	Aspirotomy
17 to 19	13 to 15 mm	Aspirotomy

Source: van Lith et al.[4]

ASPIROTOMY PROCEDURE

Ergometrine, 0.15 mg, is injected either intravenously or intramuscularly. After local disinfection of the perineum and vagina with povidone-iodine, a weighted speculum is introduced. Two milliliters of a solution of 1% lidocaine with epinephrine 1:200,000 is injected into the cervix at the 12 o'clock position. An atraumatic tenaculum then is placed on the anterior cervical lip at the instillation site, and a total of 10 ml of the same anesthetic solution is injected at the 4 and 8 o'clock positions. In addition, a total of 20 ml of the anesthetic solution is injected at the level of the internal os and the ascending branches of the uterine vessels at the 2, 4, 8, and 10 o'clock positions. Before injection, the needle plunger is withdrawn to avoid direct intravascular injection. The result of this combined para- and intracervical block, in addition to providing an excellent analgesia, is the constriction of the ascending branches of the uterine arteries. This latter factor helps to create a nearly bloodless operation.

The cervical canal then is dilated by insertion of Hawkins-Ambler tapered lightweight uterine dilators of overlapping sizes. A minimum of cervical trauma results from the gentle handling of these instruments, especially with dilatation according to the schedule in Table 23-1. For aspirotomy of a pregnancy of 14 to 19 weeks' menstrual age, a 10 mm rigid plastic suction cannula is introduced, and as much amniotic fluid as possible is aspirated. Vacuum is provided by a negative pressure of 700 mm Hg.

The van Lith/van Schie embryotomy forceps* then are inserted in closed position into the uterine cavity up to the fundus, withdrawn about 1 cm and only then opened widely, so that the uterine contents fall between the jaws. The forceps are closed gently and, by maneuvering the instrument in a rotating manner, the operator makes sure that no uterine wall is caught. The larger fetal parts are crushed and evacuated in the longitudinal axis of the cervix. The placental tissues are removed from the uterine walls. If no fetal parts are obtained by the forceps, suction is reapplied to bring these products from beyond the reach of the forceps in the uterine corners down to a place in front of the internal uterine os where they then can be grasped and removed with ease. *Grasping does not take place in a random fashion in all areas of the uterine cavity. It takes place in front of the internal os of the cervix as the uterine walls close down and contract.* A gentle curettage then is performed with a 10 mm Evans sharp curette. To assure complete evacuation of all fetal parts, final suction is reapplied with a 6 mm cannula in order to clear the fundal corners of both placental tissues and air if it is present. All products of conception are examined to confirm completeness. The duration of the procedure varies from 10 to 20 minutes.

COMMENTS

The routine injection of ergotrate preparations causes a sustained contraction of the uterine wall. This may be the reason that, in our experience, uterine perforation in the second trimester occurs only about twice as frequently as in the first trimester (Chapter 24). This is in sharp contrast to the report of Burnhill,[3] who has indicated a perforation rate 14 times higher in late vaginal abortions than in earlier abortions. Moreover, the addition of epinephrine 1:200,000 to the local anesthetic solution results in: 1) reduction of operative bleeding, 2) increase of the tolerable dose of lidocaine, and 3) absence of vasovagal responses during and after the operation (Figure 23-3).

A tachycardia of short duration almost always occurs after the anesthetic injection. It is possible that this is the reason that we see so few vasovagal reactions,[4] since atropine is *not* routinely administered to prevent vasovagal reaction. Of interest, ergotrate 0.15 mg and 30 ml 1% lidocaine with epinephrine 1:200,000 have been administered to more than 12,000 patients between 1976 and 1979 at our clinic; there have been no complications.

---

*Available in the U.S.A. from The Charles A. Fields Medical Foundation, Ltd, Chicago.

Adequate and special instrumentation are of extreme importance for a fast and safe procedure. A strong and silent suction machine facilitates quick aspiration of placental tissue and causes minimal distress to the patient. A heavy, weighted speculum, a nontraumatic, firm-grasping tenaculum, nontraumatic tapered dilators, a sufficiently long suction cannula with two or three apertures, and a strong and slender crushing forceps are essential instruments.

The procedure described in this chapter is almost painless and far less costly and time-consuming for the patient than is the case with instillation abortions. Moreover, the complication rate as reported by Beekhuizen et al. in Chapter 24 supports this technique as first choice for abortions of 14 to 19 menstrual weeks' gestation.

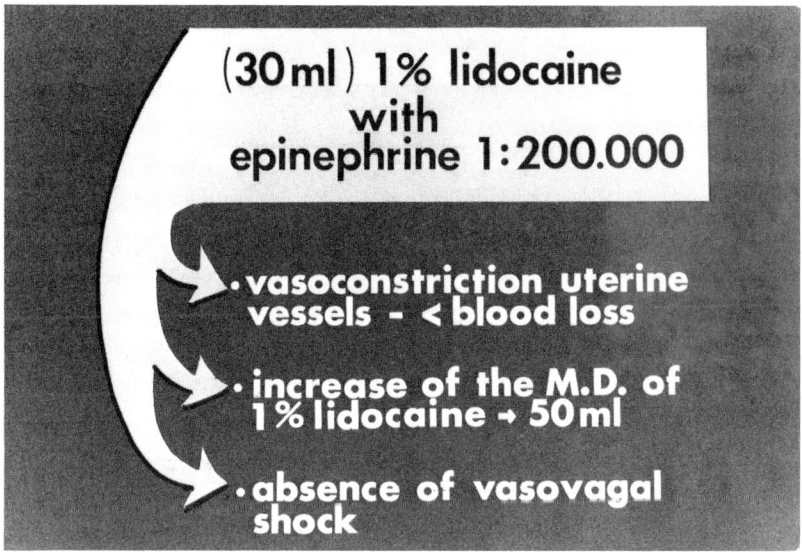

Figure 23-3 The effect of the addition of epinephrine to the local anesthetic.

REFERENCES

1. Beekhuizen W, van Schie KJ, van Lith DAF: Evaluation of Aspirotomy. Presented at the 5th International Congress of Psychosomatic Obstetrics and Gynecology, Rome, November 13, 1977.

2. Van Lith DAF, Beekhuizen W, van Schie KJ: Complications of aspirotomy (AT). A modified dilatation and curettage procedure for terminating early second-trimester pregnancies, in Zatuchni GI, Sciarra JJ, Speidel JJ (eds): *Pregnancy Termination: Procedures, Safety and New Developments*. Hagerstown, Md, Harper & Row, 1979.

3. Burnhill MS: Vaginal second trimester abortion, in Sciarra JJ, Speidel JJ, Zatuchni GI (eds): *Risks, Benefits and Controversies in Fertility Control*. Hagerstown, Md, Harper & Row, 1978, p 345.

4. Van Lith DAF, van Schie KJ, Beekhuizen W, et al: Laparoscopic sterilization under local anesthesia without premedication, in Phillips JM (ed): *Endoscopy in Gynecology.* Downey, CA, American Association of Gynecologic Laparoscopists, 1978, p 107.

24 Complications of Aspirotomy

Willem Beekhuizen
Dirk A.F. van Lith
Kees J. van Schie
Marijke du Plessis-Alblas

In 1977 and 1978, 6674 patients requested termination of pregnancy at the Center for Human Reproduction, Leiden, Holland. Two hundred forty-four patients were not treated because they were either not pregnant, or the pregnancy was too far advanced for treatment in our outpatient clinic. In all, 6430 women underwent an elective pregnancy termination. In contrast to other clinics in Holland, our clinic specializes in early second- as well as first-trimester outpatient pregnancy termination. The percent distribution of gestational ages for all abortions performed in 1978 in Holland and in our clinic is shown in Figure 24-1.

Based upon the duration of the gestation, one of two methods of pregnancy termination is selected. Up to the end of the 13th week of menstrual gestation, vacuum aspiration (VA) is used. From the 14th week, a D&E technique, aspirotomy (AT), is used. This technique represents an extension of the vacuum aspiration procedure and has been described by van Lith et al. in more detail in Chapter 23. Two-thirds of the patients were treated by vacuum aspiration alone. One-third of the patients, their pregnancies ranging from 14 to 19 weeks' gestation (Figure

24-2) were treated by aspirotomy. Patient demographic characteristics and major complications were noted on the day of abortion using standard forms provided by the Netherlands Abortion Federation.

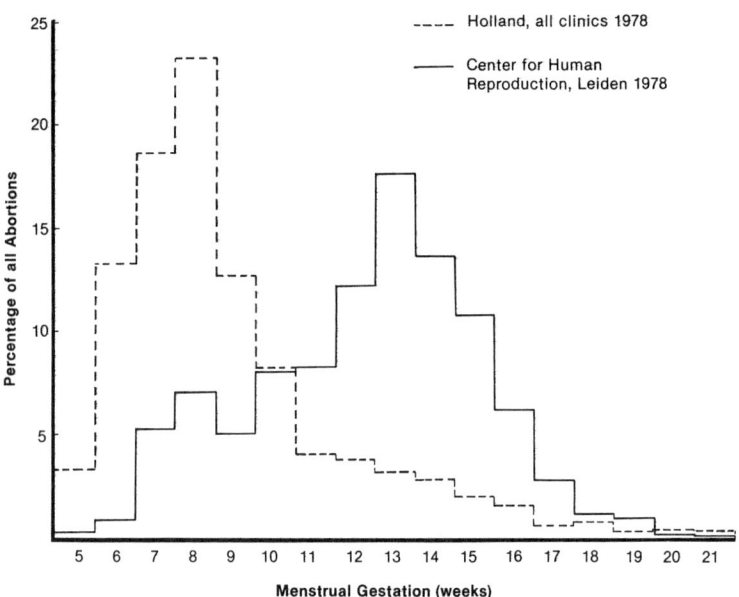

Figure 24-1 Percent distribution of gestational age by menstrual weeks' gestation: Holland, 1978, and Leiden, 1978.

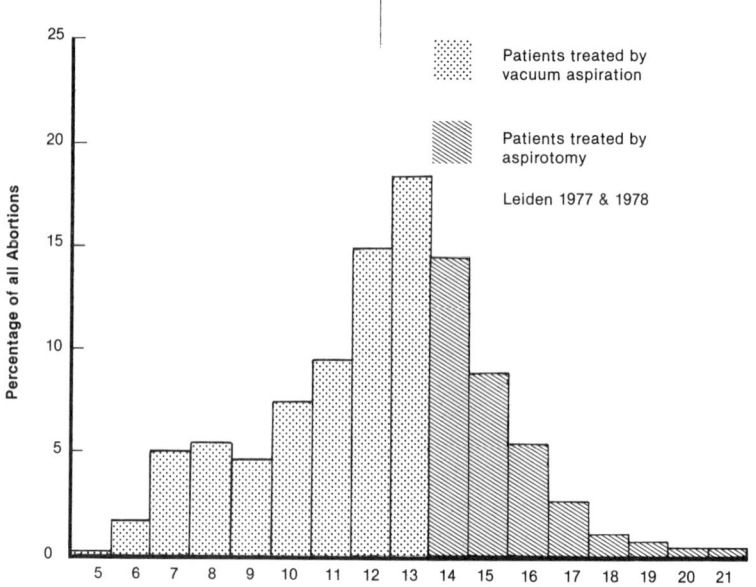

Figure 24-2 Percent distribution of gestational age by menstrual weeks' gestation: Leiden, 1977 and 1978.

RESULTS

The demographic characteristics of the women who underwent pregnancy termination by VA and AT are shown in Table 24-1. Nearly one-fourth of the patients were 20 or younger. About half of the patients were single and nulliparous. The median age and parity of all patients were 23.9 years and 0.5 live births, respectively. Almost nine-tenths of the women reported no previous pregnancy terminations. Two-thirds were not using contraceptives, while one-tenth were using either oral contraceptives or IUDs at the time of conception. Three-quarters of all patients came from West Germany to obtain an abortion in our clinic.

Table 24-1
Percent Distribution of Selected Characteristics of Women Receiving Abortion by Vacuum Aspiration (VA) and Aspirotomy (AT), Leiden, 1977 and 1978

Characteristics	VA No. = 4294	AT No. = 2136	Total No. = 6430
Age (years)			
≤ 19	21.1	26.8	23.0
20 to 24	29.7	28.7	29.4
≥ 25	49.2	44.5	47.6
Marital status			
Single	52.4	58.6	54.4
Married	40.5	33.9	38.3
Divorced/widowed	7.1	7.5	7.3
Parity			
0	48.4	52.1	49.6
1-2	34.6	31.4	33.6
3-4	13.7	12.3	13.3
5 and over	3.3	4.2	3.5
Previous pregnancy terminations			
0	87.6	89.0	88.1
1	11.1	10.4	10.9
2 or more			
Land of origin			
Netherlands	7.5	10.1	8.3
West Germany	77.0	71.1	75.0
Other	15.5	18.8	16.7
Contraception used at conception			
None	63.5	67.1	64.7
Oral	9.0	11.2	9.8
IUD	0.8	0.9	0.9
Condom	6.5	5.3	6.1
Coitus interruptus/Knaus Ogino	10.6	7.7	9.6
Other	9.6	7.8	8.9

Patients in the aspirotomy group (13 weeks and more) more often were young, single, and had used no contraception than was the case with the patients in the vacuum aspiration group ($p < 0.0005$). On the other hand, there were less significant differences between both groups with respect to parity and previous pregnancy terminations ($p < 0.05$).

COMPLICATIONS

Only immediate major complications are discussed in detail here, i.e., complications occurring either at the time of the operation or before the patient was discharged from the clinic. The 12 serious complications of this series are listed in Table 24-2.

Table 24-2
Immediate Major Complications, Leiden, 1977 and 1978

No.	Complication	Type	Weeks LMP*	Treatment	Hospitalization
1	Blood loss	1500 ml	11†	...	...
2	Blood loss	1000 ml	14	...	...
3	Blood loss	Coagulopathy	19	Transfusion	Yes
4	Perforation	Uterine	17	Laparoscopy	Yes
5	Perforation	Uterine	12	Observation	...
6	Blood loss	600 ml	12	...	...
7	Perforation	Uterine	N.P.‡	Observation	...
8	Blood loss	750 ml	15	...	...
9	Blood loss	1000 ml	14	...	...
10	Blood loss	800 ml	14	...	...
11	Perforation	Cervical	15	Observation	...
12	Perforation	Intestinal laceration	20	Laparotomy	Yes

*Weeks since last menstrual period = gestational weeks.
†Twin pregnancy.
‡N.P. = not pregnant.

The two most frequently occurring immediate major complications were blood loss estimated at more than 500 ml and perforation of the uterus. Blood transfusions were needed for one patient who also required a major operation for repair of an intestinal laceration.

The immediate major complication rate for pregnancies from 5 to 13 weeks, treated with vacuum aspiration alone, was 0.09%, or about 1 per 1000 patients. The immediate major complication rate for pregnancies from 14 to 20 weeks, treated with the aspirotomy technique, was 0.37%, about 3 to 4 per 1000 patients.

These latter figures are low, especially for a second-trimester D&E procedure.[1] Our rates for hemorrhage and perforation have been compared with the rates for major early complications reported by a WHO Scientific Group[2] as shown in Table 24-3.

Table 24-3
Percent Incidence of Hemorrhage and Perforation by Vacuum Aspiration, Dilatation and Evacuation, and Aspirotomy

Complication	VA WHO* No. = 40,000	VA Leiden No. = 4294	D&E WHO* No. = 6500	AT Leiden No. = 2136
Hemorrhage	0.10 to 3.90	0.05†	0.48 to 6.00	0.23†
Perforation	0.00 to 0.45	0.05	0.06 to 0.28	0.14

*Summary of results of various studies reported between 1974 and 1977, published by the World Health Organization, 1978.[2]
†Rates for hemorrhage of Leiden do not include delayed hemorrhage.

Minor complications, which are not listed here, include a wide variety of problems such as difficulty in evacuating the uterus, need for repeat curettage prior to discharge from the clinic, patients not being pregnant at the time of operation, tenaculum tear of the cervix, and equipment problems.

COMMENT

Many factors contribute to complications of abortion: the general health of the patient, the medications and equipment used for the procedure, the skill and experience of the operator, and the medical standards and the structure of a clinic.

In our spectrum of complications it is remarkable that there are no obvious cases of true cervical laceration, ie, laceration of the internal os of the cervix. Convulsions, hypotension, or other anesthesia problems also were extremely rare. There was one case of convulsions associated with coagulopathy. It is possible that the absence of these anesthesia-associated complications in our series, as well as the low rate of hemorrhage and perforation, is related to our modifications of the classical D&E technique, in particular the use of epinephrine and intracervical block.

Aspirotomy originally was developed by van Lith and associates[3] in 1975 and 1976 to perform early *outpatient* second-trimester pregnancy termination. AT includes four major modifications of the classical D&E technique.

1. Administration of an ergotrate preparation, IV or IM, preoperatively. This results in a sustained contraction of the uterus which may help to prevent perforation.
2. Addition of epinephrine 1:200,000 to the local anesthetic solution. This seems to prevent many minor and major anesthesia problems associated with the use of local anesthetics. Atropine is not given routinely.
3. Epinephrine in a solution of 1:200,000 gave optimal vasoconstriction and did not cause any major side effects in our series.
4. Minimal dilatation (Chapter 23, Table 23-1) and the alternating suction-crushing technique may prevent serious cervical laceration. To complete the procedure with minimal dilatation, specially developed small instruments are required, such as forceps in different sizes (Figure 24-3), curettes, etc. In our AT series, we have

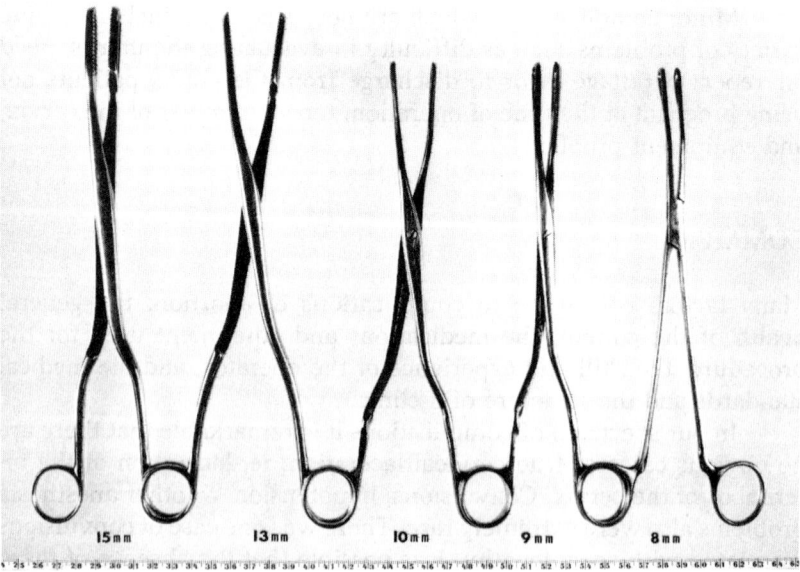

Figure 24-3 Different evacuation forceps, required cervical dilatation, and corresponding gestational age. Left to right: Sopher or Finks forceps, 15 mm dilatation required; 17 weeks and more. Smaller Sopher forceps, 13 mm dilatation required; 16 to 17 weeks. Van Lith/van Schie embryotomy forceps,* 10 mm dilatation required; 15 to 16 weeks. Aspirotomy forceps,* 9 mm dilatation required; 13 to 14 weeks (Scale at bottom is centimeters.)

*Available in the U.S.A. from The Charles A. Fields Medical Foundation, Ltd., Chicago.

noticed no cases of injury to the internal cervical os by bony parts of the fetus (calvaria, femur), possibly because of the fact that in early second-trimester—at least up to the 17th week LMP—these parts are not yet firm enough to lacerate the cervix when removed in a longitudinal axis of the cervical canal.

Further investigations are required to determine the importance of each of these above-mentioned variations in the classical D&E technique on the morbidity of the AT procedure.

The immediate major complication rate for AT in the early second trimester are within the range of complications published by the WHO for first-trimester procedures (Table 24-3). Along with Cates et al.,[4] we conclude that a differentiation by trimesters based on gestational age alone as a risk factor is arbitrary and can be misleading. Future complication studies regarding D&E procedures in late second trimester (18 weeks and more) may perhaps indicate a significant difference between these procedures and early second-trimester pregnancy termination.

REFERENCES

1. Tietze C: Personal communication, September 1979.
2. World Health Organization: Induced abortion, report of a WHO Scientific Group, Technical Report Series 623, Geneva, 1978, p 30.
3. Van Lith DAF, Beekhuizen W, van Schie KJ: Complications of aspirotomy, in Zatuchni GI, Sciarra JJ, Speidel JJ (eds): *Pregnancy Termination: Procedures, Safety and New Developments*. Hagerstown, Md, Harper & Row, 1979, pp 193 205.
4. Cates W Jr, Schulz KF, Grimes DA, et al: The effect of delay and method choice on the risk of abortion morbidity. *Fam Plann Perspect.* 9:266, 1977.

PART VII
Future Directions

25 The Future of Second-Trimester Abortion in the United States

Louise B. Tyrer

Before the legalization of abortion in the United States, it was estimated that about one million illegal abortions were performed annually.[1] At the time of legalization on January 22, 1973, the medical profession had no direct knowledge of the mechanics required to establish a service-delivery system of the extent needed for the abortion demand which soon was to become evident. It was clear, however, that there was a need to provide comprehensive medical services, diminish the health risks associated with poorly performed or criminal abortions, and eliminate the problems associated with enforced childbearing, i.e., children bearing children, short intervals between births, and grand multiparity.

Since 1973, a great deal of progress has been made both in medicine and in the programs which bring these services to potential recipients. This progress notwithstanding, certain issues remain unresolved. Most of these concern the performance of abortion at 13 weeks or later. The task which presently faces the medical profession is to develop workable strategies for the future which minimize as much as possible both the need for later abortions and the risks associated with them. Almost simultaneously with the liberalization of abortion laws, the Joint Program for Surveillance of Abortion was instituted. This effort has been continued by the abortion surveillance branch of the Center for Disease Control which now collects data on abortion performance, complication rates, and mortality. Initially, as abortion services were established, it became apparent that many women who otherwise could have obtained an abortion within the first trimester ultimately sought it at later stages of pregnancy when the medical risks were greater (Table 25-1).[2] Figure 25-1 displays the percent distribution of legal abortions by weeks of gestation in the years 1972 through 1976, and also documents the fact that, although the numbers of abortions performed from 13 menstrual weeks on has declined, there is room for additional improvement.[3] This statement is particularly true for younger women. In 1976 the US abortion ratio was 312:1000 live births; however, the ratio for women less than 15 years old was 1208:1000 live births.[4] Figure 25-2 shows the relationship of age to abortions by weeks of gestation in New York City in 1977. Since the mortality rate associated with abortions occurring at 13 menstrual weeks and beyond is higher than the mortality rate associated with pregnancy and childbirth, exclusive of abortion (Table 25-2), it is apparent that future actions should not only be directed toward diminishing the need for second-trimester abortion but also to making it safer.[2]

Table 25-1
Death-to-case Rate for Legal Abortions
by Weeks of Gestation, United States, 1972 to 1977[2]

Weeks of Gestation	Rate*	Relative Risk†
< 8	0.6	1.0
9–10	1.7	2.8
11–12	2.7	4.5
13–15	7.5	12.5
16–20	14.6	24.3
> 21	20.5	34.2
Overall	2.6	

*Deaths per 100,000 abortions.
†Based on Index rates for 8 menstrual weeks' gestation of 0.6 per 100,000 abortions.

Table 25-2
Death-to-case Rate for Legal Abortions Performed at 13 Weeks and Beyond, as Compared to Other Pregnancy and Childbirth-Related Deaths

Abortion Deaths, 13 Weeks and Beyond*	Other Pregnancy and Childbirth-Related Deaths†
14.2	10.6

*Deaths per 100,000 abortions.
†Deaths per 100,000 live births, exclusive of abortion-related mortality.

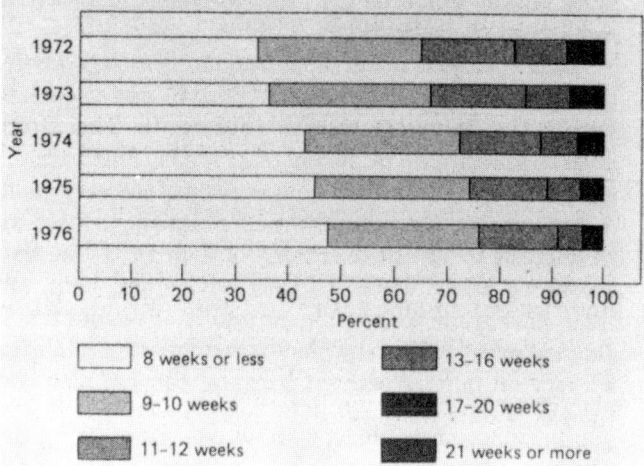

Figure 25-1 Percent distribution of legal abortions by weeks of gestation: United States, 1972–1976.

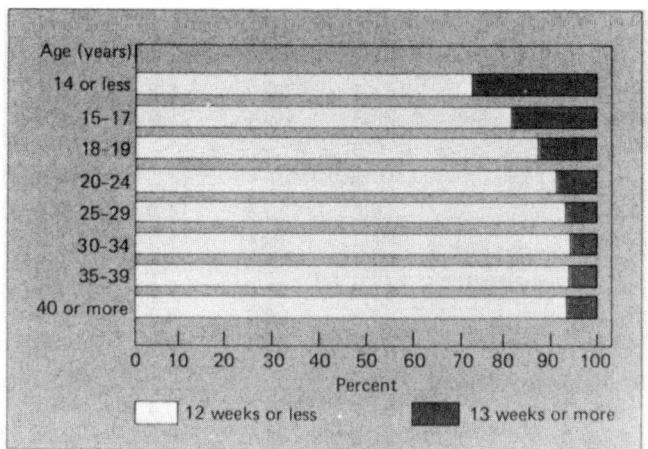

Figure 25-2 Percent distribution of legal abortions by weeks of gestation and woman's age: New York City, 1977.

Before definite strategies for the future can be proposed, the following assumptions for the next decade should be set forth in regard to second-trimester abortion:

1. As first-trimester abortion services become more readily accessible, women desiring to terminate an unwanted pregnancy will avail themselves of these services at earlier dates, thus further diminishing the overall need for second-trimester abortion.
2. As greater educational efforts are put forth to inform women of their option to terminate an unwanted pregnancy, of the increased risk associated with delay in seeking abortion, and of the ready availability of first-trimester termination services, women desiring abortion will seek this service at an earlier stage in their pregnancies.
3. The need for second-trimester abortions never will be eliminated completely. There always will be a small percentage of women who remain unclear in their minds until after amniocentesis in the second trimester whether or not the fetuses they are carrying have a congenital malformation. Additionally, there probably will always be a small number of women, often the very young, who either do not know or cannot bring themselves to admit that they are pregnant until they are past the first trimester.
4. Because there appears to be a greater risk of morbidity and mortality with certain techniques of second-trimester abortion (Figure 25-3), it can be assumed that the less safe methods will be used less frequently in the future.[5]
5. The legal and legislative challenges from those who oppose abortion will continue or intensify; they will be greater in the area of provision of second-trimester abortion than in any other aspect of this controversy.

STRATEGIES FOR THE FUTURE

Based on the foregoing assumptions and the history of legal abortion as set forth above, the following activities are proposed for the future:

- Increase the efforts to educate women about the option of abortion in the event of an unwanted pregnancy.
- Inform all women that earlier abortion is safer and easier.

- Expand the provision of contraceptive services in order to reduce the need for abortion, particularly repeat abortion.
- Educate physicians about the safest techniques of abortion after the 12th menstrual week. D&E should become the procedure of choice for termination of pregnancies under 21 menstrual weeks, not only because of increased safety but also because women will want termination in the 13th to 16th menstrual week phase of their pregnancies when they learn that D&E frees them from the trauma of a painful and unproductive labor.
- Work vigorously and ceaselessly to assure that the right of access to second-trimester abortion remains an option for the women who need it. Because of the strident opposition from a small but vocal minority to all abortions (particularly when performed in the second-trimester), this issue may well prove to be our greatest challenge in the next decade.

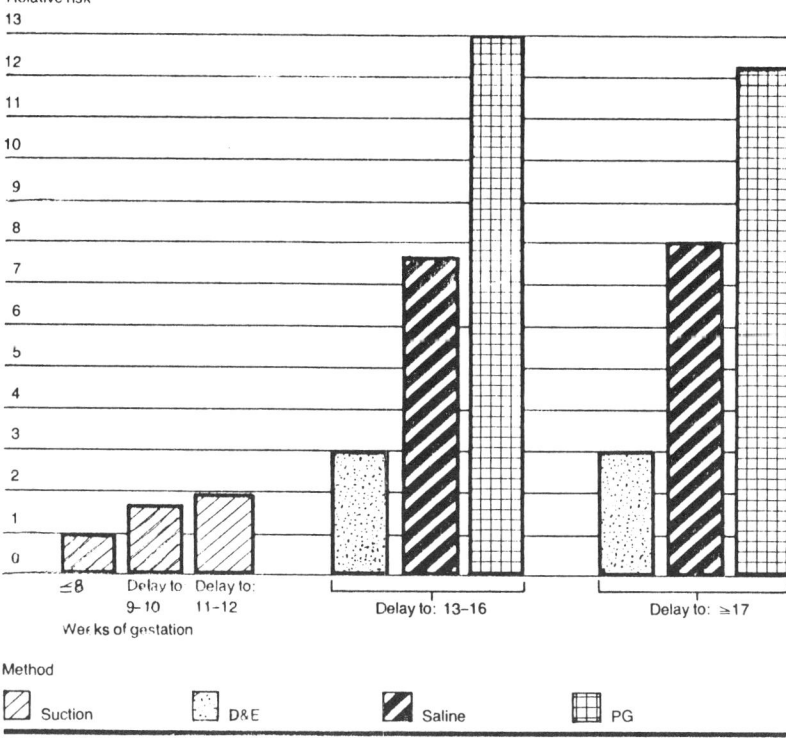

Figure 25-3 Risk of major abortion-related morbidity due to length of gestation and choice of method, compared with risk associated with suction at ≤ 8 weeks' gestation.

REFERENCES

1. Calderone MS: *Abortion in the United States.* New York, Paul B Hoeber, 1958.
2. Center for Disease Control: *Abortion Surveillance 1977.* Atlanta, *Morbid Mort Wkly Rep.* 28:25, 1979.
3. Tietze C: *Induced Abortion: 1979.* Third ed. New York, The Population Council, 1979.
4. Center for Disease Control: *Abortion Surveillance 1976.* Atlanta, issued August 1978.
5. Cates CW Jr, Schulz K, Grimes D et al: The effects of delay and method choice on the risk of abortion morbidity. *Fam Plann Perspect.* 9:266, 1977.

26 The Future of Second-Trimester Abortion Throughout the World

Malcolm Potts

PATTERNS OF ABORTION

Questions regarding the future of abortion practices in the world can be divided into two categories:

- Assertions based on abortion patterns in general, which can be made with some degree of confidence
- More speculative propositions relating to factors that often are difficult to predict, such as changes in technology, patterns of social relationships, or political emphasis

There are strong reasons to conclude that the total number of induced abortions will increase in the remaining years of the twentieth century as the number of women at risk for pregnancy and the pressures to restrict fertility increase. The number of fertile, sexually active women will continue to rise, particularly in continents such as

Asia and Latin America where half or more of the population presently is still below the age of marriage and can be expected to enter the years of maximum fertility just before the end of the twentieth century. On the basis of current projections, the number of women aged 15 to 44 in the United States will increase from 51 million in 1980 to 52.5 million in the year 2000, or only 2.9%. In Bangladesh, on the other hand, the corresponding increase will be from 20 to 34.5 million, an increase of 74% (Table 26-1). Since the majority of the women included in these projections are presently alive, the total number in either case cannot be altered extensively by any foreseeable changes in birthrates.

Table 26-1
Number of Women, Aged 15 to 44, for Selected Countries (Millions)

	1980	2000	Increase (%)
Developed			
USA	51	52.5	2.9
Developing			
Bangladesh	20.0	34.5	74.0
Brazil	26.5	45.7	72.5
Egypt	9.2	14.3	55.4
Sudan	4.3	8.5	97.6

The pressure to restrict fertility, particularly in the developing world, is likely to increase. Birthrates, which have already begun to decline in the many developing countries, are likely to fall further in the next two decades.[1] Abortion is used most frequently when a society begins to control its fertility. It is thus likely that in the 1980s and 1990s countries such as Thailand, Indonesia, Mexico, and Brazil will repeat the experiences of nations such as Korea[2] and Taiwan[3] in the 1960s. In these latter countries, rising abortion rates were observed during early stages of demographic transition. Developing countries, beginning to escape the cycle of poverty, appear to undergo the same evolution in abortion trends that occurred previously when income, educational opportunities, and other aspects of development began to expand rapidly in what are now wealthy communities. Japan in the 1950s[4] or Britain or the United States in the late nineteenth and early twentieth centuries had similar increases in abortion rates.

The total number of abortions taking place is easier to predict than the specific proportion of second-trimester operations. The simplest hypothesis to construct concerning changing patterns of induced abortion with time is that induced abortion plays a relatively more important part in fertility control at the beginning of demographic transition than it does later (Figure 26-1),[5,6] since contraceptive practice by an individual couple improves with duration of use.[7] Hopefully, a second generation of contraceptive users will be more successful with a technology than were their parents. With the passage of time, contraceptive practice improves and the need for abortion is reduced, although never eliminated. Recently, the historian James Mohr documented the widespread (and, incidentally, socially acceptable) practice of abortion in nineteenth century America.[8] The Board of Health in Michigan in 1881 stated "34%, or one third of all [pregnancies] ended in [purposeful] miscarriage." While the exact numbers are in dispute, there is no doubt that the total fertility rate for US women fell from 7.04 in 1800 to 3.56 in 1900, and there is little doubt that induced abortion played an important role in this change. Evidence from Europe parallels this observation.[9] Many nineteenth century abortions probably were performed rather late in pregnancy, just as contemporary folk methods often extend into the second trimester.[10]

While it is possible that birthrates will continue to decline in contemporary developed countries, it perhaps is more likely that they will reach a plateau at their current levels, which indeed approach the number needed for biological replacement. If this is the case, the total number of induced abortions taking place in developed countries is

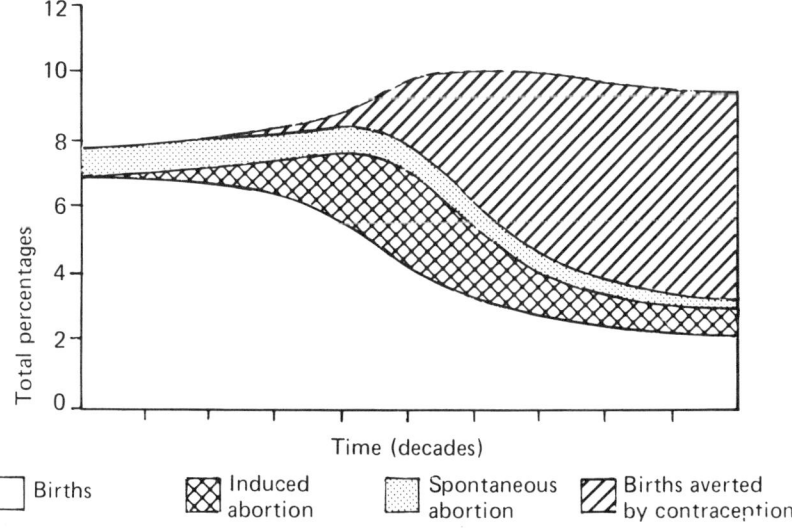

Figure 26-1 Model community using contraception and induced abortion to control fertility. Source: Potts et al.[6]

unlikely to increase and, actually, may decline as alternative methods of fertility control, particularly voluntary sterilizations, become more widely utilized. Of course, it also is possible that adverse information or, more likely, adverse reactions to misinformation, could erode the use of some of the better methods of contraception, such as the oral contraceptives, even in the developed countries, thus leaving abortion to fill some of the gap between desired and achieved fertility.

The number of third-world abortions is likely to climb dramatically in the next 20 years, both because of an increasing number of women at risk of pregnancy and because desired family size is likely to fall. Indeed, in a world seriously concerned with curbing excessive population growth and achieving rapid improvements in maternal and child health, the provision of safe and humane first- and second-trimester abortion services would seem to be one central, inescapable goal.

FACTORS AFFECTING THE NUMBER OF SECOND-TRIMESTER ABORTIONS

Within the broad overall context of induced abortion in contemporary society, it is reasonable to ask, "How many will take place in the second trimester?" The relationship between the number of second-trimester abortions and the total number of abortions varies widely from country to country and is subject to numerous external influences (Table 26-2). Clearly, as the total number of abortions rises, it is likely that some will always be second-trimester procedures. This relationship is not a straightforward one, however.

Table 26-2
Percent Distribution of Legal Abortions After 13 Weeks for Selected Countries*

Country	Year	13 Weeks or More
Czechoslovakia	1976	0.5
England and Wales	1975	17.4
India	1972–1975	23.7
Japan	1977	4.2
Sweden	1968	57.1
Sweden	1976	6.4
USA	1976	9.7

*Source: Tietze C: *Induced Abortion*, 1979: Population Council.

Biosocial

Women at the extremes of fertile life are more likely to seek termination late in pregnancy than those in the years of maximum fertility (Figure 26-2). The adolescent girl, particularly one who is pregnant and unmarried, may not recognize her conception, may deny it, or may not be able to find a source of help in obtaining an abortion until the pregnancy is well advanced. Similarly, a woman approaching the menopause, who may have regarded her family as complete 10 or 15 years earlier, may seek other explanations of amenorrhea before realizing she is pregnant; by this time the pregnancy may be well into the second trimester. Although pregnancy in these two disparate age categories represents a relatively small proportion of all pregnancies, the pressures affecting these particular groups of women may exert a measurable effect on the total number of second-trimester abortions requested. In countries such as India, where marriage is early and premarital intercourse is relatively unusual, second-trimester terminations among adolescents are likely to remain few. On the other hand, in North America or among the educated classes in Black Africa, where marriage increasingly is delayed and premarital intercourse is relatively common, second-trimester abortion among adolescents may become relatively important.

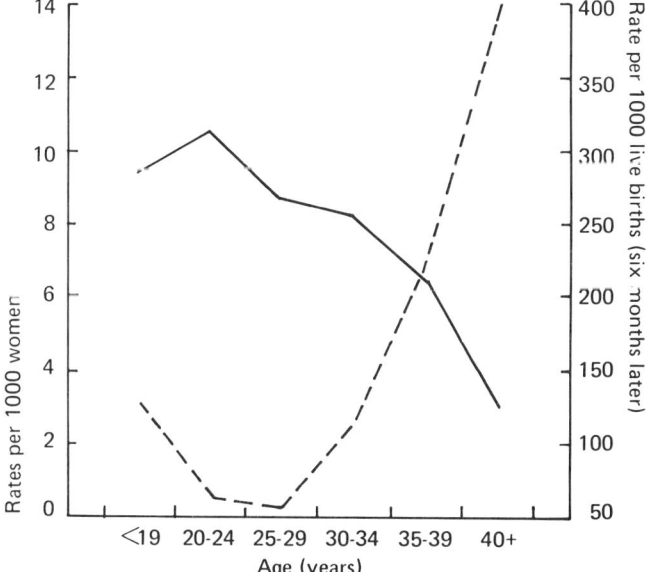

Figure 26-2 Abortion rates per 1000 women and per 1000 live births. England and Wales, 1970. Data from Kestleman. Source: Potts et al.[6]

Political

Most abortions are requested for reasons of social health rather than physical disease. In the past decade, public attitudes toward abortion have become deeply polarized in the United States. Abortion is culturally acceptable and always has been available in most of the third world, where restrictive abortion laws derive mainly from nineteenth century colonialism. When the bulk of the population is faced with the problem of living on a few dollars a day, immediate and powerful human emotions related to everyday living come into play, and philosophical or theological debates about the status of the human embryo appear to be difficult to sustain.

Among the factors which will influence the incidence of second-trimester abortion in developed countries over the next two decades, politics is likely to be key. For example, the Right to Life Movement has become politically influential in the United States, is not so forceful but, nevertheless, exists in Great Britain, has succeeded in achieving some restrictive legislation in New Zealand, and may achieve the same goal in Australia.

Conservative attitudes toward abortion often have paradoxical outcomes. The political counterattack presently being mounted against liberal abortion legislation is not immediately directed toward outlawing abortion, but rather at creating serious obstacles to obtaining it. For example, in the United States the withdrawal of Medicaid has not denied abortions to the poor in the legal sense, but it has made them more difficult to obtain and, therefore, more likely to take place late in pregnancy. Similarly, in the United Kingdom, draft legislation put before Parliament in recent years has not been a frontal attack on the 1967 Abortion Act but an attempt to make abortion referral services more difficult to run, to put restrictions on private sector operations (which, if implemented, would increase costs), and to limit abortion decision-making or surgery to a smaller number of physicians. On July 13, 1979, an Abortion Amendment Bill passed in the United Kingdom House of Commons by 242 votes to 98. It aims to make abortion more difficult to obtain by requiring a license for referral and pregnancy testing services. The regulation of advisory services could be so interpreted as to eliminate the charitable organizations which presently are a major source of service. The wording of the 1967 Act would be changed from a "substantial risk of serious injury to the physical or mental health of the woman or her children" to a "grave risk." All these moves would delay the operation for some women and, even though the draft legislation contains a clause to restrict the second-trimester abortions to "less than 20 weeks" (except in the case of severe fetal defect), the total number of second-trimester operations might rise if the legislation is ultimately enacted.

Action in the developed world affects the developing world. The restrictions placed on funds designated for US foreign assistance programs inhibits the growth of simple services which could be explicitly linked to postabortal contraceptive advice and which might, in turn, help reduce the total number of abortions occurring, as well as prevent late operations.

The interesting and often tragic paradox of the existing political situation is that the restrictions either suggested or enacted actually have little influence on the total number of abortions taking place in a community, but in reality adversely affect the ratio of first- to second-trimester abortions. Women have to spend more time obtaining the extra money needed to pay for legal but later operations; fewer centers are able to perform procedures; advertisement and referrals become more difficult. Whenever the law regarding the decision-making process is made more complex, it is virtually certain to delay obtaining a desired abortion. Evidence from Scandinavia in the 1950s and 1960s clearly demonstrates that efforts to limit decision making to certain cetegories of doctors, set up committees, or involve psychiatric or social consultants, all pushed the time of operation to later and later in pregnancy (Table 26-3).[11] Legislation inspired by a sincere, but uninformed, attempt to protect embryonic life by making abortion less accessible often increases the total number of second-trimester abortions, adds to the individual suffering of women seeking to terminate their pregnancies, confuses an already bewildered public and their elected representatives, and succeeds only in destroying the human embryo later in pregnancy.

Table 26-3
Medically Induced Delay in Granting Legal Abortion in Umea Hospital, Sweden

	No. of Abortions	Days of Investigation	Days in Hospital	Medium duration of Pregnancy at Operation (Weeks)
1963 to 1964	45	25.8	10.1	16.0
1967	127	11.6	5.6	12.6

Clinical Developments

On the one hand, as obstetric practices improve, the physical indications for abortion diminish each year. This reality is likely to continue. Although the phenomenon will not be as widespread in the developing as in the developed world, it still may have a measurable effect in poor countries. On the other hand, the number of pregnancies terminated because of fear of fetal defect is likely to increase. Amniocentesis in women over 35 is becoming increasingly common in developed countries. Fear of malpractice suits, as well as genuine clinical need, is likely to accelerate the adoption of fetal screening programs in the United States and other developed countries. These procedures ultimately will be used in the developing world, although they are likely to remain limited to prosperous urban patients.

At present, most procedures for detecting fetal abnormalities do not give satisfactory, predictable results until the second trimester. Therefore, in the short term, one may expect a rise in the number of second-trimester abortions performed for fetal indications. In the long term, however, there are no biological reasons why some of the screening tests for fetal abnormalities cannot be adapted for use in the first trimester of pregnancy. It is certainly to be hoped that by the end of the 1980s or the year 2000 at the latest, the number of second-trimester abortions performed because of a fetal abnormality will decline drastically.

It is difficult to foresee any improvement in second-trimester abortion technology that could make it as safe as an earlier operation. It is equally difficult to think of any advance that could make it as acceptable to the woman—or her physician.[12] The present range of not-too-satisfactory methods for second-trimester operations hopefully will be replaced by one which is preeminently satisfactory; such a clinical revolution unfortunately is unlikely to have a major effect on the total number of late operations. In actual fact, should a safe, successful method be found, some women might conceivably desire to use it rather than concern themselves with early diagnosis.

CONCLUSION

Most women who have to face a decision concerning abortion and most practitioners who have to perform the operation are uniform in finding early abortion ethically and emotionally acceptable. The safest, most acceptable, least expensive, and ethically most justifiable abortion is one that takes place at 10 weeks or earlier as an outpatient vacuum aspiration. With experience, health professionals have become aware of the relief early abortion brings to patients. This is not the case, however, with second-trimester abortions. Physicians know them to be considerably more dangerous than first-trimester operations. Moreover, patients who need or request second-trimester abortions often have concomitant psychological and/or medical problems.

Philosophically, the decision to have a second-trimester abortion is best made by the woman. If the total number of second-trimester abortions is likely to be partly determined by increasingly restrictive public attitudes toward abortion in general, then the philosophy of the medical profession in performing second-trimester abortions and the care, common sense, and altruism the profession displays toward the topic become critically important. Those physicians who recognize and support the need for second-trimester abortion must take special care to ensure that the woman is fully informed about the nature and consequences of the operation and has reviewed all possible alternatives. There must be no element of financial exploitation, because the image of the millionaire abortionist can be as unsettling to the general public as visions of dismembered fetuses. If the integrity of the medical profession is to survive in a difficult situation, then there must be a visible and active enthusiasm for postabortal contraceptive advice, and a consistent, unquestioning effort to attempt to improve medical services and to simplify patterns of decision making so that women have less and less reason for seeking late abortion.

The 1980s may be the decade of maximal *surgical* involvement in fertility regulation at a global level. Voluntary sterilization is being chosen on an increasingly widespread scale and probably already represents the single most important method of fertility control. In the case of sterilization, however, the number being performed is likely to peak as services finally meet ongoing needs, whereas in the case of abortion, a wider use of and greater familiarity with alternative contraceptive methods is likely to reduce numbers in the developing world, just as it did in the West and in Japan. The rate at which the world gets over the foreseeable "hump" in the total number of abortions taking place will depend more on medical and political attitudes than on predictable improvements in technique. Perhaps the 1990s will be the first decade when the surgical methods of family planning, although remaining of key significance, herald a more acceptable level of meeting genuine human needs rather than responding to the errors of the past or current emergencies.

SUMMARY

The overall number of abortions taking place is determined largely by economic and social pressures which are part of the great patterns of history and which physicians are unlikely to influence. On the other hand, the proportion of first- and second-trimester abortions taking place at any one time is the result of more parochial forces which are determined in part by policy-makers responding intelligently to expert information and advice. It is this area where physicians must continue to exert their influence.

This work was conducted under the auspices of the International Fertility Research Program and supported in part by the US Agency for International Development.

REFERENCES

1. Westoff CF: The unmet need for birth control in five Asian countries. *Int Fam Plann Perspect.* 4:9, 1978.
2. Hong SB, Watson WB: The role of induced abortion in fertility control in Korea. Clinical Proceedings IPPF, SEOR Congress:115, 1972.
3. Freedman R, Hermalin A, Sun TH: Fertility trends in Taiwan. *Population Index* 38:141, 1972.
4. Muramatsu M: An analysis of factors in fertility control in Japan. *Bull Inst Public Health,* Tokyo, 19:97, 1970.
5. Requena M: Abortion in Latin America, in Hall RE (ed): *Abortion in a Changing World,* vol 1, New York, Columbia University Press, 1970, p 338.
6. Potts M, Diggory P, Peel J: *Abortion.* New York, Cambridge University Press, 1977.
7. Westoff CF, Potter RG, Sagi PC: *The Third Child.* Princeton, Princeton University Press, 1963.
8. Mohr JC: *Abortion in America.* New York, Oxford University Press, 1978.
9. Rentoul RR: *The Causes and Treatment of Abortion.* Edinburgh, Pentland, 1889.
10. Narkavonkit T: Personal communication, 1979.
11. Ottensen-Jenson O: Legal abortion in Sweden: 36 years' experience. *J Biosoc Sci.* 3:197, 1973.
12. Edstrom K: Techniques of induced abortion, their health implications and service aspects: a review of the literature. *Bull WHO* 57:481, 1979.

27 Preventing the Need for Second-Trimester Abortion

Elizabeth B. Connell

There is no reason, logically speaking, that second-trimester abortion should not join bubonic plague and poliomyelitis as practically historic medical conditions. At this very moment, sufficient contraceptive technology is available so that by 1989 it should not be necessary to re-examine a second decade of second-trimester abortion experience.

The most pressing question is, "How can second-trimester abortion be avoided?" There are three possible answers. First, these pregnancies could be avoided altogether; second, they could be terminated in the first trimester by either medical or surgical means; and third, all pregnancies could be allowed to go to term.

AVOIDANCE OF PREGNANCY

Given the current state of contraceptive technology there is very little reason for unwanted pregnancies to occur. Although not ideal, present methods are highly safe and effective. With the proper application of this knowledge, unwanted pregnancies should be rare indeed. Unfortunately, we know for a fact that this is not the case. The reasons for this state of affairs are basically three in number: fear, ignorance, and lack of appropriate services.

There presently is a growing concern on the part of many women about the side effects of our most effective medical methods, the oral contraceptives and intrauterine devices. These concerns, which often amount to real fear, frequently are far out of proprotion to the actual risk. For example, the recent reevaluation of the cardiovascular side effects of the pill by Tietze[1] and Belsey[2] has shown that even the very low risks presently quoted are probably too high. Similarly, the fears regarding the induction of malignancy, which have deterred many women from starting the pill or have caused them to discontinue its use, have yet to be documented. To make matters more complex, widespread publicity about rare complications, such as benign hepatocellular adenoma, cholelithiasis, and pituitary microadenoma, resulting from the use of oral contraceptives, has generated widespread anxiety. Equal amounts of publicity about the dangers of pregnancy or the beneficial side effects of the pill, such as the control of irregular or heavy menses, have not been forthcoming either from the popular press or from responsible health agencies.

A number of concerns presently exist regarding the use of intrauterine contraception, particularly by the nulligravid patient. While there is clear evidence of an increased incidence of pelvic inflammatory disease (PID) in association with the use of the IUD,[3] the exact percentage of the increase, which truly is IUD-related, remains unclear. An even less clear issue is that of ectopic pregnancy. There is, at the present time, considerable doubt as to whether or not the IUD actually produces ectopic gestation, and, if so, if any one particular device produces a disproprotionate share of this condition.[4] While the current position of the FDA tends in this direction, it appears that the apparent increase simply may be a reflection of the growing frequency of pelvic inflammatory disease. A number of studies presently being conducted by WHO and others suggest that there is a cause-and-effect relationship between PID and ectopic pregnancy, but that the use of the IUD introduces an extraneous but unrelated variable.[5]

Barrier methods of contraception have been associated with negative commentary and comparatively little thoughtful consideration by the medical profession in recent years. Women often do not recognize that these methods can be highly effective if used properly. For instance, it has been shown that the combination of condom and foam, if used properly, can approach the effectiveness of the oral contraceptives.[6] Unfortunately, these methods often are poorly utilized because of certain inherent aesthetic problems and the difficulties they pose when patients attempt to ensure high compliance.

One bright spot in this somewhat dismal picture is the increasing utilization of sterilization by couples following the completion of their desired family size. Following the development of newer techniques of female sterilization such as laparoscopy and minilaparotomy, it has been suggested that many potential abortions have been averted simply because some women who had completed their families had been sterilized and thus avoided future pregnancies. If current research designed to make male and female sterilization procedures reversible is successful, this knowledge undoubtedly will give added impetus to the continued use of this method.

More important, even if adequate contraceptive services were to become available, they would still not provide the final solution. Above and beyond any medical considerations, innumerable problems remain in relation to obtaining contraceptive care by women. The degree of ignorance that women have about their bodies, particularly their reproductive functions, is amazing in today's so-called open society. Even those women who understand how their bodies work often risk the chance of pregnancy for a variety of social and psychological reasons. For example, it is clear that many women are willing to take a chance on pregnancy rather than go through the humiliation of requesting services from the current health care system. This is particularly true in the case of the very young teenager; the emotional and financial costs of obtaining contraception often are perceived as being higher than the benefits that she might receive, particularly since she frequently views pregnancy as a somewhat mystical occurrence which could never possibly happen to her anyway.

Studies have been carried out to determine the psychological reasons for becoming pregnant, even in the face of a stated conscious wish not to have a baby.[7] Included in the responses are the desire to establish a pregnancy for one's own self-esteem or that of one's sexual partner, the desire in both sexes to have unprotected sexual relations for the thrill of it, and the need to have a passive, dependent infant to care for and love. When women become pregnant, they may wish to punish their parents or sexual partners, or they may view pregnancy as a means to marriage or a way by which to hold a faltering marriage together.

Once again, considerable knowledge already exists in this area. As in the case of medical services, however, little is being done from both preventive and therapeutic points of view to implement this knowledge in order to prevent unwanted pregnancy. The complexities of doing so are quite obvious, but this is not really a valid excuse for not at least beginning to make inroads into the problem.

PROVISION OF FIRST-TRIMESTER ABORTIONS

The second option, the prevention of second-trimester abortions by doing all pregnancy termination procedures during the first trimester, is a possibility which rapidly is becoming a reality. Examination of the relevant data since abortion became legal shows a very clear trend in this direction (Chapter 1). Here again, however, the total prevention of second-trimester abortion by using this option depends on two major factors. First, all women must be made aware of the psychological and medical desirability of first-trimester as compared to second-trimester abortion. This would involve greater emphasis on the dissemination of the relative risks and benefits of abortion carried out in these two situations. As in the case of contraception, if women are to avail themselves increasingly of first-trimester abortions, services must be made available which are attractive, easy to reach, and safe. Secondly, an even greater impact would be the development of a self-administered method of very early abortion, such as a prostaglandin-bearing tampon.

TERM PREGNANCY

The third option, allowing all pregnancies to go to term, in many ways reflects certain of the aspects of the first two. If one were to assume that every pregnancy that began was a wanted pregnancy, then all normal and uncomplicated pregnancies indeed should proceed to term. There would remain, however, the abnormal gestations. At present, a major medical cause of second-trimester abortion is the need to terminate pregnancies because of known fetal anomalies. If the diagnosis of a fetal anomaly could be made early in the pregnancy rather than by amniocentesis in the second trimester, such a pregnancy could be terminated in the first trimester.

SUMMARY

At present, it is essential that services related to second-trimester abortion continue to be made available. Nonetheless, it is to be hoped that, a decade from now, second-trimester abortion will be a therapeutic memory and not a medical reality.

REFERENCES

1. Tietze C: The pill and mortality from cardiovacular disease: another look. *Fam Plann Perspect.* 11:80, 1979.
2. Belsey MA, Russell Y, Kinnear K: Cardiovascular disease and oral hormonal contraceptives: a reappraisal of vital statistics data. *Fam Plann Perspect.* 11:84, 1979.
3. Edelman D, Berger GS, Keith L: *IUDs and Their Complications.* Boston, GK Hall, 1979.
4. Berger GS, Keith L, Edelman D: IUDs and ectopic pregnancies, in Hafez ESE (ed): *Progress in Contraceptive Delivery Systems,* vol 3, IUD Pathology and Management. Lancaster, England, MTP, 1980.
5. Aznar R, Berry CL, Cooke ID, et al: Ectopic pregnancy rates in IUD users. *Br Med J.* 1:785, 1978.
6. Hatcher RA, Stewart GK, Guest F, et al: *Contraceptive Technology 1976-77,* 8th ed. New York, Irvington, 1976.
7. Stepto RC, Keith L, Keith D: Obstetrical and medical problems of teenage pregnancy, in Zackler J, Brandstadt W (eds): *The Teenage Pregnant Girl.* Springfield, Ill, Charles C Thomas, 1975.

28 Contragestational Agents

Gerald I. Zatuchni

The performance of second-trimester abortion, for the most part, represents a dual failure of society: first, the failure to fully provide birth control information, education, and contraceptive methods that are acceptable and applicable to all those who need them; and second, the failure to fully provide high quality, safe, first-trimester abortion services which are geographically and financially accessible to the women who need them. If contraception were freely and easily utilized by all segments of society, obviously there would be little need even for first-trimester abortion—only for the contraceptive failures and the few women who prefer the certainty of abortion. Logically, the need for second-trimester abortion then would exist only for genetic or true medical indications.

Fortunately, in most developed countries legal second-trimester abortion is becoming less frequent. In Sweden, for example, the mean duration of pregnancy for all abortions performed has decreased from 14 weeks in 1968 to under 10 weeks in 1976. In the United States, a similar pattern has occurred; abortion at 13 or more weeks declined from 18% in 1972 to less than 10% in 1976.[1] The number of late second-trimester abortions, never high in the US, also decreased significantly during the same years—from 1.8% to 0.9% of all abortions. Unfortunately, this decline has not been evident among all segments of society. For example, in data from England and Wales in 1973, a stepwise increase in the percentage of second-trimester abortions performed was closely correlated with the single woman's own occupation or, in the case of married women, with the occupation of the husband. In other words, the professional groups had the lowest incidence (approximately 2% to 3%), while the unskilled had the highest incidence—over 20% of abortions performed at more than 13 weeks.[1] In New York City in 1977, a different stepwise correlation existed between the mother's age and the percentage of abortions performed at more than 13 weeks; below age 17, about 25% of abortions were of more than 13 weeks' gestation, while beyond age 25, only 7% were performed at more than 13 weeks.[1]

There are numerous reasons for these downward trends and the unevenness of participation of all segments of society in these changing patterns. It is not possible to discuss all of them in this chapter. Nevertheless, it appears that progress is being made and, hopefully, within the next decade, the performance of second-trimester abortion will have become a rare event—a situation simultaneously satisfying the patients, providers, physicians, and politicians.

A major factor in the decline of the number of abortions, especially in the second trimester, is improvement in contraceptive technology for the female, as well as for the male. The immediate future is bright for new methods that would be more applicable, more acceptable, and more readily available. These include long-acting, biodegradable, injectable medications containing steroids or other substances, new barrier methods of vaginal contraception, improved and long-acting medicated IUDs, nonsurgical female and male sterilization, and potentially reversible methods of sterilization.

Even assuming that these technological innovations will be useful, there still will exist a need for better methods of pregnancy termination than are presently available. By "better" is meant nonsurgical methods that are as effective as D&E, that can be safely self-administered, particularly in very early gestation—implantation to six weeks—and that will not impair future fertility. In other words, there still is a need to search for systemic contragestational agents.

The folklore of many ancient as well as modern cultures includes the description and use of a large array of potions and remedies for the purpose of terminating pregnancy. Under scientific scrutiny, most of these naturally occurring substances have failed to produce abortion in an effective and safe manner. Even so, a few are promising. These include derivatives from a Chinese plant—Trichosanthin, a

Mexican plant—Zoapatle, and a plant found in the Amazons—Pirpiri. Anthropological studies have indicated wide usage, but unknown effectiveness, of these plants in their respective cultures for the voluntary control of fertility through early abortion. Several research efforts are presently under way to isolate and study the active ingredients of these and other plants. It may well be that their activity is derived from prostaglandin-like substances which act as uterotonic agents or as disruptors of luteal function.

In all animal species studied to date, it is clear that progesterone is absolutely essential for the beginning of life in utero. It acts as a support system for nidation and eventual placental maintenance. Beyond this early developmental stage, however, nature has relegated progesterone to a lowly status. Indeed, progesterone has no functions beyond its progestational activities and, in fact, is one of the few hormones that is not necessary for the maintenance of life. Accordingly, this hormone, its site of production, and/or its sites of activity, present meaningful targets for disruption or interference without jeopardizing any other organ systems.

THE MECHANISMS OF CONTRAGESTATION

Theoretically, there are four major mechanisms to consider in the scientific development of luteal phase contraceptives that do not exert their effect through toxicologic or teratologic means. All four mechanisms aim at interfering with progesterone synthesis or action by: 1) disrupting luteal function, 2) inactivating progesterone, 3) inhibiting the uptake of progesterone by its receptors, and 4) interfering with blastocystic support of corpus luteum maintenance.

Disrupting Luteal Function

The inhibition of progesterone synthesis may be accomplished by a direct effect on the ovary or, indirectly, through inhibition of hypothalamic-pituitary gonadotropin production and secretion. A few compounds block ovarian steroidogenesis by inhibiting the conversion of pregnenolone to progesterone. In laboratory animals, parenteral administration at suitable dosage levels of azastene, aminoglutethimide, and trilostane has resulted in 100% abortifacient capacity.[2-4] A major concern at present, however, is the potential effect of certain of these compounds on the adrenal gland, which possibly could result in decreased adrenal steroidogenesis and other toxic effects. From a clinical point of view, these drugs have the potential for utilization as luteal phase contraceptives or as contragestational agents in very early pregnancy at the time of incipient implantation. Perhaps the most appropriate time for administration of such an agent would be at the time of the missed menses.

In some species, including subhuman primates, there is evidence that a luteolytic substance indeed does exist; it is produced by the uterus and transported locally to the ovary. Apparently, prostaglandin is one of these luteolytic substances.[5] In the human, however, it now has been established that the uterus does not produce a luteolytic substance, but it is possible that certain analogs of prostaglandin may exert a luteolytic effect similar to that observed in animals. Such analogs presently are under investigation.

At the central nervous system level, a paradoxical effect has been noted regarding the control of corpus luteum formation and maintenance. The administration of LH-RH, in frequent doses, results in a downgrading of luteal activity and actual luteolysis in the particular menstrual cycle. Certain synthetic analogs of LH-RH have been shown to be even more potent suppressors of luteal function.[6]

Inactivating Progesterone

It is possible to synthesize compounds that inactivate progesterone, either by metabolic changes in the molecule itself or by binding it into an inactive form. Several compounds exhibit antiprogesterone activity, but so far they have not demonstrated a specific affinity for progesterone and interfere with other steroids as well.

A different approach is the development of an antibody to progesterone. Though it is available only in minute quantities, administration of this antibody in animals, either intramuscularly or intraperitoneally, has resulted in significant declines in serum levels of progesterone. Additional studies are in progress to determine the effectiveness of this approach as an abortifacient and to determine the optimal method of administration.[7]

Inhibiting Progesterone Receptors

Throughout the female reproductive tract and the breasts, many cells contain chemical receptors for the binding of progesterone prior to its transport through the cell membrane. These receptors act under the influence of estrogens and gonadotropins and become most numerous during the proliferative phase of the menstrual cycle. They exhibit their most marked development during pregnancy. These receptors can be "fooled" into binding compounds that are chemically similar to progesterone but that do not exert significant progestational effects. Manipulation of the natural molecule of progesterone has resulted in the development of compounds that competitively inhibit the uptake of progesterone by its receptor. However, these compounds may block the uptake of steroids other than progesterone. If a suitable compound with focused activity can be found, it is quite likely that a useful method of luteal phase contraception could be developed that would be safe and completely effective, even if fertilization already had occurred.

Interfering with Blastocystic Luteotrophic Activity

It is likely that the first hormone produced by a fertilized ovum is chorionic gonadotropin (HCG). The primary action of HCG is the stimulation and prolongation of corpus luteum function, at least until the placenta is able to synthesize its own progesterone and other hormones. Measurable levels of HCG have been observed even before implantation. HCG, or a portion thereof, is weakly immunogenic, and antibodies can be obtained that immunologically will bind and inhibit the HCG molecule. Injection of antiserum containing high levels of HCG antibodies results in abortion, at least in nonhuman primates.[8]

This particular immunological approach to contragestational activity has been hampered by the necessity of developing an antigen that is specific for HCG and that will not crossreact with other hormones, in particular, LH.

From a clinical point of view, the development of such an immunological vaccine against the establishment of pregnancy could and probably would be utilized by women who have no further desire for children. It is unlikely that an immunological method that requires sufficient and probably quite specific levels of antibody could be temporary in its action. More likely, a successful immunological approach would result in permanent infertility. In addition to the concern arising from this supposition, immunological approaches that seek to act upon endogenously produced substances may result in autoimmune diseases and other unknown effects resulting from the deposition of such antigen-antibody immune complexes. Accordingly, long-term studies of such potential agents are mandatory before their widespread use. Therefore, it is unlikely that this approach, even if effective in humans, would be available within the next decade.

An analogous but nonimmunological approach is the competitive inhibition of HCG-LH receptors in the ovary by compounds that exhibit similarities in chemical structure while having no LH effect. Administration of such peptide compounds would be expected to result in interference with luteal function (and result in inadequate progesterone synthesis) at the crucial time of implanatation. From the clinical point of view, such compounds could be administered for a few days each cycle just before the onset of the next expected menses.

CONCLUSION

There is a need for the development of a contragestational agent that is safe and effective and that will have no effects upon future fertility. Such an agent could be utilized during the luteal phase of the menstrual cycle, perhaps using the missed menses as the indicator for therapy. Research has demonstrated the feasibility of this approach, and it is quite likely that within the next decade several general methods described here will be available. The development of such luteal phase contraceptives, along with improved contraception for both the male and the female, may be the best way to prevent the need for surgically induced abortion in the first and second trimester.

REFERENCES

1. Tietze C: *Induced Abortion: 1979*. New York, The Population Council, 1979.
2. Schane HP, Creange JE, Potts GO: Comparative adrenal inhibiting and abortifacient activities of WIN-17,625 in the rat and Rhesus monkey. *Fertil Steril.* 28:301, 1977.
3. Csapo A: Anti-progesterones in fertility control: pregnancy termination, in Zatuchni GI, Speidel JJ, Sciarra JJ (eds): *Proceedings of PARFR Workshop*. Hagerstown, Md, Harper & Row, 1979.
4. Glasser SR, Northcutt RC, Chytil F, et al: The influence of an antisteroidogenic drug (aminoglutethamide) on pregnancy maintenance. *Endocrinology* 90:1363, 1972.
5. Csapo A: The "see-saw" theory of parturition. *Am J Obstet Gynecol.* 121:578, 1975.
6. Yen S: Program for Applied Research on Fertility Regulation. Semi-Annual Report, July 1979 (uncirculated document).
7. Chatterton R: Program for Applied Research on Fertility Regulation. Semi-Annual Report, July 1979 (uncirculated document).
8. Segal SJ: Immunological methods to prevent pregnancy. *Contraception* 13:125, 1976.

INDEX

Abdominal circumference (AC), fetal, 58, 62
Abortion
 availability of, 28
 delays of, 199, 203, 252-254
 factors affecting numbers of, 318-322
 fear of, 254-255
 federal funding of, 248
 future of, 312-313
 historical trends of, 222-224
 mechanically produced, 51
 methods, 7, 10-11
 nurses for, 245-246
 patient issues for, 241-242
 patterns of, 315-318
 physicians for, 246
 as public health problem, 13
 social issues of, 240-241
 spontaneous, 40
 staff issues of, 242
 subsidized, 28
Abortion Act (1967), 7, 320
Abortion clinics, Dutch, 285
 for foreigners, 287-288
 legal, 286
 other countries and, 289, 293
 as medical specialty, 287
Abortions illegal, 191
 death from, 191
Abortions, legal, 15, 79, 191
 change in trends of, 22-24
 decline of, 5, 16
 evaluation of 199-203
 reported, 16
Abortions, second-trimester
 mortality from 171-176
 safety of, 164
Abortion services
 comparative costs of, 35-36
 geographical distribution of, 33-34
Abortion Surveillance report (CDC), 200, 202
Adnexal mass, 58, 64
Aid to Families with Dependent Children (AFDC), 36
Alan Guttmacher Institute (AGI), 15, 34, 224
Amenorrhea, 7
American Civil Liberties Union, 228

American Medical Association, 223, 224
Amniocentesis, 57, 108
Amnioinfusion, 79
Amniotic fluid, 39, 53, 58
Anemia, 110
Anesthesia, 127, 128
Anker dilator, 153-154
Aspirotomy (AT), 301
 complications of, 304-305
 demographics of, 303-304
 procedure, 297
Asthma, 110

Belgium, 291-292
Biparietal diameter (BPD), fetal, 58-62
 gastational age and, 58-59
 standardization of, 59
 24-week limit and, 61-62
Blastocystic luteotrophic activity, 335
Blood pigments, abnormal, 116
Boston Hospital for Women, 168

Center for Disease Control, 15, 17, 34, 85, 172, 189, 198, 199, 200-202, 224, 310
 See also Joint Program for the Study of Abortion
Cervical lacerations, 84, 100, 110, 116, 144, 168
Cervical resistance, 75-76
Cervix, preoperative dilatation of, 100
Clinical investigation
 essential information for, 207-208
 statistical tests, errors in, 210
 study design of, 206-207
 techniques for reporting date for, 208-210
Coagulation, 83
Combination methods, 171
Congenital anomalies, fetal, 58, 66
Contraception
 barrier methods of, 279-280, 326
 demographic factors affecting, 267
 oral, 278-279, 303, 326
 possibilities of, 272-282
Cooperative Health Statistics System (CHSS), 201

Counseling
  after abortion, 262
  contraceptive, 265
  during abortion, 261–262
  late, 263
  preabortion, 260–261
Crown-heel (CH) length, 41
Crown-rump (CR) length, 41, 44, 53
Culdoscopy, 276
Curettage, 182–184

Dates, innaccurate, 64, 66
Death, 102, 191
Death-to-case rates, 17–20, 173–175
Diabetes, 179
Diaphragm, 282
Diarrhea, 96, 97, 99, 116, 169
Dilatation and evacuation (D&E), 7, 32, 100, 103, 112, 119, 120, 182–184, 301
  instillation abortion and, 130–131
  morbidity and mortality in, 128–130, 173–175
  safety of, 131, 166, 168, 198
  second-trimester, use of, 120–121
  second-trimester, techniques of, 121, 127–130
Doe v. Bolton, 203
Down's syndrome, 179

Endometritis, 168
Epinephrine, 296, 306
Ergometrine, 297
Ergotrate, 295, 306
Ethcridine lactate, 11, 92
Ethicians, 214

Fetal age, 40, 100, 251–252
Fetal growth, 40
Fetal heart beat, 114
Fetal movement, 43, 222–224
Fetal weight, 41, 43, 48, 53
Fertility Control Center (Johns Hopkins Hospital), 107, 109
  studies at, 109–112, 114, 115
Fetus, 39, 40–44
  liveborn, 171
Fever, 32, 84, 102, 168
Food and Drug Administration, 173, 326
France, 292
Free-standing clinics, 34

Gastrointestinal side effects, 150
  See also Diarrhea; Nausea; Vomiting
Germany, Western, 290–291
Gestation, multiple, 64
Glucose, hypertonic, 101
Gonorrhea, 110
Gutnick device, 154–155

Halothane, 127
Headache, 116
Heart disease, 110
Hemorrhage, 32, 83–84, 92, 100, 102, 109, 115, 144, 168, 269
Hospital cost, 16, 33
Hospital policies, 3
Human soul, 215
Hypernatremia, 83
Hypertension, 110
Hysterectomy, 7, 10, 112, 175, 276
Hysterotomy, 7, 10, 119, 175

Incest, 36
Incomplete evacuation, 100, 102
Indian Council of Medical Research (ICMR), 169
Infection, 32, 83, 84, 102, 143, 269
Instillation abortion, 130–131
International Fertility Research Program, 168, 169
Intracervical injection, 128
Intrauterine devices (IUD), 277–278, 303
Intrauterine fetal death (IUFD), 66

Johns Hopkins Hospital, 171
Joint Program for the Study of Abortions (JPSA/CDC), 129, 144, 166, 168, 169, 310

Kapiolani Hospital, 136
Kaplan Hospital, 181
Karolinska Institute, 92

Labor, induction of, 120
  laminaria and, 152–153
Lactation, 269–271
Laminaria, 11, 108, 110, 115, 127, 131
  alternatives to, 153–157
  cervical dilatation and, 138–142
  characteristics of, 136–138
  complications from, 142–144, 149

digitata, 136–137, 140, 146, 149
  infections from, 143
  japonica, 136–137, 140–141
  prostaglandin and, 146–151
  removal of, 138
  technique of insertion and,
    137–138
  uterine contractibility and,
    145–146
Laparoscopy, 64, 273, 276, 327
Laparotomy, 64, 327
Lawyers, 214
Luteal function, disruption of, 333

Maternal age, 180
Medicaid, 36, 38, 198
Membranes, fetal, 39, 52–53
Menstrual age, 40
Menstrual period, last (LMP), 58
Morbidity, comparative studies on,
  166–177
Mortality, 171–176, 225

National Center for Health Statistics
  (NCHS), 201
National Health Service (NHS), 7
National Hospital Discharge Survey,
  16
National Medical Committee
  (Planned Parenthood Federation),
  121
Nausea, 116, 169
Netherlands Abortion Federation,
  302
New Jersey State Board of Medical
  Examiners, 32
New Jersey Supreme Court, 32
New York, studies in, 169–175,
  190–203
New York City Health Code
  (Article 42), 191
New York City Health Department,
  189, 190–199
New York Times, 197
North Carolina, University of, 129,
  168
Nursing care, 131

Obesity, 110
Oligohydramnios, 66

Parity, 180
Pelvic inflammatory disease (PID),
  326

Pirpiri, 333
Placenta, 39, 48–52, 58, 62, 109
  changes in, after abortion, 51
  variations in sizes of, 48
Plantago ovata (Isapgol), 156–157
Polymers, expanding, 155–156
Population Council, 166, 198
Pregnancy, abnormality in, 57
  molar, 64
  prior, 147
Pregnancy tests, free, 22, 28
Premature labor, 119
Preterm device, 155
Products of conception, retained,
  168
Professional staff
  emotional responses of, 251–256
  social environment of, 256
Prosterone, 333
  inactivating, 334
  inhibiting receptors, 334
Prostaglandin, 10, 19, 75
  analogues, 91, 93–94, 98
  cervix and, 100
  classical, 90–91, 92–93
  extraamniotic administration of,
    90–92
  hypertonic saline and, 169
  instillation, 168
  intraamniotic administration of,
    92
  intramuscular administration of,
    95–99
  other methods and, 101
Psychological characteristics,
  227–229
Psychological trauma, 225
Psychosocial research, 225

Quickening. *See* Fetal movement

Rape, 36
Regulations, 28, 31–33, 310
  restrictive, 36
  surgery, 7
Report on Health Promotion and
  Disease Prevention, 28
Reproduction, future
  curettage and, 82–84
  dilatation and, 182–183
  prostaglandin procedures and,
    183–184
  saline procedures and, 181–182

RH testing, 31
Roe v. Wade, 28, 32, 198
Rubella, 179

Saline, hypertonic, 11, 18, 92, 101
  complications from, 83-85
  effectiveness of, 81
  instillation of, 79, 80-81, 168
  laminaria and, 146-148
  mortality from, 85
  prostaglandin and, 169-171
Service providers, influences of, 229-230
Slippery elm bark, 153
Smoking, maternal, 41
Spermicides, vaginal, 280-281
Sociodemographic characteristics, 226-227
Socioeconomic status, 6-7, 180
Sonographic studies, 53
Sonography, 49, 108
Sterilization, 7, 272-277, 327
Supreme Court, 28, 33, 37, 201, 203, 225

Term pregnancy, 328
Termination of pregnancy rule, 32
Theology, 215, 224
Tupelo *(Nyssa aquatica)*, 153
Twins, monozygotic, 45

Ultrasound, 58
Umbilical cord, 39, 43, 44-47
  differences in, 46
  looped, 45
University of California, study of, 243
  results of, 244-248
U.S. Department of Health, Education, and Welfare, 215
United States Public Health Service, 200
Upjohn Company, 173
Urea, hypersmolar, 11, 101
  administration of, 107-109
  complications from, 112, 115
  -oxytocin, 152
Urinary tract infections, 110, 168
Uterine contractility, 70-75
Uterine cramping, 116
Uterine masses, 58
Uterine myoma, 64
Uterine perforation, 100
Uterus, involution of, 267, 269

Vacuum aspiration (VA), 62, 301
Vacuum curettage abortion, 142-145
Vomiting, 96, 97, 99, 169

Warmth, sensations of, 116
Washington, DC, 230-235
Water intoxication, 84
World Health Organization (WHO), 92, 95, 165, 180, 305

Zoapatle, 333